ECONOMIC METHOD, THEORY AND POLICY

Economic Method, Theory and Policy

Selected Essays of Kurt W. Rothschild

Edited by

J.E. King

La Trobe University, Australia

E ron £ ✓
8/9/96

Edward Elgar
Aldershot, UK • Brookfield, US

Published by
Edward Elgar Publishing Limited
Gower House
Croft Road
Aldershot
Hants GU11 3HR
UK

Edward Elgar Publishing Company
Old Post Road
Brookfield
Vermont 05036
US

British Library Cataloguing in Publication Data
Rothschild, Kurt W.
  Economic Method, Theory and Policy:
  Selected Essays of Kurt W. Rothschild
  I. Title   II. King, J.E.
  330.1

Library of Congress Cataloguing in Publication Data
Rothschild, Kurt W. (Kurt Wilhelm), 1914–
  Economic method, theory and policy: selected essays of Kurt W.
Rothschild / edited by John King.
    p. cm.
  Includes index.
  1. Economics—Methodology. 2. Economic policy. I. King, John.
II. Title.
HB131.R68 1995
330'.01—dc20   95–21330
                                                                    CIP

ISBN 1 85898 249 9

Printed and bound in Great Britain by
Biddles Ltd, Guildford and King's Lynn

Contents

Acknowledgements

The publishers wish to thank the following who have kindly given permission for the use of copyright material.

Atlantic Economic Society for article: 'Micro-Foundations, Ad Hocery, and Keynesian Theory', *Atlantic Economic Journal*, **XVI**(2), June 1988, 12–21.

Australian Economic Papers for article: 'A Note on Some Economic and Welfare Aspects of Working-Time Regulation', *Australian Economic Papers*, **21**(38), June 1982, 214–18.

Banca Nazionale del Lavoro Quarterly Review for article: 'Glimpses of a Non-linear Biography', **176**, March 1991, 3–13.

Basil Blackwell Ltd for articles: 'A Note on Advertising', *The Economic Journal*, **LII**(205), April 1942, 112–21; 'The Small Nation and World Trade', *The Economic Journal*, **LIV**(213), April 1944, 26–40; 'Price Theory and Oligopoly', *The Economic Journal*, **LVII**(227), September 1947, 299–320; 'Stagflation and Intensified Inflation: A Primitive Hypothesis', *The Economic Journal*, **LXXXII**(328), December 1972, 1383–7.

Contemporary Austrian Studies for article: 'Austro-Keynesianism Reconsidered', *Contemporary Austrian Studies*, **II**, 1994, 119–29.

Edward Arnold (Publishers) Ltd for article: 'A Note on Some Socioeconomic and Normative Aspects of Risk', *Review of Political Economy*, **2**(3), November 1990, 359–65.

Elsevier Science B.V. for article: 'Political Economy or Economics? Some Terminological and Normative Considerations', *European Journal of Political Economy*, **5**(1), 1989, 1–12.

Greenwood Publishing Group Inc. for article: 'Schumpeter and Socialism' in *Schumpeterian Economics* (ed. H. Frisch), 1981, Praeger, 113–25.

Harcourt Brace and Company Ltd for article: 'Like a *Lehrstück* by Brecht: Notes on the German Reunification Drama', *Cambridge Journal of Economics*, **17**(3), September 1993, 259–66.

Introduction

It is often very difficult to calculate the extent of one's intellectual debts. Joan Robinson once wrote that she had absorbed so much from Keynes, and from Michal Kalecki, that she simply could not say what precisely she had learned from whom (Robinson (1952), p. 159). My own contact with the ideas of great economists has been – until very recently – entirely impersonal, through the medium of their published works, but I can appreciate her problem. It was not until I began to think about the historical origins of Post Keynesian economics that I realised just how much I owed to the writings of Kurt Rothschild, not only in labour economics (which has been my bread-and-butter as a university teacher for a quarter of a century) but also as an influence on my attitudes towards neoclassical price theory, the distribution of income, and the scope and method of economics in general. The present volume is by way of acknowledgement – if hardly repayment – of the debt.

Rothschild is probably best known as a labour economist. His *Theory of Wages* (1954) still reads remarkably well after forty years, its sceptical but not entirely dismissive attitude towards marginal productivity theory striking a chord with all but the most bigoted neoclassical students of the labour market and forming the basis for Rothschild's numerous analytical and empirical contributions in subsequent decades. This outstanding textbook demonstrates the breadth of knowledge, the critical edge, and the underlying good humour and tolerance which characterized the other book for which he will be best-remembered in the English-speaking world: the highly influential collection of readings, *Power in Economics* (1971). Both reveal the full range of Rothschild's interests. Neither dogmatically Marxist, nor narrowly (Post) Keynesian, nor an unqualified institutionalist, Kurt Rothschild has sympathies with many heterodox strands of political economy, and has been able to communicate with them all. At a time when the barriers between the competing rivals to the neoclassical paradigm appear to be crumbling, Rothschild's work is of particular importance.

The recently published collection of his essays, *Employment, Wages and Income Distribution* (1993), was restricted to articles on labour economics and income distribution theory, some newly translated from the German. But Rothschild has never been a narrow specialist, as can be seen from the present collection. It brings together twenty-six papers, written between 1942 and 1994, on a wide range of methodological, theoretical and policy questions. Truly Rothschild has been the hedgehog to his Austro-Keynesian friend and colleague Josef Steindl's fox.[1] In one way this has been a source of weakness, for Rothschild has perhaps too often failed to develop a brilliant insight, instead rushing on to the next issue that attracted his attention. (A prime example is the 1947 article on oligopoly, reprinted as chapter 10 below, and followed up only 46 years later in the paper reprinted here as chapter 18.) In another sense, though, this breadth has been a source of great strength. As can be seen in the papers that follow, there are few questions of any significance in modern economics on which Kurt Rothschild has had nothing of interest to say.

The book begins with a brief and characteristically modest autobiographical sketch,[2] in which he recalls the economic and political turbulence of his native Vienna in the early 1930s and the competing influences on him of Marxism and subjectivist Austrian economics. After the *Anschluss* Rothschild and his wife fled to Scotland, where he spent nine happy years. It was at Glasgow that he discovered Keynes, Kalecki, Joan Robinson and E.H. Chamberlin, whose work had a major impact on his intellectual development. Returning to Vienna in 1947, Rothschild joined the Austrian Institute for Business Cycle Research. Here he worked in the disparate fields of labour economics and international trade, acquiring (as he writes in chapter 1 below) a healthy scepticism concerning the quality of economic data and a respect for good empirical work. This experience, which lasted for almost two decades, also taught Rothschild just how difficult it was to 'prove' or 'disprove' theories in any decisive way. When, in 1966, he returned to academic life, at the new University of Linz, he found himself required to lecture on a wide and varying range of subjects, and greatly enjoyed the opportunities that this offered him. Retirement in 1985 simply increased the time available to Rothschild for thinking, researching and writing; he has been extremely active ever since.

Chapter 1 concludes with a summary of Rothschild's views on the methodology of economics. This has been a life-long concern, as is evident from the four papers on method which are reprinted here. They are arranged chronologically, but chapter 5, which explores the differences between political economy and economics, serves as a good introduction to Rothschild's ideas. He is a methodological pluralist, embracing a political economy – as distinct from the narrower 'science' of economics – whose practitioners 'must probably admit quite openly and unashamedly that they cannot *and do not want to* compete at present with the methodological and (pseudo-) scientific standards of neoclassical economics, because this would necessarily involve a disabandonment [disavowal? JK] of their research subject' (p. 46, original stress). No unified political economy is at present possible, Rothschild argues, or even desirable (p. 51). Political economy is inevitably a 'soft' science, like the other social sciences and unlike classical mechanics. But if this is a weakness, it is an inevitable weakness. As he writes in chapter 1, 'the real crisis in economics (if there is one) is a consequence of the hegemonic claims and the arrogance of the ruling neo-classical orthodoxy which tries to restrict the range of a "true economic science" to the mechanistically inspired "exact" approaches of equilibrium theory and its proliferations' (p. 12). These claims Rothschild has resisted for over half a century; on this, if on little else, he finds common ground with Hayek and the subjectivist Austrians.

On related grounds he insists, in chapter 4, that it is a mistake to insist on 'microfoundations', and that neoclassical microeconomics is in principle unsuitable as a basis for Keynesian macroeconomic theory. 'Economics is, by necessity, a multi-paradigmatic science. Several theoretical structures exist side by side, and each theory can never be more than a partial theory ... there can be no justification for a hierarchical stipulation that (Keynesian or other) macro-theories require a micro-economic foundation for macroeconomics, when the latter finds it difficult to fit macroeconomic realities into its own framework' (pp. 32–3). Moreover, 'the primitive hypothesis of optimising behaviour' should be replaced, or supplemented, by concepts of satisficing, bounded rationality, and X-inefficiency (pp. 38–9). Similar reasoning is revealed in chapter 2, a brief comment written early in Rothschild's career, taking issue with Oskar Lange on the treatment of rationality in economics. Three types of irrational behaviour should be distinguished, Rothschild argues: emotional or impulsive actions, irrationality based on ignorance, and deviations from the 'capitalist spirit' which occur when people follow a different type of rationality from that demanded of 'economic man'. There is no reason to suppose that the latter could not be modelled successfully, but neoclassical tools will not be very useful in doing so (pp. 17–19).

Rothschild broadens his attack on orthodox theory in chapter 3, where he discusses the treatment of power in mainstream economics. The entire question has been neglected by economists, he argues, since the days of John Stuart Mill, even though power enters as an argument into individuals' utility functions (where it is probably as important as wealth), and despite economic agents' use of power both to alter the outcome of market transactions and to change the operation of the market mechanism itself. Economists have been seduced by the model of perfect competition, their vision of an economy without significant power being reinforced by its aesthetic appeal; by the growing specialization of economics as a discipline and consequent separation from sociology and political science; and by the desire of the powerful to avoid public scrutiny (pp. 21–5). No matter how hard they tried, however, neoclassical theorists have not been able to exclude power altogether. It intrudes into their analysis of monopoly, albeit in a stunted form as the mere absence of competition, that is, in the restricted context of market processes and market adjustments.[3] Obviously power cannot be ignored in the analysis of collective wage bargaining, though here too its significance is distorted. Finally, power has featured prominently in the thinking of economic dissidents as diverse as Marx, the Webbs, Tugan-Baranovsky, Hobson, Oppenheimer and Henry George, together with the institutionalists and the historical economists (pp. 25–7).

There is, Rothschild concedes, no well-defined subject area for a book on power in economics, and the concept of power itself is not precisely defined. His selection of material for the book of readings is thus inevitably 'somewhat haphazard' (p. 16). It is also stimulating and provocative, containing 18 pieces, by sociologists and political scientists as well as economists, and dating from 1943 to 1968. Rothschild divides the book into seven parts, dealing respectively with the reasons for the neglect of power in economic theory; the concept of economic power (Harsanyi, Pen); property, big business and power, including a very important article by Erich Preiser on power, factor supplies and the distribution of income; managers and the techno-structure (Brady, Galbraith); the Galbraithian notion of 'countervailing power'; Baran and Sweezy on racial minorities; and inequalities in power in international economic relations. Anyone thinking about such a book would have their own complaints about Rothschild's selection of material, and he would be the first to acknowledge their legitimacy. There is nothing specifically about Fascism or Communism, for example, no representative of classical American institutionalism, and – apart from Baran and Sweezy – nothing from the substantial Marxian literature on economic power. The fact remains, however, that these are issues which economists should not neglect, but rarely feel comfortable with. And Rothschild was the one to grasp the nettle.

For a while *Power in Economics* proved influential, especially among younger economists whose ideas had been formed in the 1960s and who sought political relevance for their theorizing and a multi-disciplinary focus for their research. Then the barriers came down again. Neoclassical theory survived the radical onslaught, the various heretical tendencies themselves became increasingly sectarian and intolerant, and Rothschild's undogmatic, open, questioning approach fell out of favour with all camps. His methodological views, however, condition his own attitude towards economic theory. As can be seen repeatedly in chapters 6–18, Rothschild often concludes his theoretical papers by emphasizing the inherent limitations of any form of purely economic analysis. His own theoretical work is distinguished by its analytical modesty, empirical orientation, dissatisfaction with any rigid distinction between micro and macro, and equal impatience with disciplinary boundaries.

An early example is provided in chapter 6, a perceptive and original note on the macroeconomic significance of advertising. Marshall and Pigou denounced advertising as a form of waste, but tacitly assumed full employment. In practice, Rothschild notes, the alternative to advertising might be the idleness of the resources employed in it. Advertising should be regarded as a form of investment which, because it increases neither the output of consumer goods nor the private capital stock, is comparable to public works expenditures. It raises effective demand without increasing the supply of market goods, and has the further indirect effect of stimulating consumption. However, Rothschild argues, public works are preferable for two reasons: advertising expenditures accrue to the well-off, who have a relatively low propensity to consume; and they tend to be pro-cyclical and therefore to increase the amplitude of the trade cycle.

The implications of market imperfections are viewed from a rather narrower perspective in chapter 7. Here Rothschild draws an intriguing parallel between selling costs in the product market, which were exhaustively analysed by Chamberlin and Robinson, and the almost totally neglected phenomenon of buying costs in the market for labour. Such expenditures, Rothschild suggests, are frequently undertaken by firms wishing to alter the position or shape of their labour supply curves. They can do so since workers possess imperfect information about the employment opportunities open to them, and also because of the possibility of altering workers' preferences for places of work. Rothschild distinguishes two types of buying costs. Advertising jobs raises the elasticity of labour supply to any particular enterprise by disseminating information, thereby reducing the degree of monopsonistic exploitation; employment and output increase, while wages may rise or fall in consequence. Welfare expenditures, perhaps undertaken from what would today be termed 'efficiency wage' motives (p. 69), also shift the supply curve and reduce its elasticity. They are especially important where there exists a 'gentleman's agreement' between firms, analogous to tacit price collusion, which rules out wage competition. With the recent revival of interest in monopsonistic labour markets, Rothschild's insights may perhaps be developed into a more systematic analysis of wage collusion than he himself provides.

He paints with a much broader brush in chapter 8. Here Rothschild assesses the conventional case for free trade, which ignores the consequences of monopoly and the trade cycle. When a commodity is produced by two national monopolies, he suggests, a cut in tariffs might actually increase prices if it leads to the formation of an international cartel. More generally, the effect of free trade will be to alter the geographical distribution of industry in accordance with the relative strengths and strategic abilities of the oligopolists involved, and not necessarily in accordance with the principle of comparative advantage. The creation of a federal union will reinforce existing structural disparities and perpetuate inequalities between the constituent nations.[4] Once macroeconomic considerations are allowed for, Rothschild argues, the case for free trade is weakened further. A balanced economy may well be preferable to a highly specialized one, since specialization in commodities with a high income-elasticity of demand leaves the economy much more vulnerable to cyclical fluctuations in world demand.

In no sense is Rothschild an apologist for big business. When Kenneth Boulding defended monopoly on the grounds that stable, administered prices offered a valuable bulwark against 'hyperdeflation' and macroeconomic breakdown (Boulding 1945), Rothschild demurred, for Kaleckian reasons. As he argues in chapter 9, industrial combinations maintain profit margins, thereby reducing the wage share in national income and cutting consumption; there is a further, indirect effect via a depressed incentive to invest. The 'protectionist' policies of workers and small farmers should be treated differently, Rothschild argues, since they tend to raise the propensity to consume. Monopolistic practices can be endorsed macroeconomically only if they are necessary to avoid bankruptcies, which have a disastrous effect on business psychology and on effective demand.

Rothschild's theoretical *tour de force* is his 1947 *Economic Journal* article on 'Price Theory and Oligopoly', reprinted as Chapter 10. Here he probes mercilessly at the weakest part of marginalist equilibrium theory. Mechanistic and biological analogies are inappropriate, he suggests. 'The oligopoly-theorist's classical literature can neither be Newton and Darwin, nor can it be Freud; he will have to turn to Clausewitz's *Principles of War*' (p. 98). Strategic considerations are paramount in oligopolistic markets, and this undermines the 'wonderful master-key' (p. 98) of profit maximization. Since uncertainty is pervasive, the desire for secure profits is every bit as important as optimization, and this cannot be reduced to a species of long-run maximization. 'Any theory ... which tries to explain price behaviour in terms of marginal curves derived from *long-term* demand and cost cost curves really by-passes the problem of uncertainty, and thus the very factor which gives rise to that desire for security which the theory tries to explain' (p. 99; original stress).

Business behaviour will be very different, Rothschild concludes, where 'security maximisation' is the goal of the firm. Prices will tend to be rigid, rather than responding to every change in costs and revenues. Mark-up pricing procedures may, quite rationally, be adopted. Excess capacity will be maintained to deter new entrants. Vertical integration will grow at the expense of tendencies towards increasing specialisation. Self-finance will replace dependence on the external capital market. Although prices will normally be set at levels which discourage new competition, and held there, infrequent but vicious price wars will be fought, often to the death (pp. 100–108).

This remarkably fertile article contains the seeds of many later developments in oligopoly theory, from the 'limit pricing' models of Andrews (1964) and Sylos Labini (1962) to Cowling's analysis of reserve capacity as a competitive weapon (Cowling 1982). It is noteworthy not only for its forthright rejection of all marginalist approaches to the analysis of oligopoly, but also for an extremely prescient critique of game-theoretic analysis as static and incapable of dealing with more than three players.[5] This was all the more remarkable in view of the postwar dislocation which meant that Rothschild had not been able to read von Neumann and Morgenstern in the original, but was forced to rely on review articles (p. 97 n19). Above all, in chapter 10 Rothschild refuses to stop short at economics, narrowly defined. The big oligopolists, he observes, 'have the power to change the market situation by their own political action. ... The gap that divides selling expenditure from political activities is methodologically much smaller than the one that divides the former from production costs proper' (pp. 108–9). Both fascism and imperialism must be regarded as outgrowths of oligopoly, and 'the inclusion of these "non-economic" elements is essential for a full explanation of oligopoly behaviour and price' (p. 110; original stress deleted).

These insights proved difficult to formalize, and it was not until 1993 that Rothschild returned to the question of oligopoly in the paper reprinted as chapter 18 and discussed below. His blistering attack on the welfare properties of more extensive competition, written in 1951 and published three years later, can be found in chapter 11. Rothschild begins by noting the irony of the 'market socialism' debates, in which conservative and Marxist writers were 'united in their admiration of the competitive ideal and only divided about the question whether socialism leads away from this target or is the only way of reaching it' (p. 113). In fact, he argues, competition between large numbers of producers is wasteful on a massive scale. In monopolistic competition, unemployment and excess capacity are endemic, and are exacerbated by the presence of monopsonistic power in labour markets. Further inefficiencies arise from product differentiation and advertising expenditure. Under pure competition, in which monopoly is absent but other imperfections persist, deficient knowledge on the part of producers, consumers and workers results in considerable waste.

Even ruling out these frictions and imperfections, and assuming (totally un-realistically) that there is *perfect* competition, will not eliminate waste from unemployment, divergences between private and social cost, and consumers' inability to influence the development of new products. Rothschild foreshadows the self-criticism of the more honest modern Walrasian theorists when he argues that neoclassical theory can guarantee neither the uniqueness of competitive general equilibrium nor its attainment:

> there is no reason to assume that there is always only one equilibrium position – there may be several. To lift the whole economy from one equilibrium to another (more favourable) one will require the simultaneous and co-ordinated action of several parts of the economy which is beyond the power of the competitive mechanism. Similarly, the limitation of perspective in a competitive system will also prevent the adoption of a 'rational' investment policy through time. (p. 121)[6]

There is, additionally, an ethical dimension to consider. Competition fosters 'undesirable qualities like greed, fraud, ruthlessness, at the cost of truthfulness, readiness to help, solidarity' (p. 122). These additional moral costs must be set against the benefits of competition.

Rothschild's hostility towards unreal and excessively abstract theorizing is not confined to the work of orthodox economists. In chapter 12 he criticizes Nicholas Kaldor's early Post Keynesian growth models on similar grounds. Rothschild attacks growth theory in general for employing a very restricted range of variables, which detach it from reality; for neglecting historical, social and institutional detail, which is permissible in short-run analysis but not in long-run models; and for assuming sustained full employment. Turning to Kaldor, Rothschild objects to his technical progress function, which rests on special assumptions but has no empirical support, and raises serious doubts concerning Kaldorian distribution theory. The savings propensities of workers and capitalists, he argues, cannot be regarded as constant, or even (in the long run) as independent variables. 'They will be influenced by the way in which short-period disequilibria in saving and investment plans (which Kaldor admits into his system) have been resolved, *by the way in which the present income distribution was reached*' (p. 139; original stress). This recognition of path-dependence is repeated in Rothschild's third criticism, directed at Kaldor's minimum profit and subsistence wage restrictions on the rate of growth. Both constraints, he argues, will depend on past experience; they are 'historically grown quantities' (p. 141). Marx had recognized this, and his use of social in addition to economic elements in the analysis of growth 'has hardly been equalled ... to this day' (p. 143). Kaldor did not respond to these criticisms, but his subsequent abandonment of steady-state growth theory in favour of models emphasizing cumulative causation and dynamic economies of scale suggests that he did eventually accept their validity (Thirlwall 1987, chs. 6–7).

Chapter 13 deals with a microeconomic question with profound macroeconomic implications. It contains Rothschild's brief but effective contribution to a discussion which would soon be overtaken – 'overwhelmed' might be a more appropriate term – by the literature on 'rational expectations'. He uses a simple cobweb model of supply and demand to assess the consequences for price forecasting if it is assumed that the forecaster has partial, not complete, knowledge of the underlying economic relationships. Even roughly correct forecasting, he demonstrates, will shorten and dampen cyclical fluctuations in a dynamic world where supply and demand functions change at frequent intervals. Significantly, Rothschild does not claim that market instability will tend to disappear in the absence of shocks, nor does he suggest that forecasters are likely ever to obtain perfect knowledge of the relevant structural relations.

It is regrettable that he took these arguments no further, since he might have been able to intervene very effectively on the side of the Keynesians in their unnecessarily defensive response to the 'new classical' economists. Rothschild did become well-known for his (qualified) endorsement of a medium- to long-term trade-off between unemployment and wage inflation, a position which he continues to maintain (see King 1995, pp. 232–3) and which is much less unfashionable in the mid-1990s than it was twenty years earlier. Chapter 14 reprints an unjustly neglected sequel to his widely-cited survey article on the Phillips Curve (Rothschild 1972), in which

Rothschild takes issue with the view that a process of gradual inflation must inevitably accelerate once rising prices are anticipated by economic agents:

> Perhaps the most decisive argument against the catastrophic view is the historical experience (including the present as history) that remarkably high rates of inflation can persist for some considerable time without any tendency towards acceleration, and that hyper-inflations exhibiting such tendencies have usually not been experienced in 'normal' periods. (p. 152)

Rothschild's alternative 'primitive hypothesis' is that learning induces a once-and-for-all increase in the inflation rate rather than continuous acceleration. The simple model presented in chapter 14 generates stagflation rather than hyperinflation. Instead of resorting to mathematical overkill, accompanied by elaborate but ultimately inconclusive econometric estimation, Rothschild supports his model with unpretentious numerical simulations and a set of illustrative calculations drawn from the contrasting experiences of the Austrian economy in the cycles of 1958–61 and 1967–70. The paper is a paradigm of intelligence and technical restraint.

Although never tempted to specialize in intellectual history, Rothschild has on occasion written very perceptively on the history of economic thought. His attitude towards Schumpeter, set out in chapter 20, will be summarized below. In chapter 15 he offers an appraisal of the theory of distribution associated with Carl Menger and the Austrian school. Rothschild identifies certain crucial weaknesses in their analysis, which are independent of and no less damaging than those uncovered by the Cambridge (or Sraffian) critique of orthodox capital theory. 'The main handicap', he writes, 'was the extreme concentration [of Menger and his followers] on consumption with a neglect of production phenomena. They were only considered in so far as they contributed to gains or losses in utility' (p. 164). This defect was compounded by Menger's neglect of the conditions under which productive inputs were supplied:

> As soon as we admit the possibility of variations in factor supplies – at least in the long run – we not only have to give up the monistic 'explanation' of factor values on the basis of utility; we also have to abolish the dream of being able to divide sharply between a purely economic imputation (or functional distribution) theory on the one hand which is based on 'natural' elements, such as lands, needs, talents, technology, etc., and a personal income distribution on the other hand, where social, historical, and power elements (e.g. property rights, market power, etc.) come into play. Such a division was always beloved by the Austrian School, but it has remained typical also for many later developments in marginal-productivity theory. When the persons in control of factor supplies (including labour) can vary these supplies depending on legal and social institutions, effective economic power, etc., then it becomes obvious that we cannot have a 'purely economic' theory of social distribution processes; we require a 'Political Economy' of distribution where economic and sociological influences are combined. (pp. 166–7)

Once again, analytical and methodological criticisms are closely related.

In the two following chapters we return, with Rothschild, to the labour market. The brief chapter 16 presents a model of the allocation of time between work and leisure which, unlike neoclassical analysis, does not assume a stable indifference map. Instead Rothschild focuses upon the social process of habit formation, arguing that workers' preferences are endogenously determined, and alter in response to changes in market parameters. Shifts in tastes, Rothschild concludes, are often irreversible, making the relevant equilibria innately path-dependent. In chapter 17 he argues persuasively that 'risk-bearing' is not the exclusive prerogative of entre-preneurs, for workers are faced with risks comparable to those taken by their employers. Workers are at a disadvantage in this respect, since they find it much harder than the owners of financial capital to spread their risk. The theory of portfolio selection has little application to problems of human capital. This casts doubt on the orthodox theory of profit, Rothschild concludes. 'Risk taking is a general and widely diffused aspect of production for future markets which affects most participants in the economic game, but only some of them are in a position to demand and receive payment for taking risks surpassing a certain minimum level' (p. 185). The social (as opposed to the private) benefits of risk-seeking behaviour have in all probability been considerably exaggerated.

Appropriately enough, the final theoretical paper in this collection brings Rothschild back to the riskiest of all market environments: oligopoly. In chapter 18, first published in a *Festschrift* for Paolo Sylos Labini, Rothschild reiterates his early suspicion (see chapter 10) concerning the fruitfulness of game-theoretic models of 'competition among the few', since they require extreme simplification, and the use of restrictive *ad hoc* assumptions, to preserve any semblance of clear and definitive market solutions. As with his earlier analytical work (see, for example, chapters 12, 13 and 14), Rothschild adopts a deliberately 'low-tech' strategy in his own attempt to model oligopoly. He uses a very simple numerical model to illustrate two conflicting approaches: a secure duopoly with a unique Nash equilibrium (which he terms the Stackelberg model), and an open situation with uncertainty, incomplete information, insecurity of position, and dynamic entry possibilities (the Sylos model). This permits Rothschild to discuss the conditions under which the stronger duopolist may try to eliminate the weaker, and further to analyse the effects of changes in costs and in demand. This 'simple exercise in oligopolistic scenarios' (p. 201) is so illuminating that one is forced to regret that Rothschild abandoned work on oligopoly for almost half a century after his classic 1947 paper.

Policy questions have never been far from the surface, even in Rothschild's most abstract analytical writing, although he is never dogmatic and his treatment of social welfare and political debate is always theoretically informed. His socialist background is apparent in many of the theoretical papers already discussed, most obviously in the concluding pages of chapter 11 (pp. 119–25). They are equally evident in chapter 19, which was written under the powerful influence of Michal Kalecki. Here Rothschild's basically neoclassical analysis of points rationing ends by identifying the implications for a socialist economic system: staple foodstuffs might be distributed by straight rationing and eventually become free goods, less essential commodities could come under points rationing, while luxuries and semi-luxuries could be left to the free market. This is less ambitious than Kalecki's radically egalitarian proposal, advocated at the height of the Second World War, for the rationing of individuals' total consumption expenditure (Kalecki 1941), but it goes further than most con-temporary – or modern – market socialists would be prepared to contemplate.

Rothschild's socialism is again transparent in chapter 20, where he discusses the very personal interpretation of Marxism found in the work of Joseph Schumpeter, another important influence on Rothschild's own work. As he explains, 'while there exists any number of people who are non-Marxian socialists, there are very few specimens who can be regarded as non-socialist Marxists. Schumpeter is one of them. Or at least nearly so ...' (p. 224). Rothschild proceeds by outlining the way in which Schumpeter came to believe, like Marx, that socialism was the inevitable successor to capitalism: 'his reasoning is socialist thinking turned upside down: capitalism – according to Schumpeter – peters out not because of its inadequacy or because of its inherent faults but because of its success' (p. 231). In uncovering the Schumpeterian view of socialism and exposing its shortcomings (most especially in its conception of the state), Rothschild gives some tantalisingly brief and tangential hints of his own view of a post-capitalist future.

He is much more forthcoming in his stance on the reform of capitalism. Here Rothschild has always been a Keynesian, with a Kaleckian tinge. In *The Theory of Wages* he argued for manpower planning and an incomes policy, the latter conditional on a widening of trade union functions and a significant expansion in the economic role of the state (1954, pp. 142–3, 147). Chapters 21 and 22 reveal how, during the anti-Keynesian 1980s, Rothschild defended the Welfare State from its New Right critics and challenged the fashionable notions of macroeconomic policy impotence. Social democratic governments in Western Europe had, he demonstrated, achieved lower unemployment and higher growth rates than their right-wing rivals. If state involvement is inconsistent with neoclassical welfare economics, so much the worse for Pareto-optimality. As Rothschild argues against Yew-Kwang Ng in chapter 23, people's rejection of the price mechanism as the 'ultimate rule' of economic life is not *ipso facto* irrational. 'While preferences of the individuals are given the highest weight [by Ng] there is one preference which they are not permitted to have: a preference for non-market transactions' (p. 273). But this is neither defended nor, for Rothschild, defensible. His critique of the Pareto principle is extended, in chapter 24, to a denunciation of the injustice of the 'two-thirds society' in which a minority of the population is permanently disadvantaged. Even if the 'outsiders' are fully compensated financially by generous welfare payments, such a society denies people access to the status and social contacts derived from paid employment. It is therefore, Rothschild argues, morally unacceptable.

The last two papers dissect the outcome of recent policy decisions in eastern Germany and in Austria. In chapter 25 Rothschild points to the adverse consequences of the economic shock therapy applied to the new *Bundesländer*, which produced a severe recession made tolerable only by substantial transfer payments from the old West Germany. 'The lesson to be learnt', he comments sardonically, 'is that one can afford the luxury of a "big bang" strategy only if one has a rich uncle' (p. 285). The orthodox economic theory on which the strategy relied operates best in the context of a stable institutional structure, where marginal adjustments are made to a slowly changing environment. In the German reunification drama, none of these conditions was satisfied. The resulting economic disaster was eminently predictable from a Keynesian or institutionalist viewpoint, and the advocates of unqualified neoclassical remedies have a great deal to answer for.

In Austria full employment survived the shocks of the 1970s, Rothschild argues in chapter 26, but only as a result of conscious 'policy targeting' by a Social

Democratic government committed to the maintenance of public expenditure and willing to accept higher budget deficits. This 'Austro-Keynesianism' combined demand-side policies which encouraged investment by reducing uncertainty, with supply-side initiatives involving interest rate subsidies and generous depreciation allowances. Inflation was controlled by a combination of incomes policy and exchange rate targeting, whereby the schilling was tied to the German mark. The Austro-Keynesian experiment petered out in the 1980s in the face of both domestic and international pressures: coalition governments at home, and a global environment increasingly hostile to Keynesian demand management. Rothschild concludes that the restoration of high employment in a small Western European country today has two prerequisites. One is a 'strong political will to foster full employment supported by a broad social consensus' (p. 297). The other, even harder to achieve, is a radical change of policy in the European Union as a whole. It is difficult not to share Rothschild's pessimism on both scores.

Notes

1. This analogy is developed in King (1994, p. 431), on which I have drawn extensively in writing this introductory note.
2. See also Rothschild (1992), and my conversation with Rothschild in King (1995, pp. 217–33).
3. One is reminded here of Rothschild's insistence in chapter 10 below that the analysis of political lobbying, up to and including support for counter-revolution and world war, must be part of the theory of oligopoly price (p. 110).
4. Similar conclusions are drawn, from their analysis of regional financial markets in the European Union by Arestis and Paliginis (1993) and Dow (1994).
5. The extremely limited nature of the von Neumann–Morgenstern analysis has recently been emphasized by Philip Mirowski: 'Surely the elephant had strained embarrassingly mightily to bring forth a pathetic mouse' (Mirowski 1992, p. 143).
6. For a recent critique of general equilibrium theory along these lines, by a practitioner, see Kirman (1989).

References

Andrews, P.W.S. (1964) *On competition in economic theory*, London, Macmillan.
Arestis, P. and Paliginis, E. (1993) 'Financial fragility, peripherality, and divergence in the European Community', *Journal of economic issues*, **27**(2), June, 657–65.
Boulding, K.E. (1945) 'In defense of monopoly', *Quarterly journal of economics*, **59**, August, 524–42.
Cowling, K. (1982) *Monopoly capitalism*, London, Macmillan.
Dow, S.C. (1994) 'European monetary integration and the distribution of credit availability', in S. Corbridge, R. Martin and N. Thrift eds, *Money, power and space*, Oxford, Blackwell, 149–64.
Kalecki, M. (1941) 'General rationing', *Oxford University Institute of Statistics bulletin*, **3**(1), 11 January, 1–6.
King, J.E. (1994) 'Kurt Rothschild and the alternative Austrian economics', *Cambridge journal of economics*, **18**(5), October, 431–45.
King, J.E. (1995) *Conversations with post Keynesians*, London, Macmillan.
Kirman, A. (1989) 'The intrinsic limits of modern economic theory, the emperor has no clothes', *Economic journal*, **99**, Supplement, 126–39.
Mirowski, P. (1992) 'What were von Neumann and Morgenstern trying to accomplish?' in E.R. Weintraub ed., *Toward a history of game theory*, Durham, Duke University Press, 113–47.
Robinson, J. (1952) *The rate of interest and other essays*, London, Macmillan.
Rothschild, K.W. (1954) *The theory of wages*, Oxford, Blackwell; reprinted New York, Kelley, 1967.
_____ (1971) (ed.) *Power in economics*, Harmondsworth, Penguin.
_____ (1992) 'Kurt W. Rothschild born 1914' in P. Arestis and M. Sawyer eds., *A biographical dictionary of dissenting economists*, Aldershot, Elgar, 472–7.
_____ (1993) *Employment, wages and income distribution, critical essays in economics*, London, Routledge.
Sylos Labini, P. (1962) *Oligopoly and technical progress*, Cambridge, Mass., Harvard University Press
Thirlwall, A.P. (1987) *Nicholas Kaldor*, Brighton, Wheatsheaf.

Note: a full bibliography of Rothschild's writings in English is given at the end of this volume pp. 301–5.

PART ONE

AUTOBIOGRAPHY

Glimpses of a Non-Linear Biography *

When I was approached to contribute to the series of recollections of economists the first effect was that I began to see more clearly than ever before how ridiculously futile the idea of "rational expectations" is. Not only did I never expect to be included in the recollection sequence (and was thus taken by surprise) I also realised – looking backwards – that what had formed me and my development could not have been planned or expected beforehand – neither rationally nor irrationally. The past was always fixed and the future very, very uncertain.

When I finished secondary school in 1933 Austria belonged to the countries which were particularly hard hit by the worst depression the developed world had ever known. Unemployment (official and unofficial) was somewhere near 25 percent, wages were low, the outlook was bleak. Though I should have liked to study physics, real constraints of finance and "rational expectations" prevented me from taking this course. Studying physics would have taken a long time and would have been costly, and the chances of obtaining a job in industry or as a school teacher seemed very low indeed. So I turned to the "mass faculty" of law studies, partly because I had some interest in a career as a lawyer, but mainly because it was a comparatively short study leaving some time to earn money on the side (by tutoring secondary school youngsters) and because of the Austrian practice to regard graduates from the law faculty as suitable candidates for a wide variety of jobs in industry and administration (in addition to the narrower field of legal activities).

In those days the old tradition (lasting till 1966) still prevailed that economics and political science had no separate faculty but belonged to the Faculty of Law and were taught as part of the law curriculum (though some specialisation in their direction was

---

* Contribution to a series of recollections on professional experiences of distinguished economists. This series opened with the September 1979 issue of this *Review*.

BNL Quarterly Review, no. 176, March 1991.

possible). In fact, all the famous protagonists of the "Austrian School" – the "fathers" Menger, Böhm-Bawerk, Wieser, and the second generation Hayek, Haberler, Mises, Machlup – had taken a degree of a "doctor juris". It was this constellation which brought me into touch with economics as a subject of scientific study. Though I continued to regard the main line of my course, *i.e.* the legal subjects, as the basis for my (vaguely hoped for) future livelihood, I immediately developed a particular liking for the unexpected offerings in economics. It became the only subject in which I invested more time and effort (in the form of reading and seminars etc.) than was absolutely necessary.

This special interest had different roots. First of all in the Austria of the twenties and early thirties one lived in an atmosphere of intensive political and ideological tension which either made you escapist, withdrawing completely into a private sphere of one sort or another, or you had to become interested in the burning problems of your environment. The economic deterioration after 1929 was disastrous and social problems were spreading fast. This was happening against a background of sharp class divisions represented by a very reactionary (ruling) conservative party and an (oppositional) semi-Marxist ("Austro-Marxism") Social Democratic Party. Confrontations took place not only in the form of day-to-day political exchanges and occasional physical fights; there were also important ongoing discussions on a "higher" plane of political and economic theories and ideologies which attracted the interest of many of us in the younger generation. Shortly after I had started University the tense political situation exploded (in February 1934) and in a short civil-war-like action democracy was crushed and political parties were forbidden: Austro-Fascism was installed. The open and lively discussions on controversial political and economic issues came to an end or were driven underground. This had a dampening effect on intellectual life in the university. So when (round about 1936) economics came up in my curriculum I was immediately attracted to it because it at least touched those problems (like income inequalities, poverty, unemployment) which had played such an important role in our pre-fascist discussions and controversies.

A second reason for turning my interests towards the new subject was connected with my scientific inclinations. After the many legal subjects which had dominated the first part of my course the change to economics was quite exhilarating. Not that I had loathed the lectures and seminars in law proper; they had their attractions as exercises in logic and argumentation, and one could see their practical and social significance. But to a large extent they just meant accumulating and remembering a vast mass of material. In economics I suddenly met with an approach which had ample room for analytical reasoning and theorising of a sort which resembled those characteristics which had attracted me in physics. It was almost love at first sight.

What I have said just now must be cut back a little: it did not apply to university economics in general but rather to a certain section of it. When I started economics the "splendour" of the Austrian School had already evaporated in the university: the old generation had died, Haberler, Hayek, Mises, Machlup had left the country, the young talents in the Austrian Institute of Business Cycle Research (Morgenstern, Tintner, Wald, Steindl) were kept out of the intrigue-infected university faculties. Most of the professors and lecturers in economics were rather uninteresting and many lectures contained mainly descriptive accounts of past economic theories and of economic facts. There were only two professors who stuck out of this grey mixture: Oswald Spann and Hans Mayer.

These two were personally and theoretically as opposed to each other as opposed one can be. Spann – more a philosopher than an economist – felt himself to be in the tradition of the romantic school of German economists of the early 19th century (Adam Müller in particular) and taught (or preached) a sort of semi-mystical "holistic" theory of the economic and political "body". His theories were full of wooly aspects but appealed to conservative instincts and served as an ideological prop for Austro-fascist corporatism. Mayer, on the other hand, who had been assistant to Wieser before becoming professor, was the "heir" to the Austrian School and a strong defender of analytical theory. Since he was also a splendid expositor I fell for him right away. It is to Mayer that I have to ascribe my first *strong* desire (though felt as utopian at the time) to shift to economics and economic theory as a life-long activity and career. But though Mayer could kindle a flame it must be stressed that it was – to put it mildly – a rather one-sided picture of economic theory that we got. Mayer, who had written (and probably researched) very little in his life-time – he was *proud* of never having written a book –, was very strong on and very much in love with marginal analysis as such and marginal utility in particular. So when I came to the end of my studies in 1938

I was steeped in marginal utility theory with all its assumptions, complications, and ramifications, so that I was able to "explain" such burning problems as why a stamp collector is suddenly prepared to pay *more* for the *marginal* stamp when it comes to complete a set etc., but had learned very little about other fields of Austrian theory, let alone other theories. As far as monetary theory was concerned I remember Mayer once telling us that such a branch exists "and some books have been written about it". And that was that.

1938 came and with it Hitler and the annexation of Austria. Being a Jew (with left-wing sympathies on top of it) the question whether I should stick to legal activities or should try to shift to economics became irrelevant. Leaving the country became the only viable option. In my various attempts to find a venue for my emigration I had the extreme luck to hear of the offer of (two) scholarships for endangered students provided by the Scottish Branch of the International Students Service (ISS). Since I was prepared to consider any straw of hope I applied for this scholarship in order to finish my economic education. To my great surprise I was informed – after an interview had taken place in Wien – that I would be considered a suitable candidate (together with Konrad Singer, subsequently Professor of Chemistry in London). The procedure, however, was slow, the situation in Austria worsened, so in August 1938 I fled (after having married) to Switzerland where I was permitted to stay in Bale. After I had informed the ISS about my new abode I was informed by a young Glasgow University lecturer, representative of the Scottish ISS, that the scholarship had been granted but that it would take a few months until I would get the permit to come to Britain. The name of the lecturer was Alec Cairncross (now Sir Alec Cairncross) whose efforts then and whose friendship and advice later on provided the foundation for the successful realisation of my earlier hopes to be able to make economics my profession.

When Cairncross wrote to me in September 1938 he suggested that it would be useful if I spent the time of waiting for my visa in reading a book which had become central in teaching and discussion: J.M. Keynes' *General Theory of Employment, Interest and Money.* When I sat down in the library of Bale University to study this work of an – for me – unknown English economist my fragmentary knowledge of the English language was the least problem in my efforts to penetrate this new world. Filled with the basics of Au-ntrian-type micro-economic behaviourism I just couldn't make head or tail of what I found in Keynes' book. I got into a rather despondent mood and began to fear the day when I had to present myself in Glasgow as a partly-trained student of economics. But then the *deus ex machina* turned up in the form of a slim volume which I detected in the library: Joan Robinson's *Introduction to the General Theory*. This proved to be an eye- and brain-opener which not only enabled me to begin to understand what Keynes was aiming at, but also immediately convinced me that here was a type of perspective and analysis which permitted a far closer link between the intellectual adventure of economic theorising and the social and socialist questions of the time than I could have found in my Wien days.

So when I finally came to Glasgow in December 1938 I could enter the "Political Economy and Political Philosophy" degree course with a bit more confidence and with considerable gusto. Since my Viennese studies were partly taken into account I was able to finish my studies in Summer 1940. By that time the war was already in full swing. My first assignment after graduation was internment as an "enemy alien" when British politicians reacted nervously to some news about German spying in the Netherlands. On my way through different internment camps I also landed for several weeks in a huge and desolate former textile mill in Lancashire. There I heard that an economist from Oxford was lecturing on economics in some corner of the place. This was a welcome attraction and I joined the group. The lecturer was – so I was told – an Austrian economist named Josef Steindl. Through his talks I was for the first time introduced to Kaleckian contributions which proved equally attractive for me (and for similar reasons) as the Keynesian approach.

Thanks to the endeavours of my wife and of Alec Macfie, Professor of Economics at Glasgow University, my interlude as an internee was a very short-lived one. After about three and a half months I was released and taken on as assistant-lecturer in the Economics Department of Glasgow University. My first duty in way of lecturing was to prepare a course on monopolistic competition. This brought me into touch with the works of Chamberlin and Joan Robinson and here again I had the "liberated feeling" that economic theory can move nearer to reality and relevance than I thought possible when I was faced with the more restrictive axioms of strictly maximising individuals in a deterministic world of full competition.

Probably by that time, *i.e.* after 1940, the "formative years" had been completed. The "mixture" which – in one way or another –

continued to influence my work and my interests consisted of the Viennese background of my school and university days with its stress on the role of psychology (Freud, Adler, Menger) and social forces (Austro-Marxism), of economic theorising (in an Austrian framework with strong links to individual psychology), and of the deep impression of the two "revolutions", the Keynesian and the imperfect competition one. All this had to be seen against the background of a world of economic depression, fascism, and war, in which it did not require an extreme amount of social conscience and social engagement to regard science and scientific activity (particularly in the social sciences) as an instrument which should *ultimately* be socially relevant and not just *art pour l'art,* no matter how pleasurable that may be. Problem-orientation and relevance seemed to me right from the beginning as a desirable aim for the (individual and societal) research effort *as a whole,* though this label cannot and need not be characteristic for every single piece of research. Basic research, experiments with new ideas, trials in different directions without narrow restrictions from practical viewpoints are necessary, if our knowledge is to expand. But the ultimate subordination of the activities to relevant and humanistic ends should be – in my opinion – an essential aspect of professional ethics and should never be lost completely from sight.

My debut in the world of economic journals bore quite distinctly the imprint of the two "revolutions" which I had so recently inhaled. In 1942 I published my first two papers: "A Note on Advertising" in the *Economic Journal,* and "The Degree of Monopoly" in *Economica.* The first one expanded a Keynesian theme (effective demand), the second was a more technical contribution to the ongoing discussion on monopolistic competition. The following years were devoted to a variety of subjects (rationing, public spending, oligopoly and monopsony, problems of a small economy, wage theory, and a book on the Austrian economy), partly dictated by politico-economic interests, partly by research imperatives, and not least by the exigencies of varying lecturing requirements which were alloted to me in the (then) rather small economics department of Glasgow University. In these exploratory and exciting first years as a "finished" economist I was greatly helped by the constant and friendly encouragement of my "boss" Alec L. Macfie, Adam Smith Professor of Political Economy in Glasgow. Though Macfie, an expert on Adam Smith and deeply influenced by Frank H. Knight, did not exactly share my research interests and political leanings, he never tried to push me into certain directions, but was always a tolerant critic taking a helpful interest in what I was doing. It was also he who encouraged me – following a course on "Wages" which I had to give – to expand my notes into book form. This resulted later (when I found the time for it) in my first theoretical book, a "Theory of Wages" in 1954.

Though I felt very happy in Scotland and Glasgow University I decided to return to Wien in 1947, because it seemed to me that the reconstruction of a democratic Austria (after eleven years of Austrian and German fascism) and of a war-ravaged economy provided a sufficient challenge for such a step. My attempts – after I had returned – to enter academic life failed, not least because conditions in the universities had not changed that much since pre-1945 days. But I was lucky to be taken on as a senior research worker in the reborn Austrian Institute of Business Cycle Research, now renamed Austrian Institute of Economic Research. Its director at the time, Professor Franz Nemschak, was busy to develop the Institute into a centre of modern theoretical and empirical research and he had already collected a talented team of young economists which provided a pleasant and stimulating environment for applied economic research. It was further enriched when Josef Steindl, who had worked in the Institute before the war, returned in 1950. Soon the Institute became not only a leading centre of applied research which provided (and still provides) the bulk of studies and materials for public economic policy discussions, it also fostered the absorption and development of contemporary theoretical trends which had been neglected in occupied Austria. Quite a number of Austria's economists in universities and other research institutions obtained their "post-graduate" experience in the Institute.

For me the work in the Institute, where I stayed for almost twenty years, meant an important experience for judging and applying empirical material both in empirical and theoretical studies. The continual rerquirement to collect, estimate, analyse, and interpret a variety of data, to use them for forecasts which in turn had to be checked and to be "defended" (particularly those that were failures!), all this contributed to the development of a healthy scepticism regarding the quality of data and a respect for good empirical work, even if it were "merely" descriptive. It also helped to become more aware of the difficulties of "proving" or "disproving" theories once and for all.

The two fields which became my responsibility in the Institute were the Labour Market and International Trade. Both were connected with research interests which had become dominant before my entry into the Institute. Wage problems as such and in their micro- and macro- (or neoclassical-Keynesian) aspects were part of my Glasgow heritage and these could be linked to unemployment and income distribution problems which – after the experiences of Austria's pre-war class struggles and depression – seemed to me (and still seem) to belong to the most pressing socio-economic and socio-political problems of capitalist societies. The international aspects of a small nation's economy had begun to interest me (long before the trade-mark SMOPEC had appeared in economic literature) in connection with the possible role and development opportunities of a semi-developed industrial country like Austria in a world of frictions and imperfect competition for which the traditional international trade theory and an unsophisticated GATT philosophy seemed anything but adequate.

In 1966 the structure of Austria's university curricula was changed in order to give more scope to the study of the social sciences. These were taken out of the Faculties of Law and Philosophy and found a home of their own in the newly created Faculties of Social and Economic Sciences. In connection with this change a new university was founded in Linz with special stress on economics and social sciences and their interrelationships. When I was asked to join the "founding fathers" of the university I took this opportunity to return to academic life and teaching. I accepted a professorship in economics which I held until my retirement in 1985 without, however, breaking completely my ties with the Viennese Institute of Economic Research.

Though Linz started off as a comparatively small university with limited numbers of staff I found the working conditions rather congenial. The simultaneous development of a new university with a new and untried curriculum opened opportunities for flexibility and experiments which made the first few years rather exciting (and strenuous too). Though the high hopes of stronger interdisciplinary ties could not be fully realised, Linz was in those days an interesting place. In economics proper ("Volkswirtschaftslehre", *i.e.* theoretical and applied economies, as against "Betriebswirtschaftslehre", *i.e.* business economics which had far more students and staff) we soon could collect among others an interesting bunch of open-minded

economists with Keynesian, Kaleckian and other non-orthodox out-
looks and an interest in socio-economic developments who fitted well
into the Austrian political environment of the seventies, when a
socialist government followed a rather specific "Austro-Keynesian"
policy in which full employment remained high on the agenda, and
which was unimpressed by the various Friedman-Laffer-Thatcher-
syndromes. Among my colleagues were Professor Kasimierz Laski,
who formerly had cooperated with Kalecki in Warsaw, Professor
Hajo Riese (now at the Free University Berlin), who developed
interesting aspects of monetary Keynesianism, Egon Matzner and
Ewald Nowotny (now professors at the Technical University and the
Economic University in Wien respectively), who all provided a stimulating basis for critical discussions and new ideas.

The limited size of the faculty meant that – as far as teaching was
concerned – each one of us had to cover a comparatively wide and
varying field of subjects. This had the disadvantage of not being able to
be sufficiently expert in every lecture, but it had the advantage of being
forced to take note of developments in several branches of economic
theory which normally would escape the attention of a narrowly
specialised economist.[1] This met with my desire to aspire, *as far as
possible*, to a rather wide coverage of economic themes, though I was
aware that this cannot be achieved nowadays in the way this was possible
fifty or hundred years ago. Of course, I had and have my special fields of
interest, in particular employment, labour market problems, income
distribution, and related subjects. But problem-orientation and wider
interests induced me again and again to muster the questionable courage
and the luxury to tackle other subjects – however incomplete and
"amateurish" – when I felt that this may add something to the discussion. Just as an illustration I might mention three different book titles:
Power in Economics (1971) was a collection of papers edited by me in
which I tried to draw attention to this badly neglected factor; *An
Introduction to Disequilibrium Theory* (1981; in German) was an attempt
to show up the insufficiency of equilibrium theory and to indicate
various escape routes; *Theories of Unemployment* (1988; in German) dealt
with the core problems of my interests and presented a critical appreciation of newer theoretical approaches.

---

[1] I rember a visit of Abba Lerner to Wien in the fifties when I came to sit next to his
wife at a dinner party. Starting the table talk she asked me: "What sort of an economist
are you?" I did not quite understand what she meant. Should I answer "A good one" or
"A bad one"? But then I found out that I could satisfy her curiosity by calling myself a
"labour economist".

The courage to roam rather freely over a wide field I derived from a methodological position which I had held vaguely from an early period onwards and which I expanded a bit more explicitly in later papers. I believe (and, of course, there are others who think the same way) that economics, like other social sciences, cannot be a "hard" science comparable to mechanics or other highly developed branches of the natural sciences. The extreme complexity of the social world as well as its dynamics, the poor quality of empirical data, and the difficulties of experimenting make any attempt at reaching high levels of "exactness" futile, if one aims at more than just the construction of "logical" models. True, economics is in a better position to apply exact methods and to obtain reliable results than most other social sciences because of the comparatively limited range of actions and motives in a market economy and the strong effects of physical and monetary constraints. These opportunities for sophisticated theory and model construction should be used as far as possible as long as they serve the advance of our understanding of the economic process or certain parts of it. How much can be achieved in this way has been shown impressively by classical and neoclassical theory. But economic processes remain a complex social phenomenon all the same and any hope to obtain a single, consistent theory which can provide a basis for all sorts of economic questions and explanations is simply ridiculous. Different theories and theoretical approaches (which do not need to harden into "schools") are not a sign of weakness but the unavoidable expression of a multi-paradigmatic attack on a "fuzzy" and constantly changing subject matter which cannot be reduced to a single all-embracing theoretical framework. Of course, there are "good" and "bad" theories; but even if it were possible to weed out all bad theories there would still be a multitude of theories and interdisciplinary links, the famous "box of tools" from which one has to select one's instruments according to time, place, problem, and question.

If there is a "crisis in economics" it is certainly not because its theoretical achievements are particularly weak or compare unfavourably with the output of other social or even some natural sciences. The real crisis in economics (if there is one) is a consequence of the hegemonic claims and the arrogance of the ruling neo-classical orthodoxy which tries to restrict the range of a "true economic science" to the mechanistically inspired "exact" approaches of equilibrium theory and its proliferations. Without denying the high quality of the work done in this tradition and its achievements it is not difficult to point out the severe limitations of this approach which cannot be overcome as long as one sticks dogmatically to its basic assumptions. The philosopher Paul Feyerabend, in his study on scientific progress ("Against Method"), has amply shown how all sorts of methods, orthodox or not, *ad hoc* considerations etc. have contributed decisively to new *thinking* about problems and thus to new *insights* and theories. And more recently McCloskey has shawn ("The Rhetoric of Economics") how economists always had to use *arguments* to support their theoretical results. By making their *methods* the exclusive trade-mark of "science" rather than the intellectual quality of new and relevant arguments the neo-classical school and some of their journals have hampered theoretical progress and reduced the liveliness of intercourse. By trying to create the impression of possessing a "hard" science, a promise which could not be met, they have contributed to existing popular disappointments and doubts regarding the efficiency of economic thinking. The way out, so it seems to me, should be a far more tolerant and open dialogue between theories (and disciplines) where quality and theoretical and practical relevance should count and not narrow rules about methodological niceties.

Wien

KURT W. ROTHSCHILD

PART TWO

METHOD

The Meaning of Rationality : A Note on Professor Lange's Article

Every period has to write its " Scope and Methods of Economics." And most of us who belong to the younger generation of economists will be grateful to Professor Lange for his re-statement of this eternal subject[1] in a way, which includes many of the ideas which the development of economic theory and philosophy as well as the experiences of the world around us have forced on us. If a critical remark is added to that article it is only because to the writer it seems that the section on rationality suffers from a certain amount of vagueness which leaves it rather indefinite what was in Professor Lange's mind, and which might give rise to misunderstandings. It is hoped that this note will help to clarify this important concept.

Professor Lange rightly states that the analytical-deductive branch of economic theory depends on the postulate of rationality. Unless economic units act in conformity with some rational pattern no general theory about what would follow from certain premises would be possible. Description of what is actually happening would be the only way open to the economist.

But there *is* rationality and so there is room for theorizing. The predominant—though by no means the only—rationality of the firm is quite clear : it is the maximisation of profits. And this offers a suitable basis for deductive economics. With regard to households the position is more complicated. Professor Lange states the problem as follows :

" A unit of economic decision is said to act rationally when its objective is the maximisation of a magnitude. Firms thus act rationally, by definition. while households do so only when their prefered allocations of resources among different wants can be ordered along a scale. The postulate of rationality is the assumption that all units of economic decision act rationally. . . . The hypothesis that producing units act rationally, i.e. with the objective of maximising money profit, is verified with satisfactory approximation in the capitalist economy. . . . The situation is more doubtful with regard to households. Here the verification of the hypothesis is much more precarious, and we must expect much larger discrepancies between results of empirical observation and conclusions derived from the postulate of rationality. There seems, however, to be some difference between households operating in the capitalist economy and households of the domestic economy of the pre-capitalist societies. The dominance of business enterprises . . . has created a mental habit . . . (under whose influence) households are encouraged to order their preferences along a scale, i.e. to maximise utility. In capitalist society, therefore, the decisions of households are more likely to conform to the deductions derived from the postulate of rationality than in societies which preceded the rise of modern capitalism."[2]

The vagueness of the above passage seems to me to lie in an insufficient explanation of different meanings of rationality. Rationality in the wide sense in which Professor Lange defines it, is a *necessary* condition for the economic theory we are used to, but it is not a *sufficient* condition. For the modern economic theory of the consumer, just as the classical theory, depends to a large extent on a very special kind of rationality : the rationality of *homo economicus*. This consists above all in fixing preferences along a scale in an order, which is decisively influenced by market

---

[1] O. Lange, *The Scope and Methods of Economics*, The Review of Economic Studies, Vol. XIII (1). pp. 19–32.

[2] op. cit. pp. 30–1.

50

A NOTE ON THE MEANING OF IRRATIONALITY

prices (or the disutility or opportunity cost of getting things, under more primitive conditions).

This is indeed the " capitalist spirit " which is fostered by a capitalist environment, and which gives the present economic theory of the consumer a high degree of relevance in our society. But it would be wrong to assume that the absence of this spirit is equivalent to an absence of rationality or of an ordered scale of preferences. In fact, whenever people make considered decisions such an order of preferences must exist ; and when these decisions diverge from what economic theory would let us expect it means that their rationality is a different one from that of *homo economicus*.

Thus the maximisation of utility for the primitive man may lie in the utmost conformity with the customs, the " do's " and taboos of his tribe. To obtain the resources necessary for this aim he may take the greatest pains, while after this has been achieved even easily obtainable goods may leave him unmoved. There is nothing unrational in this and such behaviour is perfectly suitable material for a theoretical analysis adapted to it. Again, the true Christian will cease to desire a thing if his possession of it will hurt the feelings of those who have to do without it. In contrast to this, we have the rationality of Veblen's " conspicuous expenditure " society who will buy a car for $(X + 1)$ £ simply because their neighbours have bought one for X £. And if the Soviet Union tries to replace the " capitalist spirit " by the principle " From each according to his ability, to each according to his need," then they do not do it in order to kill rational behaviour, but in order to substitute a new kind of rationality for a traditional one.

The fact is that the word " irrationality " is used by economists in different ways and much confusion can result if insufficient attention is given to these differences. In particular, three meanings of irrationality should be distinguished : (1) *Real* irrationality. This term should be applied to purely emotional, impulsive actions, which, on consideration, would be rejected, even though no new information was forthcoming. Though psychological analysis may one day reveal to us the subconscious rationality of such actions, we must in the meantime—as far as economics is concerned—regard such behaviour as amenable to individual description only.

(2) Irrationality born from ignorance. Often one describes an action as irrational when an individual takes a decision which would have been different if fuller and better information had been available. This type of " irrationality " introduces a certain amount of irritation into a theory built on the postulate of rationality (which as yet cannot be supplemented by a general theory of *erroneous* choice). But if the average level of intelligence and efficiency of the economic units is sufficiently high to make such ignorance the exception rather than the rule, it can be dismissed as one of those " frictional " forces which reduce the full applicability of deductive conclusions to the real world. If, however, ignorance or mis-information are widespread or are deliberately fostered, their effects have to be particularly included into the economic framework if its conclusions are to be relevant. This will be of importance in the economics of branded goods and advertising.

(3) Irrationality as deviation from the " capitalist spirit." Very often we find references to irrationality when people do not behave according to the rules of *homo economicus*, in other words, when they follow a different type of rationality. Such deviations rob certain aspects of the " normal " economic theory of their usefulness, but they do not run counter the postulate of rationality nor do they exclude the possibility of deductive theorizing. They only require new premises which have to be provided by a sociology of the consumer or of the household in the way, which, for instance, Veblen has indicated.

Probably Professor Lange is aware of all these points. But in his article a confusion arises from the fact that his definition of rationality is wide enough to cover all actions except those which I called *real* irrationality, while when he speaks about the difference between the rationality of capitalist and pre-capitalist households he seems to think of the narrower meaning of rationality which also excludes the actions mentioned under points (2) and (3) above.

Vienna.   K. W. ROTHSCHILD.

[3]

20-30
NA
except

Introduction

Economics as a separate science is unrealistic, and misleading if
taken as a guide in practice. It is one element – a very important
element, it is true – in a wider study, the science of power.
Bertrand Russell

Economics is a social science. It is concerned with a certain
section of human relationships, and a very important section at
that. Economic activities take up, after all, a large part of the
adult's waking time, and the results of these activities play a
decisive part in determining one's standard of living and social
status. It is almost self-evident that people will be anything but
indifferent to the factors which influence their economic conditions. As in other important social fields we should expect that
individuals and groups will struggle for position; that power will
be used to improve one's chances in the economic 'game'; and
that attempts will be made to derive power and influence from
acquired economic strongholds.

Power should, therefore, be a recurrent theme in economic
studies of a theoretical or applied nature. Yet if we look at the
main run of economic theory over the past hundred years we
find that it is characterized by a strange lack of power considerations. More or less homogenous units – firms and households –
move in more or less given technological and market conditions
and try to improve their economic lot *within the constraints of
these conditions*. This model has been explored in great detail by
modern economic science and very important insights into the
working of the market mechanism have been gained. But that
people will use power to alter the mechanism itself; that uneven
power may greatly influence the outcome of market operations;
that people may strive for economic power as much as for
economic wealth: these facts have been largely neglected.[1]

1. The passionate complaint of the American sociologist, Robert S. Lynd,
raised more than quarter of a century ago, applies today with undiminished
force. In a Foreword to Brady (1943, p. 6), he wrote:
'If the American rank and file – the upwards of four-fifths of the nation

This neglect requires some comment. It is the more necessary since matters have not always been that way. Early classical 'political economy' right up to the days of J. S. Mill was fully aware of the sociological and power background of economic events. The writings of this era abound with remarks and hints at the interplay of market mechanisms and outside intervention. It was only in its later stages that the main strand of traditional economic thinking turned inwards towards 'purely' economic matters, paying increasingly less regard to extra-market and power affairs. Several factors contributed to this development and are still influential.

One of the most important causes was the complete victory of 'perfect competition' as the basic model for economic theorizing. Perfect competition was at no time – even in the days of nineteenth-century small-scale business – an adequate description of economic reality. But for two reasons it provided a great attraction for economists ever since the early days of classical theory.

One reason is a purely scientific one. With the transition from feudal conditions to capitalistic market economies, competition moved rapidly into the foreground as one of the decisive motors of economic adjustment and development. The model of perfect competition could thus be constructed with considerable justification as an abstract picture of reality permitting an intensive study of all the corollaries flowing from the working of *one*, very important economic motive force. The usefulness of this approach has been proved beyond doubt in the progress of economic theory over the past two hundred years.

But there was another reason contributing to the overwhelming

---

who are working class and small-business folk – are thus illiterate in the language of contemporary power, the case is almost as bad with those experts, the professional social scientists, whom society supports because they profess to know about men's institutions. It is no accident that, as Dr Brady points out, a world of scientists who comb their fields for important problems for research have left the problem of the power organization and politics of big business so largely unexplored. For the most part, contemporary social scientists still exhibit towards the changing business world the encouraging moral optimism of Alfred Marshall. Nor are we helped by the fact that the crucial science of economics derives its data within the assumptions and concepts of a system conceived not in terms of such things as "power" but of blander processes such as the automatic balancing of the market.'

8 Introduction

dominance of the perfect competition model. Most of the classical economists wanted an optimal development of the economic forces set free by the industrial revolution and the extension of markets. But this development was everywhere hampered by the intervention of powerful vested interests, in particular by the feudal aristocracy, who acted directly or via the government, and who were aided by entrenched commercial monopolies and similar groups. To set the potential economic energies free it seemed decisive to break down these harmful intrusions of power and influence. Hence came the strong demand for minimizing state interference (which tended to act on behalf of the 'old' interests); hence came also the predilection for a regime of perfect competition, of countless small economic units, none of which would be strong enough to bend circumstances towards its own requirements. On the contrary, each firm or household would have to accept the economic facts and in this way economic forces and development would get a free run.[2]

From the very beginning, therefore, the basic model of perfect competition was both an abstract analysis of a decisive economic force, and the Utopian formulation of a society in which power is so widely and thinly distributed that its influence can be neglected. In this way, the important social phenomenon of power receded into the background as far as the kernel of classical economic theory was concerned.

The question arises why this development was reinforced, rather than weakened in later periods. How is it that additional theoretical constructs, leaving more room for power and its influence, were not created to take the same pride of place as the competition model?[3] This question is the more pertinent, since

2. The classical ideal of a competitive economic universe with widely dispersed power is still strongly upheld as a practical programme by some schools of economists, though most of them realize that it could only be achieved by positive government efforts in this direction. Views of this kind have been particularly stressed by the so-called Chicago school in the United States (e.g. Friedman, Simons) and the Neo-Liberals of the Freiburg school in Germany (Eucken, Müller-Armack).

3. The broad attention given to monopoly and trade union questions is an important exception. But as we shall see later, this approach was also seriously limited by the preponderance of the competition model.

already in the later nineteenth century it became clear that the world was not moving towards the competitive Utopia, characterized by a passive government (in internal and international economic affairs) and the absence of monopolistic groupings and interest lobbies.

Several factors have probably contributed to the continued domination of the competitive set-up in economic thinking and the consequent neglect of power elements. They partly flow from the ways in which knowledge is passed on and developed, partly they have their roots in social and ideological causes.

The great intellectual achievement of Adam Smith, Ricardo and others in creating a closely reasoned systematic framework for analysing and interpreting the economic scene in all its ramifications was such an advance over previous speculations on social and economic matters that it provided a continuous challenge to later generations of economists. To build on this structure, to improve and refine the basic model, to apply it to new problems and situations was often more appealing than attempts to throw light – perhaps with the aid of cruder methods – on neglected, but nonetheless important, other aspects of economic life. This trend has been reinforced by the aesthetic qualities of competitive equilibrium models which ease the path towards 'determinate' solutions of the type achieved by the much envied natural sciences.[4]

Thus a traditional way of economic thinking and theorizing evolved, which rapidly advanced in explaining the mechanics of market adjustment and 'equilibrium' under the impact of competitive forces, but which had little room for such factors as

4. The fear of losing this advantage when the confines of the competition model are left was vividly expressed in a well-known passage by Hicks:
It has to be recognized that a general abandonment of the assumption of perfect competition, a universal adoption of the assumption of monopoly, must have very destructive consequences for economic theory. Under monopoly the stability conditions become indeterminate; and the basis on which economic laws can be constructed is therefore shorn away. . . . It is, I believe, only possible to save anything from this wreck – and it must be remembered that the threatened wreckage is that of the greater part of general equilibrium theory – if we can assume that the markets confronting most of the firms with which we shall be dealing do not differ very greatly from perfectly competitive markets' (1946, pp. 83–4).

10 Introduction

power, non-pecuniary motives, group behaviour and the like. Qualms about the neglect of these 'non-economic' factors[5] were increasingly suppressed in view of the rapid specialization of science. Economics could be regarded as being responsible only for the 'purely' economic phenomena while other influences – such as power – should be taken care of by sociologists or political scientists. These are, however, quite often too much occupied with other social spheres; and, at any rate inter-disciplinary cooperation has up till now not been sufficiently developed so as to achieve the necessary combination of economic and non-economic factors in the interpretation of economic events.

But it would be a mistake to regard the neglect of power elements solely as the result of traditional forces and the inner workings of theoretical expansion. The disregard of power aspects is greatly helped by the fact that concentration on the mechanics of economic and market adjustment within a given framework enables the economist to avoid the detailed occupation with facts which powerful social groups prefer to keep under a cloud of uncertainty. This desire for secrecy is in itself a real and objective difficulty. Nowhere is the analogy of the iceberg more appropriate than in this sphere: only a tiny fraction of the power play becomes visible (and that in a distorted form). But difficulties arise in other fields too, and they do not necessarily lead to a neglect of the subject.

With power, however, the discovery of the truth is not only difficult, it can also lead to clashes with entrenched interests. Thus the social scientist is faced with difficulties which are unknown to the natural scientist. At its worst, the economist facing this situation turns apologist by covering up existing power relations behind an impressive barrage of 'economic necessities' and 'economic laws'.[6] But one can escape this dilemma without

5. That some of them are called 'non-economic' is already a consequence of the traditional definitions and developments in economic science. One can easily build models of economic reality in which so-called non-economic factors become fundamental parts of the theoretical structure.

6. The sins in this direction were particularly blatant in the second half of the nineteenth century, when many economic theorists saw their main task in defending the ruling circles against the rising wave of socialist

running into trouble by concentrating on those aspects of the economic scene in which power relations are unimportant or can be taken as exogenously given. This possibility of avoiding pressures and conflicts has certainly contributed to the remarkable concentration on competitive market and equilibrium theory and the startling dearth of theoretical and applied reasoning in those fields where power and political influences cannot be disregarded.

In the preceding section we have advanced some reasons why power has been neglected in the main run of economic literature. But the neglect has never been complete. Apart from occasional sidelights on power relations, which continued in the literature even after the early classics, there have always been important exceptions to our main thesis that power questions were not properly integrated into economic analysis.

One far reaching exception arose from the fact that the discrepancy between the competitive Utopia and the realities of big business just could not be overlooked. Thus side by side with the basic competitive model, a model of monopolistic behaviour was developed. And with monopoly the question of power could no longer be shelved. Monopoly power had to be recognized as the essence of the monopoly problem, and the literature on monopoly power in theory and practice is indeed plentiful.

But what is significant in our context is the fact that monopoly power is usually discussed within the narrow boundaries set by the basic competition model. In the competition model, as we saw, the small firm is powerless in the market. It has to accept the market parameters – price, demand etc. – and can only passively adjust to it. Monopoly is usually seen as *the absence of competition* in this sense. One recognizes that larger units exist which can influence the market parameters – prices, sales – through their own isolated actions. This capacity of changing the outcome of the market process is the main content of the traditional

---

demands. Marx and Engels had easy play in disclosing the apologetic nature of some of those theories.

Later these openly apologetic intentions became less frequent. But ideological elements were and are still prevalent in many theoretical structures. See the famous work by Myrdal (1953).

concept of 'monopoly power'. While the importance of this power over prices and demand must be fully acknowledged it is, nevertheless, true to say that this power concept is a very incomplete one. It limits its attention – like competition theory – exclusively to market mechanisms and market adjustments without giving consideration to attempts at changing the conditions under which the the market process – be it competitive or monopolistic – operates.[7]

A line similar to that of monopoly theory was followed in the description of the labour market. Here, too, it was recognized that trade unions and employers' organizations did not tally with the competitive stereotype and that power elements could not be completely cast aside. But here again a large part of the traditional literature concentrated on price-setting power in a given labour market while neglecting other aspects of the power problem.

The other big exception we have to note is the fact that everything we have said so far applies only to the main stream of traditional academic economics. There have always been important schools, side-currents and outsiders who have given full weight to the power problem and to the interplay between economic and power elements. This cannot be the place to give a full account of these various systems of thought. But a few outstanding names should be mentioned in order to show that the importance of power certainly was recognized by some representatives of the economic profession.

First of all we must, of course, mention Marx and his followers. Marx inherited from the classical school not only their 'purely' economic theoretical concepts, but also their less developed attempts to see economic 'laws' in relation to the social and historical background. By laying greater stress on these aspects he formed his grand amalgam of economics and sociology, in which the drives for economic and political position, for economic

7. The restrictive interpretation of monopoly power, inherited from competition theory and limiting it to the play on the price mechanism, explains to a large extent why for a long time economists were so helpless *vis-à-vis* the problems of bilateral monopoly and oligopoly, where quite different forms of power tactics are relevant. See on this the classic new approach by von Neumann and Morgenstern (1944), and Reading 5 in this collection.

and political power are closely interwoven. The Marxist school has never lost sight of the power problem in economics, and in the writings of such Marxist 'classics' as Engels, Hilferding, Kautsky, Rosa Luxemburg or Lenin, one can find innumerable examples of such combined analysis.

Similarly, direct and indirect aspects of power have always obtained some recognition among the so-called 'institutionalist' and 'historical' schools of economic thought. Composed of scholars who were less inclined towards general and predominantly logical analysis and more interested in concrete historical situations these schools were naturally less impressed by the 'competitive Utopia' and more aware of actual power influences. Outstanding early contributors in this sphere were Veblen in the USA and Sombart in Germany, and in both these countries contributions of this type continued to appear in later periods. Some of the writings of Schumpeter belong in this group.

Then we must also mention the miscellaneous writers who came to recognize the importance of power problems in connection with some special field in economics on which their interests centred. Thus some of the students of the labour market came to feel that they would have to pay far more attention to power aspects than current economic theory was prepared to do. Sydney and Beatrice Webb or Tugan-Baranovsky can be cited as outstanding early examples. Others (e.g. Henry George or Oppenheimer) came up against the power question in connection with their studies on the continuing advantages accruing to landed property. Then, of course, writers attracted by the rising phenomenon of economic imperialism could hardly avoid dealing intensively with the problem of power. The name of Hobson readily springs to mind.

It would seem that the last few paragraphs – containing, as they do, a list of 'power-minded' economists and 'schools' – are somehow in contradiction to what has been said earlier about the neglect of power in economic science. The contrary, however, is true. The existence of these 'outsiders' and alternative schools throws into even sharper relief the lack of concern for power relations in the main body of academic economics. The amazing point is how little effect the 'unorthodox' writings had on the formulation of questions and answers in 'traditional' economics.

14   Introduction

Quite often no notice at all was taken of the outsiders, in other cases one tried very hard to fence off their influence.[8]

To some extent this cavalier treatment of outsiders could be justified on the ground that quite a number of them paid too little attention to the working of economic mechanisms and to the limits they set to the acquisition and exertion of power. But these shortcomings are not sufficient to explain fully the remarkable immunization of 'traditional' theory against the important problems raised by the 'non-official' literature. To understand this phenomenon one has to take recourse to explanations in terms of traditions, modes of thinking, and social pressures, which were treated in the first section of this introduction.

From what has been said so far it should be clear that a selection of readings to fit the title of this volume faces special problems. Normally, readings on some economic subject have to deal with a well-defined sector of economic theory and reality. The confines of the subject are comparatively easy to discern and the main problem is to pick out relevant excerpts which will give a well-balanced picture of the state of present-day knowledge and its current trends.

With the subject of power the situation is different. There are no clear cut areas which unequivocally belong to this theme. This is above all due to the fact that power elements can pop up to a greater or lesser degree in all sorts of economic situations. The problem is further complicated because 'power' is such a vague concept. In relation to economic affairs it can take on very different forms. Even if we do not bother about niceties of definition[9] and details of form we can easily see that very different things fall under the power-economics complex. Thus we can think of economic power in terms of unequal initial positions in

8. A remarkable classic in this respect is the famous article by Böhm-Bawerk (1914).

9. It may be permitted to quote an old anecdote which is appropriate in this context. It tells of a university professor in the medical faculty who tries to define 'illness' for his students. After having discussed some twenty different definitions, none of which is fully satisfactory, he continues: 'Now look, if a patient comes to me and tells me he is ill, *he* knows what he means, and *I* know what he means, and that, after all, is important.' 'Power' is probably a concept not so very different from 'illness'.

the market which permit some agents to reap special benefits *in and through* the market mechanism. Conversely, one can find situations where the workings of the market are used to derive power which may then be used for economic or non-economic ends or may even be an aim in itself. Again, a relationship arises when power – be it of economic or non-economic origin – is being used to change the institutional framework and the market mechanism itself so that its working yields different results. And, finally, added to all these objective difficulties of delineation and definition is the previously stressed fact that the whole power problem has been badly neglected in economic literature and has never been systematically treated.

In view of these circumstances any choice of readings in this field will by necessity be somewhat haphazard. No rounded picture of a closed subject can be given. The best one can hope is that a perusal of the present selection will provide a certain 'feel' for the lacunae in present-day theory, for the main aspects of the power problem, and for some of the concrete forms in which it appears.

To approach this aim a mixture of general and more special excerpts have been included. The general articles contain both critical remarks about shortcomings of ruling theories as well as positive contributions towards a better understanding of power influences. These general analyses are supplemented by investigations of power emanations in important specific areas. These items should be taken as examples and not as a complete listing of 'power-infested' economic areas.

Two limitations must be mentioned. Firstly, contributions dealing exclusively or primarily with narrowly defined problems of market power have not been included in this selection. As was mentioned earlier, the price-setting powers of monopolies or the higgling of labour market organizations have been taken up early and regularly by the respective chapters of economic theory. They are treated as the main exemptions in the basic competitive model rather than as special examples in the much wider field of power influences. In any case, this type of analysis is well established and can best be studied in its own specific context.[10]

10. Thus, relevant contributions can be found in Penguin Modern Economics series in the volumes edited by Hunter (1969) and by McCormick and Smith (1968).

The second limitation refers to the period covered. All included items have been written in the past thirty years. The exclusion of older works means that some first-rate contributions do not appear. But to go back further and, in particular, to show the ancestry of some of the ideas represented in this book would have increased the number of essential candidates far beyond the possibilities of a single readings volume. Moreover, the concentration on writings of the recent past has the advantage that the illustrations from and references to reality are still more or less significant for the world in which we live.

References

BÖHM-BAWERK, E. (1914), 'Macht oder ökonomisches Gesetz?', *Zeitschrift für Volkswirtschaft, Socialpolitik und Verwaltung*, vol. 23, no. 3–4, pp. 205–71. (Translated into English as 'Control or Economic Law?', *Shorter Classics of Böhm-Bawerk*, Libertarian Press, 1962.)

BRADY, R. A. (1943), *Business as a System of Power*, Columbia University Press.

HICKS, J. R. (1946), *Value and Capital*, Oxford University Press, 2nd edn.

HUNTER, A. (ed.) (1969), *Monopoly and Competition*, Penguin Books.

McCORMICK, B. J., and SMITH, E. O. (eds.) (1968), *The Labour Market*, Penguin Books.

MYRDAL, G. (1953), *The Political Element in the Development of Economic Theory*, Routledge & Kegan Paul.

NEUMANN, J. VON, and MORGENSTERN, O. (1944), *The Theory of Games and Economic Behavior*, Wiley.

[4]

Micro-Foundations, Ad Hocery, and Keynesian Theory

KURT W. ROTHSCHILD*

Methodological questions are a nuisance. As if it were not enough to cope with the problems of relevancy, applicability, prognostic qualities, and the like of competing theories, one is confronted with rules of procedure which are supposed to tell one what they are permitted to do or not to do. It is no secret that some of the best economists paid little attention to methodological issues because the real problems kept them busy all the time. This did not prevent them from achieving interesting and useful results. This does not mean that it may not be fruitful to get acquainted with methodological issues. But methodology becomes dangerous when it moves to the center of the stage and hampers the search for new insights and theoretical approaches.

So, if this paper deals only with methodological issues it needs some excuse. The excuse is that for quite a while now Keynesian and post-Keynesian theories have been under attack from neoclassical and neo-Walrasian[1] economists not because of differences regarding assumptions or results—here confrontations are desirable and important—but on the basis of purely ideological and methodological objections. As far as the latter are concerned, the attacks concentrate mainly on missing microfoundations and a too frequent use of *ad hoc* arguments. Because of these blemishes, the Keynesian model is regarded as poor theory (if theory at all) quite apart from its relevancy and its results.

Two quotations from authors who are by no means hostile to Keynesian views can serve as a good illustration for this attitude. In an evaluation of Hicks' path-breaking revival of equilibrium theory in *Value and Capital*, Clower [1975, p. 7] stresses that Hicks had provided an impulse for the neo-Walrasian revolution "by explicitly linking his lucid and scholarly account of general equilibrium theory wth the rather unscholarly but vastly exciting and 'socially relevant' analysis of Keynes' *General Theory*."

The second quotation comes from a paper which Hahn presented to an International Economic Association Conference on Microeconomic Foundations of Macroeconomics. Keynes' theory, said Hahn, is of interest to a practitioner of general equilibrium theory for two reasons: on the one hand it deals exactly with those questions which remain undecided in equilibrium theory (how equilibrium is reached and how signals are transmitted); but on the other hand, so he complains [Hahn, 1977, p. 25], "it [the Keynesian theory] is plainly in need of proper theoretical foundations." The use of the words "plainly" and "proper" should be noted. Though Keynes' writings are regarded as an important contribution to economic knowledge, it is regarded as obvious that certain rules have to be kept irrespective of the real insights.

It is interesting to note to what extent even authors who do not regard general equilibrium theory as a useful starting point for a realistic macroeconomic theory submit to the methodological imperatives of the neoclassical school.[2] Thus, Moss, in a book

---

*Vienna, Austria. Paper presented at the Twenty-Third International Atlantic Economic Conference, April 20-27, 1987, Munich, West Germany.

[1]The expression "Neo-Walrasian Theory" was introduced by Clower [1975] as a name for equilibrium theories without an auctioneer (neoclassical disequilibrium theories).

[2]The vague term "neoclassic" is used to denote all the different varieties of general equilibrium theory stretching from Walras and the Marginalists to all sorts of neo-Walrasianism. Common attributes are: a microeconomic and frequently static basis; decision making on rational optimizing lines; concentration on market mechanisms; converting uncertainty into risk; and neglecting the historical aspects of time.

12

31

where he develops a new macro-theory with disequilibrium tendencies and a certain affinity to Keynesian perspectives, writes that he accepts the traditional model of decision making as an axiom, because [Moss, 1984, p. 73] "it prevents the analyst from employing *ad hoc* behavioural postulates for either convenience or ideological appeal." Now, the avoidance of ideological bias is certainly an important demand, if one is aiming at a truly scientific interpersonal exchange of arguments and conclusions; but why "convenient" assumptions which may help to treat a problem in a more realistic or more tractable way (e.g., linearization of a function) should be exorcised on principle is not self-evident. This question will be reviewed later when the paper deals with *ad hoc* reasoning.

The few examples just mentioned should suffice to show that Keynesian theory is subjected to massive methodological attacks; these attacks require an answer. This paper tries to contribute to such an answer. It does not claim to be complete or to be particularly original; but the author believes (or better: is afraid) that the decisive arguments still need to be mentioned and repeated.

When one turns to the micro-foundations for (Keynesian) macro-theories, one is faced with a two-stage problem. The first touches the wider question, whether a microeconomic foundation is really needed to attach validity to a macroeconomic theory, to make it a true theory. The second question is whether such a foundation—if it is possible and desired—should build on the contents and methodology of the ruling neoclassical paradigm. The answer will be negative in both cases.

Start by considering the trivial observation that economic reality is an extremely complex and dynamic phenomenon. This has prevented economists (and the same holds for all social scientists) from coming anywhere near a "ruling" or "unique" paradigm, such as can at least be approximated in some branches of natural science.

Economics is, by necessity, a multi-paradigmatic science. Several theoretical structures exist side by side, and each theory can never be more than a partial theory; be that it deals only with a limited area (money and credit, regional economics, and so forth); or be that it aims at a global explanation, which then necessitates a concentration on a very limited selection from the numerous elements and interrelations of the system. A comprehensive economic theory covering all important economic events seems hardly feasible.

For this reason alone, one cannot expect a necessary link between micro- and macro-theory, just as one does not expect a close correspondence between a theory of exchange rates and a theory of the firm. Certainly, there will be overlaps, relationships and contradictions between various theoretical approaches, which can act as a stimulus for further research and better results. But differences in situations and differences in problems will demand different starting points in the highly selective process of choosing the proper variables and relationships.

With these facts in mind, one should recognize first of all that micro- and macro-theories are not just competing or complementary theories, but partial theories with restricted and different research programs. Taking the special case of neoclassical micro-theory, the original question concerned the possibility and uniqueness of a consistent result arising from uncoordinated individual decisions in markets with flexible prices. In the special case of Keynesian macro-theory, the problems centered on total production and employment in a dynamic and uncertain environment. These theories overlap insofar as both of them deal with the global economy, but they are different and partial theories as regards the problems and perspectives which each of them stresses.

A confrontation of these theories can help to recognize more clearly the boundaries of each approach and also lead to critical modifications in overlapping areas. One could also try to build bridges between the two approaches or even to construct some combinations in more complex super-theories. But there can be no justification for a hierarchical stipulation that (Keynesian or other) macro-theories require a microeconomic foundation to obtain full validity. One could just as well demand a macroeconomic foundation for microeconomics, when the latter finds it difficult to fit macroeconomic realities into its own framework.

A possible argument giving logical priority to micro-foundations could be the observation that macro-results must result from micro activities. But this is not conclusive. Fallacy of composition and the dependence of individual actions on the social environment prevent a simple derivation of macro-events from microanalysis. Both, micro- and macroeconomics, can act as ports of entry for theoretical analysis, each using different materials and hypotheses without establishing any methodological claims to a special foundation role.[3]

A demand for micro-foundations of Keynesian economics, which is not accompanied by a similar desire for proper macroeconomic foundations for microeconomics, implies, therefore, that one regards the ruling micro-approach as theoretically superior; therefore, it should serve as a standard for Keynesian economics and other nonorthodox model builders. That this is, in fact, a widely accepted view can be deduced—explicitly or implicitly—from many remarks which refer to this question.

As an example, Hahn, who after a discussion of certain aspects of general equilibrium theory, goes on to say [1977, p. 39]:

"This leaves at least one important matter undiscussed. That is, of course, macroeconomics, which we think of as an essentially Keynesian invention. The reason for not discussing it is that I have nothing to say. Certainly macroeconomics serves as a good 'simpler' model, which many economists feel is what we need. It also no doubt helps treasuries. But how one is to give it a theoretical foundation I do not know."[4]

If one dismisses the idea that the word "theory" is merely an expression for schools of thought which one prefers, then it is not quite easy to understand why—to use Hahn's words—a "good" model which economists see as being "needed" and which treasuries find "useful" should require theoretical foundations rather than being regarded as one theory among many. But one does not need to deal with the rather idle question of what sort of definition of the term "theory" one should adopt; there exist many definitions from which one can choose. The concern is with the question of what sort of ideas about theories, methods, and contents give rise to such doubts about the nature of Keynesian economics and to the call for a microeconomic foundation.

A closer look at the various demands for such a foundation reveals two main lines of argument. On the one hand, the vagueness and loose nature of many sectors in Keynesian and post-Keynesian literature is contrasted with the rigorous formulations and the consistent framework of equilibrium theory. On the other hand, is the complaint that the behavior of some of the macroeconomic aggregates cannot be easily (if at all) reconciled with the rational individual decision rules which form the core of

---

[3]If the demand for microeconomic foundations rests on the argument that the individual decision process should be fully specified (what Keynes failed to do), then one could as well ask for a foundation of neoclassical decision theory on the basis of psychological theories. This might lead to some unpleasant surprises. A regress to some deeper foundations could probably continue for quite a while.

---

[4]Another telling example for the tendency to deny theoretical character to a nontraditional model, which is explicitly declared to be enlightening and useful, can be found in the well-known survey article on segmented labor markets by Cain [1976].

neoclassical theory.[5] The first argument aims mainly at questions of scientific form and method; the second is more concerned with substance and consistency of contents. But, as will be shown, these two aspects are not completely disconnected.

First, consider the problems of rigor, determinateness, generality, and consistency of the systems. Without hesitation, one can concede right away that the neoclassical paradigm displays all these characteristics to a far higher degree than Keynesian and post-Keynesian theory. Also, there is no doubt that, *ceteris paribus*, science should always aim at the highest possible standards in these respects. But what remains to be considered are three important questions: (1) Since rigor, determinacy, generality, and consistency can normally not be achieved over the whole field of social sciences, the question arises how much rigor is essential and how far softer methods can be admitted without robbing the resulting structure of its theoretical character; (2) Given the necessity for some tolerance in standards, does a higher formal standard (rigor) by itself justify a claim for a higher place in the scientific hierarchy; and (3) Closely connected with these points, is one not to some extent faced with a difficult trade-off between rigor, determinateness, generality, and consistency on the one hand and certain other important demands on a theory on the other, like problem orientation, operationality, prognostic efficiency, even—*horribile dictu*—causal plausibility?

When one is prepared to take these

problems seriously, the demand for a foundation based on the general equilibrium model becomes rather questionable. The original research interest of equilibrium theory, the question whether isolated individual decisions can lead to determinate and stable market results, justified the adoption of some rather simple assumptions with regard to decision making (maximizing behavior), technology (well-behaved production functions), markets (competition), and fully flexible prices. There was no need—as far as the main query was concerned—to introduce a greater correspondence with reality or to grapple with all sorts of possible complications. On this narrow basis, it was possible to erect an impressive and intellectually satisfying rigorous theoretical structure which proved extremely effective in answering the original questions regarding the possibility and nature of a general equilibrium.

As time went on, constant improvements and extensions (imperfect competition, incomplete information, increasing returns to scale, and so on) enabled the theory to throw important light on a growing number of market-related questions. This progress was, all the time, both helped and hindered by the desire to keep the basic structure intact. It is this structure which guarantees the unified character and formal elegance of the theory.

The research program and the specific theoretical approach suited to this program enabled general equilibrium theory to achieve standards of formal rigor and exactness which are unique among the social sciences. This enabled neoclassical economists to take the methods of macro-physics, and particularly of mechanics, as the ideal to be followed, and to take these formal requirements as one of the main characteristics by which to judge the scientific quality of competing theories. This attitude was fostered by a relatively uncritical reception of certain rules and procedures which some philosophers of science had developed in

---

[5]Two quotations can serve as illustrations. With regard to the first argument [Clower, 1975, p. 8]: "Discussion of standard microtheoretical problems of household and business behavior—by Marshall as well as by Keynes—tends accordingly to be vague and, by contemporary standards, unsatisfactory." And as far as the second point is concerned [Streissler, 1977, p. 123]: "The need for a substructure of macroeconomic models built upon a foundation of individual optimisation is often argued. It is asserted that only the aggregation of individual optima can yield determinate macroeconomic results."

connection with research in the natural sciences.

However, one must face the fact that full and uncompromising formal rigor can only be maintained in purely mathematical, logical, and formal analyses (this explains why pure neoclassical economic theory proves so attractive for mathematicians). In problem-oriented, real world sciences (both social and natural sciences), compromises have to be made if they are to meet their research targets. A dogmatic adherence to the standards of rigor, generality, and determinate results may not only fail to improve theoretical insights, it might even stand in the way of constructing a more suitable framework. If the object to be investigated is very complex, if perhaps reality itself lacks precision, then a demand for ever higher standards of precision in theoretical formulations can act as a barrier for a proper analysis of the real phenomena.[6]

This touches one of the decisive points in the micro-Keynes debate. Keynes' research program was not directed towards the explanation of the miraculous mechanics of a self-regulating system. He looked for a basis that would help him to understand the forces behind the dynamics of aggregate income and employment in the very complex and changing environment of modern capitalist nations. The complexity and inherent uncertainty of the developments he wanted to analyze did not only require assumptions, concepts, and data which are different from those of neoclassical microeconomics, they also require different methods.

Without going into the question of whether Keynes always managed to express himself as clearly and precisely as possible (he did not), one should stress that the mere fact that there is less rigor in his theory than in orthodox treaties, that one can find vague propositions and open questions, does not by itself permit the conclusion that a capacity for rigorous modeling is missing. This way of presenting the subject may be—so far—the only possible method to come to grips with the complex *problematique*.

Keynes did not spend much time in stating explicitly what his methodological guidelines were. But one can extract his main ideas from his work. This has been done by several writers in much greater detail than could be done in this paper.[7] Here, this author only wants to mention Keynes' criticism regarding an excessive use of mathematics [1936, p. 298]: "Too large a proportion of recent 'mathematical' economics are mere concoctions, as imprecise as the initial assumptions they rest on, which allow the author to lose sight of the complexities and interdependencies of the real world in a maze of pretentious and unhelpful symbols." His doubts about Tinbergen's econometric models, as well as his remark that one should always keep a number of alternatives at the back of one's mind, all go to show that he was clearly aware that he had to look for special methods to meet the requirements of a difficult subject.

And these methods cannot be more precise than the object itself. It is not by chance that the question, "What did Keynes really say?," comes up again and again, and that the same question is raised in connection with Smith, Ricardo, Marx, or Schumpeter. One could almost say that it is a methodological necessity that such a question arises whenever a first-rate mind turns to a very complex theme where time, uncertainty, and expectations play an important part. A good theory must mirror these uncertainties and the shiftiness of the situations so that it is open

---

[6]Elster quite generally stresses the fact that logic may suffice in relatively simple contexts, while judgment is required and efficient when very complex situations arise. This is also true for science [Elster, 1985, p. 17]: "Within the sciences one may make a rough distinction between those which require logic above all, and those which mainly require the less formal exercise of judgment."

[7]See, for instance, Kregel [1976] and Lawson and Pesaran [1985].

to several interpretations. This does not, of course, exclude that certain parts of the complex system can be separated and treated in a rigorous fashion. The IS/LM analysis of various aspects of a fix-price economy can be taken as an example.

Yet, doubts could be raised whether such a procedure can still be regarded as scientific method, as a proper theory. To some extent, this is a question of definitions and "calling names," and insofar this is the case, the question loses interest. But it becomes important when one asks whether this is indeed a path which leads to a systematic improvement in scientific knowledge, whether this broadening of methods to include a wider rhetoric and argumentation has a serious history in economics and other sciences. And here the answer seems to be quite clear: A freedom from narrow methodological prescriptions has often proved to be an essential precondition for new insights and the birth of new theories; and this is no less true for the natural sciences than for the social sciences. The greater the complexity of a phenomenon and of its interrelated elements, the greater the importance of attacking the problem from different angles and with a variety of methods.

The importance of methodological pluralism and the dubious nature of narrow methodological prescriptions has recently been very forcefully presented by Feyerabend [1975] for science in general and by McCloskey [1985] for economics in particular. Even if one is not prepared to accept Feyerabend's spirited attack against traditional methodological imperatives in its entirety, it is hardly possible not to be impressed by his arguments and examples showing that the progress towards "truth" did not follow Popper's or other rules, but was achieved by all sorts of attempts and attacks which were suggested by the problems at hand and the questions to be answered.

Feyerabend comes to the conclusion—on the basis of investigating the progress in

physics from early times right up to modern developments—that some of the most revolutionary theoretical discoveries could only take place because some thinkers either quite deliberately acted against generally accepted methodological rules or worked against them by sheer neglect. For an economist, it is not difficult to detect here a parallel to Keynes.

This is a good place for adding a short remark on *ad hocery*. One of the reasons for demanding micro-foundations for Keynesian theories is the complaint that they tend to turn too often to *ad hoc* assumptions and are not able to derive their results from basic axioms in the same strict manner as is done in neoclassical theory. One could, of course, argue that a certain amount of *ad hoc* thinking also goes into the choice of axioms, but that would be beside the point; of concern here is that this objection against *ad hoc* reasoning is also one of those methodological rules whose absoluteness should be questioned.

One can easily agree that *ad hoc* reasoning should be regarded as unscientific when it is introduced in order to save some theory or to obtain a desired result. But the situation is very different when *ad hoc* considerations are used in a new area of research where one meets many "white spots" and has to experiment with soft hypotheses. In this case, *ad hoc* arguments which are well reasoned can be a valuable instrument in order to feel one's way into new areas and to experiment with different assumptions. *Ad hocery* of this sort is not a theoretical weakness but can be—as Feyerabend again shows with special stress on the natural sciences—a necessary element in the difficult stages of developing new theories or extending old ones.

So far, these considerations have shown that from a purely methodological point of view there seem to be no decisive arguments which would support the micro-foundation demand. Micro- and macro-theories (in their neoclassical and Keynesian form) have different perspectives and research targets which demand different strategies. None of them can claim methodological priority.

On the other hand, both theories deal with the same object—the global economy. This leads to comparisons and confrontations, particularly since general equilibrium theory has expanded beyond the original aim of explaining the complicated mechanism of a flexible market system. It has turned increasingly to a more direct treatment of those economic and policy problems which inspired Keynes' departure. Such confrontations can fulfill an important and stimulating function for theoretical development. But, one should see that this confrontation is a mutual relationship on a symmetrical and not on a hierarchical basis.

The debate between the two schools has so far not lacked vitality and provocation, and it has certainly helped both sides to improve their theoretical structures. One cannot help feeling that in this process of mutual stimulation the neoclassical micro-theory derived more benefits from the Keynesian challenge than the other way round. The micro-foundation debate at least has not yet delivered any substantial fruits for Keynesian theory.[8] This lack of symmetry is partly due to the obvious relevance of the Keynesian *problematique* which had to be taken up by a neoclassical theory turning to real world problems. But, since the basic structure of the equilibrium theory had to be preserved, there was only room for some half-hearted adjustments. These neglected several important aspects of the Keynesian and post-Keynesian research program: the problem of historical time degenerates to a sequence of temporary equilibria; uncertainty is assimilated to a choice problem with costly

information; and the role of money in a dynamic, uncertain monetary economy is played down.

On the other hand, the special case of wage and price rigidity, where neoclassical and Keynesian theories get into closer touch (and where the difficult problem of the price formation process disappears), gets a lot of attention. This taming of Keynesian theory enabled neoclassical theory to accept the Keynesian challenge without endangering the core of their theory, which was not created to deal with problems of this sort.

This brings one to the second aspect of the micro-foundations debate. It concerns not so much the methodological question but is based on the claim that only neoclassical theory can offer a consistent theory of individual decision making in the economic sphere. It should, therefore, be possible to derive macroeconomic phenomena from these micro-laws. This also applies to Keynesian theory. So here, one is faced not with methodological niceties but with the question of to what extent the neoclassical choice theory can be regarded as a relevant and valid basis for Keynesian-type macro-theories.

As in the case of methodology, one must beware of looking for simple absolute answers. Hypotheses which may be adequate in some contexts may be of no use when dealing with different problems. It shall be argued that the neoclassical decision theory and the equilibrium analysis connected with it can be regarded as appropriate for its own research program (though—as shall be indicated—to a diminishing extent), but is totally unsuitable for the Keynesian *problematique*.

Remember that the original problem of equilibrium theory concerns the possibility and uniqueness of a general equilibrium emerging from decentralized individual decisions. It is quite useful and defensible to start off with relatively uncomplicated and well-behaved assumptions, like perfect competition and individual optimization

---

[8]In spite of intensive discussions among leading economists, only meager conclusions were obtained at the International Economic Association Conference on Microeconomic Foundations of Macroeconomics. In the final summary, Lady Hicks noted [Harcourt, 1977, p. 395]: "By and large little progress has been made towards the objective of identifying the general relations between microeconomics and macroeconomics."

behavior, as long as there exists at least some link with real market phenomena. This may be the only way to achieve precise answers to the special problem under discussion. From this basis, one could hope to advance to more complicated research programs and economic problems by introducing an ever wider number of modifications and extensions.

But, from the very beginning, this process of extension was characterized by the desire and tendency to leave the basic structure of the equilibrium model as unscathed as possible. So, a strong inclination persists to stress that atomistic markets with flexible prices are not too strong an abstraction from the reality of a competitive world, and the *homo economicus* is presented as a quite plausible picture of interest-oriented behavior in the economic sphere.

It is interesting, though, that normally no demand is made for a further foundation of these assumptions by making use of newer results of psychology, sociology, and organization theory. It is, of course, true that these sciences are not yet able to deliver hard theories and results which could be easily generalized. Neoclassical theory seems to offer particular resistance against the inclusion of some interesting suggestions from these sources because they could undermine the basis on which the whole equilibrium structure rests.

It is understandable and even justifiable that one adhered to a somewhat primitive view of psychology and decision making, because it seemed to offer the key to a precise microeconomic analysis of a wide variety of microeconomic questions. This strategy was the more acceptable as the assumptions fit quite well the observable behavior of individuals and firms under the rather strict constraints of the nineteenth and early twentieth century. Most households were then under strong pressure to make ends meet in order to obtain certain obvious necessities on the basis of their meager incomes. A majority of firms had to struggle

to survive in a highly competitive environment by making some profits in order to avoid bankruptcy and loss of status. They all had to act under strong pressure to achieve certain, more or less clearly defined, essential targets.

But such behavior—acting under the pressure of essential needs and strict constraints—has the same outward appearance as the behavior in a world where individuals with given preferences and certain (but not pressing) constraints freely decide how to optimize their utility. The externally (through existential needs and small incomes) enforced behavior of spending one's income on bread and clothes could also be seen as a free choice resulting in maximum utility. The reality could, therefore, be quite easily interpreted as compatible with the neoclassical vision (though other assumptions, e.g., habitual behavior, might also have worked). In addition, the future and its uncertainty also posed no big problems as the narrowness of the resources enforced a concentration on immediate needs and actions.

All this has changed quite fundamentally in the wealthier countries. Oligopolistic structures, organizations and lobbies, state intervention, and the like have enormously expanded the room for entrepreneurial and organizational action. Households which no longer live in the neighborhood of a biologically determined standard can now decide freely about the purchase of nonessentials by saving and distributing their expenditure over time. The pressures of the past have lost their absolute character and individuals, as well as groups and firms, have a far wider range of possible choices, just as they always had in other spheres of life which are not subjected to the dismal laws of economics.

Under such conditions, the primitive hypothesis of optimizing behavior is no longer an efficient general basis, if one aims at results which are in close touch with reality. People decide under weak pressure and are surrounded by a cloud of uncertainty as to what to buy or invest today or tomorrow, how liquid their status should be in face of past commitments and hoped-for or dreaded future developments, what groups to join for collective action, and so forth. To this has to be added that in the macroeconomic environment the interrelationships between individual and group actions become very important.

The changed environment of more recent decades could provide strong arguments for a revision of the basic assumptions of traditional microeconomics and to pay more attention to various psychological and sociological elements.[9] Quite a number of ideas and approaches in this direction have been developed: satisfying behavior, bounded rationality, X-efficiency, several new aspects in the theory of the firm and of organizations, and the like. But it is obvious that there are strong inhibitions on the part of traditional neoclassical economists to incorporate such ideas. They threaten the delicate structure of their theory, together with its obvious methodological and ideological (Pareto optimality) attractions.[10]

But whatever traditional micro-theory might think about its own requirements with regard to new foundations, there can be little doubt that the existing neoclassical micro-theory cannot serve as a foundation for a macro-theory that wants to keep in touch with the realities and problems of the present day world and has already begun to develop some suitable theoretical instruments to tackle these problems. This applies not only to Keynesian theory but to all theories which have similar research programs.

One sees similar questions arising in game theory, which also originated as a consequence of certain misgivings with traditional behavioral hypotheses. One the one hand, one sees attempts to stress the parallels between game theory and traditional equilibrium theory and to marry the two approaches. On the other hand, those who take the critical content of game theory seriously realize that its new ideas of strategic and collective behavior cannot find a suitable basis in neoclassical microeconomics [Shubik, 1975].

The demand for a micro-foundation of Keynesian theory, in order to give it a secure methodological basis and to achieve consistency between micro- and macro-theory, thus seems to be ill-founded. Perfect consistency between micro- and macro-theories is at present probably unattainable in view of limited knowledge, different research targets, aggregation problems, and the like. Moreover, consistency between neoclassical micro-theory and Keynesian macro-theory is not even desirable because the former—apart from needing a revision—rests on a program of abstraction which hinders the access to those problems which have a central position in Keynesian and post-Keynesian research, *viz.*, uncertainty, time, dynamics, and money in a world of contracts and monetary obligations.[11] If a micro-foundation for Keynesian theory is deemed necessary,[12] it will have to follow a different route.

---

[9]In actual fact, neoclassical strategy tends to go in the opposite direction. To prevent a softening of their useful apparatus of rational decision making through coming into contact with the complex and not very precise insights of psychologists, sociologists, and politologists, one tries to "economize" these other sciences by forcing their material into the framework of traditional economic theory. For a critical discussion of this tendency, see Schanz [1979].

[10]How far-reaching these consequences could be can be surmised by reading Kornai's [1971] thoughtful attack on equilibrium strategies.

[11]Leaving aside the role of effective demand in Keynesian thinking, whose importance is admitted in all interpretations of his approach, one finds quite a variety of opinions regarding the specific elements of his theory. It may be uncertainty and dynamics [Shackle, 1974]; historical time and the monetary character of the economy [Chick, 1983]; or expectations and dynamics [Kregel 1976]. But all these elements are closely related, as Robinson has always pointed out.

[12]That attempts in this direction could only be an advantage can hardly be denied. That Keynes did not pay sufficient attention to this question is a criticism which is also advanced by economists who are by no means hostile to the Keynesian approach. See, for example, Kaldor, Hahn, and Solow at the Keynes Centenary Conference in Cambridge [Worthwick and Trevithick, 1983] and the paper by Salant [1985] referring to their discussions.

This is not the place to investigate the various methods with which Keynes and post-Keynesians have experimented in this field. But it cannot be denied that the need for progress in this sphere is recognized. That "animal spirits," the fragile mixture of statics and dynamics, and similar vaguely defined elements in Keynes' writings cannot be described as fully satisfactory is obvious. Further analysis has since taken place and much more is still needed. But Keynes' refusal to force a rigid pattern on a vague and uncertain world, only in order to obtain formally precise results, should remain a guiding line for this research.

REFERENCES

G. G. Cain, "The Challenge of Segmented Labor Market Theories to Orthodox Theory: A Survey," *Journal of Economic Literature*, 14, 1976, pp. 1215-57.

V. Chick, *Macroeconomics after Keynes. A Reconsideration of the General Theory*, Oxford, 1983.

R. Clower, "Reflections on the Keynesian Perplex," Zeitschrift für Nationalökonomie, 35, 1975, pp. 1-24.

J. Elster, *Sour Grapes. Studies in the Subversion of Rationality*, Cambridge, 1985.

P. Feyerabend, *Against Method. Outline of an Anarchistic Theory of Knowledge*, London, 1975.

F. H. Hahn, "Keynesian Economics and General Equilibrium Theory: Reflections on Some Current Debates," in *The Microeconomic Foundations of Macroeconomics*, Harcourt, ed., 1977, pp. 25-40.

G. C. Harcourt, ed., *The Microeconomic Foundations of Macroeconomics*, London, 1977.

J. M. Keynes, *The General Theory of Employment, Interest, and Money*, London, 1936.

J. Kornai, *Antiequilibrium. On Economic Systems Theory and the Tasks of Research*, Amsterdam, 1971.

J. Kregel, "Economic Methodology in the Face of Uncertainty: The Modelling Methods of Keynes and the Post-Keynesians," *Economic Journal*, 86, 1976, pp. 209-25.

T. Lawson and H. Pesaran, eds., *Keynes' Economics: Methodological Issues*, London, 1985.

D. N. McCloskey, *The Rhetoric of Economics*, Brighton, 1985.

S. Moss, *Markets and Macroeconomics. Macroeconomic Implications of Rational Individual Behaviour*, Oxford, 1984.

W. Salant, "Keynes and the Modern World: A Review Article," *Journal of Economic Literature*, 23, 1985, pp. 1176-85.

G. Schanz, "Ökonomische Theorie als sozialwissenschaftliches Paradigma?," *Soziale Welt*, Heft 3, 1979, pp. 257-74.

G. L. S. Shackle, *Keynesian Kaleidics*, Edinburgh, 1974.

M. Shubik, "The General Equilibrium Model is Incomplete and Not Adequate for the Reconciliation of Micro- and Macroeconomic Theory," *Kyklos*, 28, 1975, pp. 545-73.

E. Streissler, "What Kind of Microeconomic Foundations of Macroeconomics are Necessary?," in *The Microeconomic Foundations of Macroeconomics*, Harcourt, ed., 1977, pp. 96-128.

D. Worswick and J. Trevithick, eds., *Keynes and the Modern World: Proceedings of the Keynes Centenary Conference*, King's College, Cambridge, 1983.

5

European Journal of Political Economy 5 (1989) 1–12. North-Holland

POLITICAL ECONOMY OR ECONOMICS?

Some Terminological and Normative Considerations

Kurt W. ROTHSCHILD*

Döblinger Hauptstr. 77a, A-1190 Vienna, Austria

The article first tries to draw a distinction between a 'political economy' based on a distinctly interdisciplinary attitude and a predominantly 'pure' science of 'economics'. Several types of approaches to a political economy are discussed and it is argued that there are many possible ports of entry. Typical characteristics are an interest in other social sciences, a critical attitude to neoclassical rigidity, theoretical and empirical openness. The paper closes with an appeal for peaceful coexistence of good theory – political economy and economics.

1. Some terminological and normative considerations

Marxists, Neo-Ricardians, Post-Keynesians – whatever their theoretical differences and disputes may be – are probably in full agreement that they are 'political economists' in contrast to the pure 'economics' of the ruling neoclassical paradigm. But various other economists also regard their studies as political economy, while some deny that there exists any difference between 'political economy' and 'economics'. There seems to be some confusion and vagueness in the use of these labels and with regard to their possible significance. In this paper I shall first discuss terminological aspects regarding the diverse uses of the term 'political economy', and then add some (subjective) normative considerations about the characteristics which a 'proper' political economist should display.

To begin with we should note that there is a historical hiatus in the use of the two terms. In the classical period of the 18th and 19th century 'political economy' was *generally* used to describe the subject of economic theory. It had become popular after James Steuart had published his *Inquiry into the Principles of Political Economy* in 1767 and it kept its monopoly position for

*The author presented this paper at the annual meeting of the European Public Choice Society at Bergen, May 18–21. An earlier version of this paper has been published in Winfried Vogt (ed.), Politische Ökonomie heute. Beiträge zur Tagung des Arbeitskreises Politische Ökonomie im Herbst 1987, Regensburg: transfer, 1988, under the title 'Politische Ökonomie oder "Economics"? Einige terminologische und normative Betrachtungen'

more than a hundred years. The introduction of the term 'economics' coincided with the switch from classical economics to marginal theory after 1870 and gained wide acceptance with Alfred Marshall's *Principles of Economics* (1980). But the use of the new term was not consciously introduced to mark a break in theoretical development or as a programmatic declaration. Marshall was certainly more dedicated to classical theory and more of a 'political' economist than his contemporary Francis Y. Edgeworth who published a collection of his more neoclassic articles under the title *Papers Relating to Political Economy* (1925).

But the fact remains that in mainstream economics the term 'economics' more and more displaced the old 'political economy' which either fell into complete disuse or was reserved for the description of classical, Marxian, and some other 'unorthodox' theories. By the middle of our century the term 'political economy' had become a rarity. In the five years 1953 to 1957 only three books were published in the English-speaking world containing this term in their title (according to the *Cumulative Book Index*).[1] But in more recent years there has been a remarkable change. Keynesian policy, the experience of war economies, the increased involvement of the state and organisations in economic affairs and, last but not least, the growing awareness of systemic interrelations between economic, social, and political processes have brought back the usage of the term 'political economy'. In the past decade several new journals have been started which carry 'political economy' in their title and in one year alone – 1983 – 50 books with such titles were published.[2] Also, a number of economics series were renamed political economy series, mostly without any noticeable changes in programs and contents.

Thus leaving the historical development aside we are faced with the (terminological) question what 'political economy' signifies *to-day* and what its differences – if any – are with regard to 'economics'. The best way to attack this question is perhaps to turn to three queries which David Whynes poses in a book on political economy which he edited [Whynes (1984)]:

(1) Is there a genuine and clear difference between economics and political economy?
(2) Is the political economy of today the same as the 19th century specimen or a different one?
(3) Are there several 'political economies'?

Since the answers to questions (1) and (2) obviously depend to some extent on the way question (3) is answered, we take the last one first. And here the answer is not difficult: even a quick glance at what is currently called 'political economy' reveals quite clearly that several very different approaches

---

[1]This information is taken from Whynes (1984, p. 1).
[2]See footnote 1.

coexist. So much is this the case that one could be tempted to resign oneself to the definition that 'political economy is what political economists do'. But this would be too simple a solution and something more concrete will later be said on this point. In any case, the realisation that different types of 'political economy' exist make it clear that no simple answers of 'yes' or 'no' are possible when we deal with questions (1) and (2).

As far as question (1) is concerned the answer is both 'yes' and 'no'. There is a difference between 'economics' and 'political economy' in the sense that there has existed through all the years a corpus of 'political economy' characterised by a conscious opposition to the ruling neoclassic paradigm and various attempts to develop alternative approaches, methods, and theories. On the other hand, the answer is 'no' when we look at some examples of the once again fashionable use of the term 'political economy'. Here we find publications where the traditional subjects of 'economics' are enriched by a greater awareness or a mere mentioning of political and institutional influences. Similarly, with regard to question (2), we get examples where an affinity to the classical political economy is quite clearly present (Neo-Ricardians, Neo-Marxism), while other types of political economy are following new and different paths.

This brings us back to the task of indicating the possible meanings of 'political economy' to-day if it is to be more than just a fashionable change of label for traditional 'economics'. One can do this either by enumerating significant examples of political economy analysis or – more ambitiously – by developing an all-embracing definition.

Let me start with an enumeration of different political economy approaches. Bruno Frey (1977), in a book on modern political economy, makes out five distinct groups which he regards as representative of present-day thinking in this field:

(1) Marxist and neo-Marxist approaches (new left, radical economics, Cambridge capital theory)
(2) System-theoretical approaches (methodological orientation, quantity-oriented; policy science)
(3) Traditional approaches (descriptive-empirical; historical school, current economic research: Brookings, Institutes of Social and Economic Research etcetera)
(4) 'Unorthodox' approaches (critical-sociological-innovative; institutionalists; Galbraith, Myrdal, Perroux, Hirschman, Kornai...)
(5) Economic theory of politics (Schumpeter–Downs tradition of extending economic methodology to the political sphere; Black, Buchanan, Olson, Frey...).

Though this list is probably not complete and though other combinations are certainly possible I do think that this enumeration does give a fair idea of the multitude and variety of political economy approaches. It is this variety which explains why satisfactory definitions of 'political economy', trying to cover the whole field, are practically not achievable. This can be shown by giving a few examples.[3]

Thus, Lionel Robbins (1981, p. 8) in a lecture on 'Economics and Political Economy' suggests the 'Political Economy is ... concerned with the assumptions of policy and the results flowing from them'. Equally general is the description given in *Webster's New Third International Dictionary* where political economy is described as the 'modern social science dealing with the interrelationships of political and social processes'. Fuller, but also more specialised definitions are, for instance, those by Robert Heilbroner (1969) who regards political economy as a theory of social evolution in whose core the economic dynamics must be systematically combined with political and social change, or by Thomas Hutchinson (1964) who talks of the 'art of political economy' which includes elements of professional judgement and intuition, normative statements on preferences and risks, and an interdisciplinary approach.

The foregoing sketch of attempts to classify and define 'political economy' shows – so I believe – that the mere declaration of a person or a 'school' that subscribes to a political economy approach does not in itself tell us very much. Political economy is no clear-cut trade mark or paradigm. But a certain unifying bond can probably be recognised when we approach the question from a negative angle. A large number of political economists of different persuasions will be able to reach a consensus on the question as to who should *not* be counted as a political economist. This is so because most branches of political economy share a critical attitude towards the hegemonic and comprehensive claims of the ruling neoclassic edifice. This criticism is directed particularly against the extensive use of methodological individualism, of equilibrium and harmony concepts, of marginalism, against the exogenous and static character of psychological and sociological assumptions, and against the neglect of historical and dynamic factors.

When these critical attitudes are taken as a typical characteristic for a political economy stance then it is clear that – from such a point of view – the so-called 'economic theory of politics' or 'modern political economy' cannot be counted as a branch of political economy proper, quite irrespective of the quality of its insights, because this approach tries to extend the methods and axioms of neoclassical economics to the sphere of politics and sociology. Instead of aiming at a true interdisciplinary combination of economics and political science in order to gain a wider perspective – political economy – it inhales politics in order to make it a branch of economics. While this 'economic imperialism' undoubtedly opens up some

---

[3]See also Borner (1975, ch. IV).

interesting new insights and certainly helps economists to talk about politics in a language with which they are familiar, it does at the same time bar the way to overcome the limitations of a narrow economic viewpoint. In particular, the extreme axioms of economic rationality in the micro-economic field[4] and the neglect of sociology, evolution, institutions, and history in neoclassical macroeconomics are a bad starting point for missionary expeditions into the field of political and societal developments.

But even if we agree to exclude 'modern political economy' from a more meaningful definition of 'political economy' there still remains a multitude of possibilities to find a place for political economy theories outside the confines of neoclassical economics. There can be no clear-cut criterion which can tell us exactly whether a person or theory falls into the political economy group or not. Views in this regard can be more or less restrictive and can hardly be free of normative ideas about 'desirable' elements. In other words, there is room for subjective judgements and the following remarks will necessarily contain a considerable portion of personal viewpoints and judgements.

Before noting down a number of observations I want, however, to return for a moment to the question of the 'non-neoclassical nature' of a 'proper' political economy. This view does not necessarily involve an *antineoclassical* attitude. One may very well regard neoclassical economics as an interesting and useful *partial* theory as long as it is clearly restricted to its original research program: the study of the workings of a market economy with (in principle) flexible prices in a relatively simple and stable setting. In this respect the theory with its numerous modifications and developments can throw considerable light on the intricacies of such a system. The point here is that this theory with its strict axioms *adapted to its specific research subject* is hardly capable to deal with the diverse and complicated questions which turn up when we want to give more weight to the neglected political and sociological elements. Political economy cannot be a mere extension of neoclassical economics; it must find new bases and approaches. To these questions we now turn.

One (and perhaps the most important) reason why political economy of almost every persuasion cannot be happy with neoclassical equilibrium theory is a methodological one. The considerable intellectual achievements of neoclassical theory and the rigour of its results were obtained by strictly isolating the economic sector from 'disturbing' influences in its models. 'Given' frameworks and 'ceteris paribus' clauses helped and help to study the mechanics of the market system under static and dynamic conditions which *formally* resemble the patterns of mechanical physics. But the very problems of a political economy, which are connected with group interests, diverse

---

[4]"The political man was a much less predictable animal than the economic man – and he still is' [Vickers (1968, p. 8)].

forms of decision making, and above all with the evolution and interdependence of political and economic processes, cannot be attacked within the strict limitations of neoclassical economics.

Yet the exodus from traditional economics is not without a price. One has to leave behind a theoretical structure which has achieved a high degree of internal consistency and 'scientific' methodology; and one has to venture into new fields of socio-economic interdependencies and dynamic processes which cannot so easily be put into a rigid theoretical framework. What one gains (or hopes to gain) in relevance has to be purchased by accepting a much higher degree of complexity. Indeed, it was the realisation of the enormous complexity of the socio-economic sphere which induced Max Plank to switch from economics to the 'simpler' world of physics. Some economists manage to escape from this complexity by moving completely to the rarefied air of 'pure' economics where many of these complexities can be avoided. But this is a path to irrelevance, not to political economy.

This means that political economists must probably admit quite openly and unashamedly that they cannot *and do not want to* compete at present with the methodological and (pseudo-)scientific standards of neoclassical economics, because this would necessarily involve a disabandonment of their research subject. Even when aiming at the highest standards obtainable political economy will have to rely on some degree of judgement, on a certain openness, a courage to admit the existence of lacunae and gaps.[5] The use of 'rhetoric', of persuasive arguments, which McCloskey (1985) has recently so strongly recommended to economists in general, has a particular role to play in political economy. Of course, the recognition and admission that political economy must be – at least in some parts – a 'soft' science opens the door to cranks and crooks. This is a real danger. But this danger cannot be banned by taking refuge in neoclassical model building; it must be met by a high quality of critical discussion and evaluation of political economy literature.

Political Economy must be interdisciplinary. This is probably a minimal requirement for all 'real' schools of political economy, because in our world of extreme specialisation of subjects and research the very program of political economy – a marriage of economic and political factors – points to the need for an interdisciplinary approach involving several social and possibly technical sciences. This creates first of all a 'language' problem which, however, can be overcome with a certain amount of patience and effort. Much more serious for economists is the problem of the unsettled and

---

[5]"Within the sciences one may make a rough distinction between those which require logic above all, and those which require the less formal exercise of judgement' [Elster (1985, p. 17)]. The latter are those where diffuse and complex information has to be analysed. Political economy obviously belongs to this category.

'soft' nature of some of the neighbouring social sciences whose methods and results one would like to incorporate in a wider theory. If we can assume that – to change somewhat a saying by Lenin – 'a combined theory is as strong as the weakest link in its chain', then the problematique of switching from economics to political economy becomes clearly visible. With regard to this problem different strategies can be adopted.

(a) Realising the danger of contamination with the softer social sciences one can try to stick as far as possible to the hard core of economics without, however, losing sight of political and societal conditions and changes. A loose but consciously considered connection between the disciplines is maintained. Perhaps Keynes can be seen as a master of this approach. He stressed the need for keeping the influence of various (non-economic) factors and alternatives 'at the back of one's mind' and it was *for this reason* that he realised that the 'hard' results of 'economics' have to be interpreted in a 'softer' light.

> 'Too large a proportion of recent "mathematical" economics', he wrote in the General Theory [Keynes (1936, p. 298)], 'are mere concoctions, as imprecise as the initial assumptions they rest on, which allow the author to lose sight of the complexities and interdependencies of the real world in a maze of pretentious and unhelpful symbols'.

In his article 'Some economic consequences of a declining population' in the *Eugenics Review* Keynes derives from his economic analysis that the maintenance of consumption and full employment in a declining population will 'necessitate' a redistribution of income, but then continues: 'Yet there will be many social and political forces to oppose necessary change'. This 'keeping-the-other-factors-at-the-back-of-one's-mind' is probably the absolute minimum of a political economy approach which, however, has the advantage that a large part of the (viable?!) economic subsystem theory can be taken over intact.

(b) A stronger alternative consists of attempts to improve the analysis of various strategic portions of the interface of economic, political, and sociological processes by considering the different types of interests, behaviour, and processes which arise out of the interplay of these factors. This does not lead to complete new theories or even consistent approaches, but can help firstly to throw new light on some special fields, and secondly to show in an exemplary fashion in what directions one has to go in order to develop a satisfactory political economy. Galbraith and the institutionalists in general are good examples for this approach, but it can also be found in other schools (Post-Keynesians, Post-Ricardians, Radical Economists etcetera). Kalecki's famous and prophetic essay on 'Political aspects of full employment' [Kalecki (1943)] is a classical example of this way of looking at the matter.

(c) By far the most ambitious way to attack the problem of creating a political economy is the attempt to formulate a unified theory of the politico-economic process. This must involve the neglect of much detail in each separate field but can elaborate and highlight the complexities and interdependencies of the different worlds. Of course Marx's works enter one's mind immediately as a Herculean effort and tremendous achievement in this direction, but also as a reminder how difficult – if not utopian – such a task is. There is obviously no easy access to this high road, but the 'vision' (to use Schumpeter's phrase) contained in such attempts plays an important role for the development of political economy. In themselves such studies can produce important general results even if these involve a heavy loss of detail and 'precision'. Still more significant, however, is their constant reminder to 'less courageous' political economists that one should not lose sight of the holistic nature of the social, or indeed the social and natural world (if we think of the ecological problems). Even if one hesitates to tread on the uncertain ground of a comprehensive theory it is important to be conscious of the challenge such a viewpoint provides and of the questions it poses. Schumpeter, more than any other economist, had always been aware of this problematique. This is the reason why he was torn between his admiration for Walras and his theoretical rigour on the one hand and Marx and his 'vision' on the other and why he ventured into expeditions into sociological and historical questions.

Let me turn to another aspect of the political economy question. Political economy, I would maintain, has to take *in principle* a more positive and active attitude with regard to empirical work then economics as such. While general equilibrium theory and other strictly axiomatic theories can obtain meaningful and useful conclusions by the deductive derivation of logical implications, there is no escape for a 'true' political economy to introduce – directly or indirectly – empirical material at almost every stage of its analysis. Variability of the socio-political environment, dynamic processes, and genuine uncertainty play an important role in almost every type of political economy and have to appear at least as background material if not as essential elements of the basic theoretical structure. Most of the eminent classical economists and, of course, Marx are shining examples for such an approach. And Schumpeter's dictum that an economist has to master three subjects, viz. economic theory, statistics, and history[6] applies with particular force to political economy.

Political economy, more than most branches of 'pure' economics, *must* avoid degenerating into mere armchair economics. Considering the already

---

[6]It is said that, when asked which of these three disciplines he would choose if he could only study one of them, Schumpeter replied: 'history'!

mentioned openness and 'softness' of political economy a purely speculative approach carries the danger of voluntary ad hocery, wild assumptions, and emotionalism. Only a steady support of theoretical research through empirical and inductive studies can prevent the descent into unscientific and unproductive debates between differing 'philosophies'. From the point of view of political economy empirical work and case studies should obtain a far higher degree of recognition in the academic world than is presently the case. They can serve not only as illustrations for already existing theories and preconceived ideas but as pioneer studies for the steady and necessary readjustment of a political economy. This is not a recommendation for a mere accumulation of historical facts and statistical tables, for 'facts without theory'. The empirical research must be guided by theoretical consideration *and* vice versa: there must be openness in *both* directions. The main trouble in the famous century-old debate on methodology between Schmoller, the economic historian, and Menger, the economic theorist, was that the question was too much centered on an 'either–or' and that made Menger an easy winner.

Finally – before I come to a few concluding remarks – I want to turn to a somewhat less obvious (and less important) question. It is: Is 'political economy' more 'progressive' then 'economics'? This question arises because many neo-Marxists and neo-Ricardians see classical 'political economy' as a dynamic, socially critical theory of social *change* in contrast to a neo-classical 'economics' with a static, apologetic bias for the status quo.

Now, whatever the term 'progressive' may mean in this context, it is obvious that it is used in a normative way. Very generally it is meant as denoting a contrast to a conservative view-point. This leads directly to the question whether such normative evaluations are in order when scientific theories are considered. If we could have a strictly value-free social science then the question whether political economy is more progressive than economics wouldn't make sense. Both would represent research programs aiming at a theoretical explanation of certain economic aspects and could be judged by their logical consistency and empirical relevance in the same way as different meteorological theories. But we know, of course, that a complete 'Wertfreiheit' – even if desired – is not fully achievable in the social sciences (including economic theory). The choice of subjects, assumptions, and theoretical structures contains already quite unavoidably a number of implicit value judgements as to the 'importance' of this or that relationship; to this are added the more or less open biases of theorists when it comes to interpretations and policy implications of their analysis. So the question whether a theory, as it is normally presented, has 'progressive' or 'conservative' connotations is not without justification.

This normatively oriented question can be raised vis-à-vis both theoretical edifices, 'political economy' and 'economics'. And it can be seen that both can be used and interpreted in 'progressive' and 'conservative' ways (however defined). Thus when one looks at income distribution from a traditional neo-classical angle one can plead for greater income equality in view of the 'law' of diminishing marginal utility or one can stress the need for greater income differentiation by laying more stress on incentive and productivity effects. In the case of political economy different valuations and interpretations can and do creep in by way of choosing different assumptions about the 'nature' of the state, of bureaucracies, and of society in general.

But while it is true that there are 'progressive' and 'conservative' specimens in both types of theory, it is also true that different paradigms have certain inherent tendencies leading to special value implications. From this point of view it seems rather obvious tiat the neoclassical framework fosters a conservative acceptance of the status quo. The concentration on the *possibilities* of a fully functioning private enterprise market mechanism; the harmony implications of the Pareto optimum criterion; the special stress on allocative efficiency as the main standard; all this plus the usual assumption of a 'given' framework lead to a perspective in which the reality of the developed capitalist countries does appear – if not as 'the best of all worlds' – at least as the 'normal case'.

Political economy – by contrast – encourages at least *in principle* (though not necessarily in practice) some more evolutionary or revolutionary perspectives. The endogenisation (or, at least, active consideration) of the political and sociological environment; the recognition of conflict; the stress on dynamic change and the more restrictive use of equilibrium concepts all indicate that change and alternatives need consideration and that trade-offs between economic ('efficiency') and non-economic ('social') aims can exist. But as has been mentioned before there is no guarantee that specific types or interpretations of political economy will always be more 'progressive' than 'economics', and we find in fact some rather 'conservative' examples of political economy 'schools' (e.g. historical school, theory of property rights, economic theory of politics) while others represent clearly the more 'progressive' – critical stance (Ricardian-Marxian theories, Veblen, radical economics, Kalecki, Myrdal).

In conclusion I want to summarise in a very general way my personal views with regard to a 'proper' use of the term 'political economy' and its demarcation vis-à-vis 'economics'. The first and most important point to keep in mind is the fact that there is not just one political economy but that we have various political economies. This is not only a consequence of the existence of various economic theories as such, but follows above all from the fact that the interdisciplinary view-point opens up numerous possibilities regarding the extent of the non-economic elements to be included (political, sociological, psychological, historical etcetera), regarding the specific theories taken over from the non-economic disciplines,[7] and finally regarding the ways in which these elements and theories are combined.

Thus, for a long time to come (or perhaps for ever!) no unified political economy can be expected and perhaps would be – in view of the complexity and dynamics of the subject – not even desirable. This state of affairs is fully recognised by practically all people who deal with the question what is 'political economy' and what could it do? A few quotations can show this. 'We are still a very long way from an homogeneous political economy' [Whynes (1984, p. 6)]. 'Unfortunately there does not exist a simple prescription how the missing political and social dimensions are to be introduced into the theoretical structure of economics' (Borner 1975, p. 123). 'Political economists see institutions as a gateway but they do not agree on the sort of explanation to which the gate leads' (Hargreaves-Heap and Hollis 1984, p. 17).

With different political economies we also have different political economists. But as a group they have – in my somewhat restricted definition (excluding the economic theory of politics) – something in common and that is their critical attitide towards 'pure' and neoclassical economics. Once one shares this critical attitude one is on this side of the fence, but has still to choose among a multitude of alternative methods and approaches. We can, however, construct a list of minimum requirements which we would expect to be met at least occasionally (not necessarily in every piece of research!) in the opus of all economists who are to be included in the political economy category. These requirements are (and here I repeat my former remarks):

(a) An all-pervading awareness that political and other non-economic factors play an important role in shaping economic processes and results.
(b) Special consideration for certain elements which are usually neglected or not given sufficient weight in 'economics', in particular problems of power and conflicting interests, behavioural assumptions regarding the homo politicus, the role of institutions and institutional change, changing structures in the world (politically and economically).
(c) Active interest in theories and approaches of neighbouring social sciences.
(d) Some indications of interdisciplinary interrelationships.

An existence of these credentials (to a greater or lesser degree) should, in my opinion, be a prerequisite for an admission to the 'club of political economists'. The coverage of the membership will then be rather wide. It

[7]Thus the state, which necessarily has to be given a certain role in a political economy can be seen as a neutral coordinator (Keynes), as the agent of the ruling class (Marxists), as a group of homines oeconomici (economic theory of politics), as a 'rational' arrangement of society (Buchanan).

would reach from Marx to somewhere near Downs, and would certainly include economists like Schumpeter, Keynes, Kalecki, Lange, Myrdal. A considerable part of the neoclassical establishment would obviously be excluded quite apart from the question whether a political *vocabulary* is used or not. Even a frequent use of the word 'government' (or of the letter G) is not sufficient to turn neo-classical analysis into political economy.

But after having tried to draw a line between 'political economy' and 'economics' I want to stress that, of course, both are part of the wider system 'economic science' and that the frontiers between the sub-systems are fluid. This is even more true for persons who cannot be exactly divided along these lines. What is ultimately needed is good economic theory and good economists and the hope that out of the cooperation and confrontation of various attempts and approaches new and fuller insights into the socio-economic process can be gained. If a special plea for a wider use and recognition of political economy is in place to-day, it is because of the hegemonic role which neoclassical and general equilibrium economics has obtained in recent decades. It would be a severe loss, if promising work in 'non-orthodox' directions would not find sufficient support and recognition.

References

Borner, S., 1975, Wissenschaftliche Ökonomik und politische Aktion (Haupt, Bern).
Elster, J., 1985, Sour Grapes. Studies in the Subversion of Rationality (Cambridge University Press, Cambridge).
Frey, B.S., 1977, Moderne Politische Ökonomie, English transl., Modern political economy, London 1978 (Piper, München).
Hargreaves-Heap, S. and Hollis, M., 1984, Bread and circumstances: The need for political economy in: Whynes, 1984, pp. 7–30.
Heilbroner, R.C., 1969, The worldly philosophers (Prentice-Hall, Englewood Cliffs, NJ).
Hutchinson, T.W., 1964, Positive Economics and Policy Objectives (Macmillan, London).
Kalecki, M., 1943, Political aspects of full employment, Political quarterly, Nr. 4, pp. 322–331.
Keynes, J.M., 1936, The General Theory of Employment, Interest and Money (Macmillan, London).
McCloskey, D.N., 1985, The Rhetoric of Economics (Wheatsheaf, Brighton).
Robbins, L., 1981, Economics and political economy, American Economic Review, Papers and proceedings 71, no. 2, 1–10.
Vickers, G., 1968, Value Systems and Social Process (McGraw-Hill, New York).
Whynes, D., ed., 1984, What is political economy? (Oxford University Press, Oxford).

PART THREE

THEORY

act on Econ + 55-64 (1942) UK M37

NOTES AND MEMORANDA

A NOTE ON ADVERTISING

THE literature on the technical and psychological aspect of advertising is increasing quickly, and year after year a great number of handbooks on advertising are published. This flood of publications shows the importance which advertising has gained, and is still gaining, in our economic environment. And yet in economic theory advertising seems still to be the Cinderella who is not worthy of being mentioned too often. It is true that since Mrs. Braithwaite wrote her article on " The Economic Effects of Advertisement," [1] lifting the whole problem from the usual business-like or moralistic treatment into the field of economic analysis, much was done to increase our knowledge of these matters. Particularly with the publication of Professor Chamberlin's *Theory of Monopolistic Competition*, selling costs found their proper place in the theory of value. Since then further details and modifications have been added in order to complete the picture.[2]

But in spite of this progress, advertising has not received the full attention which it deserves. This is probably not so much due to difficulties in its theoretical treatment or to a lack of interest, but to the extreme difficulty of getting any reliable statistics or other material on the subject.

Up to now the theoretical approach to advertising has restricted itself mainly to the examination of the selling expenditure of the individual entrepreneur in his endeavour to maximise profits, and a description of the equilibrium arising out of the aggregate effect of the many independent actions. This is actually all that is needed in considering advertising within the sphere of the theory of value. Here we are fully justified in assuming static conditions, assuming prices and supplies of other commodities as given, and not taking into account changes in employment. This treatment is as important and fruitful as it is for the explanation of the price of a single commodity. But as the explanation of the price of a

---

[1] ECONOMIC JOURNAL, 1928.

[2] See H. Smith, " Advertising Costs and Equilibrium," *Review of Economic Studies*, Vol. II, pp. 62–5; R. M. Shone, " Selling Costs," *ibid.*, Vol. II, pp. 225–31; E. K. Zingler, " Advertising and the Maximisation of Profits," *Economica*, Vol. VII, p. 318.

single commodity is not sufficient in order to understand the
interdependence and changes in production and consumption in
a changing economic world, an appreciation of advertising as
part of the whole dynamic economic system will be different from
a purely static analysis.

In the following paragraphs an attempt will be made to indicate
some of the more general aspects of advertising.

Until recently, whenever economists spared a few lines for
the question of advertising, they tended to join the general
criticism of it and to denounce it as a misuse of productive
resources.   Marshall, after distinguishing between " constructive "
advertisements, which are used for giving information, and " combative " advertisements, which try to supplant competitors,
admits the necessity, and even the desirability, of the former, but
goes on to say that " advertisements which are mainly combative
generally involve social waste." [1]   Professor Pigou accepts this
distinction, and he, too, regards most of the competitive advertisements as a social waste.   Resources are diverted from increasing
the social product to the creation of private advantages.   A
removal of a great part of the advertising practice seems desirable.
" The evil might be attacked by the State through the taxation
or prohibition of competitive advertisements—if these could be
distinguished from advertisements which are not strictly competitive.   It could be removed altogether if conditions of monopolistic
competition were destroyed." [2]

We must note that these criticisms are made from a purely
economic point of view only, and have nothing to do with the
growing objections by the moralists, who point to the fraudulent
and vulgar nature of many advertisements and their detrimental
influence on the tastes and habits of the public.   But even without
taking into account these ethical considerations, the attitude of
Marshall and of Professor Pigou is easily understood.   It is the
logical outcome of the tacit assumption of full employment which
pervades the whole argument.   If there is full employment, it is
obvious that the habit of advertising will lock up considerable
resources in a socially useless struggle for an increased share in
total production or greater monopolistic power, instead of using
them for the production of consumption or capital goods.   The
alternative to more advertisements is, under this assumption,
more immediate consumption or better provision for future
consumption.

[1] *Industry and Trade*, 3rd ed., p. 306.
[2] *Economics of Welfare*, 4th ed., pp. 199–200.

This assumption of full employment seems to lie at the bottom of most of the common-sense and economic criticism of advertisements. This is, for instance, shown by the following passage from Professor Vaughan : [1] " But granting greater sales (due to advertising) to each member of an industry and hence lower costs, the advantage to the public does not necessarily follow. The increase in business within a particular industry cannot include a relatively large number of industries because of the limited purchasing power of the consumers. The increase of activity in one industry is apt to be at the expense of another, though unrelated, industry. Greater sales and lower costs in the one may mean fewer sales and higher costs in the other, and consequently no advantage to society."

But recent economic theory has shown that we must remove the assumption of full employment if we want to understand fully an economic system in which unemployment has become a regular feature. A static equilibrium theory based on the assumption of full employment is an ideal model for the exhibition of the economic forces in an economy of free exchange, but it is not sufficient for an explanation of the dynamics of such a system, or for those phenomena which are a consequence of premises which had not been taken into account by the classical theory.

Applying this removal of the assumption of full employment to advertising, we reach the conclusion that the alternative to advertising may not be increased production of consumption or capital goods, but idleness of the resources involved. It is true, a single publicity campaign of a big concern may only lead to an increase in its monopoly power and to a fall in total production, so that finally there will be more unemployment, in spite of the absorption of some people in the advertising and similar trades. But that would be a rather exceptional case. Very often increased advertisement for one commodity helps to increase also the sales of its substitutes. A well-known example is the increase in the sale of brooms, carpet-sweepers, and similar devices after an advertisement campaign for vacuum cleaners. But the main point in this connection is that advertising has become so general that it is doubtful whether the publicity campaign of a single firm can seriously curtail the production of other firms which spend similar sums for advertising.

Advertising must then be viewed as one of the many possible

[1] Floyd L. Vaughan, *Marketing and Advertising : an Economic Appraisal* (Princeton University Press, 1928), p. 98.

forms of investment.   But, unlike most of the other investments, which are made in order to increase profits, it neither leads to an increase in consumption goods nor in the stock of capital goods. It has thus similar effects to expenditure on charity or public works.   It creates new incomes and increases old ones, and through the well-known multiplying effect, the initial employment in the advertising trades will lead to further employment in the consumption industries, and finally in the investment industries. Regarding the effects on the employment situation, then, advertisement has one advantage over most of the other forms of commercial investment : it increases the effective demand without increasing the supply of goods.   The stimulus which the rise in price offers will, therefore, be more lasting than in the case of the usual investment in fixed or working capital.   But advertising has a second salutary effect on the employment situation, and that is its stimulating effect on consumption.   Besides creating new incomes, advertisements lead to an increased propensity to consume for *all* income receivers.   Employment is governed by two factors, investment and consumption.   The habit of advertising influences *both* these factors directly, and in a way which is favourable to employment.[1]

Leaving on one side all moral considerations, we have to admit that advertising, including competitive advertising, will help to mitigate the evil of unemployment.   Since unemployment was a fairly steady guest in our world before this war, and since most people will agree that it is to be regarded as a social evil, we can no longer conceive advertising in such circumstances as a social waste.   The difficulties which most people will still have in accepting this point are similar to those which are met when one is faced with the proposal of digging holes as a remedy against unemployment.   Advertisements and digging holes seem to be such a silly waste of productive resources.   But they are a waste only if the sole alternative were use for other purposes but not idleness.   The waste lies not in the advertisements and the holes, but in the fact that we have still an economic system which constantly allows productive resources to lie idle.   The criticisms which are levelled against useless public works and advertising should logically be directed against the economic system which forces us not only to accept them, but even to consider them as desirable.[2]

[1] I cannot think, at present, of any other expenditure which has this double effect.

[2] Once again I want to point out that the *moral* objections against advertising are valid in times of unemployment as well as full employment.

But though it is not difficult to see the connection between advertising and employment, it is extremely difficult to get an idea of the quantitative effects of advertising. We know that it is very difficult for a single entrepreneur to trace the effect of an advertising campaign on the demand for his commodity, and this in spite of the advanced stage of cost-accounting. If he is able to get only a vague idea of these effects, I think it hopeless to try a quantitative estimate of the effects of total advertising on total consumption. All we can say is that the habit of advertising must be responsible for a considerable increase in the propensity to consume. We must only look at the great power of political propaganda, which often reshapes old and fundamental habits of a population, in order to appreciate the psychological importance of repeated publicity. And political propaganda has only derived its methods from commercial advertising and transferred them to another sphere.[1]

When we turn to the investment side of advertising our task does not become much easier. Here it is the extreme secrecy which surrounds the advertising departments of most firms which makes it impossible to get an accurate idea of the annual expenditure on advertising, or even less of its fluctuations from year to year. Reliable statistics on this matter are practically non-existent, but there are various estimates which are sufficient to indicate at least the order of magnitude. Some of the estimates which have been made for this country before 1934 are quoted by Mr. Taylor.[2] They cover a wide area ranging from £70 million to £180 million per year. Without going into details, we can assume that the annual expenditure on advertising is somewhere near £100 million. Estimates for the United States vary between £200 million and £400 million.

Such an expenditure is certainly not negligible, and it may be interesting to compare the figure of £100 million with the special expenditure (central and local) of Britain on public works which expressly aimed at the relief of unemployment. Here, too, full statistics are not available, but Mrs. Hicks estimates that £14 million or £15 million were spent in the years of maximum grants, but much less in most of the other years.[3] That means that even in the years of maximum expenditure the sums spent on public

---

[1] It is interesting in this connection that Louis Degrelle, the leader of the " Rexists," the Belgian Fascists, was originally advertising manager of a firm in Brussels.

[2] F. W. Taylor, *The Economics of Advertising* (Allen and Unwin, 1934), pp. 201 ff.

[3] Ursula K. Hicks, *The Finance of British Government, 1920–1936*, p. 195.

relief works were only about a seventh of the expenditure on advertising.

Although this comparison indicates the importance of advertising expenditure for the employment situation, we must keep in mind that a hundred pounds spent on advertising have probably a less beneficial effect on employment than a hundred pounds spent on public works. In the case of advertising a comparatively large part of the initial expenditure does not go to wage-earners but to monopolists. The high prices for advertisements in many newspapers and magazines are only to be explained by their monopolistic position. There is no close substitute for an advertisement in *The Times*, since no other paper reaches the same public. The same is, of course, true of other newspapers and magazines with a great circulation, each circulating among a different set of people. Monopolistic elements enter also in the case of advertising writers and designers, and even in the case of some advertising agencies, and unusually high incomes are the consequence, at least for some of the persons engaged in this kind of work.

Thus it seems very likely that the expenditure on advertising goes to a great extent directly to people who usually save a large part of their income. This would mean that the multiplier would be lower in the case of expenditure on advertising than in the case of certain other kinds of investment, certainly lower than in the case of public works. These considerations do not, however, invalidate our previous argument, showing the importance of advertising for employment. They only point to certain modifications which limit the quantitative relation between advertising and employment, not the qualitative relation.

When we turn to an examination of advertising in its connection with the trade cycle, we are once more faced with the lack of adequate statistics. If it is difficult to get an accurate estimate of the average annual expenditure on advertising, it is, of course, still more difficult to find out how much this expenditure fluctuates from year to year. And, indeed, there are no statistics available in any country which would enable us to calculate these fluctuations. One has therefore to find some other way of getting at least a rough idea of the direction of change during a period of expanding or recessing trade. An obvious device is to measure the space devoted to advertisements in some of the more important papers and to compare it with the space in other years. This tedious task has been undertaken by various people, and I quote here three tables which have been prepared by Mr. Taylor.[1]

---

[1] *Op. cit.*, pp. 213 ff.

1. *Average Percentage Increase in Display Advertising Space in Eight London Daily Newspapers.*[1]

(1910 = 100.)

1910.	1912.	1920.	1922.	1924.	1926.	1928.	1930.	1932.
100	116	157	153	172	197	249	228	182

2. *Average Percentage Changes in Display Advertising Space in Five Leading Provincial Morning Papers.*

(1912 = 100.)

1912.	1920.	1922.	1924.	1926.	1928.	1930.
100	140	116	122	118	140	122

3. *Percentage Increase in* Volume *of Display Advertising Space in Four London Daily Newspapers.*[2]

(Space times Circulation.)   (1910 = 100.)

1910.	1912.	1920.	1922.	1924.	1926.	1928.	1930.	1932.
100	120	346	444	523	659	971	950	757

The shortcomings of these tables for our purpose are obvious. Firstly, they do not indicate directly the sums which had been invested in advertising. The price of advertising space has probably changed considerably during the period in question. But no reliable information can be obtained on this point, since the rates are usually kept secret by the newspapers, and particularly because it is usual to charge very different prices for different pages, issues, and customers. At any rate, it is likely that the money value of advertising in the above newspapers has increased more than the figures in table (1) and (2) would indicate, because with increasing circulations the price per square inch will have risen too. On the other hand, the money value will not have risen to the extent that the figures in table (3) would indicate. For there is no reason to assume that the price per square inch has increased in the same proportion as circulations, and, in addition, it is very likely that the figures relating to circulation are to some extent inflated, in order to attract more advertisers.

Secondly, the above tables need not be representative of *total* advertising expenditure. Besides omitting a great number of newspapers and all weeklies, monthlies, etc., they do not take into account small advertisements and all the other media which are used for advertising. It may well be the case that owing to changes in the relative price levels of these different media, the composition of advertising is different in times of boom from what it is in times of depression. If that were so, the above

[1] *Times, Telegraph, Mail, Chronicle, Express, News, Morning Post,* and *Mirror.*

[2] *Times, Mail, Express, Morning Post.*

figures would not be truly representative of total advertising, and still less of total advertising expenditure.

But in spite of these shortcomings the tables are not useless. After all, we must not forget that newspapers are the most important medium for modern advertising, and the above samples comprise the most important advertising papers. Moreover, there is such a marked upward trend in advertising that even a small decline in advertising space has a serious meaning, and we are fairly safe in assuming that such a decline indicates a decrease in total advertising expenditure.

We see, then, plainly that expenditure on advertising fluctuates in the same direction as investment generally. We have in all three tables a distinct peak for the boom years 1920 and 1928, and a marked decrease in advertising in the subsequent slump years. Other writers stress also the tendency of profits and advertising to expand and contract together.[1]

We must therefore conclude that the advertising habits of the business world tend to accentuate the movements of the trade cycle. This is by no means as obvious as one is inclined to think. We have already seen that one of the peculiarities of advertising is its stimulating influence on consumption, and nothing would be more logical than to increase publicity in times when a general fall in demand sets in. And, indeed, some firms adopt this procedure. The Kodak Company, for instance, usually increase their advertisement outlay when their sales decline.[2] But logic is not always the motive power in big business, and the behaviour of the Kodak Company and some other concerns seems to be rather the exception than the rule.

Generally, business men prefer to curtail their advertising expenditure in a slump. The wave of pessimism which accompanies every depression leads to a blind acceptance of the slogan : " Save wherever you can." The advertising department is a good field for the application of that motto, since the vague knowledge which we have of the effects of advertising lets the entrepreneur see in a clear light the advantages of reduced costs, while the consequences of his action are not so obvious, and perhaps deliberately under-estimated. The inclination towards a reduction in advertising will also be intensified through the feeling on the part of many entrepreneurs that their advertising is of no use against such a fundamental force as the trade cycle. If this portion of the general pessimism is important, the fluctua-

---

[1] See, for instance, Vaughan, *op. cit.*, p. 101.
[2] See Taylor, *op. cit.*, pp. 63 ff.

tions in advertising would increase with the increasing " cycle consciousness " of business men.

At any rate, whatever the reasons may be, once some firms cut down their advertising expenditure, the effect will be cumulative. If one firm diminishes its expenditure on advertising, its closest competitors will no longer feel the necessity of maintaining all their publicity, and they will cut down their expenditure as well. This will react on the advertising policy of other firms and of the firm which started the whole circle. And in this way the entire process feeds on itself.

In times of recovery the opposite takes place. Optimism returns, entrepreneurs are more willing to spend, and they usually want to intensify the upward swing in demand. Some embark on an enlarged advertising campaign, and the others have to follow suit, in order to hold their own.

Thus, as we said before, advertising will tend to accentuate the movements of the trade cycle, although to only a small extent. And it will do that in its two particular ways : by increasing or decreasing total investment (by the sums spent on it), and by increasing or decreasing the stimulus to consumption. But while we have to acknowledge the fact that the advertising practice does certainly not mitigate the fluctuations of the trade cycle, we must not over-estimate the fluctuations in advertising itself. The imperfect knowledge with regard to the effects of advertisements has made the advertising budget of many firms much less elastic than other kinds of expenditure. Very often the advertising policy of a firm is settled for many years in advance, and variations in the one direction or the other tend to be small in comparison to the total expenditure on advertising. Thus, in spite of the cumulative effects of changes in advertising expenditure, it seems likely that business men hesitate to move away too far from what is considered as the " necessary " amount. It would, then, seem that advertising contributes to the oscillations of the trade cycle, because of the typical, though illogical, reactions of business men, but that at the same time it contributes something to that " hard core " which prevents the slump from falling to still lower levels, because of the tendency to maintain a certain standard of publicity.

Here again a parallel drawn from public works, introduced in order to relieve unemployment, will give a useful illustration. Governments, infected by attitudes which may be appropriate for private investment, and influenced by certain traditional canons of public finance, have usually arranged their active unemployment expenditure in such a way that more is spent during prosperous years than during bad years. The boom of 1929 coincided with a record expenditure on public relief works in Great Britain.[1] Such a practice leads, of course, to an accentuation in the fluctuations of the trade cycle (although this is not the purpose of the public-work policy).   But we also know that the presence of public works during the slump, even at a diminished level, prevents—among other factors—sooner or later a further deterioration of the downward movement of business activity. The parallel with advertising is complete. The only thing which remains to be done is an assessment of its quantitative importance in the whole course of the trade cycle.

But for this task much more data would be required than we possess at present.

K. W. ROTHSCHILD

University of Glasgow.

---

[1] See Ursula Hicks, *op. cit.*, p. 196.

Monopsony, Buying Costs, and Welfare Expenditure

J42
D21
D43

In her *Economics of Imperfect Competition*, Mrs. Robinson devoted a considerable part of the book to a discussion of imperfectly competitive conditions in the supply of a factor of production, mainly labour. Denoting these conditions by the term " monopsony," she could show that monopsony is in many respects the counterpart to monopoly, i.e. imperfectly competitive conditions in the demand for a commodity. Under monopsony, as under monopoly, the firm will produce less than its optimum output, labour will be exploited[1] and discrimination might occur.[2]

As it has been found that one of the " natural " consequences of monopoly is the quick growth of selling costs, the obvious question arises whether we can find anything corresponding to it under conditions of monopsony. This question escaped Mrs. Robinson because she did not deal with selling costs in her treatise, while Professor Chamberlin, who in his *Theory of Monopolistic Competition* dealt extensively with this item, neglected the question of monopsony. In this paper the attempt will be made to bring these two lines—selling costs and monopsony—together.

*   *   *

Let us first remember under what conditions selling costs can arise. The main condition is absence of perfect competition. Under perfect competition each firm can sell as much as it likes at the current price, and selling expenditure would not benefit the firm that spends it. If, on the other hand, the product of the firm can be distinguished from others and the demand curve for that product is no longer infinitely elastic, then the firm might be able to increase profits by influencing the position or shape of the demand curve. This will be possible owing to two reasons : (1) because of imperfect knowledge on the side of the buyers ; (2) because of the possibility of altering people's wants by advertising or selling appeal.[3]

Now something similar to selling costs—let us call it *buying costs*—can be found under monopsonistic conditions. If the supply of labour is perfectly elastic, there is no point in spending money on obtaining it. The individual entrepreneur will be able to get any amount of labour at the current wage ; and any attempt to increase the preference of labour for a particular type of work and thus to lower its wage would have so little effect on one firm that no firm will incur any buying expenditure.

Once, however, the supply of labour to one firm is not infinitely elastic— i.e. once monopsonistic conditions exist—it might be profitable to incur buying costs in order to alter the position or shape of the supply curve of labour. Again this will be possible owing to two reasons : (1) because of imperfect knowledge on the side of workers ; and (2) because of the possibility of altering the workers' preferences for certain places of work.

---

[1] " Exploitation " is here used in the Pigovian meaning of the term.
[2] See J. Robinson, *The Economics of Imperfect Competition*, ch. 26.
[3] For a fuller discussion of selling costs, see Chamberlin, *Theory of Monopolistic Competition*, ch. 6.

62

MONOPSONY, BUYING COSTS, WELFARE EXPENDITURE   63

So far we have seen that the parallel between monopoly and monopsony is also reflected in a parallel between the essentials of selling costs and of buying costs. This parallel, however, comes to an end as soon as we turn to the *form* in which selling and buying costs are realised in our world. When we speak of selling costs we think of display advertisements, of posters, margins granted to retailers, window-dressing, etc., in short of all expenditure that will adapt the demand to the product, not the product to the demand.

Buying costs, however, will take shape in different forms. These forms can be grouped under two headings: (1) classified advertisements; and (2) what may be called " welfare expenditure," which term here includes all expenditure that improves the welfare of the employees in a factory, offers sport and club facilities, creates amenities, etc. And each of these groups is directly linked up with one of the two reasons which we gave before for the occurrence of buying costs.

Let us take each of the two combinations in turn.

First, the supply curve of labour may be rising because workers do not possess perfect knowledge of openings, wages and conditions in all firms. A small rise in wages will not attract any wanted quantity of workers, because the knowledge of these improved wage condition will only slowly filter through to the people concerned and will only reach a limited number. A rising supply curve is the consequence.

In this case the elasticity of supply can be increased by spreading information about the wages paid by a firm. Therefore buying costs in the form of classified advertisements are incurred. A small rise in wages, widely advertised, will now come to the knowledge of many workers and a great influx of workers will be the consequence. In other words, the supply curve of labour will be more elastic than before.

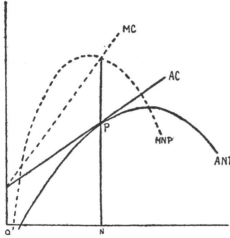

Fig. 1.

What will be the consequences of this type of buying expenditure? Let us illustrate the position with and without buying expenditure in two diagrams. (See appended diagrams). In both figures *ANP* is the average net productivity and *MNP* the marginal net productivity of labour to the firm; *AC* and *MC* represent average and marginal cost of labour respectively. Both diagrams represent a state of equilibrium for firm and industry.[1]

Let Fig. 1 represent the equilibrium of a " representative " firm before buying costs have been incurred, and Fig. 2 after they have been introduced. The consequences of publishing advertisements will be

[1] For a full explanation of the meaning of the terms and diagrams used here, see Robinson, op. cit., chs. 20, 21.

twofold : (1) the supply curve of labour (*AC*) will become more elastic; and (2) the average net productivity of labour (*ANP*) will be reduced, since from the total value produced by labour the buying costs have now to be subtracted.

From these considerations we can deduce the following consequences : the introduction of classified advertisements will reduce monopsonistic exploitation of labour and will almost invariably lead to an increase in employment (*ON*) and output. Whether it will lead to an increase or decrease in wages (*NP*) cannot be definitely said. It will depend on the amount of buying costs and the consequent increase in

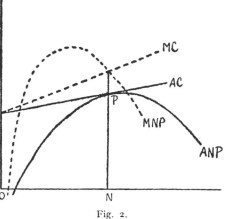

Fig. 2.

the elasticity of labour supply. The smaller the buying costs and the greater the increase in the elasticity of supply, the greater the tendency towards an increase in wages ; and vice versa. Since this type of buying costs will almost always consist of comparatively small sums, it is unlikely that the spreading of information by firms will lead to lower wages ; but it might lead to higher wages.

It is, however, the second type of buying costs which seems to me more interesting, because it throws some new light on the expenditure on the welfare of employees. *Some* part of this expenditure may be due to monopsonistic conditions.

A rising supply curve of labour may also arise when higher wages have to be offered for additional supplies of labour, because the additional workers have to pay more for transport, are reluctant to work outside their district, have a preference for their old place of work, etc. Mere spreading of information would not, in these cases, bring forward greater supplies of labour at the current or at a slightly increased wage. On the other hand it will be possible in some cases to increase the preference of all workers to work for a certain firm. This will lead to an increased supply of labour *at any given wage*, i.e. the supply curve will be shifted downwards and to the right. During this process of shifting the elasticity of the supply curve may remain unchanged, it may increase or it may decrease. This will depend on a variety of circumstances which cannot be discussed here. But since this type of buying expenditure usually aims at increasing the preferences of the workers working in the factory, it is probable that there will be a tendency towards lower elasticity.

Now perhaps this type of buying costs could have developed on similar lines as the corresponding type of selling costs. That is, entrepreneurs could have tried to influence the tastes and habits of workers by the means of modern

MONOPSONY, BUYING COSTS, WELFARE EXPENDITURE   65

propaganda. This is, however, not normally the case.[1] Rather, it seems, that entrepreneurs have tried to influence the supply of labour to their firm by spending money on the welfare of the employees. Thus a wireless set in the workshop, a garden, sports and other social activities, all this *may* be organised[2] in order to increase the workers' preferences for the firm. In so far as this is the case, in so far we can include this expenditure in the category buying costs.

A successful allocation of buying costs by one firm in advance of others will not necessarily express itself in the form of a greater labour supply at a given wage ; its success may also be shown by a lower labour turnover, or it may help a firm to get the best men in each trade so that—even if wage-rates are fixed—they will pay lower efficiency wages than the other firms.[3]

All this may sound rather artificial. We know that monopolistic conditions in the sale of a commodity are to-day the rule rather than the exception. Therefore we can easily see the wide importance of selling costs. But the supply of labour to a firm is still largely perfectly elastic. In normal times there is in a great number of occupations a sufficient reserve army of unemployed which enables most firms to obtain more workers at the current wage-rate. But we may note that even when heavy unemployment exists in a trade, for a firm located in a district outside the main supply of this particular type of labour a rising supply curve may still occur.

Another important objection is that with the spreading of collective bargaining and the general fixing of wages the supply of many homogeneous types of labour is becoming perfectly elastic.

It is, therefore, very difficult to get an idea how important this item of buying costs is. And since it is spent in the form of welfare improvements which are also induced by other factors it is almost impossible to disentangle the relative importance of monopsonistic conditions. All we can say is that they are likely to have some influence on welfare expenditure. This will be particularly true when there is a " gentlemen agreement " between employers to the effect that there should be no competitive bidding for labour. Under these circumstances there will be buying costs, particularly in boom conditions, even if wages had been fixed by collective bargaining with the Trade Unions. Once certain types of labour become scarce, employers might be able to increase profits by inducing workers from competing firms to change their employer. But they do not want to raise wages either because of some agreement or because the number of firms is so small that every employer takes into account the full repercussions of his action which would be an all-round increase in wages reducing the profits of all the firms in the industry. Under these circumstances employers will induce workers to enter their firm by offering them advantages of the type which we have denoted by the general term " welfare

---

[1] There are a few isolated instances where firms use some sort of display advertisements in order to attract workers. In these advertisements it is not so much the higher wage (if any) that is stressed, but the high prestige of the firm. This higher prestige may, however, represent some real economic advantage, viz. greater security of employment.

[2] We shall later see that there are also other forces influencing the supply of (voluntary) welfare facilities.

[3] This last point was mentioned to me by Mrs. Ursula K. Hicks.

E

facilities." Thus non-wage competition for labour will lead to buying costs exactly as the refraining from price-competition gives rise to selling costs.[1]

A few tentative remarks can now be made as to the general effects of buying costs in the form of welfare expenditure. The importance of these effects will of course largely depend on the importance of this type of buying costs. Anyway, in so far as they exist they will shift the supply curve of labour downwards or prevent if from moving upwards. That is to say, for any given supply of labour money wages will be lower than they would have been otherwise. Against this, however, we have to weigh the advantages accruing to the workers from the increased welfare facilities.

The buying expenditure will not only lower the supply curve of labour but also the average net productivity curve, since the buying costs have to be subtracted from the value of the product of labour. If the firms within the industry compete with each other and if entry to the industry is free, a new equilibrium will be reached where both the average cost curve and the average net productivity curve of labour are lowered and tangential to each other. There is not a priori reason for assuming that this new equilibrium will lead to the same or a different level of employment as the one which would exist in the absence of buying costs.

If, however, this type of buying expenditure also leads to an increased inelasticity in the supply of labour—and we have seen that there is some probability that it will do so—then it is most likely that employment will be reduced and each firm will be further away from its optimum size. Also, the greater inelasticity will lead to greater monopsonistic exploitation. Thus we see that the first type of buying costs, in the form of classified advertisements, will increase the mobility of labour, increase employment, bring the firm nearer to its optimum size and reduce monopsonistic exploitation ; while the second type of buying costs, in the form of welfare expenditure, will probably have the opposite effects. Where both types occur together the combined effects may work one way or the other.

*   *   *

It may seem strange that the welfare work of firms should be attributed to the existence of monopsonistic conditions. This aspect has, however, only been stressed because it has been neglected up to now. But buying expenditure is only one source—and mostly not the most important one—of welfare work. It may therefore not be inappropriate to give here a more complete classification of the factors which lead to *voluntary* improvements in the conditions of work.

The most important source of improvements is probably the organised pressure of trade unions and other bodies, and expression of public opinion. In a more limited field improvements may also be introduced by benevolent employers who take a personal interest in the welfare of their employees. This factor is however of a very restricted importance in these days of absentee ownership.

[1] See A. R. Burns, *The Decline of Competition*, ch. 8.

MONOPSONY, BUYING COSTS, WELFARE EXPENDITURE 67

To these two factors we have to add three others which might be called purely economic factors. That is, they will lead to welfare expenditure, the amount of which will be determined by the usual standard of profit maximisation, though the forces involved are far too complex to allow any accurate approximation to that standard. Into this category falls the improvement of conditions with the aim of increasing the efficiency of labour (while wages remain unchanged or rise proportionately less than efficiency). Then, welfare expenditure might be incurred as part of the selling expenditure of a firm. Good working conditions will help to increase sales to a socially interested body of consumers.[1] Finally, as we have shown, buying expenditure can take the form of welfare improvements.

These factors are summarised in the following list :

A. Institutional Factors.

1. Pressure from Trade Unions and other bodies.
2. Benevolent motives on the side of employers.

B. Economic Factors.

1. Increase in the efficiency of labour.
2. Selling expenditure.
3. Buying expenditure.

This classification seems to me to have some practical bearing on welfare policy in war-time. For three of the five factors listed above have lost much of their power under present conditions. With the prohibition of strikes, essential work orders and conscription of labour, the strategic position of trade unions has been somewhat weakened. With increased purchasing power, limited supplies and controlled prices, the factor " selling expenditure " loses most of its importance. And " buying costs " are also less important in times when a large proportion of the labour supply is centrally controlled and cannot be engaged in the usual ways.

Thus we see that some of the forces which induce welfare expenditure are now " out of order." There is therefore a strong case in favour of a legal imposition of welfare standards in order to secure satisfactory conditions of work for the many thousands who are now in the war industries. This has already been partly recognised by the Ministry of Labour which demands a certain minimum amount of welfare conditions from every establishment that is scheduled under the Essential Works Order. But it seems the above points show the necessity of introducing further minimum welfare standards for all industrial establishments for the duration of the war, and a strict supervision of conditions by factory inspectors who might work in co-operation with shop stewards, trade unions and the new joint production committees. This would also help to reduce absenteeism and to increase output.

[1] For this aspect of welfare expenditure, see A. C. Pigou, *The Economics of Welfare*, 1st ed., p. 749.

Glasgow.   K. W. ROTHSCHILD.

8

THE SMALL NATION AND WORLD TRADE

I

It is clear that the present war, with its profound effects on practically every part of the earth, should have provoked a good deal of discussion on the political future of the world. While the Atlantic Charter clearly states that one of the aims of this war must be the restitution of independence to all the nations who have been robbed of it by German Fascism, and thus endorses the motive which to-day combines the armies of the Anglo-Soviet-American alliance with the guerrillas and underground fighters on the Continent, many writers have put forward plans advocating the creation of federal blocs or unions which should replace certain or all independent nations. The motives which lie behind these suggestions are probably rather varied. They may range from a somewhat naïve idealism that believes that the mere invention of new and ingenious constitutional *forms* will give us that integration and co-operation of humanity for which all progressive people hope, to the reactionary plans of creating a " cordon sanitaire " between the Soviet Union and the Western democracies, thus splitting the world into powerful hostile camps which would only form the basis for World War III.

But this article is not written in order to investigate the political feasibility or desirability of any such scheme. It is designed to deal with the economic problem of the small nation and its place in a world with constantly expanding methods of large-scale production and a highly developed transport system. In books and pamphlets advocating a federal solution it is usually assumed that the abolition of frontiers and trade restrictions would greatly stimulate world trade and improve automatically the economic welfare of all people in the new federal area.[1]

---

[1] Here are just two examples to illustrate this point. Mr. Clarence K. Streit writes in his book *Union Now* (London, 1939) : " Whatever may be the merits of a managed economy the danger of managing it as a weapon is clear enough. . . . Where, under the best of leagues, trade barriers remain and any reduction in them is not only temporary but precarious, exposed to the sudden exercise by any nation of its sovereign right to denounce them because of a national emergency, these barriers vanish completely and for ever when states form a union. . . . Here again the Union of only fifteen democracies provides a base big enough to solve practically the whole world problem. Even before more countries entered the Union its influence would inevitably tend, powerfully, pervasively, to free trade and *restore prosperity everywhere on earth* " (pp. 221–2 ; italics mine).

And here an example from an English writer : " It has often been asserted

Thus, while the belief in *laisser-faire* methods is rapidly vanishing among both economists and non-economists, we see here a remnant of the (once perhaps justified) idea that the mere removal of regulations and interference will give us paradise on earth.

The reason why it is just in the international field that the advocacy of *laisser-faire* has survived is rather obvious. The frequent abuse of tariffs, quotas, and monetary methods for aggressive purposes and " beggar-my-neighbour " policies has clearly shown that the absence of *this* type of regulation would be beneficial to the vast majority of people. But the fact that certain tools are misused does not justify us in jumping to the conclusion that the removal of the tools is preferable to their proper use. That the complete removal of the tools is so widely accepted as the best solution is probably also due to the fact that the two most outstanding modern books on the theory of international trade both explicitly exclude monopolistic phenomena and problems connected with the trade cycle from the larger part of the treatment of the subject.[1] Will a consideration of them not necessitate a modification of the conclusions which were based on the assumptions of perfect competition and a highly flexible economic system in which frictional forces play only a minor part ? To this question we shall now turn.

II

It has been rightly stressed that the theory of international trade is in essence part of the theory of localisation.[2] The great advantage of free trade is then based on the fact that the absence of restrictions will allow industries to settle down in those places where the costs of production are absolutely or comparatively lower than in other places. The consequence will be an all-round increase in productivity and greater wealth for *all* the countries participating in the free international exchange of goods.

The above reasoning will, however, only be true without modification if two conditions are fulfilled. Firstly, costs of production must represent, as far as possible, " real " costs. That this condition is not realised by a competitive cost-structure

---

that complete internal free trade is an essential of federal union. *Undoubtedly* it is to the long-run advantage of the federation " (H. R. Greaves in *Federal Union in Practice*, London, 1940, p. 115. Italics mine).

[1] Bertil Ohlin, *Interregional and International Trade*, p. viii; and Gottfried Haberler, *The Theory of International Trade*, p. v.

[2] Ohlin, *op. cit.*, p. vii.

has been argued by various writers.   The criticism might be based on the divergence between private and social costs,[1] or—more fundamentally—on the huge inequalities in ownership and income which rob comparisons between different costs of commodities and factors of production of much of their meaning.[2] Important as these considerations are, they do not affect the free-trade argument to any great extent.   For as long as a country allows its internal economic life to be guided by a competitive cost-structure, there is no reason why special consideration should be given to its shortcomings when relations with foreign countries are concerned.

The second condition which is essential for the validity of the free-trade argument is that prices are equal, or at least proportional to costs of production.   Only then will free trade lead to the optimum location of industry.   If, however, the price structure is distorted through the existence of monopoly rents and profits, then the abolition of trade restrictions will only lead to a *different* location of industry, not necessarily to a *better* one.

That the existence of monopolistic elements necessitates a modification of free-trade arguments is, of course, recognised by most writers on international trade.   But very little consideration has so far been given to the practical implications of the growth of monopolistic and oligopolistic trends.   Because most writers assume that, while firms might be able to obtain monopolistic advantages within a national area behind protecting tariff walls, the creation of an international market would reintroduce the classical assumptions of free competition.[3]

But while these assumptions were probably justified in the nineteenth century, when comparatively small firms produced for a quickly expanding world market, it is doubtful how far they can be regarded as typical for the middle of the twentieth century. The growth of giant concerns, the increasing number of international cartels, the decline of population growth and the end of colonial expansion—all these factors point to the conclusion that even the world, and *a fortiori* regional blocs, is not large enough to-day to prevent the growth of a monopolistic and oligopolistic environment over a wide field of economic activity.

Once this change in circumstances is granted, a large part of the traditional free-trade reasoning has to be modified.   Thus, for instance, it will no longer be always true that the abolition

---

[1] See Pigou, *The Economics of Welfare.*
[2] See M. Dobb, *Capitalist Enterprise and Social Progress,* pp. 40, 160-1.
[3] See, for instance, Haberler, *op. cit.,* p. 144.

of a tariff on a commodity will lead to a fall in its price. The opposite might happen. Suppose that in each of two neighbouring countries a certain commodity is produced by a monopolist,[1] and that the two countries are separated by a prohibitive tariff with respect to this commodity. Each of the two monopolists will adjust his output to the demand in his home-market so as to maximise his profits. Now suppose the tariff between the two countries is removed. The combined market is now open to both producers, and we get a case of duopoly (or oligopoly). As a consequence, the outcome of the opening of the wider market will not be a nice equilibrium between the pulls of different objective economic forces, but will depend on a game of bluff, compromise, political intrigue, and so on. One very conceivable solution is that after some time of manœuvring a single monopoly will emerge. This may quite easily result in the closing down of one of the plants and the concentration of production in the other one, even if they are both equally efficient. If demand conditions in both countries are fairly similar, the output of the surviving plant, though greater than before, will be less than the total output of both plants before the abolition of the tariff. As a consequence the price of the commodity will rise in both countries.[2]

It should be noted that this result depends on the removal of the tariff. A monopolistic agreement between the two firms while the tariff still prevents or hinders the commodities from crossing the frontier, makes the above price and production policy impossible.

More generally we can say that in all cases where industries work under conditions which would mean the continuation of a monopolistic or oligopolistic environment in the larger federal

---

[1] Here, and in most of the discussion that follows, I mean by a monopolist any influential firm which controls a considerable proportion of the total output. The case where monopolistic elements are the consequence of a differentiated product produced by a large number of small firms is of less importance in this context.   For the influence of this aspect of monopoly on international trade, see Donald B. Marsh, "The Scope of the Theory of International Trade under Monopolistic Competition," *Quarterly Journal of Economics*, May, 1942, and the bibliography given there (p. 475).

[2] If total cost for each of the monopolists is given by $\pi = ax^2 + bx + c$, and the demand function in each country is $p = \beta - ax$, then the original equilibrium is given by $2ax + b = \beta - 2ax$, and the price will be $p_1 = \beta - \dfrac{a}{2}\dfrac{\beta - b}{a + a}$.

After the tariff is abolished, the combined demand function becomes $p = \beta - \dfrac{a}{2}x$. If production is concentrated in one plant, the equilibrium condition becomes $2ax + b = \beta - ax$, and the new price is $p_2 = \beta - \dfrac{a}{2}\dfrac{\beta - b}{2a + a}$, which is greater than p_1.

area, the abolition of tariffs will not necessarily lead to a reallocation of resources that will benefit the majority of those concerned. It will certainly lead to a replacement of the old pattern of industrial location by a new one. Where a greater number of smaller monopolistic industrial centres existed behind sheltering tariffs, we should now expect the slow emergence of highly concentrated big monopolistic combines.

But to what points will these new industrial centres gravitate ? To those where the economic advantages of production are greatest ? No, not necessarily. In the fight for supremacy in the new common market the victory will go to the firms which occupy the best strategic positions and which are most skilful in the application of the tactics of the poker game. But these will not necessarily be the firms which are most efficient in producing the commodity in question. Production will tend to be controlled by those firms which, through their size and weight, will have sufficient reserves to swallow smaller concerns or to force them into line. That is, production will tend to be centred in those industrial countries which provided already large domestic markets before the formation of the federal bloc.

This problem of dislocation may even become worse as time passes on and the factors influencing the location of industries change. For if new, independent producers would try to take account of these changed circumstances, a powerful concern would try everything in its power to prevent the successful establishment of the newcomers; and the giant concern of the larger federated area would be more powerful to achieve this than the smaller monopolists in the originally independent countries. The monopolist himself, however, will not readily move to those places which have become more advantageous for the production of the commodity in question. His desire to maintain the value of his capital equipment will tie him to his original place of production.[1] If we keep in mind the growing length of life of such equipment and the fact that different parts of a plant wear out at different dates, we can imagine that the period of immobility of a great concern may be found in the order of decades, not years.

Thus, to sum up the argument of this section, the creation of large federal blocs and the removal of all the tariffs between

[1] The way in which the monopolistic practice of " basing-point " prices has distorted the location of the American steel and stool using industries in the interests of the United States Steel Corporation and its investments in Pittsburgh has been admirably described by Professor Burns, *The Decline of Competition* (New York, 1936), pp. 290–371.

their constituent parts will not *in themselves* lead to the optimum location of those industries where monopolistic and oligopolistic elements are predominant. If a *laisser-faire* policy is pursued, the creation of a federal union will tend to reinforce and perpetuate the economic structure of its constituent members. The greater industrial countries will become the centres of heavy and other monopolistic industries. The smaller countries will find opportunities in the small-scale industries and in agriculture. Backward countries will remain backward just because they were backward before.[1]

Before drawing some further conclusions from our argument, we shall first have to turn to the other important factor that makes it necessary to approach the simple free-trade argument in favour of federal unions more cautiously—cyclical fluctuations.

III

When we come to this other important factor which makes considerable modifications in the classical free-trade reasoning a necessity, we are in the fortunate position to find already a considerable literature on this subject. In this country it was above all Lord Keynes who has on several occasions shown the limitations of the free-trade argument in conditions of underemployment and crisis.[2] We can, therefore, be rather short in this section.

This argument against unrestricted free trade runs approximately as follows. The classical maxim that free trade will maximise the social product was developed under the more or less tacit assumption of full employment. If this condition is not fulfilled, however, that proposition is not always correct. A country that is completely welded into the world system through

---

[1] It may be noted here that the kind of tariff which is suggested as useful in this section, viz., one that will guide the location of industries and prevent it from being distorted by monopolistic forces, is not the same as the " infant-industry " tariff. On the contrary. The " infant-industry " argument pre-supposes a high degree of competition, but realises that friction and the road from actual to potential conditions make a *temporary* tariff necessary. It is a tool to render possible the step from one competitive equilibrium to another. Under the conditions we visualise here, the new industry would be born into an oligopolistic world, and its greater efficiency would be no guarantee for its survival. To achieve this, a *permanent* tariff might be necessary which would shelter it against the aggressive tactics of the long-established monopolists. Since the necessity of a permanent tariff is frankly admitted, the main argument against the " infant tariff," viz., that once introduced it tends to stay, does not apply to our case.

[2] See particularly, *Treatise on Money*, vol. 1, ch. 21; *The General Theory of Employment, Interest and Money*, ch. 23; and Addendum 1 to the Macmillan Report.

an international currency and the absence of trade restrictions may—in times of depression—find that the policy which is necessary to keep it in the world system, *i.e.*, to maintain its external equilibrium, makes it impossible to follow a policy that would improve the employment situation, *i.e.*, to restore its internal equilibrium. If, however, the country is to some extent cushioned against the immediate and full impact of changes in the international price structure, policies can be adopted which will increase domestic employment and production without constantly endangering the external equilibrium of the country. If the country can make judicious use of tariffs, or if it can follow a moderately independent monetary policy, then it will be possible to stimulate economic expansion, even if the rest of the world is not prepared to follow suit. In this case the loss which results from the curtailment of international trade may be more than outweighed by the increase in domestic production.[1]

In addition to this argument there exists also a more general one which got more consideration in countries specialising in the primary industries, and which is based on the concept of a " balanced " economy. It points out that a high degree of specialisation, though of great advantage if international trade flows smoothly, carries with it grave dangers if demand is subject to frequent changes. In a depression not only the total of effective demand declines; the whole structure of demand is changed. Countries which specialise in the production of commodities, the income elasticity of demand for which is great, will be much more hit by a slump than others supplying goods which have a more permanent place in the fluctuating budgets of the consumers.

The lack of balance in the economy of a country which specialises for a world market is—like the problem of monopoly—a factor of far greater importance in the twentieth century than it was in the nineteenth century. The increasing amount of specialised fixed capital makes the change from one industry to another a very slow process. This slowness is aggravated in an " unbalanced " country by the absence of the necessary variety of skill and experience that is essential to give an economic structure the necessary elasticity of adjustment.

On the other hand, the suddenness and weight of modern

---

[1] This does not mean that the attempt to cure the domestic unemployment problem has to be based on a beggar-my-neighbour policy. On the contrary; if the governments of the different countries are internationally minded and keep the immense advantages of an international division of labour in mind, then the increased prosperity of any country will ultimately lead to an increased volume of world trade.

depressions as well as the growing fickleness of demand which accompanies the growing wealth of the world [1] make it particularly necessary for a country to adjust itself to new circumstances within comparatively short periods.   If this cannot be achieved, it may need a long period of deflation and unemployment to bring the country into line with the changed world situation. Here again, if the careful and limited use of trade restrictions allows the country to build up a more balanced economy, the consequent loss from international trade may be smaller than the gain derived from the greater stability of employment and production.

It will be clear how all this links up with our main theme : the effect of the formation of large free-trade blocs on the smaller countries which become part of them.   It is a well-known fact that there is no fundamental difference between the principles of international and inter-regional trade.   The *raison d'être* for a separate theory of international trade in the classical economic doctrine was based on the assumption of perfect spatial and occupational mobility of labour and capital *within* each country, and the absence of mobility (at least of labour) *between* the countries.   But in so far as full mobility is absent within a country, considerations of the type developed in the theory of international trade can be applied directly to the phenomena of domestic economic life.   This has actually been done—explicitly or implicitly—ever since Cairns developed his theory of non-competing groups.

The important thing to notice here is that for a long time to come these inter-regional problems would play a much greater part in the economic life of a federal union than in that of the large unified economic areas which have been in existence for a long time and whose political and cultural structure has reached a high degree of homogeneity.   For immobility between Holland and the United States or between Czechoslovakia and Poland is bound to be much greater than immobility between Clydeside and the Home Counties or between Kansas and New York.

Thus, even if several small countries were united in a large federal bloc, this would not solve by itself the problems touched in this section.   Entirely embedded into the unrestricted economic life of the larger economic area, they will not necessarily benefit; if the new circumstances force upon them deflationary conditions because of the type of monetary policy decided upon

---

[1] See W. B. Reddaway, " Special Obstacles to Full Employment in a Wealthy Community," ECONOMIC JOURNAL, June, 1937.

at the centre, or because of the lack of balance in their economic structure, they may become a region far more depressed than in the absence of the federation. The result will depend on the ways in which the independent countries would have used their tariff and monetary policies and on the regional economic policy adopted by the federation.

It seems indeed strange that the *laisser-faire* magic of large economic areas should fascinate some writers just at a time when economic literature and practice in large countries are giving increasing consideration to the problem of regulating industrial location and the balance between different regions. The appointment of a Royal Commission in 1937 to investigate into the " Distribution of the Industrial Population " and the Report of this Commission show the great importance which is attached to regional problems in this country.[1] Nor has the changed outlook influenced writers only; it has also left its marks on regional policies. Schemes like the Tennessee Valley Authority, or the legislation and measures adopted in Britain to deal with the problem of the depressed areas,[2] are examples of the ways in which integrated economic areas have found it necessary to interfere with the " natural " location of industry.

IV

Before concluding this article I should like to touch very briefly two further points, which have a close bearing on this subject, but which take us out of the rather artificial field of " pure economics " into the real world where political and economic factors intermingle.

We have so far dealt mainly with the effect which federation would have on those countries which would lose their independence and would become part of it. But as long as federal projects stop short of a complete world federation, we must also consider their effect on the rest of the world.

After the last war a great deal was written about the harmful effects of the thousands of miles of new tariff walls that had been created by the peace treaties. Now, there is no doubt that the multiplication of frontiers and the creation of new economic

---

[1] Thus the Report recommends the " encouragement of a reasonable balance of industrial development, so far as possible, throughout the various divisions or regions of Great Britain, coupled with appropriate diversification of industry in each division or region throughout the country " (p. 202).

[2] For a good account of these measures and the whole background of the problem, see S. R. Dennison, *The Location of Industry and the Depressed Areas* (London, 1939).

units involved serious problems of readjustment for those countries which were split up.   This is a natural result of *any* considerable change, and is hardly an argument against it.   Indeed, the same problems will arise when Germany's " New Order," this travesty of a federal Europe, is to be broken up.

But as far as the rest of the world is concerned, the fact that there are many tariffs instead of one for a certain area will cause inconvenience to traders, but it will not make trading more difficult.   This would only be true if it could be shown that small countries tend to restrict trade more than large areas.   The available evidence, however, does not point to this conclusion.[1]

If, however, a small country has not *a priori* a greater tendency towards protectionism, then, other things being equal, a larger area is clearly a greater potential danger to a smooth running of world trade.   The small country is not only more dependent on an international exchange of goods, it can also gain more from it than a large country; while, on the other hand, a tariff imposed by a large country will do much more harm to world trade than that of a small country.   It is obvious that the American Hawley–Smoot tariff of 1930 did more damage to world trade than the highly protectionist policy of Bulgaria.   And it is equally obvious that it is only a large area that has the economic power to apply an aggressive trade policy and to aim at self-sufficiency.[2]

The second point I want to make is connected with that difficult idea of " cultural autonomy," which is a favourite subject with most writers on federalism.   It is not the task of this article to find out whether the preservation of the various national cultures and traditions is desirable or not.   But let us be quite clear that any talk of giving " cultural autonomy " to the smaller countries while transferring their right of regulating their economic affairs (within the limits imposed on all international intercourse) to some *laisser-faire* mechanism of a larger area, is just nonsense.   If we mean by " cultural autonomy " something more than the preservation of picturesque costumes and out-of-date traditions which delight the traveller, then we must realise that it cannot develop unless a certain economic environment is given.

Now, if the reasoning of this article is at least to some extent

[1] See the Appendix below.

[2] Following Burky, J. B. Condliffe writes :   " Not small, but great, countries, practicing not nationalism, but imperialism, and utilizing the whole armory of economic, political and cultural weapons, are the centres of ' regressive autarky.' . . ."   (*The Reconstruction of World Trade*, p. 165).

correct, it is very likely that the economic forces released by the formation of the federation will endanger the cultural life of some of the smaller countries.   Firstly, as we saw, the heavy industries and other industries in which the degree of monopoly is high will tend to be concentrated in certain areas.   This will mean that higher incomes will also be concentrated in those areas : above all, the monopoly profits of the owners, but also the wage-level will probably be higher than elsewhere.[1]   As experience has shown, a very large proportion of these higher incomes will be spent on services which will also tend to accumulate in these areas.   This concentration of highly skilled workers and professions will give an enormous stimulus to the development of arts and science in that region.   Within a nation such concentration is of less consequence; there is enough cultural unity to make these cultural centres fruitful for the rest of the country.   But with different languages and different national traditions this becomes much more doubtful, particularly if left to chance.

Secondly, and more important, if economic depressions are allowed to recur, some of the areas inside the federation will be particularly affected owing to their economic structure and specialisation.   If such an area of heavy depression coincides more or less with a national area, the cultural potential of this country would suffer badly.   Either the best elements will migrate to other parts of the federation and leave their own country poorer in human material, or they will stay at home and become slowly tired, demoralised, cynical.[2]   The right of a country to regulate its economic life is, of course, no guarantee that this will not happen.   But it gives it the power to do its best to escape to some extent the uneven incidence of a slump in an uncontrolled world.

Finally, the question of a " balanced " economy has also a bearing on this point.   A certain amount of industrialisation and town life is essential if a country is to make its own specific contribution to our common twentieth-century civilisation, which is so permeated by the elements of natural science.   If no proper apparatus is created to supervise the regional location of industries with due regard to the general needs of *all* the constituent countries, great and small, then the developments of the

---

[1] As we saw that immobility is likely to be particularly great between the different countries, this wage-differential may be permanent.

[2] To see what regional depression can mean in human terms, see Ellen Wilkinson, *The Town that was Murdered* (London, 1939).

past will lead to a distribution of the more important industries that will leave some of the countries industrially under-developed and therefore incapable of participating fully in the cultural life of the world.[1]

V

What are the conclusions we have to draw from all these considerations ? That, at least economically, federal solutions and the abolishment of trade restrictions are always a step back ? Certainly not. This article was mainly written in order to show that the still widespread belief that the creation of larger economic areas will *in itself* solve most of our economic problems, cannot be maintained. The incorporation in a federation of a country, and particularly a small country, which has learned to manage its economic affairs more progressively and more successfully than its neighbours, would mean a loss of welfare not only for that country, but for the whole world. On the other hand, it seems also fairly clear that in a case where several countries have a similar political outlook and have reached a similar technique and success in regulating their own economic and social life, the formation of a federation would increase the area over which this regulation and co-ordination of economic affairs could be achieved and would, in all likelihood, make it more effective. The whole truth is that trade restrictions were not the cause of all the economic ills of the inter-war period; they were rather a symptom of them. Federalism and similar solutions cannot be the beginning of the " brave new world," they must be the outcome of it.

K. W. ROTHSCHILD

Glasgow University.

APPENDIX

GREAT AND SMALL NATIONS AND INTERNATIONAL TRADE IN THE
INTER-WAR PERIOD

In his book *Tariff Levels and the Economic Unity of Europe* (London, 1938) H. Liepmann has calculated tariff-level indices for the more important European nations for the years 1913,

---

[1] In the Soviet Union, where " cultural autonomy " has become a reality for scores of nationalities, this point has been fully realised and the location of industry has been accordingly planned. As early as 1923, Stalin, in a speech to the 12th Congress of the Communist Party, said : " In addition to the schools and language the Russian proletariat must do everything to ensure that centres of industry are set up in the outlying districts in the culturally backward republics—which are backward not because of any fault of their own, but because they were formerly looked upon as sources of raw material " (quoted in N. Miklaylov, *Soviet Geography*, London, 1935, p. 51).

1927, and 1931. By " tariff level " he understands a magnitude which is equal to the average of the percentages which the duties imposed by any tariff constitute of the values of the commodities subjected to that tariff. The following indices are based on the duties on a sample of 144 goods and measure the " potential " tariff level, *i.e.*, duties were taken into account even if the commodity in question was never imported into that particular country.

A word of warning must be added. To put it as shortly as possible, there is no satisfactory method of measuring tariff levels.[1] In particular, the reader should keep in mind that the absolute figures for tariff levels of various countries must not be used for comparisons of differences in the degree of protectionism. Differences in economic structure and other factors also play their part. More weight should, therefore, be attached to the ratios which the figures bear to one another.

TABLE I

The Growth of Potential Tariff Levels in Europe 1913–31.

Popula- tion in 1937 (000,000).	Country.	Absolute height.			1927 as % of 1913.	1931 as % of 1913.
		1913.	1927.	1931.		
68·09	Germany	16·7	20·4	40·7	122·0	244
43·04	Italy	24·8	27·8	48·3	112·0	195
41·99	France	23·6	23·0	38·0	97·5	160
34·92	Poland ª	72·5	53·5	67·5	74·0	93 ᵈ
24·44	Spain	37·0	49·0	68·5	132·0	185
19·65	Roumania	30·3	42·3	63·0	140·0	207
15·40	Yugoslavia ᵇ	22·2	32·0	46·0	144·0	207
15·27	Czechoslovakia ᶜ	22·8	31·3	50·0	137·0	220
9·04	Hungary ᶜ	22·8	30·0	45·0	131·0	197
8·66	Belgium	14·2	11·0	17·4	77·5	122
6·74	Austria ᶜ	22·8	17·5	36·0	77·0	158
6·32	Bulgaria	22·8	67·5	96·5	296·0	420
6·29	Sweden	27·6	20·0	26·8	72·5	97
4·20	Switzerland	10·5	16·8	26·4	160·0	252
3·63	Finland	35·0	31·8	48·2	91·0	134

ª 1913 = Russia 1913.

ᵇ 1913 = Serbia 1913.

ᶜ 1913 = Austria-Hungary 1913.

ᵈ The fall in the tariff level here is not due to a liberal tariff policy, but to the abnormally high tariff level of Tsarist Russia.

Source : H. Liepmann, *Tariff Levels and the Economic Unity of Europe*, p. 415.

It does not need any refined statistical methods in order to see that there is no obvious correlation between the size of a country [2] and its tariff policy. The generally greater increase

[1] For an account of the difficulties which have to be met, see H. Liepmann, *op. cit.*, and A. Loveday, " The Measurement of Tariff Levels," *Journal of the Royal Statistical Society*, 1929, pp. 487–529.

[2] By the size of a country we mean the size of its population. Finland with its area one and a half times as great as that of the United Kingdom is still a small country—economically—with its 3½ million consumers.

in the tariff levels of the " new " countries of Central and Eastern Europe is, of course, partly due to the attempt to rectify just those distorting factors with which we have dealt in our article.

The real orgy in nationalist economic policies began, however, after the crisis of 1929 had begun to show its effects. But for this later period tariff-level indices are no longer sufficient to show what happened. For quotas, exchange regulations, administrative protectionism took the place of tariffs or supplemented their work. Thus, for this later period we show in the following table the relative changes in the gold value of the imports and exports of the European nations for the years 1935 and 1938, as compared with 1928.

TABLE II

Great and Small Nations in Europe (excluding U.S.S.R.) and their Imports and Exports of Merchandise in New Gold Dollars.

(1928 = 100)

Population in 1937 (000,000).	Country.	Imports.		Exports.	
		1935.	1938.	1935.	1938.
—	Gold prices	41	45	41	44
2,125·60	World	35	41	34	40
132·09	United States	30	28	26	35
68·09	Germany	30	39	35	44
47·53	United Kingdom	39	47	35	38
43·04	Italy	32	29	33	41
41·99	France	39	37	30	25
34·92	Poland–Danzig	26	39	37	47
24·44	Spain	29	16	28	14
19·65	Roumania	29	41	54	56
16·80	Turkey	37	62	51	77
15·40	Yugoslavia	36	49	48	61
15·27	Czechoslovakia	29	30	29	33
9·04	Hungary	33	34	55	64
8·66	Belgium–Luxemburg	41	51	39	50
8·64	Netherlands	35	42	34	43
7·38	Portugal	51	50	53	67
7·01	Greece	37	48	50	68
6·74	Austria	29	37	32	34
6·32	Bulgaria	43	70	53	90
6·29	Sweden	48	68	46	65
4·20	Switzerland	47	42	37	44
3·76	Denmark	38	48	38	48
3·63	Finland	34	54	51	68
2·94	Ireland	37	41	26	31
2·91	Norway	44	64	49	63
2·55	Lithuania	45	78	61	91
1·97	Latvia	33	44	38	52
1·13	Estonia	32	49	38	48
1·12	Albania	50	80	40	60

Source : League of Nations, *The Network of World Trade* (Geneva, 1942), p. 101.

Again, it does not need a scatter diagram to show that we have to look for other factors than the size of countries if we want to find an explanation for the different developments in the various countries.

Quite apart from special explanations—as, for instance, the civil war in Spain, or the considerable Swedish iron and steel supplies for Germany's rearmament boom—it is necessary to try to find more general causes for the differences. This would be beyond the scope of this article, and such a study would also have to include a close examination of political and sociological factors. Here we want to conclude this note by pointing only to one more technical factor that had probably some influence on the recovery of international trade in some countries : the adoption of bilateral trade agreements. Dr. Albert Hirschmann has calculated indices of bilateralism for five countries.[1] Although this is too small a number to provide a basis for any definite conclusions, the following table seems to indicate that a higher degree of bilateralism tended to be accompanied by a greater recovery in the international exchange of goods.

TABLE III

The Degree of Bilateralism and the Recovery of Import Trade in Five Countries

(Index of bilateralism : 100 = complete absence of bilateralism, 0 = complete bilateralism)

Country.	Index of bi-lateralism 1937.	Imports in 1938 as % of 1928.
Germany . . .	21·5	39
Netherlands . . .	21·2	42
Belgium	20·8	51
Sweden	18·2	68
Great Britain . . .	17·5	47

[1] In a memorandum " Etude statistique sur la tendance du commerce extérieure vers l'équilibre et le bilateralisme," quoted in J. B. Condliffe, *The Reconstruction of World Trade*, p. 283.

9

FURTHER COMMENT

It is with a sense of surprise and expectation that one turns to a plea by a well-known analytical economist "in defense of monopoly." Have the great majority of economists been wrong in their almost unanimous attack on monopoly? Have we reached another of those turning points in economic theory when we have to revalue our judgments? Well, to anticipate the answer to these questions, it seems to the present writer that Mr. Boulding has not proved his case. Monopoly will still be in the dock.

Let us go into the case in more detail. Mr. Boulding admits the correctness of the "classical" arguments against monopoly, namely, that it has an undesirable effect on the allocation of resources between different industries and on the distribution of incomes between different persons. Were monopolies created solely in order to obtain extra profits, nothing could be said in their favor. But, he adds, this is not the only motive force behind the growing trend towards monopoly. Restrictive measures of all sorts — monopolistic combinations, trade unions, protective tariffs — have largely developed in an attempt to safeguard an economic group against the disastrous effects of deflation. With this statement few economists will disagree. In fact, most trade cycle theorists today assume that the depression period is characterized by an increase in the degree of monopoly, because of the tendency towards price-fixing and other monopolistic agreements.[1] But Mr. Boulding goes further than this. He says not only that deflation fosters monopolistic trends, but also that — as long as deflation is allowed to occur — these trends will be beneficial by preventing, through the rigidities they introduce, a bottomless deflation. He thinks that economists have not realized that under such circumstances monopoly is a sensible protection of the community against a complete breakdown, a hyperdeflation. "The unjust criticism is that monopoly causes unemployment by preventing the downward movement of the prices both of commodities and of factors of production in times when these downward movements are held to be necessary."[2]

Now, the mistake which Mr. Boulding makes is that he throws all sorts of "protectionist" policies — industrial combinations, trade unions, agricultural restrictionism, tariffs — into one pot, and claims that they *all* act as "stabilizers" in the deflation and unemployment period. It seems to me, however, that a certain differentiation is necessary when judging the effect of these various monopolistic tendencies.

Cyclical deflation is not, as Mr. Boulding clearly realizes, due to price flexibility. It is due, as he shows very lucidly, to the fact that the rate of accumulation must decline when a certain point is reached, and that — so far — we have not yet devised a mechanism in peace-time which would increase consumption sufficiently to take up the slack created in the investment-good industries. "There are only two ways to lessen the rate of accumulation; one is to increase consumption, the other is to diminish production. The sensible solution would seem to be to increase the consumption of those goods which give rise to wholesome pleasures and a high standard of life. This solution is either too simple or too sensible for us: we prefer either to increase the consumption of materials of war or to diminish production through unemployment."[3]

If, then, the deflationary unemployment can only be eliminated

1. The one outstanding writer who takes a different view is Mr. Harrod, who maintains in his essay on The Trade Cycle that the consumers' search for cheaper markets in times of depression tends to make industry more competitive.

2. Op. cit., p. 527. For a good presentation of the view that monopoly aggravates the unemployment problem in times of depression, see E. A. G. Robinson, Monopoly, Chap. VII.

3. Op. cit., p. 535.

by stimulating consumption (and investment), the controversy, monopoly vs. price flexibility, can only be decided by analyzing their relative effects on consumption and investment. If there were nothing to choose between them in this respect, none would be preferable, as far as a solution of the deflationary evil is concerned. If we deal with the economy as a whole, rather than with one particular industry, the question whether the one system or the other is to be preferred cannot be solved by drawing a line between elastic and inelastic demand, as Mr. Boulding does. For the *total* effective purchasing power in both systems will not be determined by the various elasticities of demand,[4] but by the consumption and investment decisions of the community.

But it is just because industrial combinations usually have a depressing effect on consumption that the critical attitude towards monopolies is not only justified but strengthened in times of deflation. The monopolistic agreements between firms in times of deflation aim, above all, at a full recovery of their overhead costs. That is to say, it is an attempt to keep interest on capital, depreciation allowances, and "normal" profits as far as possible stable at a time when incomes over a wide field are falling. This will increase the relative share of interest and profits in the national income, which comes to the same as a transfer of money from wages and small farmers' incomes to the higher income groups.[5] But this is exactly a tendency which will strengthen the deflationary trends. Consumption will be reduced, while the monopolists and creditors, with all the excess capacity around them, will have no incentive to invest money.

The foregoing argument explains why I said in the beginning that monopoly has not even been partly justified. At the same time, it shows why our attitude towards the "protectionist" policies of workers or small farmers in times of deflation has to be different. To a large extent their activities are only defensive, i.e., they try to hold their own in an economic environment where prices are becoming increasingly fixed.[6] If they succeeded in keeping their

4. The different elasticities of demand are an important factor in determining the *incidence* of the deflation on the various industries.

5. For an interesting theoretical approach showing how an increase in the degree of monopoly lowers the share of wages in the national income, the reader is referred to M. Kalecki, Essays in the Theory of Economic Fluctuations, Chap. 1.

6. Mr. Boulding probably overestimates the influence of deflation on the wage tactics of trade unions in his paragraph on the "standard rate" on

incomes even more rigid than prices, then the distribution of incomes would be changed from profits and interest to wages, a change which would, on the whole, stimulate consumption and thus contribute to a reversal of the deflationary process. It is only in this case that monopolistic tendencies will have that beneficial effect which Mr. Boulding claims for them in general.

Two modifications have to be added to the main argument of this paper. There *is* a way in which industrial combination in times of deflation may shorten the depression. And though Mr. Boulding does not mention this case, I think it has often been a reason for government support of monopolistic measures. Deflation means a reduction in output. Under monopolistic conditions this reduction is largely brought about by spreading unused capacity fairly evenly over the whole industry or by the "orderly" closing down of some factories. Under a competitive system the struggle for survival that follows a deflation will leave some firms with an output not much below the pre-depression level, while others will go bankrupt. Now it is quite possible that bankruptcies have a much worse effect on business psychology than the reduction of selling opportunities through price-fixing, cartellization and trustification. So far as a high mortality among firms discourages investment, quite apart from what the objective prospects for the future are, monopolistic arrangements will have a beneficial effect on employment. And this will have to be taken into account when the negative effects on consumption are considered.

The second case refers to protective tariffs. Such tariffs are, of course, monopolistic measures, with all the usual objections against monopoly applying to them. But they might be a real barrier against deflation in a world where economic policies are determined independently by sovereign national states. If a deflationary policy is followed in a foreign country, whose economic policy cannot be influenced, then a protective tariff will help the home country to isolate itself from external deflationary pressure and to adopt or continue an expansive full employment policy.

K. W. ROTHSCHILD.

GLASGOW UNIVERSITY

p. 538. The main reasons for the use of standard rates are the simplicity they introduce into the administration of collective bargains and the barrier they set to monopsonistic exploitation and discrimination. With regard to the latter, see Joan Robinson, The Theory of Imperfect Competition, Chap. 26.

[10]

PRICE THEORY AND OLIGOPOLY

I

In the theory of a capitalist market economy price has always been one of the central problems, if not *the* problem. And, indeed, for a long time it seemed as if this problem at least had found a methodological approach and a solution which might require refinements, but which by and large could provide the main answers for the purposes of interpretation, economic policy and economic forecasting. Then, with more and more refinements and reconsiderations taking place in the 'twenties, doubts with regard to the general validity of the fundamentals of price theory began to grow and spread, until finally the theory of imperfect and monopolistic competition opened new paths for the treatment of the price problem.

These new developments were and are rightly hailed as great advances, which have enabled us to get a more realistic view of the pricing process and to include in our theoretical scheme a number of cases which could only be fitted into the competitive theory by making special assumptions, such as " friction," " irrationality," " non-economic factors," etc. But, great and important as was the advance, it soon turned out that even the new theory did not provide the tools that would cover satisfactorily all major aspects of the price-making process. Within a few years from the publication of Joan Robinson's and Edward Chamberlin's standard works, descriptive economists and economic field-workers complained that the new theory did not provide a sufficiently useful frame of reference for the factual material they had to investigate and to interpret.[1] The purpose of the present

---

[1] Thus, for instance, R. L. Hall and C. J. Hitch, after discussing the results of an inquiry into the pricing methods of thirty-eight firms, came to the conclusion that " these considerations seem to vitiate any attempts to analyse normal entrepreneurial behaviour in the short period in terms of marginal curves " (" Price Theory and Business Behaviour," *Oxford Economic Papers*, May 1939, p. 32). Or, Professor Walton Hamilton, in introducing several industrial case studies carried out for the U.S. Cabinet Committee on Price Policy, says : " As the world is not all black and white, so industry cannot be set down in terms of an antithesis between competition and monopoly. . . . To set cases down along a straight line that moves from monopoly through duopoly and oligopoly to competition pure and undefiled, and to measure competitive forces by the relative number and size of sellers and buyers, is to make hypothetical economic phenomena the subject of mathematical exercises . . . the result is not a picture of pragmatic reality called industry " (Walton Hamilton and others, *Price and Price Policies*, New York, 1938, pp. 22–23).

article is to investigate the reasons for these shortcomings and to indicate some steps which might help price theory to cover some of the " irregular " cases more successfully and more systematically.

II

The great power and attraction of the neo-classical competitive price theory lay in its simplicity and determinateness. This determinateness was due to the fact that in a market of competitive small-scale enterprise, price is the outcome of impersonal forces. Demand and cost conditions could be assumed as given— at least for a single industry—and outside the control of any single firm. If, in addition, the assumption was made that firms could enter and leave the industry freely, and would try to maximise profits, then a point of price equilibrium followed with the logical necessity of a physical law. And, indeed, it was the natural sciences which provided the main signposts for the choice of terminology (stable and unstable equilibrium, the pull of the market forces, elasticity of demand and supply) and of method (mathematical approach, predominantly mechanistic and static cause— effect relationships). Quite rightly, therefore, this theoretical approach has been characterised as " value mechanics." [1]

There is no doubt that this theory was a satisfactory approach to an explanation of the price problem in the typical mid-nineteenth century market. There is also no doubt that it is still a very useful model for some of the present-day markets. But at the same time it became increasingly clear that with modern trends towards large-scale enterprise, product differentiation, advertising and trade agreements, the competitive price analysis lost much of its force. Of course, Marshall, Edgeworth and their contemporaries were aware of the existence of imperfect competition, but they treated such cases largely as exceptions. And the one case they really dealt with in detail—the pure monopoly case— is to some extent an economic monstrosity, because, strictly speaking, a pure monopoly never exists in a world full of substitutes.

Thus it was not until the early 'thirties that a new theoretical framework was created which allowed for the inclusion of the now typical non-competitive markets. The main methodological change was that price was no longer regarded as the sole outcome of impersonal market forces dictating a unique solution to the individual firms, but that it was realised that under imperfect

[1] E. G. Nourse, " The Meaning of ' Price Policy,' " *Quarterly Journal of Economics,* Feb. 1941, p. 205.

competition the firms themselves had a certain amount of freedom of action with regard to price, the nature of the product and selling expenditure. The consequence was that analysis shifted from the industrial supply and demand curves to the cost and demand conditions of the individual firms, and that price—or rather a price structure—was explained in terms of the adjustment of the firms to different and changing market situations. This meant that the analogies drawn from the world of mechanics became less applicable. Some of the new ideas, such as the " organic growth " of a firm or the survival of the most suitable business form, rather pointed to a certain affinity with biological thinking, and indeed biological reasoning and biological terminology (price environment, conditioning, ecology) found their way into economic theory.[1]

This change in price theory meant a great advance, in so far as it included a vast number of cases in the main theoretical body, which were formerly regarded as " exceptions " and had to be explained by additional factors. At the same time, with its greater scope, price theory lost some of the simplicity and determinateness which it possessed under the competitive approach. With the consideration of product differentiation, price discrimination, and advertising, " industry," " commodity," " cost " and " price " lost their exactly definable meanings, and it seemed as if the new theory would no longer be able to offer any exact solution of an " equilibrium price." This in itself need not be very tragic if the loss in simple determinateness is compensated by a greater relevance of the theory.[2] Nevertheless the strong tradition of price theory centring round a definite long-term " equilibrium price " made any idea of indeterminateness so abhorrent to the " father," and even more to the " mother," of imperfect competition theory [3] that most of their analysis was centred on those cases where determinate solutions in the mechanistic–biological sense could be most easily achieved. That is, their typical case deals with the market situation characterised by many small producers, product differentiation and free entry, which sets very definite limits to the freedom of action of the individual firm. A determinate solution is achieved by making the impersonal market

---

[1] See E. G. Nourse, *op. cit.*, p. 182.

[2] Not all economists will subscribe to this view. Thus, for instance, J. R. Hicks, in his *Value and Capital*, justifies his unrealistic assumption of perfect competition by pointing out that this is the only way of saving something from the threatened wreckage of economic theory (p. 84).

[3] I hope Professor Chamberlin and Mrs. Robinson will not object to this spiritual relationship.

forces the very powerful factor, and restricting the independent action of the firm to an adjustment to these forces—an adjustment which will be unique on the basis of profit maximisation (and survival in the case of the marginal firm).

This is, of course, a very important addition to the perfect competition model, and a useful frame of reference when we try to explain price in many of the present-day markets, particularly in retailing, but also in some small-scale industries. But, again, what can be regarded as the established body of " monopolistic competition theory " does not cover the whole field of price formation. In particular, it badly neglects the case where a small number of powerful firms compete with each other, the action of each exerting a marked influence on the position of all the others, and each of them not only adjusting itself passively to a " given " market situation, but capable of actively changing that market situation. This neglect of duopoly and oligopoly problems [1] is the more regrettable as recent investigations have shown that oligopoly is by no means an exception, but that the most typical case in industry is probably monopolistic competition, with a considerable admixture of oligopoly.[2] Indeed, the reader of the classics of monopolistic competition must be left with the impression that the problem of monopoly with which our society is faced is predominantly created by the small grocer down the street rather than by the big steel firms.

III

To say that duopoly and oligopoly problems have been neglected does not mean that there have not been frequent attempts towards their theoretical solution. But it seems to the writer that these attempts—in contrast to much of the descriptive literature on this subject—have been hampered by being too much influenced by the models of perfect and monopolistic competition, and " pure " monopoly. Yet neither of these theories can be expected to form a sound basis for the study of duopoly and oligopoly prices.

[1] The neglect is particularly noticeable in Mrs. Robinson's book. Professor Chamberlin devotes some space to these problems, but they are definitely relegated to a secondary place, and he tries hard to formulate his additional assumptions for the oligopolistic case in such a way as to obtain a determinate equilibrium price similar to that of " pure " monopolistic competition. A good critical review of the unsatisfactory treatment of the oligopoly problem in Robinson's and Chamberlin's works can be found in R. Triffin, *Monopolistic Competition and General Equilibrium Theory*, Chs. I and II.

[2] See R. L. Hall and C. J. Hitch, *op. cit.*, p. 29.

On the whole, we can divide the theories dealing with duopoly and oligopoly into two groups : [1] those presenting a determinate solution and those stressing the indeterminateness of the problem. The determinate solution, in turn, can be reached in two ways. Either it is assumed that the oligopolists do not take into account the effects of their action on the policy of their rivals, as in the famous Cournot and Bertrand solutions ; or these effects are recognised, but a determinate solution is reached with the help of additional assumptions.   The first type of approach is absolutely valueless, because it only solves the oligopoly problem by removing from the analysis its most essential differentiating aspect : the oligopolists' consciousness of their interdependence.

Those who take into account this interdependence are free from this fundamental mistake.   But in spite of this, their theories do not advance much towards a better explanation of reality, because in their desire to reach determinate solutions within the traditional framework of price theory they adopt additional assumptions which are too articificial.[2]   In particular, these theories are all based on the assumption that the oligopolists— while recognising that their price activities will call forth reactions from their rivals—acquiesce in the permanent nature of the industry's structure.   But since it is doubtless one of the distinguishing characteristics of duopoly and oligopoly that the rival firms can *actively* influence and change the market situation, these theories, too, fail to provide a theoretical framework for the interpretation of reality.[3]

In a certain way, therefore, the writers who stressed the indeterminateness of the problem made an important step in the right direction.   For they recognised that the reduction of producers to a small number meant that the market situation was no longer the " natural " price determining force of perfect competi-

---

[1] A good summary of the more important theories can be found in E. H. Chamberlin, *The Theory of Monopolistic Competition*, Ch. III and Appendix A.

[2] " The unreal atmosphere which surrounds our current theories of oligopoly may be ascribed to the fact that the assumptions are too often chosen for their analytical convenience, rather than for their actual relevance to the real world of to-day " (R. Triffin, *op. cit.*, p. 78).

[3] Thus R. F. Kahn, who amongst this group of writers makes perhaps the most serious attempt to get away from the unrealistic flavour of earlier theories, has still to depend for his solution on a qualifying statement of this sort : " I imagine my firms to be searching, by means of experiment or of trial and error, for the most profitable price and output—but not for more than that, not for the most profitable line of reaction to a change in a competitor's behaviour " (" The Problem of Duopoly," ECONOMIC JOURNAL, March 1937, p. 14).   In this way the important problem of major changes in price and output policy directed towards a fundamental change in the market situation simply drops out of the picture.

tion theory nor the strictly limiting price environment of monopolistic competition. They realised that under such conditions
the firms become active agents which have the power to change
those very market factors on which the determinate theories had
to rely for their solution.

But while thus the increasing acceptance of the indeterminateness of the problem was an advance towards a more realistic treatment of the subject, it was also a retreat from the former belief
that price theory could be sufficiently developed to deal with all
possible market phenomena. Indeed, the majority of these
writers, once they have shown the inadequacy of the determinate
solutions, take up an almost nihilistic attitude towards the theory
of duopoly and oligopoly. They may, like Chamberlin, just add a
short list of " uncertainties " to an artificial, determinate solution; [1]
or they may deny the possibility of a general theory covering
industry under oligopolistic conditions and substitute for it
voluminous case-studies describing the behaviour pattern of
particular industries; [2] or oligopolistic industry is just viewed as
a chaotic mess where practically anything may happen, and about
which economic analysis has very little to say.[3]

But, surely, the recognition of indeterminateness should have
been only the first step towards building up a more adequate price
theory for duopoly and oligopoly conditions. For the statement
that there is no determinate solution to the problem can only be a
relative one. It can only mean that the question cannot be
suitably solved *within the framework of existing price theory*, just
as the question of the monopolistic competition price could not
have been suitably solved with the industrial demand and supply
curves of perfect competition theory. But there can be no absolute
and inherent indeterminateness in this problem, any more than in
any other of the questions facing natural or social science. It has
been said quite rightly :

> " No doubt, there is a sense in which the solution is always determinate;
> it all depends on the number of variables that are considered. But it is clear
> that the variables that would have to be added to determine the solution
> might be of a very different type from the ones generally used by pure

---

[1] *The Theory of Monopolistic Competition*, 5th Ed., pp. 52–3.
[2] See, for instance, Walton Hamilton, *op. cit.*, p. 22 : " There exists to-day a
competition of big business as well as a competition of petty trade; but the ways
by which the battles for custom go on are quite different. . . . As industry
becomes the concern of human beings and of public policy, the way of its control
descends from the absolute and the imponderable *to the concrete and specific*."
(Italics mine.)
[3] This view is most forcefully represented by H. von Stackelberg's *Marktform
und Gleichgewicht*.

> economics of the equilibrium brand. Such considerations as financial back-
> ing, political influence, prestige psychology, optimistic or pessimistic slant,
> enterprise or routine-like attitude in business, etc. may well play an over-
> whelming role in determining the solution." [1]

Economists have on the whole shied away from this problem of drawing up a wider and different framework which could deal with the oligopolistic cases, because the concepts and methods used for the other market situations would be of little use. In particular, the influence of analogies drawn from mechanics and biology—so fruitful in the fields of perfect and monopolistic competition respectively—must be discarded when we deal with powerful active agents like duopolists and oligopolists. If analogies have to be used (and they may be of considerable heuristic value), then they will have to be drawn from those spheres where writers deal with moves and counter-moves, with struggles for power and position—in short, from books dealing with the general aspects of politics, and military strategy and tactics.

This is by no means a new discovery. Not only has a military terminology found increasing acceptance in price theory (*e.g.*, economic warfare, price strategy, aggressive and non-aggressive price policies), but both theoretical and descriptive economists have pointed out the appropriateness of comparing oligopolistic price behaviour with this field of human activity. Thus, Professor Pigou, in his *Economics of Welfare*, refers to the resemblance between the mutual bluff under oligopolistic conditions and a game of chess.[2] Speaking of the motives influencing the actions of big corporations, Berle and Means come to the conclusion that " it is probable that more could be learned regarding them by studying the motives of an Alexander the Great, seeking new

---

[1] R. Triffin, *op. cit.*, p. 71. It is a pity that Mr. Triffin, after thus recognising the necessity for a different approach to the oligopoly problem, and after a very able criticism of the shortcomings of the leading oligopoly theories, does nothing to advance towards the formulation of a theory of price under such conditions. He restricts himself to a refined re-classification of market situations, making extensive use of cross-elasticities of demand which completely neglect those factors which are mentioned in the above quotation. The consequence is that in the Conclusion the reader is left uncertain whether, after all, economic theory, has anything to contribute to the problem of oligopoly. (". . . The way is now open for a different type of economics. Instead of drawing its substance from arbitrary assumptions, chosen for their simplicity and unduly extended to the whole field of economic activity, our theory may turn to more pedestrian, but more fruitful methods. It will recognise the richness and variety of all concrete cases, and tackle each problem with due respect for its individual aspects. More advantage will be taken of all relevant factual information, and less reliance will be placed on a mere resort to the pass-key of general theoretical assumptions "—p. 189.)

[2] *Op. cit.*, 1st ed., p. 233.

worlds to conquer, than by considering the motives of a petty tradesman of the days of Adam Smith." [1]　The matter is put still more definitely in a recent article by Nourse :

> " While, of course, the conditioning environment imposes rigorous limitations on the price administrator's freedom of action in a capitalist society dedicated to ' free enterprise,' he devises and implements business plans in ways broadly similar to those of military command. A general must operate within the limitations of the terrain on which he fights and of the personnel and material at his disposal—to say nothing of meteorological conditions.　But at the same time, much depends too on the strategy which he and the high command devise and the specific tactics by which he and his officers seek to carry it out.　It seems appropriate, therefore, to discuss price policy in terms of business strategy and tactics." [2]

But while thus the need for a new methodological and conceptual framework for oligopolistic price theory is clearly recognised, no attempt is made to lay the foundation for such a theory. Nourse, in particular, after stating the necessity of a new approach in the clear way illustrated by the above quotation, largely spoils his case by urging more research into the thinking, prejudices, etc., of the entrepreneur in order to make possible a more proper analytical treatment of price policy.[3]　But, surely, the peculiarities of price behaviour under oligopolistic conditions are not due to any peculiarities in the psychology of duopolists and oligopolists, but to the different economic environment in which they work.　By all means let us have more research into the psychology of the business-man in all the various market situations, but the *distinguishing* feature of oligopolistic price theory cannot lie in additional psychological investigations, but in the provision of a framework which will show the actions of a " normal " businessman under the specific conditions of an oligopolistic environment.[4]

---

[1] *The Modern Corporation and Private Property*, p. 350.
[2] *Op. cit.*, pp. 189–90.　　　　　　　[3] *Op. cit.*, p. 199.
[4] A completely novel and highly ingenious general theoretical apparatus for such a solution of the oligopoly problem has been recently created by John von Neumann and Oskar Morgenstern in their book *Theories of Games and Economic Behaviour*.　Unfortunately, at the time of writing this article I had no opportunity of obtaining a copy of this important book, and I had to rely on the very capable summaries given in the review articles by Leonid Hurwicz and Jacob Marschak in the *American Economic Review* (Vol. 35, 1945) and the *Journal of Political Economy* (Vol. 54, 1946), respectively (republished as No. 13 in the Cowles Commission Papers, New Series).　Like this article, the book starts from the recognition of the inadequacy of the calculus and similar methods when dealing with the complex interdependence in oligopolistic situations.　A completely new mathematical and conceptual apparatus is then constructed, which makes this interdependence, the possibility of coalitions and collusion, of bribery, etc., an integral part of the general theory.　As the title indicates, the analogy from which inspiration is drawn is that of games.　But it is recognised that the techniques developed in the book have also a bearing on optimum military and diplomatic

The oligopoly-theorist's classical literature can neither be Newton and Darwin, nor can it be Freud; he will have to turn to Clausewitz's *Principles of War*. There he will not only find numerous striking parallels between military and (oligopolistic) business strategy, but also a method of a *general* approach which—while far less elegant than traditional price theory—promises a more realistic treatment of the oligopoly problem. To write a short manual on the *Principles of Oligopolistic War* would be a very important attempt towards a new approach to this aspect of price theory; and the large amount of descriptive material that has been forthcoming in recent years should provide a sufficient basis for a start.

Any such attempt would, of course, go beyond the limits of a single article. All that can be done in this context, therefore, is to outline some considerations to which this approach gives rise.

IV

The first point that requires reconsideration when dealing with duopoly and oligopoly situations is the motive force behind price decisions. Profit maximisation has up till now served as the wonderful master-key that opened all the doors leading to an understanding of the entrepreneur's behaviour. True, it was always realised that family pride, moral and ethical considerations, poor intelligence and similar factors may modify the results built

---

strategies (which to me seem to have a closer resemblance to oligopolistic situations than chess, poker and similar games).

There is no doubt that Neumann's and Morgenstern's approach surpasses in generality, rigour and elegance of treatment by far anything that could be achieved on the lines suggested in the following section of this article. At the same time, this very generality and rigour set, at the present stage of development of their theory, very serious limitations to the application of their theory to the price problems of the oligopolistic world. Not only are certain assumptions introduced for the sake of obtaining a more determinate solution rather than for their relevance to the real world (*e.g.*, the introduction of " mixed strategies," and the neglect of the influence which *variations* in profits may have on price policy), but it also seems that considerable difficulties present themselves when an attempt is made to deal with cases that involve more than three persons. And, above all, the theory is, at present, exclusively static. But in no market situation is the dynamic aspect, the timing of price and output decisions, so important for an understanding of " what's going on " as in the case of oligopoly.

It seems to me, therefore, that while the further development of the " pure " theory expounded in *The Theory of Games and Economic Behaviour* may some day yield a very powerful tool for treating oligopolistic price problems, its present stage justifies the simultaneous exploration of the more modest and pedestrian paths indicated in this article. Their greater concreteness and their allowance for dynamic factors may give them a greater usefulness than a more general, " pure " theory can at present provide.

on the maximum profits assumption; but it was rightly assumed that these "disturbing" phenomena are sufficiently exceptional to justify their exclusion from the main body of price theory.

But there is another motive which cannot be so lightly dismissed, and which is probably of a similar order of magnitude as the desire for maximum profits : the desire for *secure* profits.[1] This motive has, of course, not completely escaped the attention of economists. But they usually thought they could subordinate this aspect of entrepreneurial behaviour to that of profit maximisation by simply postulating that it is *long-term* profits he is trying to maximise.[2] Since, however, uncertainty is an essential feature in this changing world, it is clear that the vague knowledge a firm possesses of its demand and cost schedules cannot extend far into the future. Any theory, therefore, which tries to explain price behaviour in terms of marginal curves derived from *long-term* demand and cost curves really by-passes the problem of uncertainty, and thus the very factor which gives rise to that desire for security which the theory tries to explain.

In fact, the reasons for the neglect of the security motive are not difficult to find. They are again due to the preoccupation of price theory with the cases where numbers are large—be it a perfectly or monopolistically competitive market—or where a complete monopoly exists; because in these cases the problem of security does not arise. For the absolute monopolist security against competitors is part of the definition; and for the small competitor, for whom the security question is a very urgent one, the market conditions are such an overwhelming force that he alone cannot do anything to safeguard his position. All he can do is to try to make full use of every opportunity as it comes up. Maximisation of (short-term) profits is, therefore, a legitimate generalisation for an explanation of price behaviour in the large-number cases.

But once we enter the field of duopoly and oligopoly this assumption is no longer sufficient. For here we find neither the safety of the single monopolist nor the impotence *vis-à-vis* his environment of the small competitor. Here is both the desire for achieving a secure position as well as the power to act on this desire. How is it, then, that in spite of the growth of oligopolistic elements, economic theory has been able to neglect this additional

[1] See A. G. B. Fisher, *The Clash of Progress and Security*, p. 159 and *passim*.
[2] An even more careful formulation of profit maximisation is " maximisation of the current value of the proprietorship interest in the firm " (*Cost Behaviour and Price Policy, A Study Prepared by the Committee on Price Determination for the Conference on Price Research*, National Bureau of Economic Research, 1943, p. 275).

motive from its basic assumptions and to rely exclusively on the maximisation principle ?   The reason for this lies in the fact that some of the most conspicuous actions motivated by the desire for maximum security are identical with actions aiming at maximum profits.   Thus, above all, the outstanding trend towards monopolistic agreements can and does serve both ends, as has been clearly shown in the New Deal and other Government policies which, while aiming at increasing the stability of certain industries, soon enabled these industries to increase their monopoly profits.

There are other examples where the desire for profit maximisation and security maximisation converge on one type of action— *e.g.*, the pressure for tariffs, the desire for direct access to the political machine, etc.   In all these cases the behaviour of firms could be (so it seemed) satisfactorily explained by the " monistic " profit maximisation approach.   But there are other cases where the two motives lead to conflicting patterns of behaviour.   Where profit maximisation demands prices fluctuating with every change in revenue and cost conditions, security maximisation may demand rigid prices ; while profit maximisation should tend to create firms of optimum size, security considerations will favour the oversized firm; again, where we should expect reserve funds to be invested in response to expected returns, we may find their practically unconditional reinvestment in their own firm.

All these divergences from " expected " behaviour have, of course, been noticed, not only by descriptive, but also by theoretical economists.   But the latter have usually tended to relegate such " exceptions " into footnotes with a passing remark on security and long-term considerations, or simply to dismiss them as irrational behaviour.[1]   This *impasse* can only be overcome, and oligopolistic price theory can only be developed, if we recognise that under this market situation the security motive must be given the same pride of place as has been occupied by the profit maximisation principle for such a long time.

As soon as we acknowledge that a " struggle for position " is taking place side by side with the attempt to make the best of

[1] Thus, for instance, R. F. Harrod seems to regard the widespread adoption of the full cost principle, as revealed by Hitch's and Hall's investigation, as at least " to some extent irrational " (" Price and Cost in Entrepeneur's Policy," *Oxford Economic Papers*, May 1939, p. 3).   But, as we shall see below, this principle loses its irrational flavour once we recognise the importance of the security motive.   Of course, even if business behaviour were *really* irrational, this would not serve as an excuse for the neglect of such behaviour.   Irrationality would then have to become one of the premises of oligopolistic price theory.   But the writer believes that the existing evidence does not point towards such a necessity.

every position that is held at any special moment,[1] many price phenomena which proved awkward in the past will readily fall into an appropriate niche.   It will also mean that we have to consider price as a dynamic phenomenon.   To say this does not, of course, mean that we must expect oligopolistic price to fluctuate more than the competitive static equilibrium price.   On the contrary, as we shall see presently, oligopoly more than any other market situation makes for rigid prices.   But what it does mean is that even the most wildly fluctuating competitive price reaches at every given moment a static equilibrium, determined by the then existing supply and demand conditions; while oligopoly prices have to be interpreted not only in terms of factors that are co-existing with them, but also in relation to future changes at which the price policy aims.   Thus care has to be taken to see such price policies in their proper setting, past, present and future each given their proper weight.[2]

The background to oligopoly, then, is—as we said—a struggle. But this is, of course, not a continuous struggle.   On the contrary, most oligopolists will try to keep such struggles, costly as they are, at a minimum.   Their normal desire will be to entrench themselves in as secure a position as possible which will enable them " to hold what they hold," and—should an opportunity arise—to launch an offensive into rival territory.   Price policy will take a pivotal place in this entrenchment policy.   A price will have to be quoted that will allow the oligopolist to hold his own both *vis-à-vis* existing and potential rivals and *vis-à-vis* the consumers.   This means that in " normal " periods the price must not be so low that it provokes retaliations from the competitors, nor so high that it encourages new entrants,[3] and it must be within the range which will maintain the goodwill of the customers [4]—*i.e.*,

---

[1] That is, within the limits set by the strategic plan, short-term profits will be maximised at any given time according to the principles worked out by the current theory of value.   Atomistic competition (both perfect and monopolistic), becomes then a special case of the oligopoly theory—viz. where the individual firm has no powers of strategic planning, and where the action of the firm is reduced to pure profit maximisation.

Since the principles of profit maximisation have been fully developed elsewhere, and will be known to the reader, this article restricts itself to a discussion of the strategic aspects of the oligopolist's behaviour.

[2] " There is usually some element in the prices ruling at any time which can only be explained in the light of the history of the industry " (Hall and Hitch, *op. cit.*, p. 33).

[3] These are the dominant considerations in the conservative price policies of the oligopolists. See Hall and Hitch, *op. cit.*, p. 21.

[4] This will set a definite limit in the case of the so-called " conventional " or " charm " prices.   See C. Clive Saxton, *The Economics of Price Determination*, p. 19.

will maintain a protection against aggressive policies of the rivals.

Within these limits, and the minimum which he regards as essential for his continued stay in the industry, the oligopolist will try to quote that price which will promise him maximum profits. The freedom he has in the choice of his base price will depend on the relative strength of the factors mentioned above. In order to make his continued existence possible and worth-while, he will at least aim at a price which will cover his expected costs. Thus cost calculations become the basis from which oligopolistic price-fixing starts. To these costs will be added a profit which will be largely determined by the strength of the oligopolist's position.

If this position is weak and the obstacles for newcomers fairly small—*i.e.*, if we have monopolistic competition with oligopolistic elements—then the percentage added to costs will be determined by " normal " or " conventional " profits, because the fear of encouraging new entry will be predominant. Thus the " full-cost principle " which so startled Hall and Hitch in their inquiry, because it seemed so opposed to the principle of profit maximisation,[1] is a perfectly logical outcome of the market situation with which they were primarily concerned—monopolistic competition with an admixture of oligopoly—once we give due weight to the security considerations. When, however, the position of the oligopolists or duopolists is more powerful and not easily invaded they will not keep to the full-cost principle, but will add varying and " abnormal " profit percentages to their costs [2] in proportion to their assumed strength, or they will fix prices without reference to costs altogether.[3]

Since, therefore, the quoted price is not the mechanic result of impersonal market forces nor the essential adjustment to a constantly changing environment, but the expression of a strategic policy, it is clear that there will be a tendency for its rigid maintenance. The propagandistic value of declaring a position as a stronghold will soon evaporate if this stronghold is constantly shifted. The existence of a stable price instead of a fluctuating one will deter rivals from starting panicky price-reduction campaigns, and it will not induce newcomers to enter a booming market; consumers, too, are often supposed to prefer fixed prices.[4] Thus, the desire for building up a strategic stronghold

---

[1] *Op. cit.*, pp. 18–19.

[2] Saxton, *op. cit.*, p. 125.

[3] See, for instance, the price strategy of the American tobacco industry's giants in A. R. Burns, *The Decline of Competition*, pp. 225–9.

[4] Saxton, *op. cit.*, p. 139.

will—within certain limits—neutralise the profit maximising principle of changing price with every change in demand or costs.[1] Even a price change of one's rivals may be ignored as long as one's *relative* position in the industry is not affected.[2]

It follows : *Price rigidity is an essential aspect of " normal " oligopolistic price strategy.*

Since, however, this attempt towards a price rigidly fixed for a longish period takes place in a world where changes are constantly taking place, there is a danger that inflexibility may ultimately lead to the disaster which the price maintenance policy tried to avoid.   If one holds too uncompromisingly to a fortification, however important it may seem, while circumstances change, not only that fortification, but many more strategic advantages may come down.   In order, therefore, to reduce the rigidity, which the decision to stick to the fortress of the quoted price introduces, this price is surrounded by a variety of minor weapons which permit a more elastic policy without giving up the basic position. These additional weapons, such as changes in quality, credit and discount arrangements, salesmanship, etc.,[3] can be used to adjust the firm to some extent to changes in the " external circumstances " particularly in demand and costs.   They also serve as tools for tactical manoeuvres in the enemy's territory, testing his strength without provoking a major conflict ; or to provide a " defence in depth " against inroads from the rivals, if it is deemed possible to hold the basic position.

It follows : *Oligopolistic circumstances lead to a multitude of conditions surrounding the quoted price.*

As long as profit maximisation is regarded as the sole motive force, price can indeed be regarded as a unique expression of this desire.   But the struggle for a safe position has many different aspects, which often conflict with each other, and the oligopolistic price can therefore often only be understood as a compromise between conflicting tendencies.

The struggle for position involves not only the sales and costing departments—which alone are considered in traditional price theory—but also the legal, technical (patent rights), advertising, labour (very often the oligopolist will also be an oligopsonist), and other departments.   They all will desire certain price–output

---

[1] See Hall and Hitch, p. 33 ; Burns, *op. cit.*, Ch. V ; and the growing literature on price rigidity.

[2] *Cost Behaviour and Price Policy*, p. 278.

[3] See Nourse, *op. cit.*, pp. 193–4 ; and the chapter on " Non-price Competition " in Burns, *op. cit.*

decisions which would help them to establish a situation which from their different points of view seems to promise greater security. Prices are therefore increasingly the outcome of the different pulls of the conflicting interests of various departments.[1] And just as in the age of " combined operations " the actions of the infantry cannot be properly understood if one does not take into account the complementary actions of naval and air forces, so in oligopolistic circumstances the picture of the " price-fixing entrepreneur " has to give place to that of the price-fixing board of the heads of several departments.

It follows : *Under oligopoly the price tends to be the outcome of a variety of conflicting tendencies within the firm, which have all to be taken into account if a full explanation is aimed at.*

It will have become apparent from the discussion up to this point that the idea of a struggle is a vital aspect of the oligopoly problem. Yet all the time we have talked of a tendency towards rigid prices and rigid relative positions as the characteristics of the " normal " oligopoly situation. But there is no contradiction between these two aspects. It is the continuous existence of a *potential* struggle for a " new order " which induces the oligopolistic firm to follow the peculiar " normal " price policy which we have outlined in previous paragraphs.[2] The " normal " periods may then extend for very long stretches of time, and actual price wars—violent changes in price policy—may occur only at rare intervals. But because their possibility really dominates the situation, they must take an important place in the study of oligopoly price.

A " quiescent " price policy [3] may come to an end either through external circumstances—what we might call " changes in terrain "—or through internal stresses, *i.e.*, attempts towards a redistribution of relative shares among the rival firms. " Changes in terrain " refers to alterations in costs, demand or other conditions (affecting all the oligopolistic firms) of such decisive importance that even after full use has been made of the price-surrounding weapons (discounts, retarded delivery, etc.) the habitual price policy becomes obviously untenable. Two cases become at once apparent : one, where the terrain becomes less favourable and " closes in " on the quoted price, and the other, where new

---

[1] See *Cost Behaviour and Price Policy*, p. 43.

[2] As an American oil producer put it : " If you start real competition . . . you are up against a system of reprisals that rather deprive you of a desire to try the experiment more than once." (Quoted in F. A. Fetter, *The Masquerade of Monopoly*, p. 52).

[3] This term is taken from Saxton, *op. cit.* See pp. 129 and 133.

territory opens up offering room for expansion. Each of these cases will lead to a different pattern of price policy.

Take first the case of a deterioration in circumstances, such as a considerable rise in cost or a sharp fall in demand. Soon it would become obvious for several firms that a significant upward or downward revision in the base price would be in the best interests of profit maximisation. At the same time, the fear that rivals will not follow suit (in case of an upward change), or will more than follow suit (in case of a downward change),[1] and that thus the readjustment may deteriorate into a price-war for changed relative positions, will tend to prevent the revision from taking place. Ultimately, however, the external stresses may prove too strong for such a stubborn hold-on policy. The outcome may then be an inter-rival price war, if some of them feel prepared for such a trial of strength. With this case we shall deal below. More frequently, however, the desire for a show-down is not very strong in hard times, and the withdrawal to new, more appropriate price positions is likely to take place concurrently, co-ordinated by tacit or open agreement. Therefore the well-known growth of price-fixing agreements in depressions.

A widening of the terrain for all the oligopolists within an industry will occur when technical progress opens up revolutionary changes in cost through large-scale production methods and/or when by a significant change in price sales can be pushed forward to large numbers of previously untouched customers. This is a situation which is typical for new and expanding industries, producing semi-luxuries (*e.g.*, motor-cars), after the first stage of technical and sales pioneering has been passed. Here the desire to proceed to new, lower price positions—induced by the profit maximisation principle—will not be held back by the fear of an internal war. For here it is not a question of invading the rival's territory, but of rushing into new, unoccupied territory before the others have taken possession of it. Thus the action demanded by the maxim of maximum profits is in this case reinforced by strategic considerations, and the price pattern for such new, expanding industries is in fact one of strong price competition, followed by a rigid price policy after the new territory has been divided up and further expansion would involve an attack on rival strongholds.[2]

Finally, a quiescent price policy may come to an end, and an aggressive policy take its place, because some of the oligopolists

---

[1] See Hall and Hitch, p. 22.
[2] See *Cost Behaviour and Price Policy*, p. 281.

may attempt to improve their position at the expense of their rivals. The desire for this will always be present. For such a move would not only reduce insecurity—the danger of an attack from the others—but it would also increase future profit opportunities, even though immediate profits would be reduced. But the cost of such a struggle, the uncertainty of its outcome, and the harmful effects it may have on other aspects of the security drive (*e.g.*, public opinion), will make the actual outbreak of hostilities the exception rather than the rule. Nevertheless, such struggles are bound to occur from time to time. They may develop automatically, wanted by nobody in particular, out of the unsettling influences of the external factors mentioned before; or they may be the outcome of a well-prepared strategic plan of an "aggressive" firm.

In any case, whether a firm has aggressive designs or just wants to be prepared against an attack, the oligopolistic situation will force considerations on the firms which do not arise under either atomistic competition or pure monopoly. These considerations will not be predominantly concerned with price policy, but since they have an influence on the structure and costs of the firm, they, too, have to be brought in when oligopolistic price is examined.

Preparedness for a price war means above all to be able to continue in existence as long as possible in circumstances where price has no relation whatsoever to the realities of a situation, but is exclusively used as a weapon. To survive such a period demands a powerful position with plentiful resources. The actions taken to obtain such a position will again often conflict with those which we would expect if profit maximisation alone were taken into account. The first and foremost aim will be financial strength. Thus size will be desired for its own sake, independent of technical considerations. The indications in American studies that mergers have sometimes led to over-sized firms would be quite intelligible on these grounds. Indeed, once we add the security motive to the profit maximum motive, the " optimum size " of the firm—as seen from the entrepreneur—will usually be larger than that indicated by current-value theory. Again, the reinvestment of profits in the concern irrespective of the yields obtainable elsewhere, while being " irrational " from the maximum point of view, are easily explained as a security measure.

But size and reserves are not enough. Security must be carried forward and backward. Forward, by " immunising " consumers more and more against rival invasion through massive

[SEPT.Economic Method, Theory and Policy 107Economic Method, Theory and Policy 107

advertising. Oligopolists fail to adjust their advertising expenditure nicely to the marginal equilibria expected by the text-books, not because they lack the necessary information (this is, of course, also important), but because their advertisement is just as much a preparation for the great battle as it is an attempt at higher immediate profits.

Security is carried backward by the attempt to reduce the pressure which may threaten one's position in dangerous times from raw material and finance supply sources. The bigger oligopolists will guard against this danger either by vertical integration or at least by interlocking directorates and shareholdings. The enormous growth of interlocking directorates in recent decades—so conveniently overlooked by current theory—is indeed an essential outcome of the spreading of oligopolistic market situations. Here, again, it should be noted that our framework gives a logical explanation for developments which run counter to the principles of current theory, in this case the principle of growing specialisation.

In these and other ways [1] the fear of the coming price war or the wish to provoke one will *all the time* impress a behaviour pattern on oligopolistic firms which cannot be understood by interpreting it in terms of profit maximisation only. The actual price wars, as has been mentioned before, are not likely to occur very frequently. But when they occur, they can take on very violent forms, and price-cutting may be carried to extremes. The lower limit of short-term marginal prime costs of perfect competition fame will not be active, because here again we do not witness a maximisation of short-term profits, but a struggle for position— a fundamentally altered position in this case. The tactics and the duration of such a war will be decided predominantly by objective circumstances—*i.e.*, the strength and position of the rivals—but also to a minor extent by subjective considerations, such as their expectations with regard to each other's actions and their resistance to wars of nerves.

The " ideal " aim of a price war is, of course, complete victory —the annihilation of the adversaries. Very often, however, this may prove impossible or too costly. In such cases the superior power may be satisfied with a position which will allow him in the future to decide his strategic policy without having to pay too

[1] As one should expect in a warlike atmosphere, the desire to know what is happening in the hostile camp is often very strong. As one business-man put it in an answer to a questionnaire : " No agreement in this trade, but firms were all anxious to know what their rivals were doing " (Hall and Hitch, p. 43). This, too, may sometimes lead to interlocking directorates.

much attention to the reactions amongst his rivals.[1]   Needless to
say that this pattern of price leadership will not only occur after
a price war.   The mere fear of such hostilities may bring about
the same result.[2]

> It follows : *Price wars, while tending to occur infrequently,
> are a dominant feature of the oligopolistic situation.   They
> may be caused by external or internal factors.   The preparation
> for them, aggressive or defensive, leads to the adoption of
> measures which are peculiar to oligopoly.   The outcome of a
> successful price war or the mere threat of one may be the complete
> annihilation of a rival's independence or the reduction of his
> status to that of a price follower.*

But the quest for more secure and more advantageous positions
does not confine itself to the traditional field of economic theory.
The water-tight separation of the business-man's personality into
that of an " economic man," a " political man " and probably
several other men, is a legitimate simplification under atomistic
competition and even for small oligopolists, where any isolated
political action they may take cannot possibly have any appreci-
able effect on their market position.   The market situation and
the price of the commodity can, therefore, be quite well explained
by concentrating attention on the purely economic activities of
the firm.

But when we come to the big oligopolists, who *do* have the
power to change the market situation by their own political action,
then the separation of the economic from the political must
necessarily result in a very incomplete picture, which will not
suffice for giving us a reasonable explanation of oligopoly price.
Indeed, what is, for instance, the logic of some of the recent
American economic literature which tries to evaluate in great
detail the effects on price and output of the huge selling expenditure of big corporations, and yet never even mentions the sums
spent for exactly the same aims in the lobbies ? [3]   For the gap

---

[1] " The typical situation in British industry seems to be one where oligopolistic elements are of most importance, although there may be a large number
of smaller firms engaged within or upon the fringes of the industry, whose price-
policy is entirely dependent upon that of the price-leader " (Saxton, *op. cit.*,
p. 168).   For American conditions, see Burns, *op. cit.*, Ch. III.

[2] " A ' follow-the-leader policy ' takes the place of the older, cruder, cut-
throat competition and works just as effectively. . . . This docility of all the so-
called independents in following the leader may be seen, on more careful scrutiny,
to be the result of competitors' fear of cut-throat competition, more artfully and
sparingly exercised than in the old days. . . ." (Frank A. Fetter, *The Masquerade
of Monopoly*, p. 51).

[3] See Anna Rochester, *Rulers of America*, Ch. VIII, and the literature quoted
there.

that divides selling expenditure from political activities is methodologically much smaller than the one that divides the former from
production costs proper.[1]

The fact is that when we enter the field of rivalry between
oligopolistic giants, the traditional separation of the political from
the economic can no longer be maintained. Once we have
recognised that the desire for a strong position ranks equally with
the desire for immediate maximum profits we must follow this
new dual approach to its logical end, if we want to construct a
relevant theory. Only by acknowledging the importance of the
political factor can we account for such trends as the increasing
appointments of people who have " good connections with the
government," of first-rate experts as political advisers to great
concerns, etc., trends, which on a purely economic interpretation
can only be regarded as " irrational " and inexcusable waste.
Explicit recognition of the political aspects of the oligopolistic
struggle will also help applied economists to make their advice more
significant and more immediately useful. It will help them to
recognise the absurdity of the conclusions of a theorist like
Stackelberg, who, as an apologist of the Fascist corporate State,
regards this political form as the only means of bringing order into
the chaos of oligopolistic indeterminateness.[2] For they would
realise at once that Fascism, far from being an independent
arbiter in the oligopolistic struggle, has been largely brought into
power by this very struggle in an attempt of the most powerful
oligopolists to strengthen, through political action, their position
in the labour market and *vis-à-vis* their smaller competitors, and
finally to strike out in order to change the world market situation
in their favour.[3]

And this brings us, finally, to the most violent aspect of the
oligopolistic struggle : the attempts of the biggest oligopolistic
groupings to regroup their forces on a world scale. It is now more
than thirty years since Hobson and Lenin drew attention to the
necessary growth of imperialism with the increase in the friction
between huge oligopolies (or " rival monopolies " as they called
it). Yet in spite of the large amount of factual material that has

[1] I wonder how some of the " pure " economic theorists would deal with the
advertisements now appearing in the press against the nationalisation of certain
industries. Are they to be included in selling costs—for advertisements they
obviously are—or are they to be neglected because they represent political
action ?

[2] See his *Marktform und Gleichgewicht.*

[3] The autobiography of the big German industrialist Fritz Thyssen will be
found very revealing on this point.

been accumulating giving empirical support to this view,[1] nine
out of ten writers on the oligopolistic market situation manage to
avoid any reference whatsoever to imperialism. The consequence
is not only that a full explanation of oligopoly prices—generally
or in particular cases—becomes impossible, but also that students
of modern monopoly theory tend to become enormously worried
about the excess capacity of the small oligopolistic shop, while
they do not even realise the danger of a clash between the big
world oligopolies.

We have, therefore, to conclude that a theory of oligopoly can
be complete and relevant only if its framework includes *all* the
main aspects of the struggle for security and position. Like price
wars, open imperialist conflicts will not be the daily routine of the
oligopolistic market. But, like price wars, their possibility and
the preparation for them will be a constantly existing background
against which current actions have to be understood. And the
imperialistic aspects of modern wars or armed interventions must
be seen as part of a dynamic oligopoly theory just as much as the
more traditional " economic " activities like cut-throat pricing,
full-line forcing, boycotting, etc. For there is no fundamental
difference between the two.

> It follows : *The oligopolistic struggle for position and
> security includes political action of all sorts right up to im-
> perialism. The inclusion of these " non-economic " elements
> is essential for a full explanation of oligopoly behaviour and
> price.*

V

In an interesting article, written on the occasion of the centenary of Marshall's birth,[2] Mr. Shove pointed out how modern
conditions have largely destroyed the applicability of Marshall's
price analysis to the world of to-day.

> " It is the territory between atomic competition and absolute monopoly
> that the pure theory of the book (the *Principles*) does not cover at all satis-
> factorily.   And it is precisely this territory which has been so greatly enlarged
> by the development of the joint-stock company and the advantages (or

---

[1] There is a lot of useful information in the reports of United States Senate
Commissions and of the Temporary National Economic Committee. (See for
instance, the Report of the Nye Committee on the Munitions Industry, or the
T.N.E.C. Monograph No. 26 on *Economic Power and Political Pressure*.) This,
and a large amount of other relevant material, has been admirably presented by
Robert A. Brady in his *Business as a System of Power* (Columbia University Press,
1943).

[2] " The Place of Marshall's *Principles* in the Development of Economic
Theory," ECONOMIC JOURNAL, December 1942. It was that essay which provided
the first stimulus for the present article.

necessity) of large-scale control. The conflicts of interest within the firm; the interpenetration of interests between firms through interlocking director- ates, shareholdings, subsidiary concerns and the like; the domination of an industry by a few large units; the intermixture of public and private control as seen in the various types of semi-public corporation and of regulating boards and devices; these are the features of modern industrial structure which find little or no place in the analytical framework of the *Principles*." [1]

The newer developments in price theory have on the whole kept to this Marshallian tradition. Though they have introduced a large number of theoretical refinements it is nevertheless true that " the general theory of value and distribution as a whole has scarcely advanced at all into that part of the field at which the *Principles* stopped short. It is still concerned almost exclusively with the case of pure monopoly on the one side and on the other with atomic competition, ' perfect ' or ' imperfect.' " [2]

That the gap has not been filled is partly due to the force of tradition; partly, as Shove points out, to the increasing separa- tion of analytical and descriptive work and the itch for precise results. But the undiscovered territory must be entered by economic theory if it is not to lose all touch with reality. The tentative first step outlined in the previous section certainly looks very crude and pedestrian when compared with the polished elegance of modern value theory. But it is tentative steps of this sort which economic analysis must undertake to-day. For " it is better to be vaguely right than precisely wrong." [3]

K. W. ROTHSCHILD

The University,
Glasgow.

[1] *Ibid.*, p. 320.
[2] *Ibid.*, p. 322.
[3] Professor Wildon Carr, quoted by G. F. Shove, *op. cit.*, p. 323.

THE WASTES OF COMPETITION [1954]

BY

KURT ROTHSCHILD

Oesterreichisches Institut für Wirtschaftsforschung, Wien

I. CHANGING ATTITUDES TO THE VIRTUES OF COMPETITION

THE growing specialization of economists in this century has led to a neglect of some of the more general and sweeping questions that used to be asked as a matter of course in nineteenth-century books on economics. Today the lyrical enthusiasm or the condemning remarks that could usually be found about the beauties of competition [1] have largely vanished from most text-books and are more at home in political pamphlets than in economic treatises. The whole problem of the advantages and disadvantages of competition has, however, again come to the fore in at least some circles of economists as a consequence of the spectacular developments of economic theory in the inter-war years. Imperfect and monopolistic competition theory helped to crystallize the full meaning of pure and perfect competition and showed how rare and exceptional it is, while the Keynesian system laid bare the 'normality' of the rigidities in the present-day capitalistic system and of the stability of under-employment equilibrium.

These developments had a double effect on the old controversy about the virtues of competition. On the one hand, these more realistic models seemed to destroy the last nimbus which the idea of competition had managed to save through all the years of scepticism and criticism, by showing that so many adverse features were not occasional blemishes but were part and parcel of the way competition worked in our world. In a different way, however, the *idea* of perfect competition became cleared and got a new lease of life. For could it not now be shown that so many of the shortcomings that had been laid at the door of competition were really due to its absence ? As Professor Chamberlin said : 'The

---

[1] As a good example see the long and critical analysis of all aspects of competition in Adolph Wagner, *Grundlegung der politischen Oekonomie*, 3rd ed., Pt. I, Book Five, pp. 794-827.

301

Monopoly, Competition and Welfare

theory affords an explanation of such wastes in the economic system — wastes which are usually referred to as "wastes of competition". In fact, they could never occur under pure competition. . . . They are wastes of monopoly — of the monopoly elements in monopolistic competition.'[1] Things on earth may be uglier than one thought, but at least the ideal in heaven could now shine again in greater splendour.

Thus the strange thing happened that in the 'thirties conservative and a certain school of socialist economists were at one in their aims. While after the First World War the discussion raged between liberal and conservative defenders of free competition and socialist planners who had no high opinion of the competitive solution, in these later days one could see Hayek and Mises, and Lange and Dickinson united in their admiration of the competitive ideal and only divided about the question whether socialism leads away from this target or is the only way of reaching it. This new situation found its clearest expression in Lerner's *Economics of Control* where such old-standing distinctions as capitalism versus socialism and free enterprise versus planning fade into the background, and the only task that remains is to approach the competitive 'rule' by any means that seem appropriate.[2]

In view of this state of the discussion a critical estimate of competition and its wastes must proceed by two steps. First, we must look at competition as it really is and enumerate its shortcomings. On this list most economists will agree unless they belong to the extreme wing who deny our profession the right to pass any value judgments whatsoever, even if it is only a case of the economic efficiency of the system. To many this type of criticism will also be all that is necessary since — they would hold — we can only deal with a competition as we know it and not with some 'perfect' model which cannot be attained anyway. We shall, however, have to pass on to this further task and see whether pure and perfect competition can serve as that perfect standard to which it has been elevated by economists from various camps, and from which all wastes are measured, or whether — if we take a wider view — it does not contain itself elements

[1] *The Theory of Monopolistic Competition*, 5th ed., p. 109. The wastes referred to in the quotation are those associated with certain aspects of the 'excess capacity' problems.

[2] Lerner admits, however, that the competitive solution will not yield an 'optimum' division of income, which he sees in as equal a division as is practically possible.

Wastes of Competition — Rothschild

of waste. On this second part of our investigation we shall find far less unanimity among economists, while those who allow only a very limited scope to welfare economics (if any at all) will probably regard the whole discussion as beyond the field to be covered by economic theory.[1]

II. WASTES UNDER MONOPOLISTIC COMPETITION

Let us then deal first with competition as it is this side of heaven. To make matters as simple and short as possible we shall not go into a description of monopolistic competition or of under-employment equilibrium, but shall plunge directly into an enumeration of the more important wastes connected with these forms of competition, adding a short commentary to each item.

(1) *Unemployment.*—Not all unemployment belongs in this section. Frictional, cyclical, and structural unemployment can — as we shall see — also exist under pure and probably even under perfect competition. But there is a special aggravation of this problem stemming from the monopolistic and monopsonistic nature of actual competition. This is, no doubt, a field about which further realistic research is needed. For it has been pointed out that the monopolistic rigidities fulfil a certain positive function by preventing the whole economic system from collapsing into bottomless deflationary downward spirals.[2] But while this supports the view that a completely perfect and frictionless system of competition is a practical impossibility, it seems nevertheless true that the *growing* importance of monopoly and monopsony creates additional unemployment and with it waste. It does so by leaving productive capacity unused (see below), by intensifying cyclical unemployment through price maintenance in place of production maintenance, and finally by increasing the share of profits in national income [3] which will reduce the propensity to consume without creating a comparable increase in the desire to invest.

(2) *Excess Capacity.*—The fact that competition is not pure, *i.e.* that the demand curve facing the individual firm is not infinitely

---

[1] To them the title of this essay should already sound suspicious ; for waste is not an absolute category but necessarily involves some chosen standard in relation to which we can speak of waste.

[2] See Kenneth Boulding, 'In Defense of Monopoly', *Quarterly Journal of Economics*, August 1945.

[3] M. Kalecki, *Essays in the Theory of Economic Fluctuations*, ch. I.

Monopoly, Competition and Welfare

elastic, leads to the well-known fact of unused capacity with its corollary of non-minimum production costs and a price above marginal cost. This excess capacity can, however, only be unequivocally regarded as a waste if the different substitutes produced under monopolistic competition can be regarded as 'really' equivalent from the consumer's point of view. That is, if the situation arises, in Meade's terminology, from 'irrational' buyers' preferences,[1] it is clearly wasteful, and consumers would be better off if production were concentrated in fewer units producing at full capacity (pure competition).

But if buyers' preferences are 'rational', *i.e.* if they are prepared to pay a price for an extensive product differentiation, the situation becomes more complicated. Not all excess capacity is now a waste, and the production equilibrium of perfect competition largely loses its relevance. As Professor Chamberlin says :[2] 'The explicit recognition that product is differentiated brings into the open the problem of variety and makes it clear that *pure competition may no longer be regarded as in any sense an "ideal" for purposes of welfare economics.*[3] . . . Differences in tastes, desires, incomes . . . all indicate the need for variety and the necessity of substituting for the concept of a "competitive ideal" an ideal involving both monopoly and competition. How much and what kinds of monopoly, and with what measure of social control, become the questions.'

With this argument Professor Chamberlin has certainly disposed of pure competition as the one and only standard by which everything can be judged, and in comparison to which monopolistic competition must always be a waste. But by giving up the simple and objective minimum cost standard of competitive equilibrium he enters the field where a 'reasoned' production policy — *e.g.* so much competition and so much monopoly — has to be adopted, which has to be based on a considered judgment of (partly conflicting) welfare requirements. To this the present writer does not object. But he thinks that this process can be carried much further. Professor Chamberlin wanted to save the honour of certain cases of the monopolistic competition reality from the absolute attacks of the pure competition ideal. But

---

[1] J. E. Meade, *An Introduction to Economic Analysis and Policy*, p. 155.
[2] *The Theory of Monopolistic Competition*, 5th ed., pp. 214-215. Professor Chamberlin has later elaborated this idea. See 'Product Heterogeneity and Public Policy', *Papers and Proceedings, American Economic Review*, May 1950, pp. 86-92.   [3] Professor Chamberlin's italics.

Wastes of Competition — Rothschild

there is no need to stop here. Once we give up the lowest possible price in a free market as the ultimate criterion, we can adopt 'optimum' solutions seen from which competition as such, both perfect and monopolistic, is wasteful. But we shall have to leave this question for the next section.

Excess capacity also arises from monopolistic elements when the employer faces a supply curve of labour which is not infinitely elastic. Here no modifying remarks are necessary when we characterize the resulting under-employment and under-production as waste.

(3) *Cross-transport.*—This wasteful use of transport facilities deriving from the differentiation of products is similar in nature to the problem of excess capacity. Here, also, the distinction between rational and irrational buyers' preferences is of importance.

(4) *Failure to specialize.*—The cost advantages that are connected with specialization cannot be reaped under monopolistic competition, because the sales of a firm cannot be expanded without price concessions. To this extent insufficient specialization belongs in this section. To some extent, however, the failure to specialize and the costly maintenance of several lines of production is also owing to a desire to reduce the risks which derive from too great a dependence on the demand for one or a few products. In so far as this is the case, we have to ascribe this waste to the uncertainty of competition with which we deal in the next section.

(5) *Advertising.*—This, one of the most popular examples of 'competitive waste', is, as is now common knowledge, also the outcome of the absence of pure and perfect competition. Already Marshall distinguished between 'constructive' and 'combative' advertisements.[1] The former, whose predominant function is the spreading of information, are compatible with pure competition where knowledge is not perfect. If one regards a perfectly competitive system as the impossibility that it is, this type of advertisement will usually not be classified as a waste. In fact, it might help to reduce the waste arising from insufficient specialization by opening up expanding sales facilities.

But the bulk of present-day advertising is of the 'combative' type, *i.e.* it is connected with a differentiated product, with a partial monopoly. This advertisement can be regarded firstly

[1] *Industry and Trade*, pp. 304-307.

x   305

Monopoly, Competition and Welfare

(assuming full employment) as a direct waste of resources, and secondly intensifying waste in many cases through strengthening the monopolistic elements in competition. Against this it is sometimes held that advertisements increase consumers' satisfactions by adding to the prestige, the glamour, the desirability of the good he buys. It is, however, likely that the dissatisfaction created by advertisements in people who cannot buy the advertised goods amounts to much more. This 'psychological waste' must not be left out of account when one talks of the wastes of advertising. It is a special case of a waste which is connected with the competitive system as such.

To this we now turn.

III. WASTES UNDER 'IDEAL' COMPETITION

When we now deal with 'ideal' competition we have still to proceed by two stages. First we shall assume pure competition, in which monopoly is absent but other imperfections still exist, and finally we shall see what wastes we can ascribe to competition when even these last imperfections are removed.

(a) *Pure Competition*

(1) *Imperfect knowledge of producers.*—Producers will have an inadequate knowledge of demand conditions. This may be regarded as an inescapable fact in a world where goods are not produced to order. As such it may be a necessary waste occurring in all economic systems under modern dynamic conditions. But under competition — in contrast to planning — producers will also be ignorant about the plans of other producers. Thus there will be wasteful over- or under-investment in some industrial sectors and disparity between industrial sectors. This can lead to frictional and structural unemployment and can intensify cyclical under-employment. In view of the great and growing importance of fixed investment these dislocations will not only be of a temporary nature, but can also leave their traces for a long time.

Speculation has usually been quoted as a factor which reduces the wastes arising from incomplete foresight of producers.[1] But

---

[1] See *e.g.* Lerner, *The Economics of Control*, ch. 8.

306

Wastes of Competition — Rothschild

even if speculation is free from monopolistic elements it may not fulfil its purpose of reducing the dislocation of economic resources, because the time horizon of speculators may be short, and they may be more interested in short-period fluctuations in the sentiments on capital markets than in the long-run development of the demand structure.[1] To the wastes of competition then, at least of the free enterprise variety of competition, must be added the wastes of speculation.

Finally, imperfect knowledge of producers contributes to cyclical unemployment, no matter how we analyse the latter phenomenon.

(2) *Imperfect knowledge of consumers.*—In so far as this gives rise to monopolistic elements we have dealt with it in the previous section. But imperfect knowledge of the consumer also means that he is not an expert buyer. As a consequence, price competition has an inherent tendency towards lowering quality and pretending non-existing advantages. Experience is an insufficient safeguard for the consumer, because in many cases he will not be able to judge the adequacy of a commodity even after the purchase (protective legislation in the case of foodstuffs and drugs shows a recognition of this fact), and in other cases his purchases will be too intermittent to allow him to correct his mistakes (*i.e.* the waste) on the basis of experience.

(3) *Imperfect knowledge of workers.*—The particular imperfection of information that surrounds the labour market combined with the great obstacles to mobility (housing!) puts the worker at a special disadvantage *vis-à-vis* the capitalist in free enterprise competition, and greatly reduces the opportunities for that beneficial flow of labour from low-paid to high-paid jobs on which the competitive argument depends.

(4) *Imperfect knowledge in general.*—Quite generally the imperfection of knowledge that pervades competition in its imperfect form means that this system is based on an equilibrating mechanism which, though it corrects 'mistakes' automatically, does so only *after the event.* This is, however, in itself a wasteful mechanism, because the aim of human endeavour has always been to reduce losses by premeditated prevention of the very occurrence of mistakes. Competition, even in its most ideal *practical* form, is therapeutic, not prophylactic.

[1] See Keynes, *The General Theory of Employment, Interest, and Money*, pp. 154 ff.

Monopoly, Competition and Welfare

(b) *Perfect Competition*

We come now to our last stage where we abstract even from those frictions and imperfections which are still associated with the concept of pure competition. To talk about the wastes of perfect competition may seem in itself a waste. For, while pure competition is today probably a historical but not a logical impossibility, perfect competition could never exist.

The assumption of instantaneous adjustment would either have to mean absolutely uniform repetition in a perfectly static world, or else a state of constant vibration ; and the assumption of perfect knowledge would, as Professor Clark remarked almost twenty years ago,[1] remove competition altogether since no seller would cut his price, knowing that all competitors would follow suit and deprive him of his gain. Why then deal with such an abstract figment ?[2] Two reasons make it necessary. Firstly, because this figment is in fact being used as a standard of comparison, and secondly, because we have left for this section all wastes of competition that do not arise from monopolistic or frictional elements but which nevertheless apply to all forms of competition, perfect, pure, and monopolistic.

(1) *Unemployment.*—Once again we must mention unemployment, which can occur even with flexible prices [3] and without any disturbances due to imperfect knowledge. The income distribution can result in saving and investment schedules which yield a competitive less-than-full-employment equilibrium.

(2) *The unequal starting-point.*—The main strength of the welfare theory of competition has been in the field of distributing resources and commodities within a historically given *status quo*. But to many people the change of this very unequal *status quo* is by far the greater welfare problem. To its solution the competitive process cannot contribute. On the contrary, it tends to preserve existing disparities or even to increase them, by adding

---

[1] J. M. Clark, *Economics of Overhead Costs*, pp. 417 and 460.
[2] Professor Sargant Florence has some harsh words to say on the economists' preoccupation with artificial problems. 'Economics . . . has become more armchair, more college-conditioned and more disintegrated and isolated from the facts discussed and from other, more realistic, studies of those facts.' See 'Patterns in Recent Social Research', *The British Journal of Sociology*, September 1950, p. 223.
[3] See O. Lange, *Price Flexibility and Employment*.

Wastes of Competition — Rothschild

to the earning power of those who have already accumulated wealth and education.

This defect of competition, which applies to capitalist but not necessarily to socialist competition, has earned it the earliest and strongest attacks. In this group belong the 'infant industry' arguments of List and Carey, pointing out the differences in national development, and the demands of an endless chain of social reformers for greater equality in income and opportunity, since without it the distribution of work and production according to market valuations will not maximize welfare.[1] The most consistent approach in this direction is taken by Marx. To him, who casts his view far beyond the limits of the market, the historical disparity between a property-owning and a propertyless class becomes the dominating factor of the situation. This class monopoly over the means of production creates waste by depriving the proletariat of a greater share in the product, and in the later stages of capitalism by hampering the development of the productive forces. In comparison, the difference between competition and monopoly in the market becomes of minor significance, and affects, in the view of Marx, mainly the distribution of surplus value among the capitalists; though Lenin, writing at a later time, has given greater weight to the economic and political importance of trustification.[2]

(3) *Social cost versus private cost.*—The fact that there may be a divergence between the private costs accruing to the decision-making competitor and the social costs accruing to the community as a whole, and that accordingly projects are started which 'should not' be started, while others are left undone, though they would be 'worth while', has become so famous since its classical treatment in Professor Pigou's *Economics of Welfare* that we need not go into it.[3] Here it should only be added that this principle has a

[1] Here, as elsewhere, a certain comparison of welfare between different persons is assumed possible. Otherwise the whole discussion becomes senseless. But so becomes any argument in favour of competition. If I prefer monopoly or robbery, I should act accordingly. There is no basis on which to find out whether my action will increase or decrease total welfare because on this view no meaning can be attached to the term 'total welfare'. On this point see I. M. D. Little, *A Critique of Welfare Economics*, ch. IV, and Hans Peter, 'Welfare Economics. Ethik und doch Wissenschaft', *Finanzarchiv*, Bd. 12, Heft 1 (1950).

[2] *Imperialism, the Highest Stage of Capitalism.*

[3] A good list of examples of divergences between social and private costs can be found in Boris C. Swerling, 'Some Limitations of Competitive Equilibrium', *The Southern Economic Journal*, July 1950, pp. 38-39. Other parts of that article have also a close bearing on the subject of this essay.

Monopoly, Competition and Welfare

much wider application than the few and mostly trivial text-book examples would suggest. It would enter into almost every major decision in a planned economy.

(4) *Limited perspective.*—The horizon of a single competitor is necessarily limited, if only because his radius of action is limited. Thus competition will always return or approach to the 'nearest' equilibrium. But there is no reason to assume that there is always only one equilibrium position — there may be several. To lift the whole economy from one equilibrium to another (more favourable) one will require the simultaneous and co-ordinated action of several parts of the economy which is beyond the power of the competitive mechanism. Similarly, the limitation of perspective in a competitive system will also prevent the adoption of a 'rational' investment policy through time.

(5) *The question of consumers' sovereignty.*—When the advantages of competition are enumerated, 'consumers' freedom' and 'consumers' sovereignty' usually take an important place. There is little to be said about the concept of consumers' freedom — the freedom to choose in a competitive market — except that inequality of purchasing power greatly reduces the welfare aspect of this institution.[1] But, on closer investigation, little is left of the statement that the consumer is sovereign under competition, that he (or rather his purchasing power) decides what should be produced. The fact is rather that the consumer can influence only the output of goods already offered on the market. The initiative to introduce or withdraw a commodity rests entirely with the producer. Under a planned economy consumers may or may not have an influence on this question; under competition it is impossible.

But more than that. While competition provides a measure by which one can judge — if one wants to accept the marginal principle — whether a little more or a little less should be produced, the standard of the market fails to indicate whether a new commodity should be produced or an established product be withdrawn. For the marginal product of the factor management can only be determined in the usual way if a new firm is introduced at the margin of a large output. But if it is a firm producing a new commodity, the marginal product of management is equal to what consumers would be *willing to pay* for the firm's output (minus the amount paid to the hired factors) rather than have none of the

See above, point (2).

310

Wastes of Competition — Rothschild

commodity, and that will be more than what is *actually spent* on the commodity (minus the amount paid to hired factors).[1] Only with comparatively small changes at the margin will the two measures coincide.

Thus neither does competition establish the consumer's sovereignty, nor does it provide a standard suitable (on its own terms) for the producer. The initiative to start or stop production is to some extent left to the caprice of the producer.

This would not matter so much if consumers' wants were the purely individual wants competitive theory usually assumes them to be. It could then be left to the market at least to weed out undesired products, even if it could not start new ones. But in fact many of our wants are not at all individual affairs but depend on the goods consumed by others. Competition may put goods on the market which nobody in particular desires but which, once they are there, are bought because others buy them. Their general withdrawal would leave nobody dissatisfied [2] — for now 'the other person' cannot have it either — and would free resources for 'less wasteful' purposes.

(6) *Ethical considerations.*—When we discuss the wastes of competition there is no need to restrict ourselves to the economic sphere. We can cast our net much wider and take into account *all* the repercussions of competition. We may then come to the conclusion that while the element of competition can play a useful and constructive part in some departments of our lives, its unrestricted acceptance as the basic driving force will foster undesirable qualities like greed, fraud, ruthlessness, at the cost of truthfulness, readiness to help, solidarity. The loss of values caused by a system of competition would have to be set against its positive achievements.

---

[1] See J. E. Meade, *An Introduction to Economic Analysis and Policy*, pp. 160 ff.

[2] In reviewing Ruby T. Norris, 'The Theory of Consumer's Demand' in the *Economic Journal* of April 1943, Mrs. Joan Robinson wrote : 'Latter-day experience of the restrictions of consumption has brought into a clear light one great weakness of the traditional theory of demand . . . that is, the erroneous assumption of individualism. When a given cut in consumption has to be made, traditional theory teaches that the minimum sacrifice is imposed on consumers if the requisite amount of general purchasing power is taken away, and each consumer is left free to economise on what he feels that he can best spare. In reality, it is obvious that less sacrifice is caused by a total disappearance from the market of certain commodities, such as silk stockings, which are bought by each consumer mainly because other people have them' (p. 116). The importance of Veblen's work in this connection is obvious.

311

Monopoly, Competition and Welfare

IV. THE PRACTICAL IMPLICATIONS

The critical attitude towards competition expressed in the preceding pages will probably shock economists more than any other single group of human beings. For the desirability of perfect competition has more than anything else been the article of faith that has united many succeeding generations of economists whatever their differences may have been on other points. And as we saw in section I, even the theoretical developments of the 'thirties, which seemed like a revolution against the competitive models of the neo-classical school, left the competitive ideal unshorn, and in a way restored its reputation as an absolute standard.

This special weakness of economic theorists for perfect competition cannot be solely explained by the fact that they have inherited this belief from the fathers of modern economic theorizing — from the Physiocrats and Adam Smith. Such traditions play an important part, but they alone could not explain the persistence with which perfect competition is defended by economists of the most diverse opinions and even by those who normally refuse to pass value judgments altogether. There is another reason: and that is, of course, that competition has proved a decisive premise for the type of theorizing we are used to.[1] No matter how subconscious the connection may be: competition as an economic system is viewed favourably because one is at a loss how to produce exact theories without having some sort of competition at the basis.

But if we economists are not to remain theoreticians for theory's sake we must recognize that for many people perfect competition seems neither an approachable nor even a desirable ideal. In fact, we shall have to recognize that the ideal of perfect competition, like so many others, is a historical category, which was born out of a certain social and economic setting and cannot serve equally well at all times and all places. Its seemingly self-

---

[1] To quote a well-known passage from Professor Hicks: 'It has to be recognized that a general abandonment of the assumption of perfect competition, a universal adoption of the assumption of monopoly, must have very destructive consequences for economic theory'. (*Value and Capital*, p. 83.)
But we find already a similar sentiment expressed by J. S. Mill, who said that without competition economics could not be a science.

Wastes of Competition — Rothschild

evident validity was probably only confined to a (historically) relatively short span of time in the immediate past.

To the middle ages, with their guild system and with everybody having his 'station in life', the idea of competition as the basis of economic welfare was completely foreign. But also in early capitalism this hostile view of competition survived, partly nurtured by monopolistic desires, but to a large extent out of a generally accepted attitude. In 1745 the Fifth Edition of the *Complete English Tradesman* still expressed widely held opinions when it complained that 'this underselling practice is grown to such a shameful height that particular persons publickly advertise that they undersell the rest of the trade'. But in the following decades competition as a system and as an idea broke through, particularly in England. In those days of thousands of small-scale producers it was only in this way that the change-over to a market economy and to modern methods of production could take place. Competition, then, had an enormous function to fulfil and opened the way to a period of tremendous economic progress. But even then, free competition, necessary as it was socially, was wholeheartedly accepted as an ideology to be admired *and to be used as a guiding principle in practice* only by those who immediately and unequivocally benefited from it. Thus it became the religion of the capitalists and of the upper middle classes in expanding societies not surrounded by dangerous competitors. Nineteenth-century Britain and the United States, while the frontier expanded, are the obvious and perhaps the only examples. Among other people the belief in competition never caught deep roots. The workers and peasants, who from the beginning came to know as much of the drawbacks of competition as of its advantages, always sought means to mitigate its impact, and in their utopias there was little room for the competitive system. Similarly, the nations who entered the industrial field later or found competition by no means a predominantly agreeable influence and accepted it only with many reservations.

The situation changed again when large-scale production units began to replace more and more the typical small firm of the nineteenth century. As both defenders of giant trusts and socialists stressed (though with very different implications in mind), the old competition of numerous isolated small-scale producers was no longer possible. But neither was it necessary. For now a real alternative was opened : for the first time it became

Monopoly, Competition and Welfare

possible to run a modern industrial society on a basis which was not dominated by the competitive standard.[1] This, it seems to me, is to most people the real issue between existing capitalist competition and socialist planning, and not the question which of the two would better approach the ideal of perfect competition.[2] The moment competition became *practically* replaceable by another method its drawbacks were no longer something one was prepared to accept, however reluctantly : the whole principle had come up for discussion.

[1] This does not mean that it would be possible or desirable to do away with all elements of competition. A socialist economy will inherit people with a competitive background, and that will have to be taken into account : in certain other cases competition will continue to be regarded as the best form of economic organization. Thus we see in the Soviet Union the continuance of markets as a suitable form of distributing consumer goods, and we see new forms of competition between work brigades to enlist the (still existing or permanent ?) competitive instincts in the growth of production.

[2] The one economist who in recent times has consistently taken the view that socialist planning should mean something different from putting perfect competition into practice, is Mr. Dobb. See his 'Economic Theory and the Problems of a Socialist Economy', *Economic Journal*, December 1933, 'Saving and Investment in a Socialist Economy', *Economic Journal*, December 1939, and *Political Economy and Capitalism*, ch. VIII.

12

THE LIMITATIONS
OF ECONOMIC GROWTH MODELS

CRITICAL REMARKS ON SOME ASPECTS
OF MR. KALDOR'S MODEL

Modern growth theory has come of age. When Sir Roy Harrod in 1939 published his famous article, "An Essay in Dynamic Theory"[1], it had a startling (though—because of the —warsomewhat delayed) effect on a professional world which had been completely absorbed by considering the theoretical and practical aspects of a short-run Keynesian model. To be reminded that the successful achievement of full employment of labour and capital in one period has important implications for the full employment problem in the next period (if these periods are taken as longer intervals) was very important indeed. At this stage of economic growth theory it was quite sufficient to work with a few rough aggregates and to show what the logical connections between them have to be, if uninterrupted full employment growth is to be established in a simple model of a competitive capitalist economy.

These early growth models and many of the refinements that were later added did not aim at an explanation of the actual course of capitalist development[2]. This would not have been possible, in any case, since we do not know of any long period of full employment growth in private enterprise economies in times of peace and without massive government intervention. And a development with ups and downs yielding a certain arithmetical average rate of growth may obey rather different rules than a smoothly growing economy with

---

1. *Economic Journal*, March 1939.
2. "These theories (viz. those of Harrod and Domar), though often referred to as theories of growth, are, properly speaking, theories of the requirements of steady growth at full employment. They make no assertions with respect to the likely development of capital formation over time." See MOSES ABRAMOVITZ, "Economics of Growth", in *A Survey of Contemporary Theory*, Vol. II, edited by Bernard F. Haley (Homewood, Ill., 1952), p. 170, footnote.

the same rate of expansion[3]. What the theories did—and that was a very useful achievement indeed—was to draw the attention of economists to certain factors and influences which, while not very important in short-term considerations, must not be neglected when long-term problems are analysed.

As the theory of economic growth has expanded, it has tried more and more to give an account of the *actual* working of the economic system. But the nearer it tries to get towards a description of reality (rather than analysing the requirements for consistency between certain macro-economic aggregates under full employment conditions) the more it is hampered by the restrictions it acquired in the days of its childhood. These restrictions are:

(1) The limited number of the variables taken into account and the simplicity of their functional relationships. This is a perfectly justifiable procedure for the early stages of the theory when the stress is laid on pointing out certain important inter-relationships[4]. Niceties in detail or changes over longer periods do not matter in that context. But when a closer contact with reality is desired it is necessary to consider the influence of a wider circle of factors and to give the functional relationships a more concrete empirical content. That means that the beautiful simplicity and unity of the early growth models will have to be sacrificed.

(2) The neglect of historical, sociological and institutional factors. Modern growth theory is a child of Keynesian theory. It has shown how the fundamental concepts and relationships of Keynes' short-run model are affected by the accumulation of capital, the growth of population, technical progress, etc. But many of the historical and institutional factors which Keynes could neglect in his short-run picture (and which, therefore, do not appear in growth theory) cannot be regarded as invariable when we aim at a realistic theory of economic change stretching over longer periods. Some functions

3. People will behave rather differently in a room where temparatures vary between 0 and 40 degrees of Celsius than in a room with a constant temperature of 20 degrees, even if the long-run average is the same in both cases.

4. As Mr. Little puts it: "But growth and distribution theory have only recently again become fashionable with economists, and it may still be worth while to work out the consequences of all sorts of assumptions, even where these are outrageous..." I. M. D. LITTLE, "Classical Growth", *Oxford Economic Papers*, June 1957, p. 175.

which Keynes could take as constants will vary when we deal with longer spans of time. I admit that the introduction of history and sociology as "endogenous variables" will make our functions less simple and less elegant. But it will prevent us from assuming reliable inter-relationships where, in fact, they do not exist.

(3) A serious handicap for a realistic development of growth theory is the starting assumption of an equilibrium growth at full employment level. As I said before, this was a legitimate *analytical* device in order to point out the necessary interrelationships between different economic categories under conditions of growth. When we try to fit growth theory to the task of explaining *actual* growth, the initial assumption of a smoothly growing full employment economy as some sort of "equilibrium" is an impediment which distracts our attention from the actual mechanism of economic expansion and the factors influencing it.

In the following pages I want to illustrate these limitations of modern growth theory by discussing some aspects of Mr. Kaldor's growth model[5]. In choosing Kaldor's essay I do not want to suggest that his model is in any way inferior to other examples in this field. On the contrary; I regard Kaldor's article as a particularly stimulating and well argued piece of research. But just because he pushes the frontiers of growth theory so ambitiously outward, the limitations of the theory become more clearly visible.

I do not intend to discuss Kaldor's theory point by point. I shall deal only with some of its aspects. I must also refrain from summarising all the relevant details of the theory. The reader of this article is expected to have read Kaldor's essay. If he has not, he is strongly recommended to do so.

1. The Technical Progress Function

Kaldor's model rests basically on three pillars: a saving function, an investment function, and a technical progress function[6]. I shall deal

5. NICHOLAS KALDOR, "A Model of Economic Growth", *Economic Journal*, December 1957, pp. 591–624.

6. The problem of population growth is introduced after the working of the model has been described for a constant population. I shall restrict my remarks to the constant population model.

with the first and third of these functions. This does not mean that no problems of empirical relevancy arise in connection with the investment function. But anything that could be said in this respect would apply to almost any general investment function. Kaldor's solution—he makes long-run investment dependent on turnover and changes in the rate of profit on capital—is certainly not inferior to other assumptions in this field and superior to some of them[7].

Newer ground is broken with the technical progress function. In a short-run Keynesian model technical progress can be safely neglected. Output is simply a function of employment. But when we allow the capital stock to grow significantly, we deal with longer periods in which technical progress will also play its part. Technical progress has often proved as a rather untractable factor in growth theories, since its course seems less amenable to definite abstract formulations than some of the traditional economic relationships. One can, of course, leave it outside the economic framework and regard it as an exogenous variable. This is, however, not very satisfactory from the point of view of both theoretical perfection and practical application.

Kaldor takes the ambitious step of making technical progress an essential element in his theoretical structure. But to keep this structure manageable and determinate within the traditional frame of modern growth theory he has to adopt a very simplified and, it seems to me, rather peculiar technical progress function.

Its main feature is that it establishes a definite link between capital investment and technical progress. There is a steady flow of new ideas, and the rate of investment determines in a unique way how and to what extent these inventions are used. Technical progress, instead of being a separate (endogenous or exogenous) factor influencing the growth of income over and above the application of capital, becomes fused with capital investment into one single re-

---

7. I would, however, take exception to one argument which Kaldor advances in favour of his assumptions. At the end of footnote 2 on p. 601 he points out that his investment function is consistent with a stable equilibrium of steady growth while a certain competing formulation is not. Since the existence of a stable equilibrium of steady growth (in an unregulated market economy) has never been proved, the convenience of a function for such a steady growth model can hardly tell us anything about its realistic quality.

lationship. The form of the relationship is given by Kaldor in Figure 1 of his article, which is reproduced below. C_t and O_t represent the capital per worker and the annual output per worker at time t, so that the abscissa represents the annual percentage growth in capital per worker, and the ordinate the annual percentage growth in output per man. (With a constant population and full employment the diagram also represents the relationship between growth rates in total capital and total output.) The TT' curve represents the link between capital growth and income growth with the technical progress built in uniquely into the investment process. A certain amount of technical progress is assumed to take place independently of new capital investment. That is the reason why the TT' curve starts above the origin. The height of the curve will depend on the inventiveness of a community, but otherwise a certain constancy in the flow of new ideas is assumed.

Fig. 1

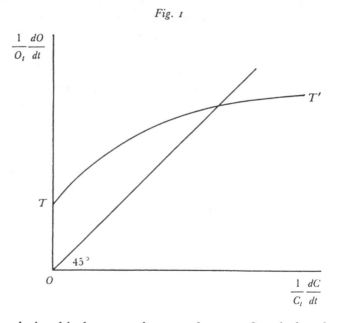

The relationship between the growth rates of capital and output determines the course of the capital-output ratio. If output grows at a quicker rate than capital, the capital-output ratio will decline and vice versa. Consequently, the capital-output ratio will decline as long as the TT' curve lies above a line drawn from the origin at an angle of 45 degrees (representing equal growth rates for capital and output), and will increase when TT' falls below that line.

To have such a compact theory of technical progress and capital investment is a great boon, if one is on the look-out for a comprehensive theory of economic growth. It permits us to concentrate our attention on the investment process pure and simple without having to worry which different forms it may take and what different consequences it may have with regard to output. As Kaldor puts it: "The recognition of the existence of a functional relationship between the proportionate growth in capital and the annual proportionate growth in productivity shows the futility of regarding the movements in the capital-output ratio as dependent upon the technical character of the stream of inventions—according as they are predominantly 'labour-saving' or 'capital-saving' in character"[8].

The only trouble with this statement is that the existence of the said functional relationship has not yet been "recognised", if we mean by "recognised" empirically tested. This relationship is a very ingenious assumption, but it is at present not more than an assumption, and a highly simplified one at that. Nor does it away with the distinction between "labour-saving" and "capital-saving" inventions. The case is rather that Kaldor has built some very special assumptions about capital-saving and labour-saving innovations into his model which result in his single-valued relationship between the capital-output ratio and net investment.

Kaldor assumes that there are some output-increasing innovations introduced all the time quite independently of any capital investment. That is, he assumes a constant flow and introduction of capital-saving devices. This gives us right from the start (i.e. before any investment takes place) an influence which makes for a fall in the capital-output ratio. As soon as investment sets in it is necessarily of a labour-saving type, since Kaldor assumes continuous full employment so that (with a constant population) there are no reserves of man-power and none must be created. Since, additionally, no spectacular new techniques are introduced, the increasing application of labour-saving devices with growing investment will lead to diminishing returns to capital and a rising capital-output ratio. The

8. *Op. cit.*, p. 597.

more investment grows, the more this rising tendency will absorb the initial reduction in the capital-output ratio until—at a certain rate of investment—the ratio begins to surpass the level attained in the previous period[9].

Kaldor has thus not done away with the ticklish problem of labour-saving and capital-saving inventions. He has only assumed a certain definite frame for them by the shape of his TT' function and by stipulating uninterrupted full employment. But is this not a rather artificial picture? Do we not have in reality a considerable pool of technical knowledge and research opportunities on which the capital investor can draw?[10] According to the choice investors make we shall obtain different technical progress functions (TT' curves) and different "points of equilibrium" in Kaldor's system[11]. This does, of course, presume that there are economic factors pulling and pushing investors into different choices. Kaldor's assumptions leave no room for such factors. Two of his assumptions help to escape this problem of varying technical forms of given quantities (or rates) of investment.

The first is the assumption of uninterrupted full employment growth. In such a state (and with a constant population) every given increase in capital yields only one possible capital-labour ratio and therefore a unique degree of "labour-savingness". This leaves (given the known technical methods) only one profitable policy open to the investor[12]: to maximise output *over the given number of workers*. Choices with regard to "capital-saving" and "labour-saving" inventions necessarily lose their meaning, if variations in labour supply are

9. For a fuller treatment of this point see the Appendix (pp. 584–586). See also FERDINAND GRÜNIG, "Substitution und technischer Fortschritt im gesamtwirtschaftlichen Wachstumsprozess", *Konjunkturpolitik*, No. 1, 1959, particularly pp. 3–5.

10. "There are many alternative production methods: (1) there are choices among alternative processes; (2) there are choices among variants within processes; (3) there are choices among varieties and grades of a given commodity produced; (4) there are choices among forms of plant or process expansion." H. B. MALMGREN, "What Conclusions are to be Drawn from Empirical Cost Data?", *Journal of Industrial Economics*, March 1959, pp. 136–144.

11. Kaldor admits the possibility of shifts in the TT' curve in times when there is a burst of new inventions or when ideas dry up (p. 598). But for normal times a single and fairly stable TT' curve is assumed.

12. Or rather to the average result of total investment activity.

ruled out and capital accumulation becomes the only variable. As soon as we permit changes in employment and various possible technical combinations between (a given quantity) of capital and labour the uniqueness of the TT' function vanishes. The same amount of capital investment can be combined with different amounts of labour and this will yield different rates of output growth and different capital-output ratios[13].

To this one can, of course, object that it is no use arguing this way, since Kaldor specifically excludes less-than-full-employment situations. But Kaldor quite obviously did not just want to discuss logical relationships within *some* model of full employment; he was out to build a long-term reference model for actual capitalist economies. The aforementioned objection will, therefore, not suffice. If employment variations *do* play a part and investment *can* create or absorb unemployment, then technical development and economic growth may take a different course from that indicated by a model of permanent full employment. If Kaldor excludes unemployment, because "an equilibrium of steady growth is inconsistent with under-employment equilibrium" (p. 594), he argues again in terms of the "traditional" growth models which *presuppose* an equilibrium of steady growth. Experience has, however, shown that such an equilibrium does not exist in free-market economies. Long-term growth is

---

13. Perhaps the gist of the argument can be put this way. (For the sake of simplicity we shall state our argument in terms of absolute quantities rather than in terms of growth rates.)

The capital-output ratio can be expressed as follows:

$$\frac{K}{Y} = \frac{K}{W} \cdot \frac{W}{Y}$$

where K, Y, W are real capital, real output and the number of workers respectively.

Now, if we assume W fixed (at full-employment level) and techniques of production determined by the amount of capital per worker (so that Y is a unique function of K/W), then K/Y is uniquely determined by K/W or simply by K. In other words, a certain amount of *absolute* capital investment will strictly determine the size of the additional output and the capital-output ratio. If we let W vary, Y will still depend on K/W (technical knowledge given) and so will K/Y. But the same *absolute amount* of capital investment will not necessarily be linked with a given amount of W so that Y and K/Y are not uniquely determined by K.

the outcome of *un*steady developments which follow rules differing from those of a full employment model.

The objection to Kaldor's unique technical progress (and capital-output) function does, by the way, also hold if we have the kind of full employment we have known since the war. If there is a public sector absorbing and releasing workers in accordance with fluctuations in the private sector, investment in the private sector will still be able to combine capital with a greater or smaller number of workers, to be more "labour-saving" or more "capital-saving"[14]. In this case, too, we can have a multitude of TT' curves rather than a single one.

There is, however, still another point in Kaldor's assumptions by which he tries to get rid of the complexities introduced by the problem of different technical combinations. He regards the choice of "techniques" as independent of changes in the share of profits and wages and of changes in the rate of profit and makes it "entirely a matter of the relative prices of different types of capital goods, which can be assumed to alter with the accumulation of capital and the progress of techniques in the capital-goods making industries" (p. 603). As an illustration Kaldor presents us with the example of a developed and an underdeveloped country, the first one using bulldozers and the second one shovels. The difference in techniques he explains by the relatively lower prices of bulldozers (in terms of shovels) in the developed country. The obvious argument that the underdeveloped country could obtain the same relative prices through international trade he tries to brush aside (in footnote 1 on p. 603) by pointing out that there may be no market for the inferior capital goods in the developed country. But this answer is not very convincing: (1) If it were true that only relative prices of capital goods (and not of labour) count, why should there be no market for relatively cheap shovels in the developed country?[15]. (2) Even if the

14. I assume that Kaldor's technical progress and investment functions apply only to the private sector. A government pledged to full employment will necessarily have to adopt different criteria.

15. If we allow wage and profit levels to enter the picture the preference for bulldozers becomes easily understandable.

Kaldor's assumption also leaves no room for the hypothesis that the development of highly mechanistic methods of production in 19th century America was due to a high supply price of labour (which in turn was closely connected with the availability of free or cheap land).

underdeveloped country imports *all* its capital goods and is thus
confronted with exactly the same price relations for capital goods as
the developed country, is it not likely—with cheap labour available—
to use shovels more often?

Kaldor does not completely deny the influence of wage and profit
changes on the choice of techniques, but he tries to belittle this effect
and he cuts it out completely when he comes to the construction of
his model. In this way the uniqueness of his technical progress
function is secured. It depends solely on the rate of investment and
establishes an unequivocal link between (full employment) growth
rates of investment and growth rates of output. When in the long run
the economic forces have established an equilibrium between these
two growth rates, the economy (output and capital) will grow at a
definite rate which is uniquely determined by the coefficients of the
technical progress function. This is Kaldor's equilibrium rate of
growth G, where

$$G = \frac{\alpha''}{1 - \beta''} = \gamma''$$

(α'' and β'' being the coefficients of the technical progress function).

From what has been said before it will be clear what, in my
opinion, the shortcomings of this formulation are. By *assuming* a
steady full employment growth and by linking the investment
process to one single technical progress function, a basic, technically
determined equilibrium rate of growth is established to which other
economic variables (e.g. savings) have to adjust. If we, however,
admit that over longer periods employment in the private sector can
fluctuate and that the form of investment will be influenced by wage-
profit relationships, then there will be no unique (technical) relationship between capital growth and output growth but several possibilities (a whole family of TT' curves). The long-term rate of growth
emerging from the events in many short-run periods (shall we call it
the "equilibrium rate"?) is not a unique technically determined
quantity, setting the frame to which other economic variables
passively adjust. It will itself be influenced by the way in which this
adjustment takes place[16]. Several "equilibrium" rates of growth

16. We can imagine, for instance, that investment and growth will take
different forms in a society where the wage share is high and the saving propensity
of workers is low, as compared with a society where the wage share is low. In the

become possible. Of course, some technical possibilities are so obvious and some technical limitations so pervasive that the differences between these rates (for a given community) will not be very great. But even small differences in growth rates can have significant repercussions.

2. The Distribution Theory[17]

With the long-term equilibrium rate of growth determined by his technical progress function Kaldor can round off his model by showing how investment and savings adjust to this growth rate. This yields him an interesting distribution theory for a growing economy, the elements of which he had already developed in an earlier paper[18]. As I mentioned before, I shall not deal with the investment function but shall restrict myself mainly to the savings function. This will also

former consumption will be high, investment will be comparatively small and mainly labour-saving (which in turn may influence the level and share of wages), income will grow slowly but perhaps smoothly. In the latter consumption will be low, income and investment will grow at high rates in periods of expansion, but be exposed to greater disturbances and set-backs. These examples are, of course, pretty far removed from Kaldor's assumptions, but they are mentioned in order to indicate how these assumptions are to be relaxed when we try to get nearer to actual growth.

17. Since this was written Professor Bombach has published an interesting article which to a certain extent covers a similar field as Kaldor's essay (GOTTFRIED BOMBACH, "Preisstabilität, wirtschaftliches Wachstum und Einkommensverteilung", *Schweizerische Zeitschrift für Volkswirtschaft und Statistik*, März 1959, S. 1–20). Some of my remarks with regard to Kaldor's theory of distribution could—with certain minor changes—also be applied to some aspects of Bombach's views. His theory is, however, less open to the criticism raised in this article, (1) because his analysis is more short-term than Kaldor's so that the assumption of constancy in the behavioural parameters is more justified, and (2) because Bombach himself stresses that his model is only meant to serve as a "Denkschema" for analysing various possible situations and not as the basis for econometric verification.

18. N. KALDOR, "Alternative Theories of Distribution", *Review of Economic Studies*, Vol. XXIII (1956), No. 2. See particularly pp. 94–100. Much of what is said in the present article is also of relevance in connection with this earlier essay of Kaldor.

Since writing this paper I have come across a short critical appreciation of this article by Kaldor: SIDNEY WEINTRAUB, *An Approach to the Theory of Income Distribution* (Philadelphia 1958), Appendix to Chap. 5 (pp. 104–107). In some points Weintraub's remarks coincide with my own observations.

enable me to say some words about Kaldor's new (or "Keynesian") distribution theory.

In equilibrium "desired" investment will not only be geared to the "equilibrium" rate of growth, savings will also equal "desired" investment. In Keynes' system the adjustment of savings to investment is achieved through changes in income and employment, a certain saving propensity being assumed. This possibility is not open to Kaldor, since he assumes full employment and can therefore not admit adjustments via the employment (and output) mechanism. The place of varying employment with a given average saving propensity is taken in his model by variations in the income distribution and a split of the average saving propensity into a wage-earners' and a profit-earners' propensity. Reduced to linearity, and calling savings S, profits P, and income Y (all in real terms), Kaldor's saving function is of the form

$$S_t = \alpha P_t + \beta\ (Y_t - P_t) \qquad 1 > \alpha > \beta \geqslant 0$$

Here α is the saving propensity of profit earners and β the saving propensity of all other income earners (wage and salary earners). Since α can be assumed to be greater than β, any shift in shares from wages to profits will increase savings and vice versa. We thus get a savings schedule dependent on income *shares* which together with the investment schedule will yield the savings-investment equilibrium together with an equilibrium of income distribution (see Fig. 2)[19].

That Kaldor deals with two separate propensities to save is definitely a step forward in comparison to the simpler notion of a single propensity to save which does not allow for the effects of changes in the distribution of incomes. But let us be clear that the gain in *realism* is small. Kaldor introduces his two propensities mainly for *analytical* reasons. He needs them in order to be able to draw up a savings schedule in a model from which he has banned all lapses from full employment.

When we deal with the (Keynesian) short run where changes in employment are probably of more import than changes in distri-

19. This diagram has to be distinguished from the similar "Keynesian" diagram (see, for instance, L. R. KLEIN, *The Keynesian Revolution*, New York 1947, p. 178, Fig. 11). In the Keynesian diagram we find on the abscissa Y and on the ordinate I and S.

bution, the use of a single saving propensity may be sufficient as a first approach. Similarly, this simplified assumption may be sufficient for a long-term model which wants to show the place of saving in the interplay of forces making for smooth growth. But if we want to grapple more realistically with long-term tendencies (and this is obviously Kaldor's aim) this simple assumption is no longer adequate, not even as a first approach; nor does the mere division of the single propensity into two meet the problem. What now becomes the main question (a question that does not matter in the short run) is the *stability* of the saving propensities.

Fig. 2

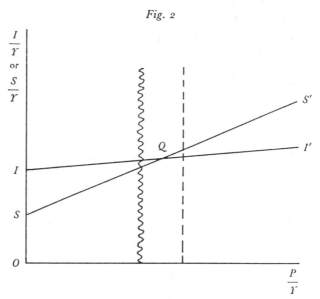

In Kaldor's system α and β are constants which have a decisive influence on the division of income between profits and wages[20]. This makes the distribution of income the unique result of certain independent psychological and institutional[21] factors. This I regard as inadmissible. α and β, the two saving propensities, cannot be

20. "For the level of profits has to be such as to induce a rate of investment that is just equal to the rate of savings forthcoming at that particular distribution of income." "A Model", *op. cit.*, p. 606.

21. KALDOR mentions the importance of company saving. "Alternative Theories", *op. cit.*, p. 95, footnote 1.

regarded as constant or even as independent variables in longer-term considerations[22]. They will be influenced by the way in which short-period disequilibria in saving and investment plans (which Kaldor admits into his system) have been resolved, *by the way in which the present income distribution was reached.* Whether in inflationary periods profits or wages push ahead more rapidly, whether prices are "administered" or free, what stratagems the trade unions apply, all this and many things besides will influence what sort of α and β will be combined with a certain income level and income distribution[23]. More than that: the α that has been established (the consumption habits of the capitalists) will have repercussions on β and possibly vice versa. In short, there are a number of historical and sociological factors (bargaining power, militancy of trade unions, government intervention, etc.) which will influence the saving propensities and the distribution of incomes[24]. They must not be neglected when we deal with long periods.

22. KENNETH BOULDING, who about ten years ago constructed a macroeconomic model of income distribution which has some points of similarity with Kaldor's theory, recognised this fact. On p. 269 of his *A Reconstruction of Economics* (New York 1950) he writes: "The dynamics of all these models is likely to be complicated by the dynamic instability of the transfer factor, and even of the consumption and investment functions themselves. They are therefore to be taken as illustrative rather than definitive pictures of the economic system, and yield us perhaps more insight than knowledge. They serve to illustrate, however, the complexities of the real world."

23. The idea that the struggle for wages may influence the long-term saving and consumption habits of entrepreneurs was expressed more than thirty years ago by MAURICE DOBB in the chapter on Bargaining-Power in his *Wages* (London and Cambridge, 1928). The following quotation gives a good idea of the views expressed there:

"...it seems logical to conclude that the level of income of yesterday, developing certain customary standards which come to be regarded as 'normal', influences to-day's supply-curve of capital as much as it influences the supply-curve of labour. The one no more than the other can be regarded as an independent variable; and the old theory, formulated as a group of equations, only remains consistent by assuming certain quantities as given (or as 'constants') which can in practice be influenced by custom and hence by arbitrary 'interference' such as that of collective bargaining or legislative action." (p. 103.)

24. Modern consumption theories pay increasing attention to historical and sociological factors. They appear, for instance, in Duesenberry's and Modigliani's models, where income peaks reached in the past and relative status in the income scale influence the propensity to save.

In terms of Kaldor's model this means that there is not a unique S_t/Y_t related to a given P_t/Y_t. Different rates of saving may be compatible with a given share of profits. In Figure 2 there will be not just one but several SS' curves. Which one will apply and what the "equilibrium" point of saving and investment will be, will depend on the path by which this point is reached[25]. The different points will not yield widely differing solutions: in a capitalist economy which is to function, the shares of wages and profits can hardly be dramatically altered. But the differences will be sufficiently important to make the assumption of a singular relationship between savings and the distribution of incomes unpracticable.

The points raised in this and in the previous section help to show the insufficiency of a closed growth model which tries to restrict itself to a few simple economic variables and relationships. Drawing together the equilibrium conditions from his technical progress, investment, and savings functions Kaldor obtains the following formula for the "equilibrium" share of profits to income (giving the equilibrium distribution of income in a steadily growing full employment economy with constant population):

$$\frac{P}{Y} = \frac{\gamma'' \dfrac{K}{Y} - \beta}{\alpha - \beta}$$

(where K is real capital). Here γ'' is given by the technical progress function, K/Y by the investment function, and α and β are the two propensities to save. As I have tried to show, at least γ'', α, and β cannot be regarded as constants in a long-term model, nor can they be regarded as independent of the actual course of the left-hand side of

25. A simple artificial example may illustrate this. Let us assume an upper class with a high income share and a high propensity to consume. Their consumption may stimulate prestige spending among the wage and salary earners so that we may have a small α and a negligible β. A more equal distribution of incomes (achieved in one way or other) may *raise* α, if the property-owning classes want to maintain their capital accumulation rather than their consumption *growth*, and the greater equality in consumption may also reduce prestige spending and so raise β. In the end we may have the same amount of saving though the relative shares have changed.

the equation (the distribution side)[26]. To explain the income distribution (and other aspects of the growing economy) one has, therefore,
to go beyond the circle of variables and relationships used so far, and
to consider how they themselves are changed in the course of economic
developement.

3. The Restricting Conditions

In this context a further point in Kaldor's model is worth mentioning,
because it helps to illustrate the influence of the historical factor.

The working of Kaldor's model is subject to two restrictions, viz.
(1) that profits should not be greater than the surplus available after
the labour force has been paid a subsistence wage-bill, and (2) that
profits are higher than the minimum required to secure a margin of
profit over turnover below which entrepreneurs would not reduce
prices, irrespective of the state of demand. Now, here again "subsistence wages" and "minimum profit margins" are not absolute but
historically grown quantities. What is regarded as a subsistence
wage or a minimum profit will largely depend on what level of
wages and profits wage and profit earners have been able to cut out
for themselves in the past. The room for smooth changes in income
distribution (at full employment) will therefore probably be much
smaller than Kaldor indicates by the waved and dotted lines in his
Figure 2. The frontiers may look more like the lines I have drawn in
my Figure 2 (p. 579). This means that a full employment adjustment
via a redistribution of incomes will soon come to an end either
because of the resistance of workers against a cut in real incomes (or
even in real income *growth*) or of profit earners against a fall in profit
margins. In the second case the result will be unemployment
(through oversaving), in the first case we may also get unemployment, if employers want to break the wage front of the workers, or
there will be a shift from investment to consumption (which may
actually stabilize the system). These limitations show that the
assumption of an equilibrium of steady full employment growth is
unlikely to be fulfilled in an unregulated capitalist economy.

26. That some dependence may exist and may disturb the working of his
model is—as far as the investment side is concerned—admitted by KALDOR.
See his "Alternative Theories", *op. cit.*, p. 98. The notation in this article differs
from the one adopted in the "Model" and used here.

The historical element in wage and profit levels is fully recognised by Kaldor when he deals in a final section with short-period developments and fluctuations. But he assumes that "long-term investment requirements and saving propensities are the underlying factors which set the standard around which these customary levels are formed, and which are responsible for the gradual change of these levels in any particular economy, or for differences as between different economies"[27]. This view seems to me to be the result of an attempt to find a way back from the modern growth models to reality. But I doubt that this is a realistic approach. The long-term investment requirements and saving propensities are the outcome of the many political and sociological pulls and pushes in the many short periods which make up the long. To be sure, these pulls and pushes take place in an economic environment which gives them only very restricted play. Economic growth models have displayed some of these restricting conditions. But this is no permanent substitute for the inclusion of a larger number of factors and influences which will give us a more realistic though less rounded picture of growth conditions.

4. Conclusion

Economic growth models of the modern type have served an important purpose. They have shown the logical relationships that must exist between different macro-economic aggregates, if an economy is to grow smoothly. In order to do this it was quite sufficient to erect the theory on a few simple assumptions and relationships. Though practical conclusions can be (and were) drawn from that theory, it was from its start not really designed to mirror actual growth in either developed or under-developed countries[28].

The attempt to bring growth theory into closer touch with

27. "A Model", *op. cit.*, p. 622.

28. It is typical that the plentiful literature on underdeveloped countries, with its more practical bent, has flowered rather independently of contemporary growth theory. In the view of ALBERT O. HIRSCHMAN "a model based on the propensity to save and on the capital-output ratio is bound to be far less useful in underdeveloped than in advanced economies... It does not really tell us much about the key mechanisms through which economic progress gets under way and is carried forward in a backward environment". *The Strategy of Economic Development*, New Haven 1958, pp. 32/33.

2

reality soon reveals that the special assumptions on which it builds and which invest it with a rounded completeness are too limited. When we deal with periods stretching over several years or even decades, many of the "given relationships" that were taken over from short-period economics can no longer be regarded as "given". They are moulded by other economic and so-called "extra-economic" influences which are themselves essential parts of the long-term development process. There must be—now that a large part of the important spade work of the young growth theory has been achieved by pioneers like Harrod, Domar, Fellner, Kaldor, Robinson, and others—a greater readiness to admit these "disturbing" factors into the discipline. This does not mean that sensational new developments are the order of the day. Classical growth theory from Malthus to Marx has worked with very definite assumptions with regard to social and sociological influences. Marx, in particular, has shown a mastership in combining economic and sociological development analysis, which has hardly been equalled till to this day. An extension of current growth analysis in these directions will help economic theory to be of more direct use to economic policy[29].

Austrian Institute of Economic   KURT W. ROTHSCHILD
Research, Vienna (Austria)

APPENDIX

Kaldor's "Technical Progress Function" takes the following simplified (linear) form in his model (see p. 604/5):

$$\frac{Y_{t+1} - Y_t}{Y_t} = \alpha'' + \beta'' \frac{I_t}{K_t}$$

Y_t, I_t, and K_t are real income, investment and capital in the period t.

It is assumed that $\alpha'' > 0$ and $1 > \beta'' > 0$. But the assumption $\alpha'' > 0$ means that all the time capital-saving inventions are applied (quite independently from capital investment), and the assumption $1 > \beta'' > 0$ means that all the investment (with population constant and employment full) is of the labour-saving type without technical invention preventing diminishing returns to capital. The

---

29. See E. RONALD WALKER, *From Economic Theory to Economic Policy*, Chicago 1943.

result is that a very special course for the capital-output ratio is mapped out. We can see this quite easily by slightly reshaping Kaldor's formula.

$$\frac{Y_{t+1} - Y_t}{Y_t} = \alpha'' + \beta'' \frac{I_t}{K_t}$$

or

$$\frac{\Delta Y}{Y} = \alpha'' + \beta'' \frac{\Delta K}{K} \tag{1}$$

Taking reciprocals of (1), we get

$$\frac{Y}{\Delta Y} = \frac{K}{\alpha'' K + \beta'' \Delta K}$$

or

$$\alpha'' \frac{K}{\Delta Y} + \beta'' \frac{\Delta K}{\Delta Y} \frac{K}{\Delta Y} = \frac{K}{Y}$$

Denoting the capital-output ratio K/Y by R, and the marginal capital-output ratio $\Delta K/\Delta Y$ by ΔR, we can write

$$\beta'' \Delta R = R - \alpha'' \frac{K}{\Delta Y}$$

and

$$\Delta R = \frac{1}{\beta''} R - \frac{\alpha''}{\beta''} \frac{K}{\Delta Y}$$

As long as ΔY is small, ΔR will be smaller than R so that the average capital-output ratio will fall. But as ΔY increases (with increasing I) ΔR will approach the first term, and since $\beta'' < 1$, ΔR will become greater than R and the average capital-output ratio will increase.

If we leave Kaldor's special assumptions we easily get a model where the capital-output ratio is more flexible and less uniquely tied to the investment process. Let us, for instance, assume that there is no autonomous supply of capital-saving inventions ($\alpha'' = 0$), and that investment can be accompanied by the invention of capital-saving methods so that (over a certain range) returns to capital can be increasing as well as diminishing (no restrictions on β'' except that it is > 0). In this case Kaldor's technical progress function reduces to

$$\frac{Y_{t+1} - Y_t}{Y_t} = \beta'' \frac{I_t}{K_t}$$

and the capital-output ratio can rise ($\beta'' < 1$) or fall ($\beta'' > 1$) with rising investment *right from the beginning of new investment*.

KURT W. ROTHSCHILD

$$\frac{\varUpsilon_{t+1} - \varUpsilon_t}{\varUpsilon_t} = \beta'' \frac{I_t}{K_t}$$

$$\frac{\varDelta \varUpsilon}{\varUpsilon} = \beta'' \frac{\varDelta K}{K}$$

$$\frac{\varDelta \varUpsilon}{\varDelta K} = \beta'' \frac{\varUpsilon}{K}$$

$$\frac{\varDelta K}{\varDelta \varUpsilon} = \frac{1}{\beta''} \frac{K}{\varUpsilon}$$

$$\varDelta R = \frac{1}{\beta''} R$$

If $\beta'' < 1$, the average capital-output ratio increases and vice versa for $\beta'' > 1$.

13

COBWEB CYCLES AND PARTIALLY CORRECT FORECASTING

K. W. ROTHSCHILD

Österreichisches Institut für Wirtschaftsforschung

I. INTRODUCTION

IN A notable article, published some ten years ago, Emile Grunberg and Franco Modigliani proved the possibility and the conditions of successful forecasting in cases where the actors on the scene are influenced by the public forecasts.[1] In addition to a generalized exposition they exemplified their ideas in the concrete frame of price prediction in a cobweb setting.[2] In a later paper Devletoglou showed how the situation is changed and how the course of events is altered once efficient forecasting has been introduced.[3] The present paper takes the discussion a small step further by investigating the consequences of introducing the more realistic assumption of less-than-perfect forecasting.

In sections 2 and 3 the cobweb situation without and with correct public forecasting is briefly summarized to serve as a basis of comparison for section 4, where partially correct forecasting is introduced. Section 5 contains a numerical comparison of all three cases. The notation and exposition used in the following sections are somewhat different from those employed by Devletoglou (who in turn deviates from the Grunberg-Modigliani notation), but the results in section 3 are essentially the same as those reached by him.[4]

II. COBWEB WITHOUT FORECASTING[5]

Let D_t and S_t be the quantities demanded and supplied in a given period, p_t the price of the product, and p_e the price expectation in a given period which influences the preparations for the next period. The supply for the coming period (currently produced) is a function of the expected price. At this stage we assume that the price expected for the next period is equal to the currently realized prize ($p_e = p_t$).

As the basis for all our further considerations we use a simple cobweb system with linear demand and supply relationships. We obtain the following supply and demand equations

$$S_{t+1} = m_s p_t + b_s , \qquad (m_s > 0) \quad (1)$$

$$D_t = -m_d p_t + b_d . \qquad (m_d > 0, b_d > 0) \quad (2)$$

We now introduce the condition that in each period the quantities supplied must be cleared by the market:

$$S_{t+1} = D_{t+1} . \quad (3)$$

This gives

$$m_s p_t + b_s = -m_d p_{t+1} + b_d \quad (4)$$

[4] His results *look* slightly different, because he conducts his analysis in terms of quantity fluctuations, while here price fluctuations are used throughout. Also, his final parameters refer to a quantity → price relationship, while in this paper the price → quantity relationship is maintained.

[5] For a full description of the cobweb case see M. Ezekiel, "The Cobweb Theorem," *Quarterly Journal of Economics*, February, 1938, pp. 255–80 (reprinted in American Economic Association, *Readings in Business Cycle Theory* [Philadelphia, 1944], pp. 422–42), where also references to earlier developments are given. A simple and concise statement of the cobweb theorem can be found in W. J. Baumol, *Economic Dynamics* (New York, 1951), pp. 108 ff.

[1] E. Grunberg and F. Modigliani, "The Predictability of Social Events," *Journal of Political Economy*, December, 1954, pp. 465–78.

[2] *Ibid.*, Sec. II.

[3] E. A. Devletoglou, "Correct Public Prediction and the Stability of Equilibrium," *Journal of Political Economy*, April, 1961, pp. 142–61.

300

or

$$p_{t+1} = -\frac{m_s}{m_d} p_t + \frac{b_d - b_s}{m_d}. \quad (5)$$

The solution of this equation is

$$p_t = \left(-\frac{m_s}{m_d} \right)^t \left(p_0 - \frac{b_d - b_s}{m_d + m_s} \right) + \frac{b_d - b_s}{m_d + m_s}, \quad (6)$$

where p_0 is some initial value of p. The price p_t will oscillate round the central value $(b_d - b_s)/(m_d + m_s)$. The oscillations will diminish, and p_t will move toward a stable equilibrium, when $m_s < m_d$. When $m_s = m_d$ we get permanent oscillations between two values. Finally, when $m_s > m_d$ we obtain an "explosive" solution.

III. CORRECT FORECASTING

We now introduce forecasting. With Grunberg and Modigliani we assume that the forecaster has full knowledge of the underlying relationships, including the agent's reaction to his own forecast. By taking this reaction into account he can make certain that his forecast comes true.

In our cobweb setting the supply decision is now no longer dependent on present prices alone but is influenced to a greater or lesser degree by the predicted price. We denote by P_t the price predicted in period $(t - 1)$ for the period t, and introduce the requirement equation that our forecast shall be a correct one:

$$P_t = p_t. \quad (7)$$

Let us now assume that the price expectations of the producers are a weighted average of present and predicted prices:

$$p_e = aP_{t+1} + (1 - a)p_t, \quad (8)$$
$$(0 \le a \le 1)$$

where a is a given parameter known to the forecaster. Supply is now influenced by the expected price as given by equation (8), and our supply equation becomes

$$S_{t+1} = m_s aP_{t+1} + m_s(1 - a)p_t + b_s.$$

Using equation (7) this can be written as

$$S_{t+1} = m_s ap_{t+1} + m_s(1 - a)p_t + b_s. \quad (9)$$

From the marketing condition (3) it follows that

$$m_s ap_{t+1} + m_s(1 - a)p_t + b_s$$
$$= -m_d p_{t+1} + b_d \quad (10)$$

or

$$p_{t+1} = -\frac{m_s(1 - a)}{m_s a + m_d} p_t + \frac{b_d - b_s}{m_s a + m_d}.$$

The solution of this equation is

$$p_t = \left[-\frac{m_s(1 - a)}{m_s a + m_d} \right]^t \times \left(p_0 - \frac{b_d - b_s}{m_d + m_s} \right) + \frac{b_d - b_s}{m_d + m_s}. \quad (11)$$

Equation (11) shows the path of p_t in a cobweb situation with partly accepted (correct) forecasting and should be compared with equation (6), where forecasting plays no part. It can be seen that the oscillations will always be smaller in the forecasting case. Partially accepted correct forecasting will not remove the oscillations, but will reduce their amplitude and will permit a much quicker progress toward the equilibrium level. In particular, forecasting will frequently change an "explosive" situation into one of converging oscillations.

When $a = 0$, the forecasts are ignored and equation (11) degenerates into equation (6). The cobweb cycle then takes its uninhibited course, and that course is exactly described by the forecasts. When, on the other hand, the forecast is fully accepted, $a = 1$ and the first part of equation (11) vanishes. The forecaster announces the equilibrium price, this forecast is taken at its full value by the producers, and equilibrium is immediately established. No oscillations occur.

IV. PARTIALLY CORRECT FORECASTING

Let us now consider the more realistic case of expert forecasters who have a fair knowledge of the underlying relationships but are not able to make exact predictions.

Their forecasts will deviate from the actual event by some error term which we shall assume to be free from any systematic bias. Equation (7) becomes now

$$P_t = p_t + \delta_t . \quad (\delta_t \gtreqless 0) \quad (7')$$

Making use of equations $(7')$ and (8) our supply equation becomes

$$S_{t+1} = m_s a(p_{t+1} + \delta_{t+1})$$
$$+ m_s(1 - a)p_t + b_s . \quad (12)$$

Introducing the marketing condition (3) we get

$$m_s a(p_{t+1} + \delta_{t+1}) + m_s(1 - a)p_t + b_s$$
$$= -m_d p_{t+1} + b_d \quad (13)$$

or

$$p_{t+1} = -\frac{m_s(1 - a)}{m_s a + m_d} p_t$$
$$+ \frac{b_d - b_s - m_s a \delta_{t+1}}{m_s a + m_d} .$$

The solution of this equation is

$$q_t = \left[-\frac{m_s(1 - a)}{m_s a + m_d} \right]^t$$
$$\times \left(p_0 - \frac{b_d - b_s - m_s a \delta_t}{m_d + m_s} \right) \quad (14)$$
$$+ \frac{b_d - b_s - m_s a \delta_t}{m_d + m_s} .$$

Comparing equation (14) with equations (11) and (6) we see, first of all, that even if the forecasts are not quite correct they will exert an equally strong damping effect on the original cobweb cycle as correct forecasts. The big oscillations at the "beginning" of the cycle, when the current price is far removed from equilibrium, will be greatly reduced and an "explosive" cobweb cycle (with $m_s > m_d$) will frequently be transformed into a convergent cycle.

But in another respect incorrect forecasting differs in its effects not only from correct forecasting but also from the non-forecasting case: the "equilibrium value" itself is not stable. It contains the term $m_s a \delta_t/(m_d +$

m_s), that is, there will be continuous random fluctuations round the stable long-term equilibrium. These fluctuations should, however, be in practice fairly small. Not only are the forecasting errors (δ) multiplied by $m_s/(m_d + m_s) < 1$; the other multiplier (a) contains a self-regulatory mechanism to keep the whole deviation term within narrow bounds. For if the forecasting errors are large, the amount of confidence placed in them will quickly dwindle. A large δ tends, therefore, to produce a small a and the expression $a\delta$ will tend to be small. When δ becomes too big the forecast tends to be ignored, a will become zero, and we are back at the uninhibited cobweb cycle of equation (6).

We see now that less-than-perfect forecasting stabilizes extreme situations just as efficiently as correct forecasting. But when the equilibrium zone is approached, its effects are slightly destabilizing. Even when the stable equilibrium point is reached, where the other cobweb situations stay put, forecasting errors will make the price bounce off again in later periods.

The whole situation is illustrated in Figure 1. The lines D and S present the "true" demand and supply schedules. If the price stands originally at p_0, an uninhibited cobweb will work itself up to $\bar{p}$ with violent fluctuations and then remain static at that point. A forecaster who has exact knowledge of D and S and of the reactions of the suppliers to his forecast, can accelerate the path toward $\bar{p}$ and then keep the situation there. The forecaster with incomplete knowledge does not know the exact course of D and S. There is an insecurity region, indicated in the diagram by the lines drawn parallel to D and S. As long as the initial price is far away from equilibrium (like p_0), these insecurity regions do not matter and the forecaster can give a strong "lead" toward equilibrium. The oscillations are damped, the path is shortened. But once the quadrilateral $KLMN$ is reached the forecaster can no longer proceed toward $\bar{p}$, and even if this point is reached he does not know that this price could provide a stable equilibrium.

Thus he will continue to use a bit of "hunch" and prices will move $\bar{p}$ with p_1 and p_2 as extreme limits.

The case of partially correct forecasting seems to be the only one that is compatible *in the long run* with *partial* acceptance of forecasting $(0 < a < 1)$. For continuously correct forecasting would sooner or later

If stabilization is the aim, it could seem that incorrect forecasting is worse than no forecasting at all.[7] With no forecasting one would have to put up with some lively fluctuations in a disequilibrium position, but (barring "explosive" cycles) one would have a good chance to come to a permanent rest after some time. With incorrect forecasting

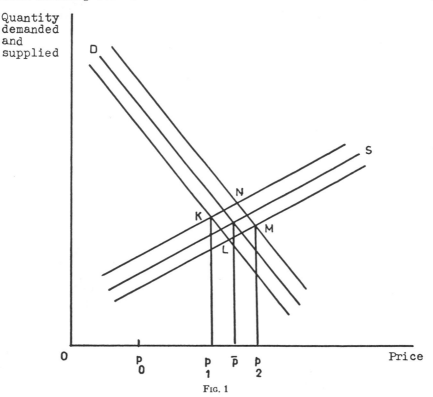

Fɪɢ. 1

lead (through a "learning" process) to complete acceptance of the forecasts.[6] With it the cobweb problem of oscillating price movements would disappear. When, however, forecasts are correct within certain limits only, then it is understandable that producers will use them more cautiously and take the current situation (or some other data) as an additional signpost.

[6] See Grunberg and Modigliani, *op. cit.*, p. 470; Devletoglou, *op. cit.*, p. 145.

playing a part, this rest could not be achieved. This argument would be of some

[7] The remarks in this section are exclusively concerned with forecasting in a cobweb setting. In other dynamic processes the forecasting problem can acquire different aspects. See Devletoglou, *op. cit.*, Sec. II; M. C. Kemp, "Economic Forecasting When the Subject of the Forecast Is Influenced by the Forecast," *American Economic Review*, June, 1962, pp. 492–96; and the comments on Kemp's article by A. C. Chiang, E. Grunberg, and F. Modigliani in *American Economic Review*, September, 1963, pp. 730–40.

force only if the basic supply and demand conditions were comparatively stable. In a dynamic world, however, they are likely to shift at frequent intervals. Stable equilibriums of yesterday may be considerably off the mark tomorrow. Under such conditions roughly correct forecasting finds its justification. It can shorten and dampen the strong disequilibriums that are constantly created in a changing world. During quieter periods it will have little to offer or may even add some disturbances. These should, however—if the errors remain within reasonable limits—not be of great significance.

± 20 per cent of the equilibrium price ($\bar{p} = 50$). In all three cases I let the cycle start with an initial price of $p_0 = 70$.

The following results are obtained. Whereas the pure cobweb cycle exhibits price deviations of 10 per cent or more (from the equilibrium level) up till "year" 6 and still has some 4 per cent to go to reach its stable level by period 10, the 10 per cent stage is reached as early as period 1 when forecasting is applied, and equilibrium is approached in period 3. With correct forecasting the situation then remains unchanged at its equilibrium level from period 4 onward.

TABLE 1

THE EFFECTS OF FORECASTING ON THE COBWEB CYCLE

ACCEPTANCE BY THE PUBLIC	NATURE OF THE FORECAST	
	Correct ($\delta = 0$)	Less than Perfect ($\delta \neq 0$)
Forecast ignored ($a = 0$)	Cycle runs its uninhibited course	Cycle runs its uninhibited course
Forecast partially accepted ($0 < a < 1$)	Oscillations damped. Quick approach to stable equilibrium	Oscillations damped. Permanent irregular movements around the equilibrium
Forecast fully accepted ($a = 1$)	No oscillations. Stable equilibrium	Large oscillations removed. Permanent irregular movements around the equilibrium

V. A NUMERICAL EXAMPLE

In conclusion I give a numerical illustration of the cases described in sections 2–4. Let the parameters of the supply and demand schedules take the following values:

$$m_s = 0.8 \,, \quad b_s = 20 \,, \quad m_d = 1 \,, \quad b_d = 110.$$

In the forecasting cases I assume that the expected price (p_e) is formed by giving equal weight to the current price and the predicted price, that is, $a = \frac{1}{2}$. In the case where forecasting errors occur I have let the error vary randomly between 0 and 9.[8] This means that the errors have been kept within less than

Less-than-perfect forecasting, on the other hand, continues with small irregular movements[9] which do not come to an end when

[8] The error terms for the single periods as shown in Table 1 (δ) were taken from two-figure random numbers in R. A. Fisher and F. Yates, *Statistical Tables for Biological, Agricultural and Medical Research* (London, 1957), p. 126. The first digit was used to determine the size of the δ's, the second digit to determine their sign (even numbers, positive values; uneven numbers, negative values).

[9] These are no longer of the regularly alternating type of upward and downward movements as in the pure cycle. The price falls, for instance, for two periods from 2 to 4 and rises from period 6 to 8.

the price happens to hit the equilibrium value (e.g., in periods 7 and 10).

VI. SUMMARY

The effects of public forecasting on the cobweb cycle under different conditions have been investigated. They are all contained in equation (14) from which the different special cases can be derived by varying the values of α and δ. Table 1 summarizes the results of the previous sections.

[14]

STAGFLATION AND INTENSIFIED INFLATION.[1]
A PRIMITIVE HYPOTHESIS

I

Two developments have recently made an appearance in a number of developed capitalist market economies: the rate of inflation has tended to be higher over the cycle as a whole compared with earlier periods, and inflationary tendencies have preserved considerable strength even in periods of stagnation. These two phenomena have not existed long enough to permit a reliable analysis of the forces behind them. We are at present reduced to a discussion of possible hypotheses.

An obvious explanation could be that the acceleration and intensification of the inflationary tendencies is the result of a learning process. People have at long last begun to grasp the true nature of the permanent post-war inflation and are beginning to anticipate further developments in their price- and wage-setting decisions. Such an interpretation would take up the arguments of some early anti-inflationist writers, who—in the fifties—maintained that the creeping inflation could only be a transitory stage on the path to ever higher rates of inflation. As soon as people had realised the true nature of the inflationary process they would try to maintain real (future) earnings by steadily increasing and mutually intensifying their monetary claims. In this view the present tendencies could mark the beginning of this secular intensification of the inflationary process.

Against this view one can advance all the arguments which were already under discussion when the first danger warnings were uttered some fifteen years ago. In particular, one could stress that the rigidity of a large sector of monetary transactions enforces thinking in monetary terms and hinders a full and quick anticipation of inflationary developments; that inflation has not developed with such regularity as to permit the formation of reliable and strongly held anticipations; and that monetary institutions could be expected to become more restrictive when expectations lead to a dangerous acceleration of inflationary processes. Perhaps the most decisive argument against the catastrophic view is the historical experience (including the present as history) that remarkably high rates of inflation can persist for some considerable time without any tendency towards acceleration, and that hyper-inflations exhibiting such tendencies have usually not been experienced in " normal " periods.

II

In contrast to the " catastrophic " view discussed above I shall present a primitive hypothesis " explaining " stagflation and intensified inflation which

[1] I am indebted to the Editors of this JOURNAL for some useful suggestions.
1383

is based on different assumptions. It also presupposes a learning process, but this process leads to a once-for-all change in behaviour (which we are experiencing just now) without any necessary further intensification. The simple assumption I am going to make is that people (firms, trade unions, etc.) have learned over the past twenty years *and are now taking into account* (*a*) that inflation will continue, and (*b*) that recessions will be short-lived.

I shall use a very simple " model " in order to illustrate my hypothesis. Let us assume that price changes (mainly changes of " administered prices ") are dependent on wage changes and on the current phase of the business cycle.[1] Writing p and w for percentage changes in prices and wages respectively, and denoting the cyclical factor by k_t we can write

$$p_t = a\,w_t + k_t \qquad . \qquad . \qquad . \qquad . \quad (1)$$

where a is a parameter and t is a time index. For wage behaviour we assume that variations are geared to price changes (with a one-period lag) and to the cyclical phase. The wage-change equation thus takes the form (with b as a fixed parameter and m_t as the cyclical factor)

$$w_t = b\,p_{t-1} + m_t \qquad . \qquad . \qquad . \qquad . \quad (2)$$

With regard to the size of the parameters a and b we make the following assumptions. Wage changes react with a certain delay to price changes and we can assume that negotiators will then endeavour to recover the lost ground. So b will be somewhere near 1.[2] In the price-change equation we have not taken into account technical progress and the rise of labour productivity. Labour unit costs will rise less than wage rates and we can take care of this by assuming that $a < 1$, and sufficiently smaller than 1 to assume that $ab < 1$. This condition ensures that the basic wage–price–wage process does not by itself lead to a cumulative inflationary spiral. For, combining equations (1) and (2) we obtain

$$p_t = ab\,p_{t-1} + a\,m_t + k_t \qquad . \qquad . \qquad . \quad (3)$$

i.e., apart from the contribution to inflation of the cost-push factors, m_t and k_t, any other inflationary price development ($p > 0$), would (provided $0 \leqslant ab < 1$) gradually die down ($p \to 0$).

Next we introduce some simple assumptions with regard to cyclical cost-push behaviour. Let us assume that there are four cyclical phases which follow each other in regular yearly procession. We might label them: recession (stagnation), recovery, boom, late phase of the boom.[3] According

---

[1] The business cycle may consist of fluctuations in growth rates and need not comprise actual recessions. The above assumption would be covered by mark-up pricing where the margin varies with market conditions.

[2] In most studies of Phillips-type wage-change relations the coefficient of the price-change variable is less than 1. But we do not need such a strong restriction.

[3] Both the four-year spread and the characterisation of the cycle has some resemblance with post-war developments. But the above scheme is only meant as a rough illustration of a principle.

to the phase, price and wage demands are raised or lowered.   We assume, to begin with, a stable pattern of these cyclical responses so that

$$k_0 = k_4 = k_8 = k_{4n}$$
$$k_1 = k_5 = k_9 = k_{4n+1}$$
$$k_2 = k_6 = k_{10} = k_{4n+2}$$
$$k_3 = k_7 = k_{11} = k_{4n+3}$$

and correspondingly with m_0, m_1, m_2 and m_3.

With the k- and m-values remaining stable a long-term equilibrium pattern of cyclical price movements (and corresponding wage movements) will emerge which is independent of the initial rate of price and wage increases. A simple way of obtaining the long-term " equilibrium " values of the price rises [1] is to submit equation (3) to an iteration process.   Writing $c = ab$ and $u_0 = am_0 + k_0$, $u_1 = am_1 + k_1$, $u_2 = am_2 + k_2$ and $u_3 = am_3 + k_3$,

we get

$$p_1 = cp_0 + u_1$$
$$p_2 = cp_1 + u_2 = c^2 p_0 + cu_1 + u_2$$
$$p_3 = cp_2 + u_3 = c^3 p_0 + c^2 u_1 + cu_2 + u_3$$
$$p_4 = cp_3 + u_4 = c^4 p_0 + c^3 u_1 + c^2 u_2 + cu_3 + u_0$$

In the last line we have substituted $u_0 = am_0 + k_0$ for $u_4 = am_4 + k_4$ taking into account the regularity of cyclical responses.

Now, once price increases have reached their permanent pattern, the price rise in the recession period 4 will be equal to the price rise in the previous recession period 0.   For equilibrium conditions we have, therefore, $p_4 = p_0$.   Substituting this condition in the last equation above, we obtain $p_0 = p_4$ and hence $p_0(1 - c^4) = c^3 u_1 + c^2 u_2 + cu_3 + u_0$ or [2]

$$p_0{}^* = \{u_0 + cu_3 + c^2 u_2 + c^3 u_1\}/(1 - c^4) \quad . \quad . \quad (4)$$

We see that the price rise in the recession period is dependent on the strength of the interplay between wage and price movements (a and b) and on the cyclical reactions in *all* periods, though the influence of the current period is strongest.

By starting an analogous iteration process with p_2, p_3 and p_4 respectively, we reach the equilibrium values for the other periods of the cycle

$$p_1{}^* = \{u_1 + cu_0 + c^2 u_3 + c^3 u_2\}/(1 - c^4)$$
$$p_2{}^* = \{u_2 + cu_1 + c^2 u_0 + c^3 u_3\}/(1 - c^4) \quad . \quad . \quad (5)$$
$$p_3{}^* = \{u_3 + cu_2 + c^2 u_1 + c^3 u_0\}/(1 - c^4)$$

Now, let us assume that the price cycle has been in force for some time,

---

[1] The equilibrium pattern will be almost reached after very few periods when the product $a . b$ is small.

[2] The asterisk refers to equilibrium values.   In this case we have the equilibrium value for price increases in recession periods.

and that the k- and m-values are sufficiently high to ensure a (stable and repetitive) price inflation over the cycle as a whole (though not necessarily in each period).

We now introduce our hypothesis that a learning process sets in which consists of a realisation that the recession periods never last long and that price inflation continues in the long run. This realisation could induce people to maintain greater pressure for price increases in the recession period than they were prepared to exact in previous years of reduced growth. The reactions in the other periods could remain unaffected. In terms of our " model " we would get a once-and-for-all change in k_0 (and possibly m_0). This change would immediately " explain " stagflation: people would maintain demands and resist declines in a bad year in view of their newly gained experience. But it would also lead—through lag effects—to higher price increases in all the other periods though with smaller effects in the boom periods than in the recovery period.[1] Thus we get—through the change in k_0 (and/or m_0)—a simultaneous transition to stagflation and in-tensified inflation. But there is no tendency towards further cumulative deteriorations or " expectation " processes. After a while the price cycle settles permanently at a higher " equilibrium " level.

Let us illustrate the above " model " with some simple numbers. We assume that $a = 0.83$ and $b = 0.9$ so that $c = 0.75$ and that the cyclical components k_t and m_t have, to begin with, the following values:[2] $k_0 = -1.05$, $k_1 = 0$, $k_2 = 0.1$, $k_3 = 0.5$; $m_0 = 0.9$, $m_1 = 0.6$, $m_2 = 0.6$, $m_3 = 1.8$. The corresponding values of the u_t will be $u_0 = -0.3$, $u_1 = 0.5$, $u_2 = 0.6$ and $u_3 = 2.0$. When people have " learned " about the " brevity " of recession and the permanency of inflation they shift their behaviour. The shift is reflected in k_0 becoming zero. The equilibrium price cycles before and after the change can be derived from equations (4) and (5) and are shown in the following table:

Price Changes and Wage Changes in Percentages

		Recession.	Recovery.	Boom.	Late phase.	Average price change over the cycle.
Prices	Before	2·56	2·42	2·42	3·81	2·80
	After	4·09	3·57	3·28	4·46	3·85
Wages	Before	4·33	2·90	2·78	3·97	3·50
	After	4·91	4·28	3·81	4·75	4·44

[1] As can be seen from equations (4) and (5) the effects of changes in k_0 and m_0 on the equilibrium inflation rates in the recession, recovery, boom, and late period respectively are:

$$\frac{d p_i^*}{d k_0} = c^i \frac{d u_0}{d k_0} \Big/ (1 - c^4) = c^i \Big/ (1 - c^4); \quad \frac{d p_i^*}{d m_0} = c^i \frac{d u_0}{d m_0} \Big/ (1 - c^4) = a c^i / (1 - c^4); \quad i = 0, 1, 2, 3$$

[2] The model has the (at least for Austria) realistic structure of wage behaviour adjusting rather slowly to the change in the cyclical situation.

I have not tried an empirical test of the hypothesis contained in this note and it may be too early for that.   But the Austrian experience seems at least not incompatible with the above assumptions.   Taking into account that

" Cyclical phases " and Price Changes in Austria

Cyclical phase.	Year.	G.N.P.*	*p*.†	Year.	G.N.P.*	*p*.†	Year.	G.N.P.*	*p*.†	Change in rates of inflation from 1958/61 to 1967/70 in percentage points ‡
" Stagnation "	1958	3·0	2·3	1962	3·7	4·4	1967	1·4	4·0	1·7
Recovery	1959	4·4	1·1	1963	4·4	2·7	1968	4·9	2·8	1·7
Boom	1960	8·3	1·9	1964	6·1	3·8	1969	6·6	3·1	1·2
Late phase	1961	5·4	3·6	1965	5·1	5·0	1970	8·2	4·4	0·8
				(1966	5·2	2·2)				
Average price increase over four years			2·2			4·0			3·6	1·4

* Annual rate of growth of real G.N.P. excluding agriculture and forestry.
† Annual percentage increase in consumer prices.
‡ Difference between the last and the first *p*-column.

there is a considerable lag between the cycle phase and wage responses in Austria (so that the inflationary rates are lowest in the recovery period) we find that the change from the cycle in the late 'fifties (1958–61) to the cycle in the late 'sixties (1967–70) has led to a higher inflationary rate with the increase being more marked in the stagnation and recovery phase than in the boom and late phase.   The cycle in between, 1962–65, (1966 was an " abnormal " year and should be disregarded) does not quite fit the pattern.

                                                        KURT W. ROTHSCHILD

Institut für Volkswirtschaftslehre und -politik,
   Hochschule für Sozial- und Wirtschaftswissenschaften,
      Linz.
Date of receipt of final typescript: June 1972.

11

Distributive Aspects of the Austrian Theory

K. W. ROTHSCHILD

Less than twenty years ago, in December 1952, when the state of distribution theory was discussed at the Annual Meeting of the American Economic Association, William Fellner could point out that the marginal-productivity theory in one form or another was the dominant approach in this field.[1] Only a few years later Kaldor and Joan Robinson produced their new macro-economic models of income distribution,[2] and nowadays a comment on contemporary distribution theory would have to be more differentiated than in 1952. Nevertheless, we can assume that a theory that occupied a dominant place in academic economic teaching for more than half a century and even today—side by side with other theories—plays an important part, must have been an impressive scientific and intellectual achievement.

Who was the father of this theory? Unfortunately, fixing paternity is even more complicated in the field of science than it is in the case of natural offspring. Theories may have several fathers and a multitude of grandfathers; disputes about their relative contributions to the birth of the child can—as we know—occupy generations of writers dealing with the development of economic doctrine. The present writer does not wish to claim any special niche for the Austrian School among the ancestors of the marginal

---

[1] 'By contemporary distribution theory we presumably mean a qualified marginal productivity theory; that is to say, a combination of the marginal productivity theory with other analytical elements' (W. Fellner, 'Significance and Limitations of Contemporary Distribution Theory', *American Economic Review*, 43 (1953), Papers and Proceedings.)

[2] Already in 1950, Boulding had advanced similar ideas in his *A Reconstruction of Economics*.

productivity theory. But that it occupies a prominent place in this ancestry can hardly be doubted. What this place has been and how it differed from other positions will be indicated in this paper.

If, at the previously mentioned A.E.A. Conference, Fellner had been asked who should be regarded as the creator of the marginal productivity approach to distribution theory, he would in all likelihood have named John Bates Clark. In several articles published in the 1880s and particularly in his grand opus *The Distribution of Wealth* (1899) Clark had advanced the marginal-productivity approach with such force that subsequent writers on distribution theory preferred to take their lead from him. This was so although Clark's marginal analysis appeared several years after the basic steps towards a consistent marginal approach had been taken. But in contrast to the founders of the marginal-utility school Clark concentrated on the distribution problem while they were mainly occupied with finding a basis for a general theory of value and price.[3] Yet as far as the fathers of marginal analysis—Jevons, Walras, Menger—*were* concerned with the distribution problem (or the problem of price formation for factors of production) they did advance ideas that already contained all the essential elements of the marginal-productivity theory.[4]

Among these fathers it was certainly Menger who was most acutely aware of the distributional implications of the new theoretical approach. Though he did no more than indicate his ideas in this field, he did it in a form that in many respects has a more modern look than much that has been written later (not excluding J. B. Clark's work). If Menger's analysis is to be criticized it is along lines that apply equally to contemporary models of the neoclassical school.

In contrast to Menger's teachings on value and price we find that the sailing was less plain for his ideas on distribution. The problem was not neglected by the Austrian School, but—as we shall see later—it was partly side-tracked by less important issues. The theoretical debate concentrated on the so-called 'imputation problem', the problem of imputing the values of finished goods to

---

[3] Clark's 'rediscovery' of the marginal-utility theory did not reach the standards of the earlier works of the founders of the marginal-utility school.

[4] The founding fathers in turn had of course forerunners too; but they seem to have been only partially acquainted with their works. Apart from the relevant ideas already contained in Ricardo's differential rent we might name above all Thünen, Longfield, von Hermann, von Mangoldt, and Gossen.

Distributive Aspects of the Austrian Theory 209

the factors of production. Both Böhm-Bawerk and Wieser dealt extensively with this problem in their main works which appeared towards the turn of the 1880s,[5] and it was Wieser who contributed the term 'imputation', just as he had contributed the term 'marginal utility'. The differences in the approach of Böhm-Bawerk and Wieser, and some contradictions in their 'solutions', led to a sporadic discussion in the following years which occasionally shed more heat than light. In the years before World War I the interest flamed up again and the problem was intensively discussed right through the 20s. Almost the entire younger generation of the Austrian School took part in the debate, and several German economists also contributed to it. In addition to special tracts on the imputation problem by Mohrmann, Hefendehl, Stephans, and Haydt, there are relevant articles by Schumpeter, Broda, Kleinwächter, Landauer, Liefmann, Schönfeld, Hayek, Diehl, and Mahr. A certain climax in the discussion was reached when Hans Mayer published his well-known article on 'Zurechnung' (imputation) in volume viii of the fourth edition of the *Handwörterbuch für Staatswissenschaften* in 1928. At the beginning of the 30s the discussion, which had become rather esoteric, began to die down. A special Austrian School of distribution ceased to exist; its lasting contributions had become absorbed in the general ideas of the world-wide marginal-productivity theory.

After this glance at the 'epochs' of the distributional discussion in the Austrian School I want to give a short sketch of the essential ideas contained in the basic works. Our starting-point is Menger, not only because the centenary of his *Grundsätze der Volkswirthschaftslehre* (1871) provides the reason for this symposium, but also because both Böhm-Bawerk and Wieser built on his foundations.

When we are going to evaluate Menger's share in distribution theory we must not forget that he had planned three additional volumes to follow his *Grundsätze*. They should have—among other things—dealt with the distribution problem. But they never appeared. Thus we are left with a mere outline of Menger's ideas

[5] Böhm-Bawerk's *Die positive Theorie des Kapitals* and Wieser's *Der natürliche Werth* both appeared in 1889. Wieser's essential ideas can already be found in his *Ursprung des wirthschaftlichen Werthes* (1884), and to some extent even in an earlier paper which he presented in a seminar in 1876 ('Über das Verhältnis der Kosten zum Wert', contained in F. A. Hayek, ed., *Wiesers gesammelte Abhandlungen* (Tübingen, 1929)).

in this sphere, as they are expressed in his considerations about the valuation of 'goods of higher order', i.e. of productive goods.

The really path-breaking idea of Menger's was that he was prepared to apply his new theory of value quite consistently not only to the explanation of final good prices but also to an explanation of prices of productive goods. This he regarded as a central task of his work. In the Foreword to this *Grundsätze* he writes (pp. ix, x):

We have given special attention to the analysis of the causal connections between economic characteristics of final products and their respective production elements. We have done this not only in order to state a comprehensive price theory which is in the nature of things and which covers all price phenomena (and therefore also interest, wages, rent, etc.) *under one unified viewpoint*, but also because of the important insights which we can gain in this way concerning some other economic processes which so far have remained completely unexplained.[6]

The unified viewpoint, at which Menger aimed, was achieved by regarding productive goods as not yet fully ripened consumption goods. This enabled Menger to establish a link between the value of productive goods and the consumer's utility to be expected from them. Menger thus completely broke away from the classical cost approach and tried to subsume the problems of value, price, allocation, and distribution *for the set of all goods* under the single principle of utility and marginal utility. Though—as we shall note later—this reduction to a single principle ultimately turned out to be a drawback in Austrian and related distribution theories, there can be no doubt that Schumpeter was right in regarding this complete reversal of the then ruling classical views as 'a genuine stroke of genius'.[7]

Of course, Menger was not the first person to think along these lines. Thus, the following significant remarks were written as early as 1832 in a book by Friedrich Benedikt Wilhelm von Hermann, whose works are frequently quoted by Menger:

. . . only the immediate value in use is the true basis of demand; a merely indirect value, stemming from utilization in the technical process or for further sale, cannot *in itself* give rise to a desire or to a willingness to pay a price. The things which do not yield immediate satisfaction

---

[6] My italics.
[7] J. A. Schumpeter, *History of Economic Analysis* (New York, 1954), p. 913.

Distributive Aspects of the Austrian Theory 211

but only serve as material, activity, or tool for the production of consumption goods, obtain demand only through the goods for which they
act as means. With every product we also desire the means for its
production, and the price of the finished commodities reacts back on the
price of the semi-manufactures and raw materials from which it is made.
Tools and machines, too, are only desired to an extent which depends
on the goods which can be derived from them. Only a small part of
labour—the services—has immediate use value; the larger part obtains
value only as an element of the commodities to whose production it has
contributed.[8]

But there is a distinctive gap between Menger and his forerunners; it shows up in the consistent way in which he followed
these earlier thoughts to their logical conclusion. This enabled
him to lay the foundation for many of the later developments in
distribution theory.

Both the consistency and the depth of Menger's pioneering
efforts are remarkable. The *consistency* is shown in the radical
departure from the traditional classification of production factors
into land, labour, and capital. Scarcity and indirect contribution
to utility are the characteristics common to all factors of production;
so there is no need to lay down their number or to define them by
physical, technological, or other qualities. All that is required is
the economic category of 'goods of higher order', the factors of
production x_1 to x_n of the modern production functions.[9] Particularly when Menger refuses to grant any special status to land,
whose qualities of immobility and near-constancy differ from
those of other factors only in degree, he is far ahead of his time and
has an absolutely modern appeal.

The *depth* of Menger's thinking becomes apparent when he
turns to the question how the utility or value of the consumption
goods is transferred to the productive goods. Here he came up
against the well-known difficulty that productive goods are
normally complementary. To find the individual values of the
jointly used factors of production one had to solve the problem of

[8] F. B. W. von Hermann, *Staatswirthschaftliche Untersuchungen* (1832),
quoted in H. Lehmann, *Grenznutzentheorie* (Berlin, 1968), p. 82.

[9] Menger's subdivision of goods 'of higher order' into those of 'second',
'third' order, etc., was less fruitful, particularly since the same good may belong
to different orders depending on the concrete circumstances. This subdivision
did, however, play a part in underlining Menger's stress on the role of time in
'roundabout' processes of production, and on the opposite movements of the
production process and the valuation process.

imputing the final value to the factors involved. This was a problem that had not existed in the real cost approach of the classical school.

In his search for a solution to this problem Menger made another pioneering contribution which has no parallel in the contemporary publications by Jevons and Walras: he recognized the analytical significance of the possibility of factor substitution, the possibility, that is, of achieving the same output with different combinations of the factors of production; in other words, he had a clear vision of the iso-product curve of modern neo-classical production and distribution theories. Fixed coefficients were to be regarded as an exception, which was illustrated by the case of chemical combinations, an example which is still a favourite in present-day textbooks.

It is true [Menger writes][10] that we can obtain quantities of goods of lower order only by the use of *complementary* quantities of goods of higher order. But it is equally true that the quantities in which the goods of higher order have to be combined in the process of production are not rigidly fixed in the way which is typical for chemical combinations, where only a certain quantity of one material together with a similarly fixed quantity of another material results in a desired chemical compound. We know from general experience that a given quantity of a good of lower order can be produced by goods of higher order which may be combined in very different ratios. Yes, we even find quite often that one or several goods of higher order which act as complementary goods with reference to another group of goods of higher order, may be dispensed with altogether without destroying the capacity of those other goods to produce the good of lower order in question.

The consideration of substitution between factors of production opened the way for a solution of the imputation problem. Menger applied the same method he had used in the explanation for the value of a consumption good unit: the value of a factor is equal to the utility lost when one unit of this factor is withdrawn. It is a marginal utility, because the least important needs will be left unsatisfied, if—as Menger assumes—economic actions are planned 'rationally'. The imputed value of the productive good is not derived from the immediate loss in consumption goods and their utility, but will be equal to that (smaller) loss that results *after* the remaining complementary productive goods have been reallocated

[10] *Grundsätze*, p. 139.

Distributive Aspects of the Austrian Theory 213

in an optimal fashion. Optimal allocation means—in full analogy to the norm for a rational consumption plan—that productive combinations are applied, step by step, to the provision of steadily falling marginal utilities until the allocation process comes to an end owing to the scarcity of the existing factors of production.

These—in a nutshell—are the main lines of Menger's thought as far as the pure theory of distribution is concerned. They also formed the basis for the subsequent discussions within the Austrian School. The affinity to the marginal productivity theory is clearly visible, though Menger did not apply the principle of diminishing (physical) returns. In his work this is completely overshadowed by the principle of diminishing marginal utility.[11] Similarly, the question raised by later economists whether the values imputed to the individual factors would ensure an exact distribution of the entire value of the final product (Euler's theorem), is not even hinted at in Menger's writings. On the other hand, they contain several details that indicate that Menger might have introduced some valuable ideas into the theory of distribution, if he had carried out his planned elaboration of the subject. Thus Menger displays his general insight into the importance of time and uncertainty also in connection with the imputation problem. He stresses that the imputed value of a productive good would not depend on the *present* value of the finished goods flowing from it in the future, but on the value to be expected at the time of completion. The role of time is also underlined in connection with the disposal of goods of higher order for lengthy production processes and with regard to the underestimation of future needs. Here one can already recognize the outlines of those ideas that later acquired major significance in Böhm-Bawerk's theory of capital and interest.

One cannot help but admire the originality and width of Menger's concepts. But this admiration should not blind us to certain weaknesses in his model. Some of these weaknesses are peculiar

[11] This neglect of the law of diminishing returns is surprising because the classical economists had studied just this phenomenon in the single case where they took account of the possibility of factor substitution, viz. in the increasing application of labour and capital to a given amount of land. With his refusal to regard land as a special case and with his insight into the ubiquity of substitution opportunities Menger should have been on the way towards a generalization of the classical law of diminishing returns. His failure to do so may have been the consequence of a certain neglect of real-output phenomena on which a few words will be said presently.

to the Austrian School, but some have remained characteristic for the neo-classical and marginal-productivity theory until this day.

The weak spots in Menger's distributional concept are to a large extent the pendant to the positive elements in his analysis. The very consistency and logical acuteness with which Menger ensured acceptance for his new concept of utility led to a dangerous neglect of other aspects. This becomes particularly apparent where the distributional question is under discussion. Frequently one has the impression that Menger and the Austrian School were more concerned with the problem of fitting factor prices and distribution neatly into the framework of the utility theory that they had constructed in the realm of consumer behaviour, than with a realistic analysis of the social-distribution process. Utility or marginal utility of the final product *and utility alone* should be the basis of the total theory. It is obvious, Menger says in his *Grundsätze*,[12] that 'the value of goods of higher order will depend *under all circumstances* on the expected value of goods of lower order'. And fifty years later we find a passage in an article by Hayek which very clearly reveals the dominant motivation in the entire Austrian imputation discussion:

. . . if we are able [he writes] to derive the importance, which an individual under given circumstances attaches to the various factors of production, from the utility of the final product, *then it becomes possible to build the distribution theory on the basis of the subjective value theory.*[13]

This motivation led to a certain one-sidedness which ultimately turned out to be a handicap for the Austrian variant of distribution theory. The main handicap was the extreme concentration on consumption with a corresponding neglect of production phenomena. They were only considered in so far as they contributed to gains or losses in utility. It is no accident that the 'law' of diminishing (physical) returns found no place in the early Austrian distribution theory. It was hypnotized by the *loss of utility* that would be caused by the withdrawal of one factor unit. The *loss of production* was only an analytically necessary link in this question; as a problem in itself it was not regarded as *economically* interesting. In this respect the Austrian School differed sharply from the marginal-distribution theory developed in the United States, particularly by Stuart Wood and J. B. Clark, which followed the traditions of

12 p. 124 (my italics).
13 F. A. Hayek, 'Bemerkungen zum Zurechnungsproblem', *Jahrbücher für Nationalökonomie und Statistik*, 124 (1926), p. 2 (my italics).

Longfield and Thünen by concentrating on production processes and diminishing returns.[14]

The stress on final utility as the 'ultimate' or 'true' explanation of factor prices and distribution might—under certain aspects—be regarded as a quest for 'deeper' insights; in practice, however, it led in a direction which did not prove very fruitful or operational. While the principle of marginal utility has the advantage of being plausible and open to immediate experience when applied to an explanation of *individual* valuations and allocation decisions in the sphere of private consumption, it acquires a very artificial appearance when it has to serve as the central cause of *social* distribution processes. The 'rational' individual producer, who so allocates his means of production as to maximize his utility, always played far too big a role in the Austrian debates on the distribution problem. The pure theory of imputation had a tendency to provide harmonious and rational *norms* for the economic plan of a Robinson or of a collective economy free from group conflicts and the problems of interpersonal comparisons of utilities. In this theory there was no room for the numerous distributionally relevant processes which we experience in a dynamic, poorly informed, non-equilibrium world populated by conflicting groups.[15] In a large part of contemporary welfare economics and in the social indifference curves of some current models we see a continuation of these modes of theoretical thinking.

Menger's fight against the classical cost approach and his endeavour to make utility the sole explanatory element of factor values created an unnecessary opposition against the use of

---

[14] Writing U for total utility, x for the output of consumption goods, and v for the factor input in the production of x, we can say that Menger and his followers tried to link the valuation of the factors to the magnitude $(dU/dx)(dx/dv)$ without paying too much attention to the separate elements of this product. The American School, on the other hand, was highly concerned with marginal physical productivity dx/dv.

[15] What is said here applies with full force only to the pure theory of imputation which served as the basis and starting-point for the analysis of the distribution problem. It is true that Menger, Böhm-Bawerk, Wieser, and many other Austrians were well aware that in the real world many other factors have a strong influence on the outcome of the distribution process. In their writings we often find pertinent remarks on these influences. There is also a tendency to distinguish between imputation as the basic force and actual distribution as a secondary stage (Böhm-Bawerk). But the fact remains that the pure theory of imputation acted as the main guide for marshalling the 'essential' facts for a treatment of distribution by factor shares.

additional elements in the Austrian School. Though Menger created a logically more impressive basis for distribution theory than Marshall, it was the latter's eclecticism that ultimately offered more room for realistic research.

If utility was to be regarded as the *sole* cause of factor costs, the scarcity of the factors had to be taken as given. Only in this way could their values be made a pure imputation problem. Classical theory, on the other hand, had—with the exception of land—never assumed such a constancy of factor quantities. Jevons, too, considered the variability of labour supply when he introduced the idea of disutility of labour. But once we allow factor supplies to vary the distribution problem acquires new aspects. Though the connection between final utilities and factor values does not disappear, we can no longer explain the latter *exclusively* by the former. This problem was largely eschewed by Menger, Böhm-Bawerk, Wieser, but also by Clark and later representatives of marginal productivity theory by taking the supplies of factors of production as more or less given.[16]

As soon as we admit the possibility of variations in factor supplies—at least in the long run—we not only have to give up the monistic 'explanation' of factor values on the basis of utility; we also have to abolish the dream of being able to divide sharply between a purely economic imputation (or functional distribution) theory on the one hand which is based on 'natural' elements, such as lands, needs, talents, technology, etc., and a personal income distribution on the other hand, where social, historical, and power elements (e.g. property rights, market power, etc.) come into play. Such a division was always beloved by the Austrian School, but it has remained typical also for many later developments in marginal-productivity theory.[17] When the persons in control of factor

[16] Menger—writing in 1871!—does seem far removed from social reality when he suggests that the supply of labour services is more or less determined 'by nature'. 'The value', he writes, 'which leisure may have for the worker is normally overestimated by far. For the great majority of people employment activities are a source of joy, being a true satisfaction of needs, and they would be carried out—though to a slightly lesser degree or in some modified form—even if these people were not forced by poverty to expend their strength' (*Grundsätze*, p. 149). In this respect Böhm-Bawerk was more realistic when he defended the assumption of constant labour supplies by pointing towards the modern organization of factory employment (*Positive Theorie des Kapitals*, 4th edn., vol. i, pp. 225–6).

[17] In this respect Menger and the Austrians compare favourably with Clark, who tried to justify the actual income distribution on the basis of his 'pure' imputa-

Distributive Aspects of the Austrian Theory   217

supplies (including labour) can vary these supplies depending on legal and social institutions, effective economic power, etc., then it becomes obvious that we cannot have a 'purely economic' theory of social distribution processes; we require a 'Political Economy' of distribution where economic and sociological influences are combined.[18]

Menger, in his pioneering spirit, carried the process of purifying the economics of distribution from all historical and sociological elements further than most of his immediate successors. Against the background of present-day neo-classical theory which has a similar leaning towards 'pure economics' and model perfectionism he, therefore, appears more modern than many later representatives of the Austrian School. Thus, as we remarked earlier, his change from the classical factors of production to generalized goods of higher order was a first-class analytical achievement; yet it pushed into the background a distinction which the classics regarded as important and which is certainly not irrelevant: the distinction between the different positions of the various socio-economic classes (land owners, capitalists, workers) in the distribution process. And it is probably no accident that the classical factors of production reappear in the writings of Böhm-Bawerk, who—and the same applies to Wieser—paid considerable attention to the problem of power. Particularly in his well-known article 'Macht oder ökonomisches Gesetz?'[19] Böhm-Bawerk anticipated many later developments in wage and distribution theory, like monopsony and other 'disturbances' of competitive equilibrium. But neither Böhm-Bawerk nor Wieser incorporated their ideas about social and power influences in the concepts of their 'pure' distribution theories, to a short description of which we shall now turn.

tion theory. The representatives of the Austrian School were—at least in principle—always aware that the imputation rules could not deliver any ethical guidance with regard to a 'proper' income distribution.

[18] See in this connection the remarkable article by E. Preiser, 'Besitz und Macht in der Distributionstheorie' in E. Salin (ed.), *Synopsis. Festgabe für Alfred Weber* (Heidelberg, 1948). An English translation 'Property and Power in the Theory of Distribution' appeared in *International Economic Papers*, 2 (1952); reprinted in K. W. Rothschild (ed.), *Power in Economics* (Penguin Economic Readings, 1971).

[19] E. Böhm-Bawerk, 'Macht oder ökonomisches Gesetz?', *Zeitschrift für Volkswirtschaft, Sozialpolitik und Verwaltung*, 23 (1914); English translation: 'Control or Economic Law?' in *Shorter Classics of Böhm-Bawerk* (Libertarian Press, 1962).

218   *Distributive Aspects of the Austrian Theory*

When Hayek, in the introduction to his edition of Menger's collected works, writes that '. . . it is not unduly to detract from the merits of these writers [Böhm-Bawerk and Wieser] to say that the fundamental ideas of the Austrian School belong fully and wholly to Carl Menger',[20] he is certainly right as far as the distributional aspects of the new theory were concerned. This is not to mean that the two authors did not develop any essential new ideas. Wieser, for instance, dwelt on the important idea of opportunity costs[21] and extended the concept of rent to all factors of production. He was thus the precursor of theoretical ideas which showed their full value only several decades later. Böhm-Bawerk enriched the debate on distributional problems in a most original manner through his work on capital and interest[22] (which we shall, however, not pursue here, since it is the subject of another contribution to this Symposium). But the fact remains that in spite of all additions and modifications which Wieser and Böhm-Bawerk contributed they adhered in principle to Menger's approach of explaining factor values by working backwards from consumer utilities and by applying marginal analysis.

Of the two Wieser was the author who certainly aimed at a formally more elegant solution which in some respects foreshadowed later developments in input–output analysis and linear programming. Like these approaches Wieser was thinking in terms of discrete productive activities with fixed technical coefficients and constant returns to scale. In this respect he differed from Menger who was inclined to regard the factors of production as highly substitutable in the production of each single commodity. Wieser, on the other hand, related to each commodity just one method of production. But factors of production could still be combined in any desired proportion (thus making general full employment possible) through variations in the product-mix in the total economy. In the differences between Menger and Wieser we can already perceive—in vague outline—the confrontation between the substitutionalists with their continuous pro-

---

[20] *The Collected Works of Carl Menger*, vol. i (London, 1934), p. v.

[21] Here Wieser, for once, was not the creator of the new *terminology*. The expression 'opportunity costs' comes from D. I. Green ('Pain Cost and Opportunity Cost', *Quarterly Journal of Economics*, 8 (1894)).

[22] Böhm-Bawerk's views on capital as a wage fund and his considerations of the time factor also induced him to define the equilibrium wage as the *discounted* marginal product of labour.

Distributive Aspects of the Austrian Theory 219

duction functions (Menger, Cobb-Douglas, neo-classics), and those economists who tend to think in terms of a finite number of production plans with possible discontinuities and 'corners' in the aggregate production function (Wieser, Walras, Leontief, activity analysis).[23]

Just like Menger, Wieser wanted to derive the unit values of a fixed quantity of production factors from the marginal utility which depended on those units. He was, however, opposed to Menger's 'loss principle', i.e. the attempt to 'solve' the problem by alternative withdrawals of units of the different factors of production. He argued that the values should not be ascertained by a method which disturbs the productive process, but that the imputation problem must be solved 'under the assumption of undisturbed property conditions'. The 'productive contribution' of the factors should be obtained from an analysis of the current production process.

This aim he tried to achieve through the simultaneous consideration of the production activities when all the factors of production are 'rationally' allocated and fully employed.[24] He assumed that the values of the final products (consumption goods) are already known. If production is carried on 'rationally', the marginal utilities depending respectively on the different factors of production would have to be the same in all activities. Since the factors are combined in different proportions in different activities, we obtain the possibility of imputing to each of them its value even though the factors always appear as complementary goods. In the famous Wieser equations we meet three factors and three activities (consumption goods). Let us call the factors X, Y, Z, their unit values (the marginal utilities depending on these units) x, y, z, the products produced by them A, B, C, and the unit values (marginal utilities) of these products a, b, c. Then, if we stipulate that the utilities produced must be completely distributed among the factors we only require the input coefficients for the three activities

[23] The affinity of Wieser's equations to ideas of activity analysis becomes more clearly visible when they are met in the changed form in which they were presented by Stigler. See G. J. Stigler, *Production and Distribution Theories. The Formative Period* (New York, 1941), pp. 166–7, 178.

[24] Full employment of all factors can always be achieved in spite of fixed co-efficients through a variation of activities. Whether the full-employment solution coincides with utility maximization is another matter. With Wieser this problem does not arise because he starts off with the *assumption* that an optimal combination has been reached.

in order to calculate the 'productive contribution' of the factors. Denoting the input coefficient of factor X for the production of one unit of A by a_{XA} and using analogous symbols for the other input coefficients, the Wieser equations take the following form:

$$\begin{pmatrix} a_{XA} & a_{YA} & a_{ZA} \\ a_{XB} & a_{YB} & a_{ZB} \\ a_{XC} & a_{YC} & a_{ZC} \end{pmatrix} \cdot \begin{pmatrix} x \\ y \\ z \end{pmatrix} = \begin{pmatrix} a \\ b \\ c \end{pmatrix}.$$

From these three equations the values x, y, z, i.e. the values of the factors of production, can be obtained.

Wieser's solution can be regarded as an important analytical supplementation and modification of Menger's ideas. In the event, however, Wieser seemed to create more problems than he was able to solve and his contribution created heated discussions on the imputation question. Some of the controversies were due to the insufficient mastery of the tools of analysis which was typical for many participants in the debate. It prevented them from recognizing the full implications of their theories, which—in their economic content—acquired increasingly complex structures. This lack of familiarity with analytical techniques applied even to the outstanding representatives of the Austrian School, with Menger and Schumpeter being slightly exceptional cases.[25] Most of them were sharp thinkers, but their training in the law faculties forced them to find simple forms and casuistic approaches for their—in many respects—mathematically orientated theoretical considerations.

This lack of analytical 'sophistication' was the cause for Wieser's misconception that his solution to the imputation problem by way of the 'productive contribution' was fundamentally different from Menger's and Böhm-Bawerk's 'loss principle'. Though the Austrian School was marginalist to its bones, it was unused to thinking consistently in terms of infinitesimal changes.[26] If Wieser

---

[25] The big exceptions, of course, were Auspitz and Lieben, who had a training in mathematics and were able to use more sophisticated techniques. But they were never integrated into the Austrian School and its discussions. (Professionally they were active in industry and banking.) At least to some extent their outsider position was due to this very use of more mathematical methods.

[26] If we exclude Auspitz and Lieben, Schumpeter was the first—within the Austrian School—to apply infinitesimal calculus consistently in this field. Otherwise he followed more or less the ideas of Böhm-Bawerk. See his 'Bemerkungen über das Zurechnungsproblem', *Zeitschrift für Volkswirtschaft, Sozialpolitik und Verwaltung*, 18 (1909).

Distributive Aspects of the Austrian Theory 221

had moved in this direction he would have recognized the equivalence of the two solutions, which is proved in the following paragraphs.[27]

Let us assume there are n factors which in n activities produce n consumption goods. Technical conditions are given by the matrix $A = [a_{ij}]$, where a_{ij} is the (fixed) input of factor i per unit of output of commodity j. The values (marginal utilities) of the n consumption goods are known and equal to $p_1, p_2, \dots p_n$.

Let us now turn to Wieser's solution. It consists in the simultaneous imputation of the unit values of the consumption goods to the factors used in the production of each unit. Writing $x_1, x_2, \dots x_n$ for the unknown unit values of the factors we obtain the general Wieser equations:

$$a_{11}\,x_1 + a_{21}\,x_2 + \dots + a_{n1}\,x_n = p_1,$$
$$a_{12}\,x_1 + a_{22}\,x_2 + \dots + a_{n2}\,x_n = p_2,$$
$$\cdot \quad \cdot \quad \cdot \quad \cdot \quad \cdot \quad \cdot \quad \cdot \quad \cdot \quad \cdot$$
$$a_{1n}\,x_1 + a_{2n}\,x_2 + \dots + a_{nn}\,x_n = p_n. \tag{1}$$

As can be seen, the coefficients of x are the transposed matrix of the input coefficients A. We can, therefore, express Wieser's equations by the following matrix and vectors:

$$A'x = p, \tag{2}$$

whence we obtain as the solution for the vector of factor values

$$x = (A')^{-1}p. \tag{3}$$

We now want to show that Menger's 'loss principle' yields the same result. First of all we have to determine total output when all factors are fully employed. Writing y for the vector of the physical outputs of the n consumption goods and v for the vector of the given quantities of the n factors of production, we have

$$Ay = v, \tag{4}$$

from which we obtain $\quad y = A^{-1}v. \tag{5}$

Let us write Y for the *value* of total output. Then

$$Y = y'p. \tag{6}$$

[27] The equivalence was already hinted at by F. H. Knight, 'A Note on Professor Clark's Illustration of Marginal Productivity', *Journal of Political Economy*, 23 (1925). See also Stigler, op. cit. The proof given here is slightly different and more general.

Now, the factor values are to correspond to the value which is gained or lost when there is an infinitesimal change in the quantity of a factor:

$$x = \frac{\delta Y}{\delta v} = \frac{\delta(y'p)}{\delta v}. \tag{7}$$

The vector product in the numerator of the right-hand term can be adjusted as follows by using equation (5) and transposition:

$$y'p = v'(A^{-1})'p = v'(A')^{-1}p. \tag{8}$$

We thus get

$$x = \frac{\delta(y'p)}{\delta v} = \frac{\delta(v'(A')^{-1}p)}{\delta v} = I(A')^{-1}p = (A')^{-1}p \tag{9}$$

since A and p are constants and $\delta v'/\delta v$ is equal to the unit matrix. As can be seen, equation (9) leads to the same result as equation (3).

The analytical insufficiency also meant that Wieser had to adopt unnecessary constraints in his exposition in order to come to terms with the complexities of the problem. Wieser was fully aware that there exist more activities (products) than factors of production. But in order to arrive at a 'determinate' solution he simply assumes that the number of *relevant* production plans is exactly equal to the number of factors. Similarly, his *assumption* of linear and homogeneous production functions secures the full and exact distribution of the commodity values among the factors of production. In his more concrete considerations Wieser distinguishes between the above 'general imputation' and a 'specific imputation' which arises when a factor has no alternative use. In this case he follows Ricardo and derives the value as a residual (after deduction of the values of the 'cost' factors). Finally, Wieser simplifies his problem by assuming that the marginal utilities of the consumption goods—the outcome of an optimal allocation process—are already known. The full solution demands, of course, the simultaneous determination of consumer utilities and factor values from given needs and technological data. This weakness in Wieser's analysis was criticized as early as 1893 in Wicksell's *Über Wert, Kapital und Rente*. There and in later writings Wicksell made important contributions in giving a more precise shape to some of the distributional ideas of Wieser and the Austrian School.

The basic structure of Böhm-Bawerk's contribution to the problem of imputation and distribution—and only the basic structure can be dealt with here[28]—is less 'elegant' and less unified than Wieser's theory; but in its cruder form it leaves more room for the consideration of additional elements. Starting from the same premises as Menger, Böhm-Bawerk distinguishes four cases. Case I refers to activities where all the factors are used in fixed proportions and none of the factors can be used in any other productive combination. In this case the full value of the produced commodity goes to the 'final piece' (*Schlußstück*), the last of the complementary factors to join the combination. For without it the other factors are completely valueless. Which factor will take this place depends on the 'concrete situation'.

In case II the factors of the limitational group can also be used elsewhere, but the alternative use yields less utility. This outside utility fixes an 'isolated value' below which the valuation of the factor in the more efficient combination cannot fall. The actual valuation will then lie between this minimum and a maximum, which is equal to the total utility of the combination minus the isolated values of all the other factors (with alternative uses). Which factors will have to be content with the minimum and which factor will obtain the maximum once again depends on the 'concrete situation'.

Case III, which Böhm-Bawerk regards as the most frequent one, allows for the substitution of factors between various processes of production. Factors now not only have alternative uses with a corresponding minimum price; they can also be replaced by factors from other branches so that the upper limit is no longer the previously described maximum but the utility forgone when a replacement factor is withdrawn from other activities. In an economy with a high division of labour and numerous productive combinations minimum and maximum limits of factor values will tend to approach each other. In this case the typical 'cost goods' are obtained which move freely between the different branches of industry. Finally, we have case IV which deals with combinations of such cost goods with irreplaceable factors which have no or only limited alternative uses. The cost goods obtain their general substitution value while the remainder is divided among the

---

[28] As already mentioned, a multitude of different ideas and hypotheses can be found in both Wieser's and Böhm-Bawerk's writings when they turn to more concrete considerations on the formation of wages, interest, and rent, or when they deal with problems of economic policy.

specialized factors according to the rules of case I and II, depending in detail on the 'concrete situation'.

Böhm-Bawerk's casuistic treatment does not—as Mayer correctly remarked[29]—result in a rounded theory of distribution. Nowhere does he indicate the interdependence between the structure of production and the formation of factor values; he takes the structure as given. In Böhm-Bawerk's approach the distinction between imputation and distribution becomes particularly sharp. The imputational 'rules' discussed above can lead to different valuations for one and the same factor depending, for instance, whether it is a 'final piece' or not. There is, therefore, no definite sum of imputed values which is exactly equal to the value of the produced consumption goods. The correspondence between end values and factor values is brought about in the distribution process where the 'concrete situation' determines the effective valuation. Under atomistic competition there is a tendency for a convergence of imputation and distribution.

While Böhm-Bawerk's theoretical structure may be unsatisfactory when judged in terms of model building, it does show a sense of realism which is characteristic of Böhm-Bawerk and which is missing in many later works of the marginal productivity school. With his stress on the 'concrete situation' Böhm-Bawerk cleared the way for a fuller consideration of institutional and bargaining elements in the distribution process of a world which is anything but transparent, flexible, and perfectly competitive. It is certainly no accident that Böhm-Bawerk, in the already mentioned article 'Macht oder ökonomisches Gesetz?', was more capable than other economists of his school of dealing sympathetically with some criticisms of the marginal-productivity theory, though of course he, too, did not accept these criticisms.

With this short exposition of the basic distributional concepts of the 'Big Three' of the Austrian School we have outlined the essence of the distributional theory of the Austrian School as a whole in so far as it can be clearly distinguished from other theories. This also applies to later developments. The discussion of the imputation problem which continued till to the end of the 20s of our century was mainly occupied with real and imagined contradictions in the writings of the 'fathers', with attempts towards greater clarity and

---

[29] See his article 'Zurechnung' in *Handwörterbuch der Staatswissenschaften*, 4th edn., vol. 8 (1928), p. 1218.

precision, and with delimitations against competing views. Some questions—like the problem of the exact exhaustion of final values through the imputed factor incomes—remained unsolved to the end of the debate.[30] But on the whole a coherent picture had been achieved, and a monograph on the Austrian imputation discussion published in 1931 could pronounce with some justification (and with some exaggeration) that 'the solution of the imputation problem has been . . . completed'.[31]

In those days of the 'completion' of the debate a number of important new developments took place in the fields of cost and marginal productivity theory, building on the pioneering work of the Austrians, of Wicksteed and Marshall, Wicksell and Clark, Pareto and others. In 1926 Sraffa's path-breaking article on 'The Laws of Returns under Competitive Conditions'[32] was published which set off a high-level discussion on cost and production functions. At the beginning of the 1930s these thoughts were consolidated in the works of Chamberlin, Joan Robinson, Stackelberg, Erich Schneider, and others. At the same time Douglas and Hicks published their treatises on wage theory which raised the marginal-productivity theory to a new level. The time had passed when an Austrian School could present a special brand of distribution theory. What it had produced in original ideas and pioneering efforts was now—together with elements from other sources—part and parcel of a unified general development.

[30] Hans Mayer stipulated for equilibrium a distribution of total utility to the various factors of production '*in the same ratio* as output is reduced by alternative withdrawals of their last units' and he stated that 'the quotas of utility so obtained represent the utility of the last factor units or their *marginal utility*' ('Zurechnung', op. cit., p. 1223). In this way, of course, no problem of incomplete or over-exhaustion can ever arise.

[31] E. Haydt, *Die ökonomische Zurechnung* (Leipzig and Vienna, 1931), p. 130.

[32] *Economic Journal*, 36 (1926).

[16]   176 - 80
[1982]

J22
J38

A NOTE ON SOME ECONOMIC AND WELFARE ASPECTS OF WORKING-TIME REGULATION*

K. W. ROTHSCHILD

Institut für Volkswirtschaftstheorie und Volkswirtschaftspolitik Johannes Kepler Universität Linz

I.

On the labour market the services of employees are sold at a certain price, the wage rate. But, as we know, for most primary workers this is not simply a question of supplying the desired ("optimum") quantity of working hours at the going hourly wage rate according to given preferences for income (market goods) and leisure (non-market activities). To picture individual labour supply as a simple application of utility maximising behaviour, as is normally done in labour theory texts[1], is obviously unrealistic in many cases. People can decide whether they are prepared to work at the going wage or not, but they have to accept a given standard time (with some limited variability where suitable part-time or over-time alternatives are available). Similarly, in collective bargaining we find continuous adjustments in pay arrangements while standard working hours are fixed separately at lengthy and irregular intervals.

Labour supply cannot be freely adjusted because the requirements of factory discipline and short-term rigidities in working-time arrangements make such flexibility of choice difficult and costly. This raises some economic and welfare problems which are not sufficiently considered when the "lumpiness" and separateness of working-time arrangements are neglected.

The fact that "leisure" cannot be acquired like other goods in single units but only in predetermined lumps means that on the labour market optimal choice is not possible for many individuals. He or she cannot equate the marginal substitution rate between goods and leisure with their relative prices. Some people would be better off if they were allowed to work longer at the current hourly wage rate, others if they could cut down their working-time. This obviously raises the question of the "best" strategy for regulating standard working-times (through law or collective bargaining). The problem is further complicated when we take into account the possibility that preferences are not constant and may be influenced by the imposed division of time between market work and other activities. Economic and welfare developments in the longer run may then depend not only on the extent but also on the frequency of working-time arrangements. To these issues we now turn.

*I want to thank the members of a staff seminar at Monash University and an unnamed referee for some very valuable suggestions.

[1] For the usual theoretical and diagrammatic treatment of utility-maximising choice between income and leisure see for instance Perlman [3, pp. 4–7].

214

II.

In the following remarks we restrict ourselves to the general fixation of standard working-times (per week, year) and neglect the additional questions arising from over-time and part-time arrangements. The first problem is whether or not a change in standard time arrangements should be undertaken. Since many individuals are probably not in an optimum position but may be deviating in different directions (some wanting more, some fewer hours) there cannot be a simple answer. This is fundamentally a political (distributional) problem of social welfare. Experience in growing economies seems to show that from time to time there is broad support for additional leisure rather than additional income.[2] But we have little information on which to base our decisions on the "optimal" extent, timing and frequency of such adjustments.

The frequency of adjustments can be important from another point of view, *viz.* when we take into account habit formation and changing preferences in a dynamic setting. If—for technical and institutional reasons—working-time cannot be con-tinuously adjusted according to given preferences, then most people (*i.e.*, those who would prefer to obtain part of their rising standards in the form of shorter working-time) will be pushed towards a higher goods-leisure ratio than corresponds to their optimum choice. This may be later corrected when an adjustment of working-time becomes politically possible. But the extent and nature of this correction will not be independent of the frequency of such adjustments. Different adjustment strategies (with regard to frequency) will yield different long-term expansion paths of the desired goods-leisure relationship.

The reasons for this are twofold. First, leisure is not only a substitute for market goods, it is also a complementary good needed for the utilisation and enjoyment of some markets goods.[3] In periods where additional leisure cannot be obtained the productivity-based rise in real wage incomes will by necessity turn towards (sub-optimal) market goods which are not too time-intensive. Getting used to them will reduce the need and the desire for leisure as compared with the initial ex-ante position. And—secondly—habit formation will quite generally make the "involuntarily" chosen market goods indispensable once one has become used to them. People will no longer be willing to trade goods against leisure at the same rate as before. While there can be comparatively high ex-ante flexibility in choosing new combinations of extended uses of goods and leisure, this flexibility is probably low for combinations already reached and to which one has become adjusted (voluntarily or by force of circumstance).

---

[2] A recent survey among Californian employees asking for preferences between a 2 per cent pay increase and equally costly working-time reductions (10 minutes per day or 50 minutes one day a week or 5 additional days paid vacation or earlier retirement) showed that only 14.3 per cent of the 746 respondents preferred the pay increase while the remaining 85.7 per cent voted for some form of working-time reduction (55.6 per cent for a longer vacation). These results come from Best [2]. here quoted from the December 1980 Bulletin of the Swiss Society for Futures Research.

[3] See on this the classic article by Becker [1]. Becker is, however, concerned with (static) equilibrium choice in a world where market goods and non-work time are used in combination and/or compete with each other. Working-time—in his analysis—is freely variable.

178 Economic Method, Theory and Policy

These ideas are illustrated in Figure 1 using the traditional goods-leisure-choice diagram. On the abscissa the total waking time available to an individual is given by $O\overline{T}$. Working time is measured from $\overline{T}$ towards the origin. The ordinate indicates the amount of market goods ("goods" for short) that can be obtained through work and wage incomes. The wage rate per time unit is indicated by the slope of a straight line passing through $\overline{T}$, like $\overline{T}W_0$. The line shows what combinations of leisure (measured from the origin along the time-axis) and market goods are available at the given wage rate. I_0, I_1 etc. are indifference curves showing the preference structure with regard to goods and leisure.

FIGURE 1

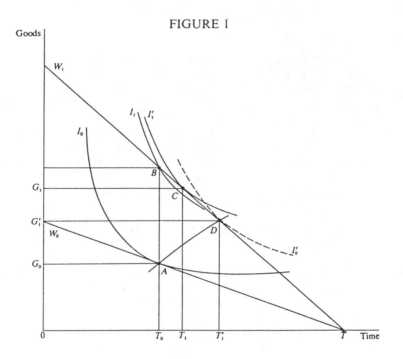

Let us now turn to our case. We start with an initial "historic" position where a "representative" individual is in "equilibrium" at point A. The ruling wage is given by $\overline{T}W_0$ and the prescribed standard time is $\overline{T}T_0$. The individual's preferences are indicated by the two indifference curves I_0 and I_0'. The I_0 curve has a "sharp" turn at point A indicating the strong preference for the habitual and partly complementary relationship between currently consumed goods and leisure. Neither is easily substituted for the other.

But for extensions of the standard of living there is considerable flexibility for a balanced expansion of output and leisure. When it comes to a choice between new types of goods and non-market activities the two sectors become more substitutional and the typical indifference curve beyond the historical standard will be flatter as represented by I_0'. If the rise in productivity per man-hour leads to a rise of the real wage rate from $\overline{T}W_0$ to $\overline{T}W_1$ in the course of several years then — with continuous adaptation of wage rates and working-time — the "optimal" expansion path would lead from A to D, working time would fall by T_0T_1' and consumption (production) of goods would increase by G_0G_1'.

Now assume instead that the standard working-time remains fixed at $\overline{T}T_0$ during this whole period and only comes up for revision after the real wage had reached $\overline{T}W_1$ (and stayed there for some time). Because of this institutional constraint the "typical" individual could not move from A to D but instead from A to B. This involves a "forced" intake of goods at the expense of leisure and the adoption of a consumption-mix based on the limited availability of leisure. So when working-time adjustments come up for discussion at point B the indifference curve system represented by I_0' is no longer applicable. The new "historic" position ruling in B has produced a "corner" at B limiting the possibilities for an ex-post substitution of leisure for goods. The historically acquired ("enforced") new preference structure is presented by the indifference curves I_1 and I_1'. An "optimal" working-time adjustment carried out at this stage will only lead from B to C instead of D. The working-time reduction will only be T_0T_1, but the growth in consumption (production) will be G_0G_1.

III.

Our considerations of habit formation and dynamic evolution of preferences have shown that not only the extent, but also the frequency of working-time adjustments has an influence on the goods-leisure choice and on the structure of consumption. A few tentative remarks can be added to this general observation. First, the frequently expressed warning to workers that pressing for shorter hours involves a sacrifice in material standards loses some of its force. If a generally growing standard of living is coupled with a smooth and continuous adaptation of working hours, alternative habits and alternative expansion paths become available permitting higher welfare levels consistent with a (comparatively) lower material standard. Secondly, as far as a fast and exponential growth of material production with its concomitant absorption of limited resources is regarded as undesirable, a strong case could be made for giving a much higher priority to continuous working-time strategies than has been the practice up till now.[4]

It is more difficult to draw any general economic or welfare conclusions with regard to the structural effects of different working-time strategies. As we have seen the greater the intervals between consecutive reductions in standard working-time the stronger will be the trend towards time-saving goods, while time-using goods will have a better chance when the adaptation is more continuous. But there is not much else we can say. Apart from some striking examples (growth of tourism) we know very little about these effects and we know even less whether there are any general characteristics

---

[4] This assumes that current prices do not reflect fully long term resource limitations and that policy considerations with regard to exhaustible resources are desirable.

(*e.g.*, service or manufacturing orientation, technological innovation, resource utilisation, labour intensiveness) distinguishing classes of time-saving, time-using and "neutral" goods which could be of economic interest. There may be room for some pioneering research in this area.

REFERENCES

1. G. S. Becker, "A Theory of the Allocation of Time", *Economic Journal*, vol. 75, 1965.
2. F. Best, "Work and Leisure in the Future" in: World Future Society, *Through the '80s*. Washington, 1980.
3. R. Perlman, *Labor Theory* (New York: Wiley, 1969).

17

Review of Political Economy, 2.3 (1990), pp 359–65

A note on some socioeconomic and normative aspects of risk

Kurt W. Rothschild *University of Linz*

In economic literature risk taking is usually discussed with special reference to capital risks and profits. It is argued that in an uncertain world all economic agents are exposed to risks. Workers in particular, face risks of income losses and obsolescence of human capital. But the effects of and rewards for risk taking are unevenly distributed between capital owners and dependent employees. This leads to critical questions about the normative aspects of risk taking propensities.

Risks and risk taking play an important part in economic reality and in the writings of economists. In a world of uncertainty and with actions and their consequences reaching into the future, risks of some sort or another are bound to occur.[1] In economic literature the problem of risk turns up in different connections. As part of 'positive science' it has become very prominent in microeconomic studies of decision making because of the realization that traditional assumptions of optimizing behaviour in a fully transparent and certain environment are a poor guide to actual behaviour. Of longer standing is the partly descriptive, partly apologetic reference to risk bearing as an explanation of and justification for profits. Finally, on a more normative plane, a positive attitude towards risk taking is not untypical for economists because its existence is regarded as an important motor of growth in a dynamic society surrounded by uncertainties. Thus it cannot be said that economic theory has neglected the problem of risk. But in both its positive and normative aspects the approach to risk is normally narrowed down to the special risks connected with capital accumulation and entrepreneurial output decisions. Yet risk is a universal phenomenon in modern life and to reduce risk considerations to the entrepreneurial sphere leads to a

---

[1] Here and in the following risk will be understood in the wider sense of refering to *any kind* of uncertain outcome. The difference between risk in a narrower sense ('calculable risk') and 'true uncertainty' (see, e.g., Knight, 1921; Keynes, 1937) which can be very important in certain connections, will be neglected because it is of minor importance in the points to be touched in this article.

biased picture of reality. The following reflections are intended to illustrate this view.

Let me start with some illustrations which show how risk is often narrowed down to capital risk from the very beginning or by definition. That this should be so in more business-oriented encyclopaedias is perhaps understandable. Thus Greenwald's *Encyclopaedia of economics* (Greenwald, 1982) mentions risk (including uncertainty) only in connection with 'risk premium for investment', and risk is similarly tied to investment and insurance in Ammer's *Dictionary of business and economics* (Ammer, 1977). But the same delineation is typical of more theoretically oriented texts both in the past and today. Sticking for the moment to encyclopaedias we can have a look at both the old and the new Palgrave (Higgs, 1926; Eatwell *et al.*, 1987). Risk as a special article appears only in the old Palgrave and its author is nobody less than Edgeworth. 'Indemnity for risk', he writes, 'as explained by Mill, forms one element of gross profits . . . Risk, as an element of profit, appears in its purest form – most detached from labour of super-intendence – in the case of joint stock undertakings.' In the new Palgrave a corresponding passage can be found in Benjamin Friedman's article on 'Capital, credit and money markets':

> . . . because of its durability, capital necessarily exposes those who hold it to whatever uncertainties characterize both the production process and the demand for wealth-holding in the future. Not just reward but risk too, therefore, are inherent features of capital that must accrue to some holders, somewhere in the economy, if the economy is to enjoy the advantages of production based in part on durable capital inputs (Palgrave, 1987: Volume I, p. 321).

To give just one more example let me quote a passage from Arrow's Yrjö Jahnsson Lecture in 1965: 'In a capitalist world . . . the owner of a business typically is supposed to assume all the risks of uncertainty, paying out the unexpected losses and enjoying the unexpected gains' (Arrow, 1965: 46).

The perspective contained in these and similar quotations creates the impression that – at least as far as the economic process is concerned – only a small part of the economic agents is faced with and threatened by uncertainty and risks. But is this really true? What about the 'dependent labour force'? Can they act in a transparent world? Do they not have to make risky decisions?

I shall in a moment argue why workers (as a short expression for employees in general) have to assume risks and to make risky decisions which are in principle not so very different from those made by capital owners albeit under different circumstances. But before I do this I want to quote another well-known economist, because I think that this quotation will help to understand why it has become so plausible and so accepted to concentrate on capital ownership and entrepreneurial decisions when risk and its consequences are discusses. The quotation comes from an essay by Shackle and runs as follows:

Thus one economic role which somebody must perform is that of bearing uncertainty, both in its subjective aspect of experiencing feelings and in its objective aspect of reaping factual consequences . . . Uncertainty is inherent in production, but it does not follow that all who take part in it need bear uncertainty; those who wish can contract out of uncertainty . . . If . . . some agree to accept from the others a stated money payment and to surrender to these others all their rights in the product, we can say that at the date when the contracts are made the planned operation has two quite different meanings for the two groups of producers. To one group it means an income of known size, for the other group it means the unknown difference between the total of the contractual payments and the price for which the product will exchange (Shackle, 1955: 82).

From this passage it becomes clear how risk can be allocated so unilaterally to the capital side. It becomes plausible as long as we restrict our time horizon to the relatively short stretch of time of production and sales which coincides with the length of wage contracts. During this period the risks of revenue fluctuations fall ostensibly on the entrepreneurs alone. Even in this case it is not necessarily the full story. The *burden* of the risks may be divided between employers and workers if the contract can be used to induce workers to work for a lower wage than they would regard as acceptable in the absence of such contracts.

But the decisive objection against the view expressed above rests on a recognition that the problem of uncertainty and risks covers a much wider area than short-period production processes combined with fixed wage contracts. When longer periods and wider decisions are considered we find that employees are faced with risks comparable to those of employers and that they cannot 'contract out' of such risks even if they wished to do so.

When we speak of capitalists' (or employers') risks we usually think of two types of risk: 1) the risk of investment, i.e., the danger of 'freezing' liquid funds in capital goods which may not be fully utilizable later on; and 2) to enter (with given capital resources) definite commitments regarding production which may later fail to bring the hoped for results in output or revenue. But workers are faced with similar risks and risky decisions. Indeed it is strange that the widespread use of the concepts 'human capital' and 'investment in human capital' in the theory of wage differentials has not led to the obvious inclusion of human capital whenever risk is discussed in connection with investment. A person's choice of what to train for and for how long is a much trickier and more long-term decision than many decisions concerning capital investment. While the opportunity costs of lost income during the training period have received sufficient attention in the attempt to explain income differences, the risks of 'sinking' investment in a particular skill and the opportunity costs of having refrained from taking up some other or more generalized training are hardly mentioned. Moreover, this is not just a single (though great and decisive) risk at the beginning of one's career. With training and learning on the job becoming increasingly important, acceptance of work in a given firm is also an uncertain and risky decision which can have important effects on the nature and extent of further accumulations of human capital.

But workers may also be fully exposed to a firm's risks with respect to the success or failures of production programmes. True, during the wage-contract period they can normally expect to receive a fixed income. But when we look beyond the contract period their fate is often closely bound up with the successes of the firm. When the firm runs into difficulties wages might fall and – more importantly – workers may be dismissed. In this case, not only will it take some time to find a suitable new job; the special skills which the workers had acquired in the interests of the old firm may also be of limited value in other firms. The decision to join a particular firm (instead of another firm) is a risky investment *and* production decision which can result in permanent losses to the workers concerned.

So far the argument has been that an extended interpretation of risk and uncertainty leads to the (perhaps obvious) conclusion that in a dynamic economy which produces for an uncertain future practically all active agents are subject to risk, and that some of the risks with which workers are faced are not so very different from those which are normally regarded as typical risks of capital.[2] But while the risks are not unsimilar, there are considerable differences in the way they can be met and how the different groups are affected.

One of the great advantages in the case of capital risks are the numerous possibilities of spreading the risks. While some spreading of risks is also possible in the case of human capital through flexible learning and training, the opportunities never come near the possibilities of portfolio selection in the realm of financial and real capital. Added to this is the greater mobility of capital both in the spatial sense and regarding different uses. When some capital is lost the remaining part can usually be transferred fairly easily to other uses and can form the basis for a new start. A partial obsolescence of human capital can mean that the person as a whole can never return to his/her former status, because accumulation through learning has biological and time constraints which do not apply in the case of capital ownership.

These circumstances alone suffice to explain why workers may feel more vulnerable to risks and show more risk aversion than capital owners. More decisive, however, are the differences arising from the uneven distribution of

---

2 Economists with a strong interest in social problems were always aware of the uncertainties and risks to which workers are exposed. They were deeply concerned about the *special* risks of propertyless workers. Thus, in his introduction to the *Economics of welfare* Pigou wrote: 'The misery and squalour that surround us . . . the injurious luxury of some wealthy families, the terrible uncertainty overshadowing many families of the poor – these are evils too plain to be ignored' (Pigou, 1920: VII). And a few years later we find an even stronger formulation in a book by Douglas, Hitchcock, and Atkins on the worker in modern society (Douglas *et al.*, 1923; here quoted from Hardy, 1923: 337): 'Indeed it can be said with a certain degree of accuracy that the worker assumes all the risks of the employer and in addition bears some unique to himself'.

wealth. While all persons have – subject to their natural talents – equal chances to decide on the development of their human capital, taking up risks with regard to capital as such is only open to owners of capital. At the same time the possession of capital greatly lightens the burden of risk taking. If the available capital is sufficiently extensive, risking part of it does not involve a great threat to fundamentals in the case of loss. On the other hand, persons who have to rely on their work income plus some modest savings and social security provisions experience far greater direct set backs when they become victims of risky developments. In addition, capital owners can avoid some risks in a way which is not open to noncapitalists. The special risks of sinking capital in 'frozen' forms and of entering specific production processes can be avoided by investing in fixed interest securities and 'living' on capital. No such choice is open to the owner of human capital. He must throw it into the uncertain production process (and maintain and accumulate it there) if he wants to survive decently at all.

If the arguments about the universal presence of risks and their uneven effects and incidence are accepted, two traditional economic viewpoints are in need of a critical interpretation. The first concerns the representation of profits (or part of profits) as a reward for risk taking. While this interpretation can be accepted in so far as some profits may be necessary to induce capital owners to submit their capital to riskier ventures, it is definitely beside the point when it creates the impression (as it usually does) that risk taking as such can – like other services – always demand a certain price. The global picture is rather different. Risk taking is a general and widely diffused aspect of production for future markets which affects most participants in the economic game, but only some of them are in a position to demand and receive payment for taking risks surpassing a certain minimum level. Workers are by necessity all the time risk takers when choosing their training and jobs, and they cannot opt out of risk. Individual capital owners can 'wait' and can permanently avoid entering the riskier fields, and have, therefore, to be specially induced to accept risks. It is the uneven bargaining position which determines whether risks are rewarded or not, and not the existence or burden of risks as such. This becomes even more obvious when we add occupational and health risks to the risks of income, capital and job security.

The point just mentioned refers to the explanatory aspect of risks in the economic discourse. The second point is connected with a normative aspect. Distinguishing between risk-loving entrepreneurial types among capital owners on the one hand, and more or less risk-averse workers and rentier-type capitalists on the other, the existence and growth of the first group is regarded to be important and desirable as the (sole?) source of innovation and economic progress. Even when one disregards Schumpeter's lyrics about the heroic pioneer-entrepreneur, a general tendency among economists to regard a greater supply of risk-loving entrepreneurs as an undisputed advantage is quite visible. But having seen that risk aversion among workers is probably not just a personal trait but may rest on solid reasons, the position becomes a bit more complex. When talking of risk-loving we have to pose the question 'whose risk, whose love?'. Let us look a bit more closely at this question.

A higher risk propensity of entrepreneurs will probably have two more or less direct consequences. On average and in the long run, more risk taking will lead to higher economic growth rates both because of accelerating effects on process (higher technical efficiency) and product innovations (higher competitiveness). This is the main argument in favour of positive risk attitudes among entrepreneurs. At the same time, however, a higher risk propensity will normally be accompanied by greater microfluctuations around the trend. Birth and death rates of firms will be higher, and booms and recessions may exhibit greater amplitudes because of infectious waves in risk-taking levels.

Now, while the first effect – higher growth rates – leading on average to higher profits and wages can count on a community of interests of employers and employees, this will not be the case as far as the second effect is concerned. There are several reasons for this. First of all there is the problem that at the enterprise level the question of whether a riskier course should be followed or not rests exclusively with the employer. The employees are 'enforced' risk takers since they cannot easily shift to a less adventurous firm in a heterogeneous labour market. The *spread* of risk taking among entrepreneurs is, therefore, much more in line with their individual risk preferences than is the case with employees who are driven into passive acceptance.

More generally, a dominance of risk strategies with constant dangers of failure looks quite different from the capitalist and labour point of view. For the capitalist risks have a more or less symmetric appearance. Big losses may occur, but there is also the chance of big gains. Capital may get lost, but it may also be multiplied. Moreover, in many countries the losses of one year can be counted against the profits of following years when it comes to paying income tax. The picture is less balanced as far as the worker is concerned. While he/she is equally exposed to losses of income and (human) capital as the capitalist in case of failure, his/her possibilities of above-average gains in the case of success are limited. True, he/she may benefit from higher wages when the firm becomes more profitable; but there exist few possibilities for an extended accumulation of (human) capital. The odds are weighted against him/her, and this is a further reason (additional to those mentioned before) for a risk-aversion bias among workers. Given this risk-aversion bias a worker may be prepared, as the contract wage theory indicates, to accept a lower wage in return for (implied) job guarantees by the employer, i.e., he/she is prepared to pay an insurance premium to the risk-loving and risk-deciding entrepreneur in order to induce him to take some of the burdens from his/her (the worker's) shoulders which are caused by risks which he/she would not have chosen.

Seen in this way the norm that a higher risk-taking propensity among entrepreneurs is always superior to a lower propensity can no longer be regarded as generally acceptable. Differences between nonhuman and human capital and in the initial distribution of wealth, unequal weight in decision making, and asymmetries in the distribution of gains and losses all contribute to different risk consequences for capital owners and dependent employees. From the point of view of the latter a certain degree of risk aversion is a 'rational' reaction to the realities of the environment. The norm corresponding to their situation cannot be to aspire to a maximum of risk-loving attitudes among entrepreneurs, but rather to an 'optimal' level which takes account of the trade off between the advantages of the growth-fostering effects of risky strategies and the drawbacks of their destabilizing effects.[3]

References

Ammer, C. and **Ammer, D.S.** 1977: *Dictionary of business and economics.* New York: Free Press.

Arrow, K.J. 1965: *Aspects of the theory of risk-bearing.* Helsinki: Yrjö Johansson Lectures.

Douglas, Hitchcock and **Atkins** 1923: *The worker in our modern society.* Chicago: University of Chicago Press.

Eatwell, J., Milgate M. and **Newman P.,** editors, 1987: *The new Palgrave: a dictionary of economics.* London: Macmillan.

Greenwald, D. 1982: *Encyclopaedia of economics.* New York: McGraw Hill.

Hardy, C.O. 1923: *Risk and risk-bearing.* Chicago: University of Chicago Press.

Higgs, H. editor, 1926; *Palgrave's dictionary of political economy,* revised edition. London: Macmillan.

Jonas, H. 1979: *Das Prinzip Verantwortung. Versuch einer Ethik für die technologische Zivilisation.* Frankfurt.

Keynes, J.M. 1937: The general theory of employment. *Quarterly Journal of Economics* 51, 209–23.

Knight, F.H. 1921: *Risk, uncertainty and profit.* New York: Macmillan.

Pigou, A.C. 1920: *The economics of welfare.* London: Macmillan.

Shackle, G.L.S. 1955: The economist's view of profit. In *Uncertainty in economics and other reflections,* Cambridge: Cambridge University Press.

---

[3] Starting from a psychological and ecological perspective the philosopher Jonas (Jonas, 1979) reaches a similar conclusion. He argues that a slowing down of technical change could - by reducing risks - diminish existing fears and lead to higher welfare levels.

18

188 - 204
[1993]

10 Oligopoly: Walking the Sylos-path

not an
Econ t

D43

K. W. Rothschild

1 INTRODUCTION: TYPES OF OLIGOPOLY THEORY

While monopoly and competition have – over the course of years – submitted to fairly clearcut definitions, analytical frameworks, and 'solutions', oligopoly by its very nature remains obstinate and insists on presenting itself as a multi-faceted phenomenon which cannot be forced into a single unified theory. Thus it is not surprising that many different approaches to the oligopoly problem co-exist and that discussions about the applicability and relevance of old and new approaches in different situations are neverending.

There are probably many useful ways of achieving some systematic order for the multitude of oligopoly theories; the following double partition does not claim to be unique or comprehensive. It is only regarded as a useful entry to the subject of this chapter.

I suggest that one can divide oligopoly theories into two different groups in two different ways. Firstly, the essence of oligopoly (or duopoly: the two will be treated as equivalent) can be viewed from two different angles. On the one hand, oligopoly may be seen as a stable market form, in contrast to and apart from monopoly and competition. The appropriate research task becomes then to study the specific interdependences and modes of reaction emerging in such a situation. This is fundamentally a static problem where the usual (neo)classical assumptions of profit-maximising behaviour and the search for equilibrium situations (if any) can be fully maintained. Comparisons with 'pure' competition are a natural by-product of this approach, which is typical for the Cournot–Bertrand–Chamberlin–Stackelberg tradition.

Against this we have an approach which sees oligopolistic groups as precarious formations whose privileges (if any) are constantly threatened by potential entrants. The essence of the oligopolistic problem is then not the *absence* of normal competition as such but the *maintenance* of a special position in a competitive environment. This perspective, which links up with early classical views of competition and which necessarily involves a

155

more dynamic approach, moved massively into the forefront after the Second World War. Belonging to those remarkable phenomena of independent 'multiple discoveries' the middle of the fifties saw the simultaneous publication of the oligopoly theories by Sylos Labini (1956)[1] and Bain (1956) which were immediately recognised as an important advance by Modigliani (1958). These publications – and particularly Sylos' extensive treatment – set off a tremendous expansion of this approach to the oligopoly problem, so much so that some years ago a paper on 'Recent Developments in Oligopoly Theory' given to the American Economic Association restricted itself – because of space limitations – exclusively to this entry problem (Dixit, 1982: p. 12).

The second division of oligopoly theories which I want to mention runs along methodological lines. It is best characterised by the treatment of oligopoly in *The New Palgrave* (Eatwell *et al.*, 1987, Vol. III: pp. 701–8). The eight pages devoted to oligopoly there are equally divided between an article 'Oligopoly' (by Sylos Labini) and an article 'Oligopoly and Game Theory' (by H. Sonnenschein). These two contributions are not treatments of two different theories *about* oligopoly. Many of the oligopoly problems are the same in both articles, and game theory can be applied to both the Cournot and the Sylos approach. The bipartition is based on methodology. The fact that in oligopoly strategic behaviour occupies a place quite unknown in traditional competition and monopoly theory meant that the instruments of game theory developed by von Neumann and Morgenstern in the forties, with its stress on strategic action, looked like a godsend for oligopoly theory, and has in fact proved to be an important tool in tackling various aspects of oligopolistic behaviour. But important as the game-theoretic approach is in opening up new vistas and as a critical counterweight to more 'pedestrian' methods, it cannot be said to be a dominant alternative. The hope that game theory would deliver more definite and singular 'solutions' than 'traditional' (i.e. not *explicitly* game-theoretic) oligopoly theories has to be given up in view of the many different 'decision-trees' and assumptions that can reasonably be suggested with the consequence that 'results are very sensitive to the details of the model' (Sonnenschein, 1987: p. 706).

Even so, game theory might still be regarded as a superior basis because it provides a consistent framework for an analytical approach. Thus, Dixit – in his survey paper already mentioned – claims that 'the new (game-theoretic K. W. R.) work can be characterized by its . . . formulation of logically consistent sets of assumptions and equilibrium concepts to replace earlier ad hoc concepts' (Dixit, 1982: p. 12). Now while it is true that game theory represents a sophisticated and consistent 'paradigm' to study 'rational' strategic behaviour, we must also see that this has been achieved at a cost. As in some other fields of economic theory, the search for ambitious standards of theoretical rigour, analytical tractability, and 'equilibrium' solutions have enforced a concentration on very high levels of abstraction and on a number of rather simplified assumptions, such as very specific attitudes towards risk, high degrees of information regarding the structure of games and strategies, etc. On this basis interesting and useful analytical models can be built and multiplied. They can contribute a lot to our knowledge and to further research. But they cannot be the full story. Firstly, in some game-theoretic models which try to tackle rather difficult strategies the analytical task can only be solved by making such extreme simplifications that their ultimate relevance becomes doubtful. Sylos Labini's plea (in his discussion of some 'old' oligopoly theories) to stick to some 'real world' elements of price determination because 'otherwise we would run the danger of remaining in the fantastic world of reaction curves and conjectural variations – a world where everything might and nothing need happen' (Sylos Labini, 1969: p. 34) seems also justified in some of these cases. Furthermore, game-theoretic models frequently have to introduce *ad hoc* considerations about the assumptions they include regarding the details of their elements and this means that a choice between different 'solutions' remains just as necessary as in the more 'open' approaches of other oligopoly theories. Finally, as soon as the essential elements of incomplete information and uncertainty are introduced the results multiply and become less definite (see Bonanno, 1988).

This shows that the methodological shift to game theory does not alter the fundamental picture of oligopolistic variety and uncertainty. Relying exclusively on the roads which can be opened up with the game-theoretic paradigm contains the danger that some behavioural actions and reactions[2] and some exogenous influences which may be particularly important in this field may get lost. Keynes' insistent demand that in the theoretical analysis of the extremely complex economic reality one should always try to keep quite a number of additional factors 'at the back of one's head' can sometimes be better met in more 'open-ended' models and a judicious experimenting with *well-argued ad hoc* elements than by adhering to a more rigid set of assumptions. What is lost in formal rigour and 'definite' results may be compensated or even more than compensated for by greater opportunities for linking theory with reality and real needs. It seems to me that such a *methodological* position can be detected in Sylos' work when he develops his main ideas about oligopolistic 'equilibrium'. 'The problem is complicated not only because we have introduced so many assumptions, but because we must consider alternative adaptation reactions. For this reason mathematical treatment appears rather difficult (at least to me) and, because it would compel us to adopt greatly simplified assumptions, the result might not repay the effort' (Sylos, 1969: p. 41).

In the following pages I want to present a specific oligopoly (duopoly) problem, viz. a homogeneous market with a big and a small oligopolist in a 'leader' and 'follower' position,[3] in a 'Sylos approach' (dynamic entry problem, 'open' model) and – for the sake of comparison – in a (let us call it) 'Stackelberg approach' (secure duopoly, unique 'Nash' equilibrium). Though the treatment will be simple it is hoped that the possibilities and opportunities (and weaknesses) of the 'open' approach become visible.

2   THE INITIAL POSITION

To begin with we have to state the framework within which we want to discuss our case. We shall try to keep the assumptions as near to Sylos and as simple as possible without endangering our access to the essential aspects of the approaches in question. But it should be kept in mind that the forms of leadership (if any) and of reaction patterns would have to be modified if other (equally simplified and 'plausible') assumptions were adopted.[4] There is no escape from the multiplicity of oligopolistic scenarios.

Our assumptions, then, are as follows. A given homogeneous good can be produced by two different and generally-known techniques, a 'big' and a 'small' technology. In both cases producers face the same *type* of cost function

$$C = K + vX,$$

where X represents the quantity of the good produced, C is the total money cost of production, K are the fixed costs of a plant (including all overheads) and v are the variable costs per unit of output (wages and materials). In other words, we assume constant variable and marginal costs per unit (v) and falling total average cost (economies of scale). The plant has a maximum capacity M so that $X \leq M$. Using the index 1 for the 'big' technology and the index 2 for the 'small' one, the difference between the two technologies is characterised as follows:

$$M_1 > M_2$$
$$K_1 > K_2$$
$$v_1 < v_2$$

$$C_1/M_1 < C_2/M_2$$

The last inequality states that running at full capacity the big technology (big firm) is more efficient than the small technology (small firm). This is not self-evident and need not be the case. As we know, the question about the relative efficiencies of small and big firms remains on the research agenda and has recently met with renewed interest. But in our presentation this assumption of positive economies of scale effects will be maintained.[5] This also provides the basis for the further assumption that a 'big' firm (using the 'big' technology) obtains a leadership position *vis-à-vis* the 'small' firm. Both its greater efficiency and its size (usually combined with greater financial reserves) represent a threat potential which induces smaller firms to adopt a passive follower strategy.

We can now turn to our concrete (numerical) example. We have two firms, a big one (Firm 1) using the 'big' technology and a small one (Firm 2) using the 'small' technology. The cost functions of a big and a small plant are respectively:

$$C_1 = 24\ 000 + 140X_1$$
$$C_2 = 2\ 000 + 160X_2$$

The respective capacity outputs per plant are

$$M_1 = 8000; \quad M_2 = 1000$$

The two firms work in a market with the following demand conditions more or less known to the producers:

$$P = 920 - 0.08\ X$$

where P is the market-clearing price of the homogeneous good and $X = X_1 + X_2$.

We can now derive right away the unique 'solution' of the Stackelberg case where the two duopolists take their position for granted and follow the usual profit maximisation procedure (under the leadership constraint). Using the same symbols for costs as before and adding π for profits and $P = A - BX$ for the demand function we get

$$\pi_1 = PX_1 - K_1 - v_1X_1 = [A - B(X_1 + X_2)]\ X_1 - K_1 - v_1X_1$$

$$\pi_2 = PX_2 - K_2 - v_2X_2 = [A - B(X_1 + X_2)]\ X_2 - K_2 - v_2X_2$$

Profit maximisation for firm 2 is derived by differentiating the second equation and setting it equal to zero:

$$\frac{d\pi_2}{dX_2} = A - BX_1 - 2BX_2 - v_2 = 0$$

This yields

$$X_2 = \frac{A - v_2 - BX_1}{2B}$$

This is the 'reaction function' of firm 2. It shows the optimal output decision once the output of the leader (X_1) is given. Knowing this reaction behaviour the big firm's profit equation becomes

$$\pi_1 = \frac{1}{2}[AX_1 - BX_1^2 - X_1(2v_1 - v_2) - 2K_1]$$

which leads to

$$\frac{d\pi_1}{dX_1} = \frac{1}{2}[A - 2BX_1 + v_2 - 2v_1]$$

Setting the term in brackets equal to zero we obtain the profit-maximising output for the big firm (X_1) and substituting this in the reaction function yields the corresponding optimum output of the small firm:

$$X_1 = \frac{A + v_2 - 2v_1}{2B}; \ X_2 = \frac{A - 3v_2 + 2v_1}{4B}$$

With $A = 920$, $B = 0.08$, $v_1 = 140$, $v_2 = 160$ we obtain the 'equilibrium' values contained in line 1 of Table 10.1. As we can see, these yield an output of 5000 for the big firm, leaving an 'excess capacity' of 3000 units. For the small firm the optimal quantity is 2250 which is more than the

Table 10.1

	X_1	X_2	X	P	π_1	π_2
1	5 000	2 250	7 250	340	976 000	399 000
2	4 925	2 188	7 113	351	946 225	376 900
3	5 319	2 409	7 728	353	1 108 947	458 937

Notes: 1: $K_1 = 24\,000$, $K_2 = 2\,000$; $v_1 = 140$, $v_2 = 160$; $P = 920 - 0.08\,X$
2: Like 1 but: $v_1 = 154$, $v_2 = 176$
3: Like 1 but: $P = 971 - 0.08\,X$

maximum output of one small plant. But this can be overcome by adding two further small plants (leaving an excess capacity of 750 units). This will add further fixed costs (of 4000) which do not change the optimum point, which depends only on marginal (= variable) costs. The duopoly price is 340 and the combined profits of the two duopolists amount to 1375 000. They could be increased to 1877 250 by combining in a monopoly, closing down the less efficient smaller firm, and selling an output of 4875 units at a price of 530. But the assumption is that for reasons of independence, mistrust, prestige, or what-have-you, such a combined policy is not introduced.[6]

We turn now to the alternative approach which we call the 'Sylos approach' for short. Again we have two firms, a big one and a small one ('big' and 'small' always including technologies), but the perspective changes. The two firms are no longer (primarily) concerned to exploit to the maximum their present duopolistic hold on the market. Their main worry is to protect their sheltered position against potential intruders.[7] Within this constraint they want to earn 'good' or 'satisfactory' profits, which should be above the 'normal' profits which are regarded as an essential long-run minimum, but need not necessarily be maximum profits which may not be targeted for various reasons (insecure information, habit, 'peaceful coexistence', etc.).

Thus we cannot expect a unique 'solution' as we had in the previous case. Rather, a number of possible constellations can be envisaged and this is certainly more in line with reality. We start off with *one possible* constellation which we can regard as inherited from past history or as a *prix crié au hasard* (Sylos Labini, 1969: p. 36). This case is pictured in line 1a of Table 10.2. Both firms (with one plant each) produce at full capacity (where the respective average costs reach their minimum). The output equals $M_1 + M_2 = 9000$ units which can be sold at a price of 200. The resulting profits are 456 000 for the big firm and 38 000 for the small one. Is this a 'viable' long-run constellation?

The first question to be asked is whether the profits are sufficient to keep the firms in production. In order to answer this question we have to know what the normal rate of profit is. Designing this 'normal' rate with R we shall assume throughout the following considerations that $R = 5$ per cent. The numerical specifications of our example show that both firms earn a profit which lies well above 5 per cent.[8]

The second question is whether the constellation is threatened by new entries. To answer this question we introduce the idea of a critical price level, the 'entry-preventing' price. If a potential competitor can expect to sell his technologically determined capacity output at a price which will

Table 10.2

	X_1	X_2	X_3	X	P	π_1	π_2
1a	8 000	1 000	–	9 000	200	456 000	38 000
1b	7 500	1 000	–	8 500	240	726 000	78 000
2a	8 000	1 000	–	9 000	200	344 000	22 000
2b	7 289	911	–	8 200	264	777 790	78 168
3a	8 000	1 000	–	9 000	240	776 000	78 000
3b	8 000	1 000	1 000	10 000	171	224 000	9 000
3c	7 250	1 000	1 000	9 250	231	635 750	69 000
3d	8 250	1 000	–	9 250	231	719 750	69 000
3e	8 000	1 250	–	9 250	231	704 000	84 750
3f	8 000	1 000	–	9 000	240	774 200	76 200

Notes: See the notes to Table 10.1; 3f: like 3, but $K_1 = 25\,800$, $K_2 = 3800$

yield at least normal profits then he will be prepared to enter the market. The price below which entry becomes unprofitable is called the entry-preventing price. The incumbents who want to prevent entry will take this into account when setting their prices or quantities. Using our previous notation the entry-preventing price (Pe) of an outsider can be calculated from the formula

$$Pe = (K/M + v)(1 + R),$$

i.e. the price he expects must cover at least average total costs plus a normal rate of profit. Using this formula and our data we obtain entry-preventing price levels of 150.2 for the big firm and 170.1 for the small firm. With these 'critical' price levels no entry will take place in our situation (line 1a, Table 10.2). For if a small firm were to enter the market, output would rise from 9000 to 10 000 and this would send the price down to 120 (see the demand equation on p. 159). This is well below the entry-preventing price of 170.1. The case is even more disadvantageous for a big firm.[9]

We see, therefore, that the 'historical' situation depicted in line 1a (Table 10.2) is a viable one: profits are 'sufficient' and there is no threat of entry. But other possibilities may exist. One possibility could be that the more efficient firm tries to eliminate the weaker firm in order to capture the entire market for itself. This introduces Sylos' second 'critical' price level, the 'elimination price'. This price corresponds to the variable costs of the firm to be eliminated. Below this price this firm will stop production. After a longer period (when the fixed equipment has disappeared) the victorious firm can raise its price to the new entry-preventing level and reach higher profits. Whether such a policy pays depends on the loss of profits in the beginning, the higher profits obtainable later, the length of the intervening period, and the discount rate used.[10]

When coexistence is maintained and desired, other viable positions with higher profits (for both firms) may be obtainable and may be found by experimenting, learning or through perfect information. Taking our example and assuming that output can only be changed in lots of 250 units we obtain a 'menu' of alternatives as given in Table 10.3. In the rows we have alternative output levels of firm 1 (the big firm) while the columns contain different output levels of firm 2. In each box three figures are given: the first states the price at which the combined output can be sold on the market (given the previously stated demand conditions), and the second and third figures show the profits of firm 1 and 2 respectively. The situation from which we started out (line 1a in Table 10.2) is shown in the lower right-hand corner where both firms produce at full capacity. All the other boxes represent constellations where one or the other or both firms cut down production. Of the combinations shown, only those below and to the right of the thick line are 'viable' positions if new entry is to be prevented. In all

Table 10.3

Output 1 \ Output 2	250	500	750	1 000
7 250	320 1 281 000 38 000	300 1 136 000 68 000	280 991 000 88 000	260 846 000 98 000
7 500	300 1 176 000 33 000	280 1 026 000 58 000	260 876 000 73 000	240 726 000 78 000
7 750	280 1 061 000 28 000	260 906 000 48 000	240 751 000 58 000	220 596 000 58 000
8 000	260 936 000 23 000	240 776 000 38 000	220 616 000 43 000	200 456 000 38 000

these positions price does not rise above 240 and sales do not fall below 8500 units. A new (small) entrant would add another 1000 units which would drive the price down to 160 which lies below the entry-preventing price. Going beyond this line, where further output restriction brings higher profits for both duopolists, is excluded because of threatened entry. With a price of 260 and sales of 8250 units a further 1000 units would bring price down to 180 which would permit profitable production for a new firm.

As can be seen from Table 10.3 the initial 'historical' position from which we started is not the optimal one among the viable constellations as far as profitability is concerned. Other combinations yield better results. For firm 1 the 'ideal' solution would be to maintain full production while firm 2 reduces output by 500 (50 per cent of its capacity). But this would give no advantage whatsoever to firm 2 whose profits would be unchanged. The ideal solution for firm 2 lies in the opposite direction: maintaining its own output while firm 1 reduces output by 500 (= 6.25 per cent of its capacity). This would still leave firm 1 with much higher profits than in the initial position so that this constellation can be regarded as a particularly 'acceptable' solution in a 'peaceful' duopoly environment with an entry-preventing strategy. This constellation is summarised in line 1b in Table 10.2 and will serve as an alternative benchmark to the full-capacity case (line 1a) in the following section. At a price of 240, 8500 units are sold. This compares with a price of 340 and 7250 units in the 'sheltered' Stackelberg case and with a price just over 170 and 9370 units in the 'contestable market' case where fixed costs are not sunk costs.

So far we have looked at the firms as quantity setters. Since mark-up pricing is a well-known phenomenon in oligopolistic markets, we shall have to consider such behaviour in the following section where changing costs are discussed. Now, the size of the mark-up (meaning here mark-up on variable costs) will be influenced by various factors: role of fixed costs, normal profits, potential competition, cyclical factors, etc. But *in the short run* the mark-up shows a tendency to remain constant for various reasons (habit, ease of calculation and, particularly, prevention of price wars between oligopolistic rivals),[11] and thus is a 'historic' magnitude. If we assume that the situation contained in line 1b of Table 10.2 has lasted for some time, we can regard the mark-ups involved in this situation as firm-specific (short-period) constants. Writing Q for the mark-up we have, by definition:

$$P = Q.v \quad \text{or} \quad Q = P/v.$$

Substituting the values from Table 10.2 we obtain for the two firms:

$$Q_1 = 1.71 \text{ and } Q_2 = 1.5.^{12}$$

3   A RISE IN COSTS

Having established an initial position we can now proceed to a discussion of the effects of exogenous changes. Higher costs are discussed in this section and an increase in demand in the following one.

Our simple assumption is that variable costs rise for all firms (incumbents and potential competitors) equally by 10 per cent while fixed costs remain unchanged. Average variable and marginal costs now become 154 for big plants and 176 for a small plant. The change in the Stackelberg case is again unequivocal and is immediately obtained by substituting these new values in the 'equilibrium' equations given on pp. 159–60. The results are shown in line 2 of Table 10.1. As one would expect, prices rise and output and profits fall as compared with the initial position.

The road is less certain when we turn to the Sylos case. Starting with the 'suboptimal' case of line 1a in Table 10.2, where both firms produced at full capacity, a possible strategy consists in sticking to these output decisions in spite of the cost increases. A motive for this might be that uncertainty exists whether higher prices might not induce some 'inconsiderate' person to enter the market. There can also be the long-term motive to keep one's absolute share in market demand. This output-maintaining policy is a *possible* policy because the oligopolistic profits in the initial situation (1a) were well above normal profits. Line 2a in Table 10.2 shows the results of such an output-maintaining full-capacity strategy. With unchanged output and demand conditions price remains unchanged at 200. Revenue is therefore unchanged. Because of the higher variable costs profits fall (by 25 per cent for firm 1 and 42 per cent for firm 2) but being still above the 'normal' 5 per cent they are 'sufficient' to keep the firms in production. The entry-preventing situation is now *strengthened* since, with the higher cost, the minimum entry price has gone up to 187 for a small firm which lies far above the price of 120 which would result from an output expansion of 1000.[13]

Next we turn to mark-up strategies. Since in this case capacity output is not regarded as a fix-point, we take as initial position the 'optimal' constellation of line 1b. The proportional rise of variable costs for all firms fosters a tacit understanding that these costs will be passed on by everybody so that no loss of market *shares* has to be feared. With constant mark-ups on variable costs the market price will be raised from the initial 240 to 264 (plus 10 per cent) and the position of line 2b (Table 10.2) is reached. With the rise in price demand falls by 3.5 per cent from 8500 to 8200. Assuming that this decline is divided proportionately between the two firms we obtain their respective output and profit data in line 2b. *Both* firms are now producing below capacity, but their profits are slightly *higher* than before the cost increase because fixed costs have remained unchanged while price has been set in line with higher variable costs. The viability of the new situation is secured since entry-prevention remains intact. A new (small) firm would extend output from 8200 to 9200 with a consequent reduction in price to 184 which lies below the (new) entry-preventing price of 187.

Other viable constellations can easily be constructed, based on intermediate strategies, changes in fixed costs, mark-ups etc., but the two examples should suffice to show that even a slight consideration of entry-prevention and uncertainty opens the road to a multitude of viable 'solutions', some of which run counter to the 'plausible' results of the secure, profit-maximising duopoly case where (in our case) cost increases lead unequivocally to higher prices, lower output and *lower* profits.

4   HIGHER DEMAND

We return now to the original cost conditions as given on page 159, but assume that demand increases. We replace the previous demand equation $P = 920 - 0.08\,X$ by a new one: $P = 971 - 0.08\,X$. The Stackelberg solution given in line 3 of Table 10.1 and compared with line 1 (the old demand conditions) yields the expected results: the higher demand leads to higher outputs in both firms and to higher prices, with a consequent clear increase in profits.

The 'Sylos' cases, discussed in Table 10.2, are again samples from a variety of possibilities. When demand increases, market clearing prices for existing outputs would go up. But charging these prices would immediately attract competitors since the old prices were chosen with an eye on entry-prevention. With costs and mark-ups unchanged, firms will stick to their old prices. If they were previously producing at full capacity (1a, Table 10.2) the output, price, and profit situation of both firms will remain unchanged. But since in the new demand position customers would prefer to buy 9638 units an excess demand of 638 units will exist.[14] When the initial position is characterised by excess capacity (1b, Table 10.2) then the increase in demand will call forth additional supplies and we arrive at the situation 3a in Table 10.2. Price remains fixed at 240; but firm 1, which before found it profitable to keep production down to 7500 units, can now increase profits by extending output to full capacity without having to lower the price. Nothing is changed for firm 2 which had already been working at full capacity. But in this situation, too, the market is not in equilibrium. At a price of 240, 9138 units are demanded, so that excess demand on a smaller scale still exists.

But both these constellations are precarious. With the increase in demand and higher market *equilibrium* prices, the former entry-prevention effects are lost at the old price levels. Opening a new small firm and adding another 1000 units of output would bring total output to 10 000 which would now catch a market price of 171 which lies above the entry-preventing price of a small firm (170.1; see p. 162). Several 'scenarios' are now possible. If the incumbents are 'slow' and fail to react to this loss of entry-barriers a third firm can be set up and the oligopoly structure has changed from two to three firms. The immediate effects are shown in line 3b. Output will increase to 10 000 and the price will be forced down to the market equilibrium of 171. Profits to the incumbents have fallen sharply, but are still 'sufficient'. The new third firm earns the same profits as the existing small firm (9000). Rather paradoxically, therefore, the result of a demand increase can be a *fall* in price in consequence of a break-up of a 'petrified' oligopoly structure.

The new situation is 'viable', in so far as the incumbents earn (slightly) above-normal profits and the new price secures entry-prevention. But better positions can be reached by 'experimenting' with new prices and mark-ups. Assuming again as before (see p. 163) that output can only be changed in lots of 250, a new and 'peaceful' position can be reached if the big firm makes an even sharper reduction in its output than in the initial position. Cutting it down to 7250 and thus reducing total output to 9250 pushes the market price up to 231. Profits are now not much lower than in the initial position (see line 3c). But note that the price is still below the level which ruled before the demand-rise (240). The new situation is viable, because adding another 1000 units would bring the price down to 151 which is below the entry-preventing price.[15]

Other consequences of a rise in demand follow when the incumbents react more quickly to the threat of new competitors. One obvious way is the provision of additional capacity (one small plant) before an outsider steps in. Then the 'optimal' viable position (keeping out further entry) can be shared by the two duopolists rather than by three firms. Whoever comes first in installing the new plant will have an advantage. Line 3d assumes that firm 1 adds an additional (small) plant, in line 3e it is firm 2 which acts more quickly. In both cases total output must not be reduced below 9250 (price not be raised beyond 231) in order to keep outsiders out. This threat continues to keep prices and profits below the initial position (line 1b),[16] but profits are – at least for the big firm – higher than if a third firm had captured the extra demand (line 3c).

If stability of mark-ups and prices (at unchanged costs) are regarded as important (for whatever reasons) a secure position for the incumbents can be achieved by erecting stronger barriers against entry. This can be done in different ways, e.g. through advertising,[17] through service networks, trade associations, etc. which become *necessary* additional costs if the product is to be saleable. As an example, let us assume that – after the increase in demand – the big firm (the 'leader') introduces additional 'necessary' accessories which add another 1800 to fixed costs. These have now to be met by every firm that wants to market its output. Fixed costs now climb to 25 800 for a big firm and 3800 for a small firm compared with 24 000 and 2000 in the initial position. This increases the entry-preventing price for a big firm from 150.2 to 150.4 and for a small firm from 170.1 to 172.[18] These entry prices turn the fixed-price constellation into a viable position; it is contained in line 3f, Table 10.2. Compared with the position before the demand increase (line 1b, Table 10.2) firm 1 will extend output to full capacity. With a combined output of 9000, supply will remain below demand at that price (9138 units), but new firms will not enter, since another 1000 units would take output to 10 000 units, depressing prices to 171 which is now below the entry-preventing price. Profits of the incumbents will be slightly depressed by the higher fixed costs, but will still be much higher for the big firm than in the case of entry-prevention via a reduction of the market price (lines 3d and 3e). For the small firm the results depend on which route would have been taken in the price-reduction case, but being in the follower-position it cannot escape the additional costs once the big firm has decided on such a course.

5   CONCLUDING REMARKS

The foregoing simple exercise in oligopolistic scenarios which took its cue from Sylos Labini's pathbreaking work (without, however, matching its richness) is meant to show how the introduction of insecurity of position, slight degrees of uncertainty and incomplete information, sequence of actions, etc., can result in very different outcomes of which only a few have been illustrated in the above examples. By contrasting them with the seemingly exact and unique results which can be obtained from models on traditional profit-maximising lines, one comes to a greater awareness of the well-known indefiniteness and multiplicity of oligopoly situations which cannot possibly be captured in one or even a few neat and 'exact' models.

While such models may be (and are) useful to highlight certain elements of the oligopolistic situation and their logical consequences, any 'exact' solutions delivered by them have only provisional validity (see the quotation from Sonnenschein, 1987 on p. 156). Openness of approach can be important. From this point of view case studies, numerical and graphic exercises, and so on, have a role to play in addition to or in place of more 'exact' but less open analytical models – more so in the sphere of oligopoly than in other branches of price and market structure theory.

Notes

1. In 1956 there appeared the first edition of Sylos Labini's work in Italian, to be replaced by a revised edition in the following year. An English translation appeared in 1962 and a revised edition in 1969 (Sylos Labini, 1969). Quotations in this article refer to this last edition.
2. Including such 'unorthodox' elements like satisficing behaviour, X-inefficiency, habit, bounded rationality, prestige, etc.
3. At this stage we do not have to distinguish between price or quantity leaders. Since we assume that the firms know the market demand conditions they can translate prices into quantities and vice versa. The distinction becomes important when we turn to attitudes under changing conditions, when we have to distinguish between price *or* quantity rigidities.
4. With regard to alternative variants of leadership and their causes see Ono (1982) and the literature quoted there. See also Ono (1978).
5. This is in line with Sylos' original assumptions in his book. Later (Sylos, 1987, Vol. III: p. 704) he has stressed that recent developments in technology, work organisation, and demand differentiation have reduced the weight of scale economies. Specialisation and differentiation have gained in importance for oligopolistic market power.
6. This, by the way, shows that also approaches adhering to profit-maximising behaviour occasionally stop short of the full consequences of this axiom by introducing (*ad hoc*? realistically?) additional factors.
7. With this assumption Sylos' approach was, of course, an important forerunner of the more recent theory of contestable markets (Baumol *et al.*, 1982), the main difference being that the latter theory puts the stress on the relative insignificance of sunk costs and the opportunities for quick and profitable raids into oligopolistic markets while Sylos and others are more aware of the remaining barriers to entry. See on this also Dixit (1982, pp. 15 ff) and Davies and Lee (1988).
8. The total outlays are 1 144 000 for the big firm and 162 000 for the small firm.
9. The reasoning here assumes that the insiders stick to their previous output levels after the entry of the new firm. This assumption, which has been named *Sylos Postulate* by Modigliani (Modigliani, 1958: p. 217) has been called into question by several writers (see e.g. Dixit, 1982: p.12). But it seems not an unrealistic assumption. Partly it may reflect real behaviour by

170   *Market and Institutions in Economic Development*

      the incumbents who want to maintain their hold on the market. But it is also sufficient that potential competitors act on this belief, which may just be a 'worst case strategy'.

10.   In our example the situation looks as follows. The elimination price is 160. At this price demand expands to 9500. To fill this demand the big firm must add two small plants and reaps a profit of 132 000 compared with 456 000 before the price-war. After the disappearance of the rival factory, one of the small plants can be closed and production can be reduced to 8375 with a price of 250. This deters entry (since a supply of 9375 would depress prices to 170 which is below the entry-preventing price) and enables the surviving firm to make profits to the tune of 887 750.

11.   See on this Okun (1981: p. 165); Bhaskar (1988: p. 382).

12.   Incidentally, these artificial values are not unrealistic. In an article on prices and incomes in manufacturing Sylos Labini calculated mark-ups on variable labour and material costs of 1.8 for Italy and 1.75 for the USA for 1953 (Sylos Labini, 1979: p. 14).

13.   This fact that entry-prevention is *strengthened* when incumbents stick to their output (and prices) after costs have increased makes such a strategy more plausible when uncertainty and fear regarding potential entrants exist.

14.   The excess demand may involve waiting lists, black markets, search activities, etc. In an open economy the additional demand may be satisfied through imports (Sylos Labini, 1979: p. 5).

15.   A further cut in production to 7000 units (total output: 9000) with a market price of 251 is precluded because that would encourage new entry, since another 1000 units would leave prices still at 171.

16.   The small firm can increase its profits if it extends its capacity (line 3e).

17.   Since we are dealing with a homogeneous commodity advertising may seem out of place. This is true if we look at homogeneity in its widest (economic) sense. If we restrict it, however, to the physical aspects of the good, trade marks and advertising may play an important part (see, for instance, the retail sales of petrol).

18.   Fixed costs at full capacity (K/M) rise from 3 to 3.23 and from 2 to 3.8 respectively. Remembering that normal profits are 5 per cent the entry price for the small firm is obtained from

$$P = (3.8 + 160) \cdot 1.05 = 172.$$

References

Bain, J. S., (1956) *Barriers to New Competition* (Cambridge, Mass.: Harvard University Press).

Baumol, W. J., Panzar, J. C., Willig, R. D. (1982) *Contestable Markets and the Theory of Industry Structure* (San Diego: Harcourt Brace Jovanovich).

Bhaskar, V. (1988) 'The Kinked Demand Curve', *International Journal of Industrial Organisation*, Vol. 6, pp. 373–84.

Bonanno, G. (1988) 'Entry Deterrence with Uncertain Entry and Uncertain Observability of Commitment', *International Journal of Industrial Organisation*, Vol. 6, pp. 351–62.

Davies, J. E. and Lee, F. S. (1988) 'A Post-Keynesian Appraisal of the Contestability Criterion', *Journal of Post Keynesian Economics*, Vol. 11, pp. 3–24.

Dixit, A. (1982) 'Recent Developments in Oligopoly Theory', *American Economic Review*, Papers and Proceedings, Vol. 72, pp. 12–17.

Eatwell, J., Milgate, M., Newman, P. (eds) (1987) *The New Palgrave* (New York: Stockton Press).

Modigliani, F. (1958) 'New Developments on the Oligopoly Front', *Journal of Political Economy*, Vol. 66, pp. 215–32.

Okun, A. M. (1981) *Prices and Quantities: A Macroeconomic Analysis* (Oxford: Basil Blackwell).

Ono, Y. (1978) 'The Equilibrium of Duopoly in a Market of Homogeneous Goods', *Economica*, Vol. 45, pp. 287–95.

—— (1982) 'Price Leadership: A Theoretical Analysis', *Economica*, Vol. 49, pp. 11–20.

Sonnenschein, H. (1987) 'Oligopoly and Game Theory', in Eatwell *et al.*

Sylos Labini, P. (1956) *Oligopolio e progresso tecnico* (Milano: Guffré).

—— (1969) *Oligopoly and Technical Progress* (revised edition) (Cambridge, Mass.: Harvard University Press).

—— (1979) 'Prices and Income Distribution in Manufacturing Industry', *Journal of Post Keynesian Economics*, Vol. 2, pp. 3–25.

—— (1987) 'Oligopoly', in Eatwell *et al.*

PART FOUR

POLICY

19

207-22

RATIONING AND THE CONSUMER
By K. W. ROTHSCHILD

[1945]

I

IN this war rationing was not only introduced at a much earlier stage than in the last war; it also covers a much wider range of goods. Furthermore, in addition to 'straight' rationing of various commodities, which alone was used in the 1914–18 war, a new method has been evolved: point rationing. Under this method several commodities—usually, to some extent, substitutes—are grouped together and a certain value of points is allotted to each of them. Then everybody is given a certain number of points at regular intervals, which he can spend on the commodities within the group according to his own choice. Usually, but not necessarily, there is also some price control with regard to the point-rationed goods.

At present, there are four different point-ration schemes at work in this country. One comprises all articles of clothing, clothing material, etc., the second scheme rations certain foodstuffs, like most tinned food, dried fruit, rice, cereals, etc., the third relates to soap, soap flakes and similar products, and finally all chocolates and sweets are distributed in exchange for points.

The advantage of point rationing in these cases is fairly obvious. In the case of staple foods, like sugar, meat, fats, etc., straight rationing is a perfectly satisfactory method, since practically everybody consumes these commodities in more or less stable quantities. Rationing here secures a just distribution of the scarce quantities after prices have been fixed, which in turn is necessary in order to prevent these essential goods from going to the people with the highest incomes.[1] But if rationing is extended to less essential goods or to commodities where a wide variety of related goods serves the satisfaction of the same want, straight rationing is a very crude and unsatisfactory method. For, in contrast to the staple foods, different consumers will want to consume these commodities in very different proportions, and if no choice is allowed to them a black market in coupons and rationed goods is bound to arise. Point rationing, by

---

[1] In other words, price-fixing prevents unfair distribution in response to inequalities in income and wealth, while rationing prevents unfair distribution in response to time available for queuing up or to the influence people might have in the grocer's shop.

giving people a fairly wide choice between related substitutes over-comes this difficulty. At the same time, by restricting the total amount which can be obtained by a single consumer, it can secure a fair distribution of these commodities.

II

The advent of modern economic theory was marked above all by a rewriting of the theory of value. What determines the value of a commodity to an individual and how an individual will behave in a market where different commodities are offered at given prices, these were the questions treated by most economists in the second part of last century and in the beginning of this century. The problem was approached in two different ways. The one, chosen by the Austrians, by Jevons, Marshall, and by others, is the marginal utility approach;[1] the second, which has been developed by Edge-worth, Pareto, and more recently by Hicks and Allen, is the method of indifference curves.[2] Both these theories, in spite of certain shortcomings with regard to their psychological foundation and their assumptions as to people's rationality of choice, give us a satisfactory model of a consumer's behaviour in a free market.[3] Given his income, his utility schedules, or his preferences, and the prices ruling in the market, we can say how he will spend his income.

The introduction of straight rationing and the consequent limita-tion of the free market do not raise any important difficulties in the treatment of consumer's choice. The effects of rationing can be shown by either of the two approaches mentioned before. In what follows we shall, however, use the method of indifference curves only, because it seems to the writer that they permit a more satis-factory demonstration of the problems at hand.

Here, then, is the 'behaviour' of a consumer under straight rationing. In Fig. 1 let X represent the rationed commodity, and Y 'money', or 'purchasing power in general'.[4] OL represents the

---

[1] See F. Wieser, *Natural Value*; A. Marshall, *Principles of Economics*, 3rd Book.

[2] See Pareto, *Manuel d'économie politique*; J. R. Hicks, *Value and Capital*, Part I.

[3] We have only to assume a free market from the consumer's point of view, i.e. he must be able to get any amount of a commodity at the current price. Monopolistic or govern-mental restrictions on the supply side leading to price-fixing or similar policies do not affect the theory of consumer's choice. (They leave unaffected the 'freedom of the con-sumer', though they affect the 'sovereignty of the consumer').

[4] See Hicks, op. cit., p. 33.

amount of X that could be bought with a given income, and OM is this income measured in £'s (or the amount of all other commodities taken together that can be obtained with that income). In the absence of market restrictions this consumer will reach a a position of equilibrium at the point P, buying the amount ON of X (the price of this quantity being SM) and spending OS on all other commodities.[1]

Suppose now that rationing is introduced. If the amount of X allowed to a consumer is greater than ON, the amount consumed

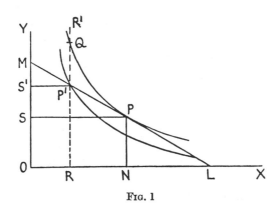

FIG. 1

before the introduction of rationing, then nothing will be changed and the consumer will spend his income as before. In most cases, however, rationing will mean a curtailment in the consumption of the rationed commodity, and this is the situation illustrated in Fig. 1.

Let OR be the amount of X allowed to every person. Then it will no longer be possible for a consumer with income OM to reach the point P, where LM is tangent to one of the indifference curves. Instead, a new equilibrium is given at the Point P^1, where LM cuts RR^1, the 'ration line'. (RR^1 is a parallel to OY through R.) This is a perfectly stable equilibrium, since P^1 lies on the highest indifference curve that can be reached under the given conditions. It will be noted, however, that P^1 lies on a lower indifference curve than P—i.e. if rationing is effective the consumer will be worse off than he would have been in a free market, provided prices and income are the same in both cases. He will now consume less of the

[1] Ibid., p. 16 and *passim*.

rationed commodity—*OR* instead of *ON*—and more of other commodities[1]—*OS*[1] instead of *OS*.

By drawing lines parallel to *LM* and by drawing a family of straight lines through *M* we can see that both the income-consumption curve[2] and the price-consumption curve[3] will coincide with the line *RR*[1] as long as *ON* is greater than *OR*. This is, of course, only the diagrammatic expression of the fact that any increase in income has to be spent entirely on non-rationed goods, and that in the case of a change in the price of the rationed commodity no substitution is possible. In fact, every such price change can only produce an income effect; rationing has reduced the substitution effect to zero.

Finally, with the help of the diagram we can also show by what means we can restore to a consumer the same 'amount of satisfaction' which he enjoyed before rationing was introduced. In Fig. 1, the consumer will regain his former amount of satisfaction at the point *Q*, where the ration line *RR*[1] crosses the indifference curve containing *P*, the pre-rationing point of equilibrium. He will only be able to reach this point if the line *LM* is raised until it passes through *Q*. This can be achieved in three different ways: (1) We can raise the consumer's income (this would be represented on the diagram by a line parallel to *LM* and passing through *Q*); or (2) we can reduce the price of the rationed commodity (a line passing through *M* and *Q*); or (3) we can reduce the prices of the other commodities (a line passing through *L* and *Q*). These three methods can also be combined.

This last paragraph shows that even in cases where incomes go up to the same extent as a truly representative cost of living index,[4] this will still leave the income receivers worse off, if rationing has been introduced.[5]

---

[1] 'Other commodities' includes saving.
[2] Hicks, op. cit., p. 27.
[3] Ibid., p. 30.
[4] The Ministry of Labour Index understates the rise in the cost of living.
[5] The problem of devising an index number that would take account of the effects of rationing is dealt with by E. Rothbarth in 'The Measurement of Changes in Real Income under Conditions of Rationing', *The Review of Economic Studies*, Vol. VIII, No. 2, and N. Kaldor, 'Rationing and the Cost of Living Index', ibid., Vol. VIII, No. 3. The latter article, which came to my notice only after this was written, uses the same diagrammatic approach as I do in Fig. 1.

III

The foregoing analysis has summarized in a convenient form facts about straight rationing which are by now common knowledge of all housewives. Let us now turn to an examination of consumer's choice under point rationing where the situation is a little more complex. If we take *all* the commodities which come under one of the point schemes as one group and all the remaining commodities as another group, we can apply immediately the method which we used in the case of straight rationing. Only that we have now to enter the whole group of point-rationed goods on the x-axis and all the other goods on the y-axis. The rest of the analysis can follow the same lines as in the case of a single-rationed commodity.[1]

The interesting case, however, is the behaviour of a consumer with respect to the choice between commodities which belong to the same point scheme. For here a new problem arises which occurs neither in a free market nor under straight rationing. In a free market the consumer has a given income, and he exerts his choice by spending this income on various goods with given prices. Under rationing, in so far as it is effective, he has no choice at all. Under point rationing he has to make a double choice. He will have a certain amount of money which he is prepared to spend on the point-rationed goods, taking account of their prices; and he will have a given 'income' of points which he can spend on the same goods, though this time it will be their point-value that will influence his choice.[2] How, then, can we illustrate the consumer's behaviour under these conditions?

There are three cases we have to consider. For the sake of simplicity we shall restrict our analysis to the case of two point-rationed goods.

(1) *The choice of the consumer is mainly influenced by the point-value of the commodities.*

In Fig. 2 let X and Y be the point-rationed commodities purchasable with the same type of coupons. Let the line LM represent

---

[1] There arises, however, a slight complication owing to the possibility of changes in the relative prices of the point-rationed goods.

[2] The rationale of this double currency lies, of course, in the inequality of incomes. The introduction of points has the purpose of leaving the consumer free choice and at the same time preventing the 'plural voting' of the higher incomes. If there were absolute equality of income there would be little need for point rationing, though straight rationing might still be retained for certain staple foods as part of the health policy of a country.

the amounts in which these two commodities can be bought at their current prices with that proportion of the total income which the consumer wants to spend on these two goods,[1] and let *lm* be the amounts of these commodities that can be obtained at their current point values with a given point-income. As far as prices and money-income is concerned the highest amounts of satisfaction will be reached at the point *Q*, while with regard to point-value and point-income, satisfaction will be maximized at *P*. As points as well as

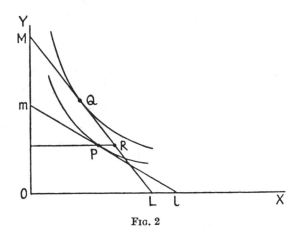

Fɪɢ. 2

money have to be given up in order to obtain the commodities, it is clear that in this case *P* will be the point of equilibrium, as no higher indifference curve can be reached under the given conditions.

It can easily be seen that in the case of point rationing we get, in addition to the price consumption and income consumption curve, a point-value consumption and point-income consumption curve. In the case considered just now only the latter two will effectively influence the amount and relative proportions in which the two commodities are consumed. Changes in their prices or in the consumer's money-income will leave his demand for *X* and *Y* unchanged. They will only influence the size of the surplus of this part of his income which will be available for the purchase of other goods. If we draw a line parallel to *OX* through *P* to cut *LM* in *R*, the size of

[1] This proportion is a function of the total income, of the prices of the point-rationed goods, and of the prices of all other commodities. It can be obtained with the help of the previously mentioned diagram, containing all the point-rationed goods on *x*-axis and the other goods on the *y*-axis. Or, alternatively, with an indifference surface of three dimensions.

this surplus can be expressed as $PR \times p_x f$, where PR is a quantity of X equivalent to a segment of the same size on the x-axis, and p_x is the price of one unit of X.[1]

In practice, we should think that this case is the typical one with regard to all point-rationing schemes for people with higher incomes. It will also be fairly generally typical with regard to rationing of sweets and soap, where the rations and the controlled prices are comparatively small with regard to the proportion of income usually devoted to these goods.

In so far as this case prevails it is clear that desired changes in the total or relative consumption of the point-rationed commodities can only be accomplished by changes in the consumer's point income or in the relative point values of the articles.[2] Small changes in the money-income of the consumer or in the prices of the goods would leave the position unaffected; though such changes might be used to divert purchasing power from or to other goods.

(2) *The choice of the consumer is solely influenced by the prices of the commodities.* This is the exact counterpart of the previous case In Fig. 2 let now *lm* represent the combinations of the two commodities which can be bought with a given proportion of the consumer's income, and *LM* the combinations he can obtain with his point-income. *P* will be the point of equilibrium, and the consumer will have a surplus of unspent points. Changes in point-values or in point-income will leave his total and relative consumption unaltered; they will only affect the amount of his unused coupons. He will, however, react to changes in the prices of the point-rationed articles and to changes in his money-income. It is the price-consumption curve and the income-consumption curve that will be relevant in this case.

It is clear that if this case is a very frequent one, the point rationing scheme has failed. For it would mean that prices have been allowed

---

[1] Actually, the consumer will 'settle down' at a point slightly above *P* on the line *lm*. This will lead to a small loss in satisfaction, but this loss will be balanced by the greater money surplus which he will retain. If, on the other hand, the line *LM* were less (negatively) inclined than *lm*, the point of equilibrium would be slightly below *P*. Only if the line *LM* is parallel to *lm*, i.e. if the prices of the two commodities are in the same ratio as their point-values, will the point of equilibrium coincide exactly with *P*. Thus we see that it is not quite correct to say that in this case it is only the point-values which guide the consumer in his choice. Prices will also have some influence—though a much smaller one than in the following two cases.

[2] Both these methods have actually been used repeatedly since the introduction of the various point-rationing schemes.

to rise to such an extent that they—by themselves—prove an effective check to consumption. But that would mean that an unduly large proportion of these goods goes to people with higher incomes. And this is exactly what the rationing scheme should prevent. A large amount of unused coupons should, therefore, always be a warning signal that the prices of the rationed articles have risen to such an extent that rationing has become largely ineffective as a means of distributing equally a limited amount of goods. There is, however, one exception to this. Unused coupons may be the consequence of an increased readiness for saving: if this leads to a reduction in the proportion of income devoted to rationed articles, no social or economic disadvantage is indicated by the existence of unused points.

In practice, we should expect this case to occur in the lower income groups, particularly with regard to the clothing rationing scheme, and to a minor extent with regard to point-rationed food-stuffs. This will be particularly true where a small income is connected with a large family. For, while in the case of point-income a 100 per cent family allowance is paid for every dependent, there is no corresponding provision for an addition to the money-income.

(3) *The choice of the consumer is influenced by both prices and point-values of the commodities.* This case is illustrated by Fig. 3. Let the lines *LM* and *lm* have the same meaning as in case (1) above. Then, as far as prices alone are concerned, the consumer would be 'in equilibrium' at the point *R*, while with regard to point-values *Q* is the point of equilibrium. Neither of these points can, however, be reached as coupons as well as money have to be given up in exchange for the commodities. It can easily be seen that equilibrium will be reached at the point *P*, the point of intersection of the lines *LM* and *lm*, since *P* lies on the highest indifference curve that can be reached under the circumstances.

There are a few conclusions we can draw from the diagram. Firstly, both the price-consumption curve and the income-consumption curve coincide with *lm*, while the point-value consumption curve and the point-income consumption curve coincide with *LM*. Then, in this case the consumer, though effectively influenced in his choice by the introduction of rationing, will always consume *more* of one of the point-rationed articles than he did previously and less of the other one, and will spend the same amount of money as he did in pre-rationing days. Thus, though here, too, rationing 'transfers' the consumer to a lower indifference curve, he will have no surplus money to increase his consumption of other goods.[1] Finally, if we may venture a psychological deduction from a simple diagram, we should guess that the consumer will find it more difficult than usual to make his choice. For, though P represents a stable equilibrium —the only maximum that can be achieved—we are so much accustomed to choose with the help of one medium only that these double influences will probably have a disturbing effect. On the one hand,

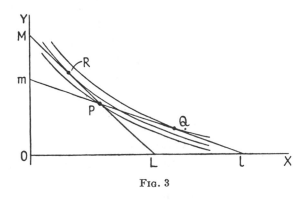

FIG. 3

prices tell us to buy more of Y and less of X while point-values induce us to buy more of X and less of Y. Thus, torn between two conflicting tendencies we may land at P in a slightly irritated mood.[2]

[1] Of course, it is quite likely that he will reduce the proportion of his income devoted to the rationed articles once he notices that he cannot get the same total satisfaction from them as before. But to that lower proportion the above analysis can again be applied. Only that now every change in point-values or point-income, which shifts the consumer to another indifference curve, will probably also lead to an alteration in the proportion of income devoted to these commodities, i.e. every change in the position of lm will cause a change in the position of LM. This will mean that the various consumption curves will take a more complicated course than that mentioned above.

[2] Pawlow, the famous Russian physiologist, once trained a dog to associate one type of behaviour with a circle and another type with an ellipse. Each of these geometric figures elicited the wanted reaction from the dog. Then Pawlow made the ellipse more and more like a circle. Finally, when the ellipse became almost indistinguishable from a circle, the dog did not act in the 'ellipse' way or in the 'circle' way, but began to whine and showed signs of nervous disorder. The indices to which he was used failed to give him a clear guidance.

Something of this sort might happen to consumers in the case we discuss here. Perhaps this is the explanation of some unusual forms of talk which can be occasionally overheard in shops. But I am afraid psycho-analysis will find this explanation far too simple and obvious as to be acceptable.

It should be noted that, if it were considered desirable, the occurrence of this third case could be avoided. All that is necessary is to make the ratio of the point-values of the rationed articles equal to the ratio of their prices. Then *lm* becomes parallel to *LM* and case (3) could not arise. But such a policy would rob the point method of much of its elasticity and simplicity which are its main advantages.

If we try again to estimate the importance of this case in practice, it seems that it, too, will be particularly common in the clothing group and to a lesser extent in the food group. But it will be representative for many medium-income receivers as well as for consumers in the lower-income groups.

This brings to an end our examination of consumer's choice under point rationing with the help of indifference maps. We said already that this method as well as the marginal utility method presupposes a certain rationality of choice. This assumption is sufficiently realistic to make the theory a workable basis for the explanation of actual happenings. But various writers have shown that individuals often are rather irrational in their choice, and have shown how these 'irregularities' affect the results of the above theories. There is no need to repeat these arguments here. But we may add two types of consumer's behaviour which are peculiar to point rationing and which cannot be shown with the apparatus of indifference curves.[1]

On the one hand, the necessity of giving up points as well as money in exchange for certain goods makes the purchase of these goods a less convenient affair than the purchase of unrationed goods. People will sometimes buy unrationed goods and leave their points unused in order to save this additional bother, though with regard to prices alone they might have preferred the point-rationed articles. On the other hand, it seems that for many people a good becomes more desirable as soon as it is rationed. This type of person may take more of the rationed goods than he would have bought in a free market, just in order to use all his coupons. Fortunately, for the pedantry of the economic theorist, these two tendencies work in different directions so that we can assume that in a large group of consumers they will cancel to some extent.

---

[1] These two deviations from 'perfect rationality' were pointed out to me by my wife.

IV

Let us now step down from the abstract heights of indifference curves and let us try to get some information on the effectiveness of rationing from some of the statistics that are available.

With regard to straight rationing it is fairly simple to get some idea of its effectiveness. In the Ministry of Labour Gazette of December 1940 the results of a family budget inquiry were published which covered the expenditure of 8,905 working-class families in four selected weeks in 1937–8.[1] This report also gives the average quantities of principal foods bought by those households. This gives a convenient basis for comparing the actual consumption in 1937–8 and the official rations at the present time (September 1942), for an average working-class household (consisting of 3·77 persons, of which 0·99 are children under 14 years).

Article	Average quantity consumed in 1937–8	Rations in September 1942
	lb.	lb.
Bacon . . .	1·4	0·9
Butter ⎫	1·8 ⎫	0·5 ⎫
Margarine ⎬ Fats	0·7 ⎬ 3·0	0·9 ⎬ 1·9
Lard ⎭	0·5 ⎭	0·5 ⎭
Sugar . . .	4·8	1·9
Jam and Marmalade .	1·0	0·9
Tea . . .	0·7	0·3
Cheese . . .	0·7[2]	1·9
Meat . . .	s. 4/8	s. 3/10

This table shows that for the *average* working-class household rationing has been effective on the whole.[3] As some less important foods, which are not included in the above list, are not or only rarely available or very expensive at present, we must assume that the potential demand for the rationed commodities would probably

[1] It also included non-manual workers with salaries up to £250, but excluded cases of long-continued unemployment. In January 1941 the results of an inquiry into the expenditure of agricultural workers' families was published, but these results are less relevant here, since food rationing affects these households only to a limited degree.

[2] This does not include cheese sold by the box or packet, which is, however, included in the ration.

[3] The only exception (if we take fats as one group) in the above table is the cheese ration, which has been increased considerably during Summer 1942, in order to compensate for a reduction in point-rationed foods. The fact that a large part of the consumers did not make full use of this increase in their cheese ration—in spite of the scarcity of other foods—throws some light on the strong influences of habits on our consumption pattern and the consequent low substitutability of one 'commodity' for another.

be somewhat higher to-day than in 1937. But even so, I think the table shows that—apart from sugar and tea—the rations come fairly near to peace-time consumption and are still very generous if compared with the heavy cuts in rations in Germany.[1] It seems that there is still some margin for further cuts should changes in the military and shipping situation make it necessary. This margin could be widened by adopting the German method of differential rationing, i.e. fixing different rations for heavy workers, sedentary occupations, children, etc.[2]

It has, however, to be borne in mind that the above comparison relates only to the average consumption of working-class households and that no figure for the dispersion of consumption is given. We must, therefore, expect that the gap between pre-war consumption and the present rations will be greater the higher up we go the income scale, while for many families with smaller incomes (and these will include many dependents of soldiers) the gap will be smaller or, in the case of some commodities, consumption will fall below the ration level. Thus, for instance, if we take the 'typical' budget of an unemployed worker with wife and four children in York in 1936,[3] we can see that their consumption fell short of their present rations in all foods except tea, butter (but not fats taken as one group), and sugar. Again, in a survey of saving and spending habits in Blackburn and Bristol in 1940, Mr. Madge found that a considerable number of families did not take their full meat and bacon ration, because prices were too high.[4]

If we take into account the importance of these basic foods under straight rationing for a proper diet and the scarcity of other valuable means of nutrition, it is clear that everything should be done to enable *every* family to obtain their full rations. Whether we want to base our policy on the principle of 'equality of sacrifice' or on the less ambitious idea of an 'iron ration', in both cases further investigations into the present consumption of lower-income groups seem to be essential. The results would probably point towards the

[1] See H. W. Singer, 'The German War Economy, VI', *Economic Journal*, June–September 1942.

[2] There have been some attempts in this direction, e.g. lower meat ration and no tea for children, extra cheese ration for agricultural workers and miners, and extra allocations of meat for factory canteens. But this process could be carried further.

[3] Given in B. Seebohm Rowntree, *Poverty and Progress*, p. 188.

[4] Charles Madge, 'The Propensity to Save in Blackburn and Bristol', *Economic Journal*, December 1940, p. 443.

fixing of a national minimum wage or towards further subsidizing of essential commodities.

When we now turn to the point-rationing scheme of foods and its effectiveness, it is far more difficult to get any accurate picture. Let us, however, try again to make use of the results of the Ministry of Labour inquiry into working-class budgets. In the case of the foodstuffs with which we are concerned here, we have, however, no information with regard to the quantities consumed. All that is given is the amount of money spent on different groups of related foodstuffs. These groups do, of course, not always correspond exactly to the grouping adopted by the Ministry of Food in its point-rationing scheme.

We shall, therefore, have to proceed as follows. We take the expenditure (1937–8) in each of the groups which contain at least one point-rationed food (i.e. items no. 15, 16, 17, 21, 28, 32, 46, 49, 52, 57, 58 in the table on p. 304, Ministry of Labour Gazette, December 1940) and see how much the same amount would buy of point-rationed foods in the corresponding group at current controlled prices (September 1942). We can then calculate the number of points necessary to obtain this quantity and compare it with the actual point-income of the family. The number of points needed will, however, depend on whether the given sum of money is spent on cheap or expensive varieties of the rationed commodity. We have, therefore, taken two limiting cases: (1) all the money is spent on the cheapest variety obtainable in each group, (2) it is spent on the most expensive variety. In the first case, the number of points necessary would be 28·1, in the second case it would be 19·9. The actual point-income of this average family per week is 18·9. Under both assumptions, therefore, point rationing is seen to be effective.

It can easily be seen that the above approach is open to grave objections. We have assumed that the same amount of money as in 1937 would be spent to-day on point-rationed foods at *to-day's* prices. This is obviously unrealistic. Wages and earnings have increased considerably since 1937, and we can safely assume that a greater amount of money would be spent on point-rationed foods to-day. Some allowance for this fact has, however, been made; because, as we said before, the groups used in the Ministry of Labour survey do not match exactly with the Ministry of Food point-rationing groups. As a matter of fact, six out of the eleven groups used contain also commodities which are still available without points. By assuming that *all* the money, in every group, is spent on point-rationed food only, we have, therefore, made some allowance for increased expenditure in this group. There is of course no guarantee that this allowance is of the right size. But it means that the above figures are at least of some guidance for our purpose.

As in the case of straight rationing, the above figures show only the effectiveness of point rationing with regard to an average household. If we turn again to the budget of the unemployed family in York,[1] we see that the consumption in one week in 1936 (here we have the actual quantities consumed) would cost 9 points to-day as compared with 30 points at the disposal of that family for the same period.

Some further information in this direction is given by a small inquiry kindly undertaken by Mr. Charles Madge. At the end of August 1942, 117 families on a working-class housing estate in Leeds were asked several questions with regard to point rationing. These families were divided into three income groups, viz. (*a*) those with up to 15*s*. per week per person[2] to spend on housekeeping exclusive of rent and rates, (*b*) those with from 15*s*. to 20*s*. 10*d*., (*c*) those with more than 20*s*. 10*d*. Of these 117 families 11 per cent in the lowest-income group, 8 per cent in the medium group, and 9 per cent in the higher group did not use up all their points. This, too, seems to point towards a policy that would enable even the lowest-income groups to make full use of their rations.

In the previous part of this paper we have shown that under point rationing three types of consumer's behaviour are possible, and we have tried to state quite generally under what conditions each type is likely to arise. In this connexion, too, Mr. Madge's inquiry has given interesting results. To the question, 'When you decide what to get on points, which is usually more important, the price or the number of points?', the following answers were given:

Income Group	Price		Points		Both		Don't know	
	No.	%	*No.*	%	*No.*	%	*No.*	%
Lower	12	34	14	40	7	20	2	6
Middle	7	14	32	65	9	19	1	2
Upper	3	9	25	76	5	15	0	0
Total . . .	22	19	71	60	21	18	3	3

[1] See above, p. 78.   [2] Children under 14 were counted as half-person.

Since the answer 'Points' corresponds to our theoretical case (1), the answer 'Both' and 'Don't know' to case (3), and 'Price' partly to each of the three cases, but particularly to (2), we see that our previous generalizations made from *a priori* assumptions (and before the results of this survey were known) are to some degree borne out by these statistics.

So much for the effects of the point-rationing scheme for foodstuffs. Similar considerations could be applied to the rationing of soap and sweets, and, above all, to the very important clothing-rationing scheme. But this would take us too far. All we can say, in passing, with regard to the latter scheme is that it, too, seems to have been effective for a large proportion of working-class families, though probably not in the lower income levels. This was shown by the drop in sales of goods coming under this scheme in May 1942, which normally used to be a good month. This drop was ascribed to the exhaustion of clothing coupons in the hands of the consumers.[1] On the other hand, as the price of, for instance, fur coats is very high, and most women have a potential 'want' for this commodity, we must assume that case (3) rather than case (1) must be typical for most working-class households which use up all their clothing coupons.

V

In conclusion, we might try to point out future possibilities of rationing schemes. State control of industry and economic life in war-time has always stimulated interest in the methods and scope of a planned economy.[2] The present experience in consumer's rationing could also be usefully employed in a centrally planned economic system.

The difficulty of such a system, if guided by socialist principles, is that it aims at equality and also at maximum efficiency. Each of these principles, however, demands a different system of income distribution. It seems to me that this problem could be satisfactorily solved by using rationing schemes, at least in the earlier stages of a socialist economy.

The basic staple foods, for which demand is fairly uniform, and for which 'optimum' quantities could be fixed by dieticians, could

---

[1] See *Board of Trade Journal*, 4th July 1942, p. 315.

[2] See, for instance, the literature on planning which sprung up in Central Europe after the last war. Some important contributions are mentioned in the bibliography to F. A. Hayek (ed.), *Collective Economic Planning*.

be distributed by straight rationing and free of charge so that everybody could obtain these essentials, whatever his income may be. As society gets richer, rationing in this sector could be abolished altogether and these staples could become free goods.[1]

Then a wider variety of goods, which are either not quite so essential as those in the previous category or the demand for which depends on individual taste, could come under point-ration schemes.[2] Every commodity in this group would have a certain point-value and every person would obtain a certain point-income, which would increase with every increase in the country's productivity (in this sector). A very low money price may also be fixed for these goods, but this is not essential. Some system would have to be found to translate money costs into point costs, and then changes in demand or supply would be reflected in changes in relative point-values. In this way equality and consumer's choice could be secured in this sector.

Finally, there would be the unlimited field of less essential commodities, semi-luxuries, luxuries, etc., which could be distributed in the usual way in a free market at money prices and bought by people who have unequal money-incomes. The great variety of goods obtainable in this sector would make it worth while for everybody to try to get a high money-income. Thus the money incentive to efficiency would be kept intact while at the same time the rationing schemes would secure equality and free choice with regard to the essentials of life.

---

[1] This system is already used in certain socialized sectors, e.g. use of roads, elementary education, etc. But in the fundamental question of our daily bread we are still very far from this stage.

[2] There would be a limit to the number of point-rationed goods because of the inconvenience it would mean to the distributive organizations.

20

Chapter Seven

Schumpeter and Socialism

KURT W. ROTHSCHILD

INTRODUCTION

To deal with the relationship Schumpeter–Socialism is no easy matter. Not only has socialism acquired so many different shades and meanings—witness the miraculous capacity of the Left to split and resplit on 'fundamental' issues—that the question 'What sort of socialism?' arises. There is also the difficulty that Schumpeter's capitalism is not of the usual sort. And there is finally the baffling question as to the exact message of Schumpeterianism. Like all great social scientists, Schumpeter was fully aware of the complexity of the real world and made—quite deliberately—ample use of qualifications, of 'buts' and 'ifs', so that it is not always easy to state uniquely 'what Schumpeter *really* meant'.

Even the answer to the rather simple question whether Schumpeter was a socialist seems not to be so obvious as one would think. Edgar Salin, in his introduction to the German translation of *Capitalism, Socialism and Democracy* states firmly 'Schumpeter is a socialist' though he hastens to add that 'no socialist, be he a Marxist or a Fabian, will detect his socialism in Schumpeter's writing' (Schumpeter, 1950a, p. 8). At the other end of the scale Joan Robinson (1943), after having read the very same book, finds that 'Professor Schumpeter, as many tart phrases reveal, has little love for socialism, and none at all for socialists' (p. 381).

While I believe that there can be no doubt that on this point Joan Robinson was much nearer to the truth than Salin,[1] there remains the fact that

---

[1] 'I do not advocate socialism.' Thus wrote Schumpeter in a manuscript on whose final edition he worked on the day before he died (see Schumpeter, 1950b, p. 447). Although Schumpeter often hesitated to advocate (rather than explain), it is certain that all through his life he adhered to the above attitude on the basis of his convictions.

113

Schumpeter could evoke such different impressions among his expert readers. And even more important is the fact that—whatever Schumpeter's attitude may have been—his writings had an important and stimulating influence on the deliberations of socialist economists; much more so than the works of other 'bourgeois' economists. Thus we find in Paul Baran's important neo-Marxist analysis of *The Political Economy of Growth* (1957) that Schumpeter is quoted quite as often as Engels, viz. 14 times, as compared with 36 quotations from Marx, 18 from Lenin and seven from Keynes.

The reasons for this ambivalent status of Schumpeter are not difficult to find. All through his life Schumpeter was attracted to the same kind of questions and problems which had been foremost in the minds of Marx and some of the classical economists: to the 'magnificent dynamics'[2] of economic development. This and the openness of a tolerant mind brought him into close contact with Marxian thinking and the capitalism–socialism problem.

If we want to oversimplify we could say that while there exists any number of people who are non-Marxist socialists, there are very few specimens who can be regarded as non-socialist Marxists. Schumpeter is one of them. Or at least nearly so, because Sweezy is probably right when he defines more carefully that the 'Schumpeterian system (is) comparable in its scope to Marxian social science, though not to Marxism as a whole' (Sweezy, 1951, p. 120). At any rate it will be advisable to deal separately with Schumpeter and Marx (in the third section) and with Schumpeter and socialism (in the fourth section). The two aspects are, of course, in many ways interwoven. But the differentiation is useful. In the first case we meet warmth and sympathy (intermingled with Schumpeterian irony), in the second aloofness and cool analysis. But before going into these matters I want to say a few words on Schumpeter himself.

SCHUMPETER HIMSELF

To understand fully Schumpeter's special position *vis-à-vis* both Marx and the capitalism–socialism problem, one has to be aware of his background and of the values that underlie his 'grand designs'. Such a biographical and psychological detour not only helps us to get a clearer insight into Schumpeter's ideas but it is also in the best Schumpeterian tradition. In his brilliant biographical essays (Schumpeter, 1951) as well as in his monumental posthumous *History of Economic Analysis* (Schumpeter, 1954) he usually introduces biographical and historical material to make the evolution and contents of specific theories more intelligible.

---

[2] The term is used in Baumol (1961).

From what one knows about Schumpeter[3] there seem to me to be two outstanding characteristics which leave their mark in all his work and in his likes and dislikes: a certain old-world 'romanticism' and a stupendous intellect. While the intellect was a gift of Nature, the romanticism grew out of the circumstances of his upbringing. In his formative years he was exposed to the full blast of the feudal remnants and the glamour of the Habsburg empire which must have seemed outdated to many Western observers even in those days. The ten-year-old boy, coming already from a well-to-do background, is presented with a titled stepfather high up in the military hierarchy. The values he derives from (and probably admires in) him are fortified by the aristocratic–conservative influence of the *Theresianum*, the exclusive school to which he is promptly sent and which greatly impresses him. After taking his doctorate at Vienna University he spends several months in England where—at least on his visits to Oxford and Cambridge—he is again in touch with an aristocratic–individualistic atmosphere. Finally, his first academic appointment which came after a prolonged stay in the monarchic circles of pre-capitalist Egypt, takes him to a chair in the University of Czernowitz, a town in the less-developed, semi-feudal east of the Habsburg empire.

Thus, up to the age of 28—and by that time the young genius had already worked out the main lines for his future research—Schumpeter, the great theoretician of capitalism and its development, was steeped in an atmosphere of aristocratic and pre-capitalistic sentiments which he liked and which shaped him. This led to a persevering nostalgia for his young days, for Czernowitz, and later—when he had moved to the United States of America—for Europe. It must also have contributed to some of his lovable habits of chivalry, good conversation, exquisite dress, etc., which had an air of bygone days.

But, above all, this basic make-up coloured his theoretical interests and his work. His elitist and romantic views lie behind his very idiosyncratic picture of the heroic entrepreneur–pioneer who is the prime mover of development and around whom capitalism is more or less defined. This point will come up when we deal with the capitalism–socialism problem. His aristocratic aloofness,[4] together with his intellectual honesty, also eased his openness towards Marx. Just as some aristocratic circles in old Austria found it easier than the immediately threatened petty bourgeoisie (for which the aristocracy

---

[3] See in this context various contributions in Harris (1951), particularly Haberler, and further Schneider (1970), Kirsch (1979) and März (1964). The last-mentioned work also contains an interesting section on Schumpeter and Marx.

[4] 'In his personal life he refused to compromise with bourgeois or proletarian standards of respectability' (Smithies, 1951, p. 13).

116   KURT W. ROTHSCHILD

had little esteem) to understand the social question and the socialist aspirations of the working class, so Schumpeter felt less tied than many of his colleagues to the possessing bourgeoisie (*Besitzbürger*) as such and felt no obligation to 'refute' or ignore Marx and socialism.[5]

SCHUMPETER AND MARX

The two economists who were held in particularly high esteem by Schumpeter were Walras and Marx.[6] In them he found the two qualities which he valued most, developed to highest perfection: analysis and vision. Walras had come nearer to a natural-science-like system-analytic[7] structure of economic transactions than anyone before. But it remained a static picture. Marx, on the other hand, had—again more than anyone before—provided a grand vision of the movement of the economic and social system as a whole and had done it—in contrast to the Utopians—as a scientist, because he provides the underlying analysis.

That Walras usually got the highest marks in Schumpeter's evaluation of economic doctrine, higher not only than Marx but also higher than Smith, Ricardo and Mill (although Schumpeter's work was more akin to Marx) is again, I believe, to be explained from the personal background. The quality admired in Marx—vision (paired with analysis)—was not in short supply among Schumpeter's talents. In this respect he surpassed his contemporaries by head and shoulders all through his life. When it came to 'exact' formal-mathematical analysis, his other beloved child, he did—in spite of all his achievements—come up against difficulties and could not quite reach the exacting standards he had set himself (see on this Samuelson, 1951). So Walras' achievement impressed him most, because it seemed so difficult to obtain. There is thus no contradiction between this extreme admiration for Walras and Schumpeter's famous dictum that if he had to choose only one of the three qualifications essential for a good economist—viz. theoretical analysis, statistics, and history—it would be history (see his remarks in Schumpeter, 1949a), which moves him, of course, nearer to Marx than to Walras.

---

[5] 'Schumpeter had been the enfant terrible of the Austrian school of economists. Steward to an Egyptian princess, owner of a stable of race horses, onetime Finance Minister of Austria, Schumpeter could look at the prospects for bourgeois society with the objectivity of one whose feudal world had come to an end in 1914' (P. A. Samuelson in his *Newsweek* column in 1969, quoted in Samuelson (1980)).

[6] See the Foreword of Elisabeth Boody Schumpeter to Schumpeter (1951, p. ix).

[7] Already in his early work on the essence and contents of theoretical economics Schumpeter had a clear idea of the need for system analysis (see Schumpeter, 1908, pp. 28–9).

The vicinity to Marx in the grand design of Schumpeter's life work is quite obvious. Like Marx and in sharp contrast to the spreading neoclassical allocation theory he always kept the vision of an endogenous dynamic movement of the entire economic system foremost in his mind. Static analysis may open up useful insights into particular problems and it may be a necessary stepping-stone in building a dynamic theory, but it can never be a substitute for it. Marx and Schumpeter were also more or less of one opinion with regard to the underlying force which leads to constant economic change. It is technical progress and innovation in the widest sense, the development of the productive forces.

From this common basis of a dynamic, long-term approach follows a whole series of further similarities. The long-term dynamics free the onlooker from a narrow preoccupation with a given historic system and from the tendency to regard given conditions as the absolute standard. Every system is in a state of flux and liable to change. This is no less true for capitalism than it was for feudalism. Thus to regard socialism as a *possible* follower to capitalism was to Schumpeter—again in stark contrast to many of his neoclassical, static, and partly apologetic colleagues—quite an obvious viewpoint. That he also regarded socialism as the *likely* or *necessary* sequel to capitalism was by no means obvious and here the vicinity to Marx is—as we shall see later—spurious, because the expected mechanism is quite different.

The stress on long-term endogenous change is also responsible for similarities in methodology. If economic systems change in the course of history, historical and sociological problems cannot be relegated to a 'given' framework. They have to be included into the analysis. This explains why Schumpeter did not join in the *Methodenstreit* in which his colleagues from the Austrian school were so heavily engaged, and why he always had a high regard for Gustav Schmoller (see Schumpeter, 1926). But what he missed in Schmoller and what he found (and admired) in Marx was the combination of historical vision and economic analysis. And though Schumpeter did not aim at the extreme synthesis of history, sociology and economics,[8] which we find in Marx, he nevertheless was always aware of their interrelationship and gave them due consideration.

His two classical sociological essays on imperialism (Schumpeter, 1919) and social classes (Schumpeter, 1927) carry particular weight in this respect. Not only do they show his capacities in this field, they also carry programmatic character in showing that an understanding of change in economic systems requires an active knowledge of sociological and historic forces. In their *content* these essays are not in line with Marxist literature but they certainly are written in a Marxian *context*. In the essay on imperialism, Schumpeter

---

[8] See his remarks on the relationship, but separateness of economics and sociology in Schumpeter (1908, pp. 539–41).

examines critically the neo-Marxist views of Otto Bauer, Emil Lederer, and Rudolf Hilferding, who had been his debating partners in his student days in Böhm-Bawerk's seminars; and in the essay on social classes, the perennial Marxist question regarding the transition from one epoch to another is treated with special reference to the transition from feudalism to capitalism.

In the more restricted field of the dynamics of the capitalist process itself we again find some decisive similarities between the viewpoints of Schumpeter and Marx. The weight given to technical progress and growing capital intensity helped them to recognize the in-built tendency towards large-scale organization and monopoly. Although they differed in their *evaluation* of this tendency, they were at least free of prevalent illusions about a possible return to a competitive and romantic world of small-scale free enterprise.

Again, their dynamic outlook helped them to recognize the unavoidable shifts and shocks in economic and social structures, and prevented them from viewing the economic process merely in terms of equilibrium. Disturbances and adjustments are essential elements in this picture; and so they could accommodate business cycles in the core of the economic process at a time when other economists relegated this theme to specialists, outsiders, or historians. It is not by chance that Schumpeter made *Business Cycles* (1939) his magnum opus and gave it the significant subtitle *A Theoretical, Historical, and Statistical Analysis of the Capitalist Process.*

But here again, though making the cycle a *normal* element of the capitalist economy is a common characteristic of Schumpeterian and Marxian thinking, they are far apart with regard to the explanation of the cyclical mechanism. Schumpeter finds it in more or less exogenous waves of technical inventions which then go through the fluctuating endogenous process of innovation (by the 'true' capitalist leaders) and imitation (by the rest). As far as Marx has a business cycle *theory*, it is an endogenous theory with underconsumption and wage-cost elements.

Finally, on a more philosophical plane, the holistic and interdisciplinary approach which Schumpeter shared with Marx made both of them sensitive to the role of ideology in social theorizing. Schumpeter never doubted that 'vision' without 'ideology' is impossible, and he had full understanding for Marx's stress on ideological elements. He only scolded him for not being sufficiently aware of and critical *vis-à-vis* his own ideological bias. The same can, by the way, also be said of Schumpeter, at least with regard to some elements in his thinking. He may also have missed the Marxian argument that the ideological commitment of a *disprivileged* class eases the way towards a 'realistic' vision, while entrenched interests tend towards mystification.

So far we have stressed—in 'desperate brevity' (to use a favourite Schumpeterian expression)—the 'Marxist' streak in Schumpeter. Before I go on to point out a few of the major differences, I want to venture a hint about the way in which Schumpeter himself may have seen his relation to Marx. When one reads the chapter on the Marxian system in the *History of Economic Analysis* (1954, Part III, Ch. 1) one cannot help noticing the warmth with which Schumpeter tries to explain the personal achievement of Marx to an audience whom he probably assumed to be hostile, indifferent, or dogmatic when it comes to Marxian economics.

Particularly in section II of this chapter he stresses Marx's incessant zest for work and study—not always under favourable conditions—leading from philosophy and sociology to economics, and the enormous amount of knowledge acquired and utilized. All this knowledge—so said Schumpeter—was subordinated to the lifelong task of throwing more light on the fundamental problems of capitalist and general economic evolution, the main vision and ideas of which had already been acquired at the early age of 29 when Marx wrote the *Communist Manifesto*. Though always drawn by his alert mind ('in which scholarly coal did not put out the fire') to many other problems, the analytic urge drove Marx always back to his basic theme. His main writings are to be seen as a constant attempt to revise, improve, and extend the 'great vision', and it was natural that with such an enormous task at hand, which could not be fulfilled in a lifetime (if ever), there should remain behind contradictions, lacunae, and 'heaps of disorderly manuscripts' (Schumpeter, 1954, p. 387). To understand what Marx wanted to say and did say, it is not sufficient—so Schumpeter insists—to read excerpts from his writings. One should go carefully through all the volumes of *Das Kapital* and of the *Theorien über den Mehrwert* (*Theories of Surplus Value*).

Does this account not fit to an an amazing extent the life, work, and aspirations of Schumpeter himself? The incessant devotion to work, the early semi-intuitive vision and insight into a comprehensive scheme of things, and the steady return to its central problems, the undying enthusiasm for new knowledge and further analysis, a life which is too short to give the finishing touches to a theoretical work, and a structure which has to be seen as a whole to be fully appreciated. The parallels are obvious. And although Schumpeter leaves no doubt that he does not agree with most of the details of Marx's analysis, and although he certainly did not approve of Marx's aggressive polemics, one cannot help feeling that Schumpeter was not only impressed by Marx's stature but to some extent tried to shape himself in a similar manner.[9]

But let us return to the theories themselves and point out some of the major

---

[9] In contrast to Marx, Schumpeter wanted to remain purely analytic in his scientific writings and leave the formulation of aims and policy recommendations to the reader. (See for instance his programmatic remarks in this respect in the Introduction to *Business Cycles* (1939).) But, of course, being a human being—and one with strong personal values at that—he did not always manage to stick to these standards.

differences between Marx's and Schumpeter's approach to economic development. On the methodological plane the main difference is that Schumpeter's approach—and here he betrays quite distinctly his affinity to the Austrian school—is individualistic, while Marx starts from a collectivist or group basis. For Schumpeter macroeconomics should be based on microeconomics. For Marx the sociological groups are the central objective of research.

This difference is clearly revealed in the diverging views of the capitalist entrepreneur and the process of technical change. Schumpeter's picture is—as mentioned before—a heroic–romantic painting of a small band of gifted, innovating entrepreneurs who are the driving force behind economic growth. They are not necessarily capital owners. But in a free-market capitalist society with credit creation they can get hold of resources and through their innovative advance they can create firms, temporary monopolies, high profits, and so *become* capitalists or *remain* capitalists in the usual sense. The block of 'imitator-capitalists' try to follow up and *may* thus be able to survive. The individual entrepreneur (in the narow Schumpeterian sense) is thus the motor of technological progress and of the steady (though cyclical) rejuvenation of capitalism. His initiative comes from such aristocratic motives as love for a dynastic future, will to victory, but—of course—also from interest in material gain.

In the Marxian view it is technical progress that is the driving force. It is the 'natural' product of a thinking and working mankind, though it may be helped or hindered by more or less appropriate institutions. In competitive capitalism a capitalist class which is characterized by ownership of the means of production has the ability to introduce innovations and is—by threat of economic ruin—driven to do it. Profit and accumulation are the aims of a capitalist class that wants to survive in such an environment, though the social and power status flowing from ownership is also recognized as a motive for innovative expansion.

Technical progress and the innovating capitalist play, therefore, a decisive part both in Marx's and Schumpeter's dynamics (see on this in particular März, 1964, pp. 384–5), but their roles tend to be reversed; and Schumpeter's innovating capitalist is a rather special phenomenon.[10] To some extent

---

[10] It may be worth while to indicate the other dominant prototypes of the capitalist in economic theory. In static neoclassical theory the capitalist is owner and manager combined, acting in a transparent world. His desire for profit makes him a perfect accountant. He sees to it that resources are efficiently allocated according to the best technical knowledge currently available. The Keynesian entrepreneur is seen as acting in the dynamic environment of the short and medium period with uncertainty as the dominating feature. His wish for survival and profits is hemmed in by existential fears caused by an uncertain future which he overcomes when his animal spirits are strong enough or when institutional and policy action reduce uncertainty. A special distinction between pioneering and imitative behaviour *à la* Schumpeter is not decisive.

perhaps Marx *and* Schumpeter have underrated the force and the *problematique* of technical progress. Marx did not see—as Schumpeter 80 years later easily could—that the terrific growth in productivity would permit exploitative capitalist relations to be accompanied by sharply rising living standards among the working class. Schumpeter underrated the economic impetus issuing from the *diffusion* of technical progress, and the autonomous force of technical expansion in old as well as new, in 'entrepreneurial' as well as in bureaucratic–managerial enterprises. Both were, therefore, rather blind (in their 'prophecies') with regard to the *general* problems of high industrialization and rapid technological change beyond the capitalism–socialism question, to the problems of the speed and direction of technical change which seem to gain in importance in our days.

SCHUMPETER AND SOCIALISM

We now turn to Schumpeter's socialism. Again we shall have to be very brief. Once we leave Marx aside the idea that Schumpeter *personally* had any likings for socialism can be quickly dropped. He made no secret of it that he had an 'ingrained dislike of socialism' (Harris, 1951, p. 45). But—unlike many of his colleagues—he never turned into primitive anti-socialism and he tried to keep an open mind with regard to both the theoretical and the practical aspects of socialist economics. His non-dogmatic thinking permitted him to be both against nationalization and in favour of a capital levy and a mixed economy in post World War I Austria. He thus managed to be *persona non grata* to socialists and to conservatives alike (Kirsch, 1979, pp. 147–8). His *Capitalism, Socialism and Democracy* (1942) 'is full of ironic twists that provide cold comfort for anyone who agrees with him. Capitalists, socialists, and intellectuals are all provided with strong emotional grounds for rejecting the argument' (Smithies, 1951, p. 16).

His dislike of socialism did not prevent him from arriving at his famous conclusion that capitalism will give way to socialism. In this point where he seems to be near to the beliefs and aspirations of Marxist and non-Marxist socialists he is in fact further away from them than anywhere else. This is so because not only is he more saddened than exhilarated by this prospect, but above all because his reasoning is socialist thinking turned upside down: capitalism—according to Schumpeter—peters out not because of its inadequacy or because of its inherent faults but because of its success.

When it comes to this question of the long-term 'March into Socialism' (Schumpeter's (1950b) last address to the American Economic Association) we should be aware of the very special terminology used by Schumpeter. He deals with the—to him likely—movement from *Schumpeterian* capitalism to *Schumpeterian* socialism. 'Capitalism' as he defines with admirable brevity in his *Business Cycles* 'is that form of private property economy in which innovations are carried out by means of borrowed money' (Schumpeter, 1939, p. 223). Capitalism is, therefore, endangered and on the decline when the environment becomes unfavourable to the unfettered development of the private, innovation-prone individual.

Socialism, on the other hand, is seen as a system in which the control over the means of production and over production itself is exercised by a central authority, or where—more generally—the economic affairs of society belong to the public sphere rather than to the private one (Schumpeter, 1942, p. 167).

The main thrust of Schumpeter's argument has always been that there are strong forces to move from the above-mentioned prototype of capitalism to the above-mentioned prototype of socialism. He realizes, of course, that there are other types of socialism and all sorts of mixed forms; but starting from his 'vision' of capitalism he sticks to his conclusion that 'there is a long-run tendency towards socialism in our sense'.[11] This tendency does not stem from any inherent incapacity of present-day capitalism to 'produce and distribute the goods'. It comes from the self-destroying forces created by the very success of Schumpeterian capitalism.

There are four main factors at work. They are:[12]

1. The success of private business in creating a high level of production has laid the foundation for high living standards and bureaucratization and has undermined the social and political position of an obsolescent business class.
2. The 'rationality' of capitalist activity destroys the habits of subordination which preserved the hierarchy at the firm and society level.
3. The growing administrative tasks have created a political system and an intellectual class which tend to be hostile to large-scale business.
4. '[I]n consequence of all this, the scheme of values of capitalist society, though causally related to its economic success, is losing its hold not only upon the public mind but also upon the "capitalist" stratum itself' (Schumpeter, 1950b, p. 449).

These factors spoil the environment in which the 'true', unfettered capitalist–innovator can initiate that creative destruction of old structures which is the essence of Schumpeterian capitalism. Stabilization policies, attempts towards reducing income inequality, antitrust legislation, public controls in labour

---

[11] This quotation comes from Schumpeter (1949b, p. 375), where he discusses labourism as a first step towards socialism.

[12] This concise enumeration follows Schumpeter's (1950b) summary of his ideas (pp. 448–9). Some of the following remarks also refer to the very typical statements contained in this article.

and money markets, security legislation, a growing sphere of public enterprise, all these are seen as a decay of (Schumpeterian) capitalism and as a steady movement towards socialism of which one may approve or not.

What seems to me to be important is not that these Schumpeterian contours of the long-run tendencies of capitalism are—terminologically, emotionally, and above all with regard to the envisaged processes—in obvious contrast to almost all 'schools' of socialism. This could only be a challenge to discuss more intensively the diverging viewpoints. The real difficulty with Schumpeter seems to me to lie in his peculiar delineation of 'true' capitalism and his views of the state.

Because of his narrow definition of dynamic capitalists and capitalism on the one hand and his concentration on the textbook example of centralized socialism on the other, Schumpeter leaves a rather wide grey zone in between on which he is rather vague. According to his view we have already left capitalism proper but have certainly not yet reached the other pole. While Schumpeter realizes that in this in-between zone different things may happen—labourist capitalism, a Catholic-inspired organization on the basis of *Quadragesimo Anno* (Schumpeter, 1949b, p. 373, 1950b, p. 447), etc.—he seems to have no doubts that all these are only stages on the way to socialism.

Had he seen the capitalists first and foremost as the property-owning class they are, rather than as two distinct groups of innovators and imitators, he might have pondered more about the primitive fact that privileged groups are not prone to give up their privileges. The consequences of this have to be seen in relation to the role of the state. On this point Schumpeter is again much nearer to Marx than to most conventional economists or to Keynes. He never falls into the error of viewing the state as the impartial arbiter administrating the common good. He sees the people and the power influences behind governments and bureaucracies. But the pioneering role he played in analysing the motives of politicians and bureaucrats and in laying the foundations for the new *Economic Theory of Democracy* (Downs, 1957), while no doubt very important and enlightening, led him too far away from the Marxist–socialist concern about the role of the state in the class struggle. The possibilities and mechanisms of using the state in the interest of privileged groups do not get sufficient weight in Schumpeter's analysis.[13]

Thus he has little to say on the questions which agitate socialist factions when they try to evaluate present-day developments, e.g. with regard to the existence or non-existence of state-plus or state-contra monopoly capitalism. In particular, once history has left the special brand of Schumpeter's competitive, heroic, conquering capitalist–innovator behind, he is so hypnotized by the avenue heading towards socialism that he pays little attention

---

[13] For an interesting non-Marxist view on these matters, see for instance Barlett (1973).

to possible side-ways, round-about ways, etc., which can in the meantime lead to other 'capitalisms' leaving the basic power structure intact. This, I think, explains the strange ommission of a proper economic analysis of the fascist past and of possible fascist futures in Schumpeter's writings.

It cannot be stressed sufficiently that the 'strictures' contained in the last few paragraphs apply exclusively to the main contours of Schumpeter's vision. When one goes into the details of his writings there is a wealth of ideas, hints, and information that is of immediate relevance for current debates on capitalism and socialism. Schumpeter's observations on the proper time and the personal requirements for a successful transition to socialism, on bureaucracy and democracy in socialism, on socialism and labourism, are always stimulating and well worth considering whether one agrees with them or not. And, above all, when one enjoys Schumpeter's enlightened— though by no means indifferent—analysis making full use of 'bourgeois' and Marxian contributions one begins to divine what economic science could have been and could be if people like him and a few others—like Lange, Kalecki, Joan Robinson—had dominated the scene.

REFERENCES

Baran, P. A. (1957) *The Political Economy of Growth*. New York: Monthly Review Press.
Barlett, R. (1973) *Economic Foundations of Political Power*. New York: Free Press.
Baumol, B. (1961) *Economic Theory and Operations Analysis*. Englewood Cliffs, NJ: Prentice-Hall.
Downs, A. (1957) *An Economic Theory of Democracy*. New York: Harper.
Haberler, G. (1951) Joseph Alois Schumpeter, 1883–1950. In *Schumpeter—Social Scientist* (Ed.) Harris, S. E. pp. 24–47. Cambridge, MA: Harvard University Press.
Harris, S. E. (Ed.) (1951) *Schumpeter—Social Scientist*. Cambridge, MA: Harvard University Press.
Kirsch, H. (1979). Joseph Alois Schumpeter. *Journal of Economic Issues*, **13**, 141–57.
Kowalik, T. (ed.) (1964) *On Political Economy and Econometrics. Essays in Honour of Oskar Lange*. Warsaw: Polish Scientific Publishers.
März, E. (1964) Zur Genesis der Schumpeterschen Theorie der wirtschaftlichen Entwicklung. In *On Political Economy and Econometrics. Essays in Honour of Oskar Lange* (Ed.) Kowalik, T. pp. 363–87. Warsaw: Polish Scientific Publishers.
National Bureau of Economic Research (1949) *Conf. on Business Cycles*. New York: National Bureau of Economic Research.
Robinson, J. (1943) Review of *Capitalism, Socialism and Democracy*. *Economic Journal*, **53**, 381–3.
Samuelson, P. A. (1951) Schumpeter as a teacher and economic theorist. In *Schumpeter—Social Scientist* (Ed.) Harris, S. E. pp. 48–53. Cambridge, MA: Harvard University Press.
Samuelson, P. A. (1980) The world economy at century's end. Paper given at the *Sixth World Congress of the International Economic Association*, Mexico (to be published).
Schneider, E. (1970) *Joseph A. Schumpeter. Leben und Werk eines grossen Sozialökonomen*. Tübingen: J. C. B. Mohr.
Schumpeter, J. A. (1908) *Das Wesen und der Hauptinhalt der theoretischen Nationalökonomie*. Berlin: Duncker und Humblot.

Schumpeter, J. A. (1919) Zur Soziologie der Imperialismen. *Archiv für Sozialwissenschaft und Sozialpolitik*, **46**, 1–39, 275–310.

Schumpeter, J. A. (1926) Gustav v. Schmoller und die Probleme von heute. *Schmollers Jahrbuch für Gesetzgebung, Verwaltung und Volkswirtschaft im Deutschen Reich*, **50**, 337–88.

Schumpeter, J. A. (1927) Die sozialen Klassen im ethnisch homogenen Milieu. *Archiv für Sozialwissenschaft und Sozialpolitik*, **57**, 1–67.

Schumpeter, J. A. (1939) *Business Cycles. A Theoretical, Historical, and Statistical Analysis of the Capitalist Process*. 2 Volumes. New York: McGraw-Hill.

Schumpeter, J. A. (1942) *Capitalism, Socialism and Democracy*. New York: Harper & Row. Quotations from 4th Edition, 1965. London: Unwin University Books.

Schumpeter, J. A. (1949a) Historical approach to the analysis of business cycles. In *Conf. on Business Cycles*. pp. 149–62. New York: National Bureau of Economic Research.

Schumpeter, J. A. (1949b) English economists and the state-managed economy. *Journal of Political Economy*, **57**, 371–82.

Schumpeter, J. A. (1950a) *Kapitalismus, Sozialismus und Demokratie*. Einleitung von Edgar Salin. München: Francke. 3rd Edition, 1972.

Schumpeter, J. A. (1950b) The march into socialism. *American Economic Review, Papers and Proceedings*, **40**, 446–56.

Schumpeter, J. A. (1951) *Ten Great Economists*. New York: Oxford University Press.

Schumpeter, J. A. (1954) *History of Economic Analysis* (Ed. from manuscript) Schumpeter, E. B. New York: Oxford University Press.

Smithies, A. (1951) Memorial: Joseph Alois Schumpeter, 1883–1950. In *Schumpeter—Social Scientist* (Ed.) Harris, S. E. pp. 11–23. Cambridge, MA: Harvard University Press.

Sweezy, P. M. (1951) Schumpeter on imperialism and social classes. In *Schumpeter—Social Scientist* (Ed.) Harris, S. E. pp. 119–24. Cambridge, MA: Harvard University Press.

[21]

236-53
[1982]

Zeitschrift für die gesamte Staatswissenschaft (ZgS) 138 (1982), 565–582
Journal of Institutional and Theoretical Economics

Observations on the Economics, Politics, and Ethics
of the Welfare State

by

Kurt W. Rothschild*

Wien

1. Welfare State and "Soziale Marktwirtschaft"

It is a good scientific tradition to start with precise definitions and demarcations of the object one is going to analyse. But we also know that in trying to do this one can run quickly into considerable difficulties when the object under consideration is a complex phenomenon exhibiting a wide variety of elements in diverse combinations. Any definition then either is so wide as to be almost meaningless or – by trying to be more exact – runs into the danger of excluding important fringe cases which are of immediate relevance.

The Welfare State is, without doubt, such a complex phenomenon. In order to avoid both the errors of the first and of the second kind (mentioned above) I shall refrain from attempting or reproducing a clear-cut definition. Rather, with the aid of some general remarks on the genesis and role of the Welfare State and of a (debatable) juxtaposition of "Welfare State" and *"Soziale Marktwirtschaft"* I shall try to give a basis for a common understanding of the relevant aspects which we should have in mind when we deal with Welfare State problems.

If we tend to give the term "Welfare State" the widest possible coverage then we have to include all cases where public bodies (central, regional or local government) take direct action with regard to some major area of social welfare, such as poverty, health, old age, education, housing etc. If we adopt this very wide definition then the Welfare State, being more or less coincident with the term social policy, has an ancient history, at least in all industrial countries. With the decline and break-up of traditional forms of social support in families, guilds, small communities etc. following the industrial revolution the stage for a new social problem was set and the need for a Welfare State – in its widest sense – was born or greatly intensified. Public action became imperative because the traditional structures were weakened or ceased to exist, and because

---

* Dr. Kurt W. Rothschild is Professor of Economics at the Johannes-Kepler-University, Linz, Austria.

the market could not, did not, or did not sufficiently provide for social needs that were regarded as minimal or desirable requirements.

The roots of the modern Welfare State – taken in its widest sense – are therefore to be found in the deep and fundamental changes in the social fabric accompanying and following the industrial revolution. *Some* turn to the Welfare State became unavoidable[1]. In some cases the steps were taken reluctantly and against considerable resistance from entrenched interests (vide the Poor Law history in 19th century Britain), in other cases there were sudden forward leaps (as witnessed by the famous Bismarck initiative).

But whatever the attitudes, whatever the motives behind the public actions – and they were varied – public involvement in social action became accepted. With general acceptance a certain growth of social expenditures becomes almost automatic quite apart from any pro-Welfare-State sentiments[2].

As a scheme becomes installed it may – by its very nature – need time to reach its full scale. Compulsory education for instance, when it comes into force will lead to growing staff and expenditure until as many cohorts of children's age groups have entered school as there are years of compulsory education. Similar developments follow when old age pensions are introduced on a (partly) contributory basis where successive age groups acquire slowly the right to full pensions. Social expenditure growth, once it is started, also follows from the diffusion of information about the existence of these services. The degree of utilisation spreads. Then there are ratchet effects. Standards that have been reached acquire the character of bench-marks; they serve as a starting point for new targets and it is usually difficult to sink below them. Finally, there is Parkinson's Law: the bureaucracy springing up in and around the Welfare State has a tendency to maintain and increase its status.

All these tendencies contributed to an expansion of Welfare State activities in absolute, if not in relative terms (relative to GNP) in practically all industrial countries quite irrespective of their political "denomination". The latter could influence the speed of the development, the frequency of set-backs, etc., but the general tendency was more or less universal. In the first half of the 20th century the Welfare State (in the widest sense) was an established fact. Social policy had become an acknowledged public activity well above 19th century levels.

When we want to deal with the Welfare State that has come under heavy fire in recent years in political and economic discussions, then we have to concentrate on developments in the second half of the 20th century; they may require a more restricted definition of the Welfare State.

This new stage is characterised by a sharp and continuing rise in social expenditure in almost all developed industrial countries after World War II, not only in absolute terms but also as a percentage of a quickly growing national

---

[1] See LAMPERT [1980], pp. 30ff.
[2] See on this, particularly for more recent times, WILENSKY [1975].

income. The state became more involved in providing social welfare not only because of higher demands with regard to traditional tasks (health, education, unemployment, old age pensions etc.) but also because activities were extended to new spheres of public welfare. The problems of different groups of handicapped and disprivileged persons got more attention, the needs of large families and anti-poverty programs in general were given more prominence, and with the growing awareness of pollution and other disadvantages arising from technological and economic advance the welfare tasks had to cover compensation and protection measures affecting the total population and not just poorer or disadvantaged sections.

The distinctive up-turn in public social and welfare expenditures was triggered off – just as the similar development after World War I – by the deep social and political upheaval that is characteristic for war and post-war periods. The enormous sacrifices demanded from the population and the shake-up of established hierarchies lead to a strong popular demand for a more egalitarian society, for more "social justice". This pressure in turn leads to a wider awareness of social needs and opens the way for the political realisation of improved and extended welfare activities which otherwise might have needed years of hard political struggle. Socialist and conservative parties alike were prepared to support programs of social reform and expansion. And – as we noticed before – once welfare programs are started (or extended) they maintain a certain momentum because of widening coverage, information, and because of historical linkages with achieved standards. Thus the push emanating from the post-war political and social scene provided a strong built-in tendency for the preservation and expansion of social expenditures all through the fifties and sixties.

But while the post-war socio-political factors acted as an impetus to increased welfare activities in all countries irrespective of their political and socio-economic set-up, the fundamental ideologies, interests, and beliefs underlying these activities were different. These differences became increasingly important as the momentum of the post-war push lost its force; and they have become particularly prominent with the onset of the economic dislocations and the decline in economic growth rates which we have experienced in recent years. It is in this context that the term "Welfare State" can be given a more restricted and a more pointed meaning.

With regard to the social and welfare activities of the state and other public bodies we can distinguish two broad attitudes, each of which contains a number of sub-varieties. For a lack of better terms let us call the two standpoints progressive-radical and conservative. It is predominantly a political division, but since economics, particularly when it deals with policy questions, seldom manages to remain value-free in its assumptions and propositions, it also deeply affects the writings of economists.

To put it very succinctly we can say that from the conservative point of view the existing economic system of a more or less free-market capitalist society is basically all right but needs social cushioning, partly because there are socially and economically undesirable side-effects in market economies which should be mitigated, partly because social expenditure is a politically necessary insurance premium to prevent discontent among the less privileged groups of society.

Social expenditure is seen as a burden – necessary, but a burden nonetheless – which should be kept within narrow bounds and should, as far as possible, not be allowed to interfere with the functioning of the basically favoured market system. The political concession element in this attitude leads to ups and downs in the acceptance or negation of welfare expansion. More is granted in times of social unrest and in post-war periods (e.g. Bismarck, or *"Soziale Marktwirtschaft"* after World War II), while roll-backs are attempted in politically more quiet times. On the whole there is a hope that, with growing wealth and income, social inequities and problems will become less important or will simply be due to individual choice, so that public social activities could be reduced (relatively if not absolutely) in the longer run and more could be left to the market.

The progressive-radical attitude is usually characterised by a strong and positive engagement for welfare activities, mainly because dynamic free-market processes are regarded as a constant source of social problems, inequities, and disruptions which cannot be overcome by individual action in the market place or only in an incomplete and inefficient way. The socio-economic dynamics produce winners and loosers, and society must provide protection and opportunities for the disprivileged and compensation for victims of change. Social services are not seen as a burden, but as rights of citizens which should be extended as society gets richer and can afford improved social services.

There is no question of subordination of welfare policy under the imperatives of a market economy. Social policy is seen as a separate integrative objective to be distinguished from economic policy[3]. The two are of course not independent from, and may clash with each other; but there ist no hierarchy giving predominance to a given economic system (like in *"Soziale Marktwirtschaft"*). The welfare aim stands in its own right. Welfare system and economic system needs have to be confronted and possible clashes have to be overcome by political action and compromise.

What I have called the "progressive-radical" view (or views) can be – in my opinion – best be equated with the "Welfare State" in a more restricted sense. It then no longer covers all countries and policies which provide for some social needs – this, as we saw, is now the general case – but is reserved for attitudes and policies which take an in principle positive and expansionary stand on public welfare activities[4]. It is this view that has come under rather heavy

---

[3] See on this and on the other points in this paragraph TITMUSS [1968], particularly Part III.

[4] As I said before, there are no hard and fast "recognised" definitions for various labels. After the war there was for conservative political-ideological reasons a great demand for describing capitalism in "mollifying" terms like people's capitalism, welfare

attack in more recent times, not only from conservative circles, which are in principle opposed to it, but also more generally because of the greater pressure of economic problems that have arrived with recession, oil price developments, and the decline in productivity growth. The clash between the economic imperatives and the Welfare State seems to have sharpened. Let us turn to this problem.

2. Economic Problems of the Welfare State

The distinction between different basic attitudes with regard to social involvement on the part of the state is a significant element when we deal with the economic aspects of the Welfare State. We should differentiate between the "economics of the Welfare State" and the currently widely discussed "economic problem of the Welfare State". The "economics of the Welfare State" should only comprise the positive analysis of the functioning of existing Welfare States – in the widest sense of the word – free of all normative undertones (as far as possible). In this respect the theoretical and empirical studies of economists should in principle be able to converge. When it comes to the so-called "economic problems of the Welfare State" a clash of values is usually involved. Here the attitude to the Welfare State in the narrower sense – described in the previous section – becomes important.

If one tends to regard most of the social problems as individual faults, which society cannot or should not repair (beyond a certain level dictated by general social and political considerations) one will discern economic problems and barriers at quite a different level than if one is prepared to give equal weights to welfare goals and economic efficiency. To give a simple illustration (which does not claim to be realistic): suppose that the same total national product could be achieved with alternative levels of employment (or unemployment), because the fear of unemployment drives employees to work harder when unemployment rates are higher. Leaving aside the transfer problems connected with unemployment benefits the two alternatives could be regarded as equivalent from a purely economic standpoint, while the Welfare State protagonist

---

state, social market economy, social state, post-capitalist era etc. These terms were often used rather loosely and were more or less interchangeable. The two expressions which obtained a more definite and durable meaning were *"Soziale Marktwirtschaft"* and "Welfare State". The *"Soziale Marktwirtschaft"* with as much or more stress on market economics as on social welfare, was largely the creation of Müller-Armack (see e.g. MÜLLER-ARMACK [1946]; for an overview see WATRIN [1979]). The idea of a comprehensive welfare state spread mainly in Great Britain. The origin of the term Welfare State is uncertain but its first appearance in print was probably in a pamphlet by Archbishop William Temple published in 1941. In that pamphlet ("Citizen and Churchman") he wrote: "In place of the concept of the Power State we are led to that of the Welfare State" (see SLEEMAN [1973], p. 1). The term came into general use after 1945, particularly in connection with the popularisation of Lord Beveridge's proposals (BEVERIDGE [1942]).

will heavily vote in favour of the high-employment alternative[5]. He would do so even if this involved a somewhat lower output, because in his dualist system there are trade-offs between social and economic goals.

This ideological factor behind much of the discussion about the economic problems of or the economic limits to the Welfare State must be kept in mind. But whatever stand is taken, the underlying "positive" economics of the Welfare State should be considered and taken into account by *all* participants in the debate. Unfortunately, the theoretical and empirical infrastructure is far from being an accomplished, reliable, and undisputed body of knowledge. Thus, problems also arise from our incomplete and controversial perception of actual and potential processes. In the following notes on economic problems of the Welfare State I shall deal with both sorts of problems: those stemming from uncertainties about the behaviour of economies under the influence of social intervention, and those following from different attitudes with regard to social and "purely" economic goals.

The main thrust of the presently fashionable attack on the "Welfare State" stems from the economic argument that state interventionist welfare activities tend to reduce economic efficiency and thus output. In the end more welfare activities may lead to less welfare because there may be less produce to be distributed. Since these arguments have gained so much weight in recent years and since they have driven many welfare-oriented politicians into a purely defensive position, let me begin at the other end by pointing out efficiency-increasing aspects of welfare expenditure, i.e. those aspects which make welfare activities desirable from a "purely" economic point of view.

The important thing to remember is that from the very beginning public social expenditures were not just interferences in a smoothly working market system in order to satisfy certain extra-economic social or political aims. There was always also another source: the failure of markets to function "properly" and efficiently. This is a field well worked over by some economists and need not be treated here in detail. But it must be stressed that the whole theory and policy problematique of externalities, public and merit goods is highly relevant to the "economics of the Welfare State". And it is not mere chance that the present theoretical trends centering on models of continuous and harmonious general equilibrium, which leave little room for non-optimal external effects and thus mobilise for privatisation and against public and merit good approaches, coincide with general attacks on the "proliferation of the Welfare State".

Yet everything points in the direction that the problems of externalities, "market failures" etc. are increasing rather than decreasing. The rapidity and

---

[5] "In a sense, the biggest commitment to economic planning in the Welfare State of the Western countries is that they are all now pledged to preserving 'full employment', though the definition, as well as the form, of the commitment varies" wrote Myrdal more than twenty years ago (MYRDAL [1960], p. 49). He also wrote "It is safe to predict that in none of the Western countries will a period of severe unemployment ever again be tolerated by the people" (p. 50). Never say "Never"!

the volume of technical innovatory processes and the ecological problems arising from our limited environment lead to massive side effects which are not
or not sufficiently digested by market signals and market processes. This raises
a host of problems which fall outside the complex of welfare expenditures. But
these are also involved as more and new groups of disadvantaged persons are
added to the "classical" cases of social action.

Many welfare services (including "classical" expenditures on health, unemployment etc.) are – as Titmuss has pointed out[6] – in essence compensations
for social "disservices", "diswelfares", originating in market processes which
fall heavily on *some* people while others reap the benefits of change and development. An economic accounting scheme which does not take sufficient note
of such negative elements (economic "bads" are not deducted or are even
added like economic "goods") consistently underestimates these problems.
Once they are taken into account – with the aid of new types of national
balance sheets or the additional use of social indicators – the efficiency-aug-
menting effects of some welfare expenditure would become apparent.

Further positive efficiency effects can be made out when we think in dynamic
terms. While some welfare recipients can be regarded as permanent recipients
(e.g. old age pensioners) and therefore as an "economic loss item", there are
other cases – education, illness, unemployment etc. – where the welfare provisions are temporary and in the nature of investment, maintenance and repair
costs. A good health service or an active labour market policy may be expensive budget items but they may be economically justified because they prevent
the loss of human capital investment. A positive efficiency effect stems also
from the fact that the provision of social services for the "victims" of change
will reduce political and economic resistance to change. This contributes to
higher productivity[7].

A further efficiency argument can be found when the afore-mentioned juxtaposition of "purely" economic and social welfare targets is kept in mind. If our
ultimate aim is something like utility or social welfare then the usual measures
of economic efficiency and economic results cannot – by themselves – be the
only and decisive indicator. We must distinguish between economic welfare –
"ecfare" in Little's terminology[8] – and "total welfare". The latter includes in
addition to market-provided goods and services a number of environmental
and institutional factors which influence the conditions under which persons
have to work and live. They do not figure properly in economic balance sheets
and are often not easily controlable through individual market action.

Most important in this connection is that social welfare is also a distributional problem. Different distributions of a *given* volume of goods and services lead
to different levels of social welfare, partly because *all* people might prefer and

---

[6] See TITMUSS [1968], p. 133.
[7] See ABRAMOVITZ [1981].
[8] See LITTLE [1950].

be better off with certain redistributions (e.g. provisions of minimum health standards) or because the positive welfare effects of some measures (e.g. anti-poverty programs) are "obviously" greater than the negative effects (falling on the tax payers). This latter view-point is unacceptable to those economists who insist on the impossibility of inter-personal utility (or welfare) comparisons. But while one must admit that there is no simple and unique measure for making such comparisons, it does not follow that no meaningful comparisons are possible at all. Particularly, when we do not deal with single individuals but with groups of peoples characterised by common welfare-relevant characteristics (e.g. family size) the problem becomes more tractable. Here individual idiosyncrasies and absurdities loose their force: it is the averages that count.

Even if social sciences had nothing to say about relative welfare effects of public transfers and expenditures, one could not avoid making such comparisons on a political plane on the basis of subjective value-oriented priorities and judgements. These conflicting judgements cannot (and should not) be avoided and are part of a democratic political process. But social science can contribute studies and analyses of group actions and group behaviour which provide useful insights into the relative welfare effects of public welfare activities[9].

This is a path that could help to give welfare accounting a chance vis-a-vis the predominant pure economic accounting and would be more productive than denying the possibility of any meaningful comparisons. The latter attitude has made Pareto-optimal welfare economics such a sterile branch of economic theory which has nothing to offer to Welfare State economics. Direct welfare judgements would also be a better way than the practice-oriented escape route of cost-benefit analysis where (an unattainable) precision is suggested by hiding value judgements behind seemingly exact money values attached to various welfare activities. This (in contrast to the more defensible cost-effectiveness analysis which compares actual costs with real results) can only lead to technocratic politics. "Expertise" would reduce the room for democratic action in a field where further objective precision becomes impossible and where subjective and moral-political factors become more decisive.

The arguments considered so far were advanced in order to stress that welfare expenditure – if it is "wisely" chosen – can (1) have positive effects on economic production by maintaining and improving human capital, and (2) increase total welfare beyond the purely economic welfare by counteracting adverse consequences of the market process and by "improving" the distribution of welfare. Fig. 1 is a simple illustration of this idea. On the abscissa we measure welfare expenditure as a percentage of GNP, on the ordinate economic welfare (GNP) and total welfare (economic and social welfare). The curves show what levels of welfare can be reached by different amounts of welfare expenditure. (It is assumed that welfare expenditure is following an optimal path.) As welfare expenditure is increased from 0 to A its positive effects on

---

[9] See SIMON [1974] and the literature quoted there.

138/3 (1982)   *Observations on the Economics, Politics, and Ethics*   573

the production process exceed the negative effects (to be discussed presently). So total welfare increases both because of higher production and the growth of other welfare effects. In the range *A B* the further increase of welfare expenditure has a dampening effect on production; but the decline in total economic welfare is more than compensated by other welfare effects. Beyond *B* the negative production effects outweigh the non-economic welfare effects so that total welfare declines.

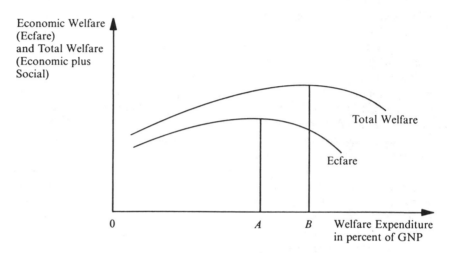

Fig. 1   Welfare and Welfare Expenditure

Even if a high level of social welfare were a generally accepted political aim (which it is not, with special interests often taking precedence) we can easily see why the *extent* of welfare expenditure must remain a contentious issue. There can be different ideas about the importance of economic and other types of welfare. This would lead to debates within the range *AB*. It would seem, however, that a general consensus should exist that welfare expenditures are to be increased when they are below *A* and reduced when they are above *B*. But even these issues are clouded by the fact that the shape and relative position of the two welfare curves are only vaguely known and are also dependent on the time horizon adopted. The trade-offs between economic and non-economic welfare are hotly debated and the positive or negative effects of welfare policies on economic production are similarly open to discussion when quantitative results are required.

The *nature* of the positive effects on productive efficiency has already been mentioned. It remains to point out the negative effects of welfare policies.

Negative effects can arise on two ends of the welfare system: on the financing (burden) side and on the reception (benefits) side. In both cases is it a question of economic responses to (positive or negative) economic stimuli. We are thus in the central domain of economic theory. The problem of financing the welfare services raises the well-known question of disincentives connected with higher taxation. There must be a point where additional taxation reduces entrepreneurial activities and labour supplies to such an extent that the positive effects of the welfare activities are more than offset by reduced output and growth. Moreover, the basis for future welfare activities could be undermined by this effect.

Against this one must keep in mind that up to a point well designed taxes need not reduce or may even encourage productive (income creating) efforts; and that more money for welfare can be obtained by reducing other types of public expenditure so that the relative merits of different government activities have also to be considered ("guns or butter"). All these problems turn up in the economic and political theories of Public Finance which thus become an integral part of any "Theory of the Welfare State".

The second group of negative effects arises from possible disincentives connected with the receipt of welfare benefits. The fact that income can be obtained without offering effort in exchange can reduce the will to provide such effort or can act as an inducement to simulate incapacity where it does not exist. Some of this can be avoided by a proper design of benefits; but some misuse will persist. Here again economic theory and empirical studies concerning labour supply behaviour can provide the student of the Welfare State with the necessary theoretical tools.

There are some further effects of Welfare State activities which may be – according to circumstances – positive or negative. They, too, can be analysed in the framework of traditional economic theories. As an example we might mention the possible effects of higher taxation and greater social security on the propensity to save. The changes in propensities will have to be estimated and their economic effects have to be evaluated in relation to expansionary or contractionary long-term tendencies.

The main outcome of this section should be that the economics of the Welfare State require the application of various branches of economic theory in a field were hard facts and clear-cut results are difficult to come by and where the – unreliable – results have to be evaluated and discussed against a background of different political and ethical beliefs and targets. There should be consensus on the idea that – because of positive and negative elements in welfare politics – there can be too little or too much welfare policy. This view can be shared by people who hold rather different opinions regarding the desirable extent of welfare activities in the wide interval between "too little" and "too much".

The growing economic difficulties in recent years have made the burden of welfare activities more visible and there is presently a tendency to stress the question whether there is not too much Welfare State. A quick look at the facts does not give any evidence that so far high welfare activities have led to negative economic results. If we take public expenditure on health and education as a proxy for welfare activities in general and calculate rank correlations for 16 developed industrial countries[10] we obtain the following results. When we compare the *levels* of per capita public expenditures on health (education) with per capita GNP we obtain rank correlation coefficients of $r = 0,71$ (0,74) which are significant at the 5% level (which is reached – with 16 observations – at a value of 0,51)[11]. This positive correlation is what we would expect, with the "causation" running from high living standards to higher welfare standards which one can afford. But the results do away with any assumption that we have already reached a stage of impoverishment through "too much" welfare spending.

More interesting is perhaps a look at *developments*. When we take the period 1970–1976/77 and the same countries as before (with the exception of France) we find (1) that in *all* countries real public expenditures on health and education have grown faster than real GNP (from an average of 8 per cent of GNP in 1970 to 9,8 per cent in 1976/77), and (2) that a comparison of the ranks with regard to real health plus education expenditure *growth rates* and real GNP *growth rates* is $r = 0,33$[12]. This is not significant at the 5% level so that no definite influence can be observed. But what interdependence there is, is positive, i.e. higher rates of expansion in welfare expenditures have certainly shown no tendency whatsoever to hamper economic growth.

There is thus no alarming evidence that welfare activities have reached a stage where the "too much" problem is evident. The present backlash against "welfarism" cannot be supported by clear-cut evidence on harmful economic effects. It is partly the result of a wave of conservative and middle-class sentiments which highlight the importance of "personal success" and take elitist and restrictive views on social policy[13], and partly a consequence of widespread economic (inflation) and budget problems which have fostered a demand for retrenchment policies. In the present political climate of anti-inflation and military expansion sentiments these are directed predominantly towards the wide field of social and welfare expenditures.

The pressure of these present trends, as well as the longer-term problem that there are limits to an "efficient" extension of welfare expenditures, make the

---

[10] Australia, Austria, Belgium, Canada, Denmark, Finland, France, Germany, Italy, Japan, Netherlands, Norway, Sweden, Switzerland, UK, USA.

[11] The calculations are based on data contained in SIVARD [1980], Table III. See Table 1 in the Appendix. It should be stressed that there are several weaknesses involved connected with the limitation to health and education expenditures, with the fact that there are national differences with regard to public or private provision for health and education, and with the well-known difficulties of comparisons between different national budget and GNP data. But since we are only dealing with ranks the correlation coefficients can serve as a rough orientation.

[12] The calculations are based on US ARMS CONTROL AND DISARMAMENT AGENCY [1979]. See Table 2 in the Appendix and the remarks in note 11.

[13] See WILENSKY [1975], pp. 34ff., 115f.

question regarding the proper *types and methods* of welfare provision – which can be more or less costly – particularly important. Here again we are faced with a problem that cannot be answered on a purely technocratic plane. It is not just a question of using "the" most efficient method, but also a question of the political and moral side-effects connected with various solutions. To these problems we shall now turn.

3. *Alternative Principles and Methods in Welfare State Activities*

Even if one has a positive attitude towards Welfare-Statism there is reason to worry about growing absolute and relative costs. To some extent the relative rise in welfare costs (relative to GNP) is more or less unavoidable as long as one does not want to reduce the extent of welfare activities. This is so because – as in some other fields of public and private services – the scope for productivity increases is usually smaller than in manufacturing, agriculture, finance, and trade. Thus with real contributions unchanged the relative cost of welfare services will rise.

Even where possibilities for mechanisation (computerisation etc.) exist it might not always be advisable to use them if the *humanitarian* rather than the economic aspect of social aid is the main target. Since some of the activities are directed towards disprivileged groups who get a rough deal anyway, the *quality* of the service in form of adequate human sympathy and contact may be at least as important as the material provisions. This requires personal social work which cannot be easily mechanised or streamlined.

Of course, with growing national income the relative burden of welfare expenditures could fall as the amount of real welfare needed declines. Experience so far shows, however, that this will probably be a slow process. Not only does growing production create new social problems and does not solve (automatically) the phenomenon of absolute and relative poverty; there is also a tendency towards rising standards in welfare aspirations. Once the North-South problem is taken seriously this would be even more true.

With these "built-in" tendencies towards growing welfare costs, the task of eliminating *avoidable* cost elements becomes urgent. Here we can distinguish between reforms which increase the efficiency of existing services and those which try to accomplish savings by changing the basic principles of some services.

Let us talk of the pure efficiency questions first on which there can be little disagreement. They are questions about organisation and about misuse. The growth of welfare state activities has created a welfare state bureaucracy with all the problems connected with this form of organisation. Here again the welfare state theory does not have to develop special hypotheses but can lean on existing theories about bureaucracies, public administration, and organisational behaviour. The bureaucratic drive for status and expansion in combination with the income wishes of the "welfare industry" (doctors, teachers, industrial suppliers etc.) can lead to unnecessary and costly developments (similar to the "military-industrial" complex).

There is no point in grieving about the failures of bureaucracy; there are not only failures, and bureaucracy is the form of organisation which (for the moment?) is probably an essential element in our world of big, complex social structures. But awareness of the problem can stimulate our theoretical and political endeavours to increase the efficiency of bureaucracies[14] and keep them under expert and democratic control. The growing interest in health and hospital economics is a promising sign. In the much longer run we might be able to develop welfare systems which rely more on solidarity and group action than on state regulation. The latter would then only provide the framework for group activities and could act as the "ultimate" social underwriter. We would then – in the words of Myrdal – advance from the "Welfare State" to a "Welfare Culture"[15].

Another problem of wastage is misuse of welfare services through unnecessary or unjustified claims. Misuse certainly exists. This is also true of other social and economic, indeed of most human institutions, but in the case of some social benefits the opportunities and incentives for such misuse are relatively great. Economies could and should be sought through designing controls and special forms of welfare application which would reduce the scope for misuse.

But the protagonist of welfarism should not be drawn into the presently fashionable tactics of welfare antagonists who seem to be *solely* interested in high-lighting misuses like work-shy recipients of unemployment benefits, healthy persons swallowing medicines etc. These allegations are often less motivated by a desire to reduce misuse but rather by the wish to reduce the welfare system as such. But we do not give up taxation because of tax-evasion or markets because of monopolistic distortions etc. In fact *every* system of complex social arrangements has its own special advantages *and* drawbacks. By concentrating on the one rather than the other it is always possible to produce a case for or against the institution under discussion.

We deal with quite different questions when we turn from cost reduction strategies through the elimination of bureaucratic waste and misuse of services to attempts of finding alternative, low-cost forms of welfare provision. Since the *method* of providing welfare services very often has important effects on the *quality and socio-political content* of these services we are here again in a

---

[14] See on this GLENNERSTER [1975]; WIDMAIER [1976], Kap. III.

[15] "I would insist on the relevance of the utopian, decentralised and democratic state where, within the bounds of ever more effective overall policies laid down for the whole national community, the citizens themselves carry more and more of the responsibility for organising their work and life by means of local and sectional cooperation and bargaining with only the necessary minimum of direct state interference" (MYRDAL [1960], p. 79).

field where clashes of values and ideas can and do occur and where no simple "technological fix" can be expected.

Two major questions arise in this context which come up in connection with a large number of welfare arrangements: the choice between universalist and selectivist approaches, and the choice between flat-rate or earnings-related benefits.

Let us take the universalist-selectivist dilemma first. The attraction of a selectivist solution – provision of services to the "poor" only – is obvious from a money-saving point of view. If we want to enable everybody to enjoy certain standards of health, education etc. it will of course be cheaper to provide these free or on a below-cost basis to the lower income-groups only and let the others pay for themselves.

Such a solution has, however, administrative, social, and moral effects. A restriction of services to lower income groups requires some sort of means test for the applicants. This involves administrative and individual costs (in money and time). They must be set against the savings achieved by excluding the better-off people. But this will not normally be a decisive barrier. More important are the social, psychological and moral implications.

Means test solutions create two kinds of citizens. To the already existing social hierarchy connected with the unequal distribution of incomes, further subdivisions are now added between welfare petitioners and others. In some cases – poverty relief, for instance – this is unavoidable. But in cases like old age, family allowances, health, education etc. non-discriminatory solutions are possible.

The "stigma of the means test" (TITMUSS [1968], p. 134) is a psychological burden and sometimes prevents needy people from applying for the benefits to which they are entitled. The desired effects (e. g. health maintenance) are then not achieved. Also, the exact fixation of means test limits creates difficult problems. If they are fixed too low the welfare targets will be missed. If they are fixed too high the desired saving in costs will be small and a universalist solution (avoiding administrative costs) might be cheaper. Again, means-test-based benefits create a serious marginal tax problem at the dividing line. When the decisive income limit is surpassed the benefits disappear completely. Where such a situation exists (e. g. means-test-based family allowances, means-test-based pensions etc.) there ist the danger of strong disincentive effects on work and self-provision. This problem can be mitigated or overcome by introducing income-related *graduated* benefits (often found in housing subsidies) or – more fundamentally – through a negative income tax. But these schemes are difficult to handle and involve high administrative costs. Finally – though this is not a necessary element of means test solutions – such systems tend to generate a "keeping people out" attitude among a suspicious bureaucracy and there is also a tendency that "services for poor people tend to be poor services".

All these considerations explain why in many cases universalist approaches are preferred and used. However, in the present restrictionist climate we experience growing demands to extend the use of selective methods. This would reduce costs, but it would also – as has been shown above – reduce the quality and utility of some social services. If economising were really essential, selection should – as far as possible – not be carried out on an individual basis discriminating benefit recipients as "supplicants", but should be oriented on some objective criterion (like old age, family size, underdeveloped region etc.) where claimants could receive their benefits as a matter of right without humiliating procedures. Such methods will, of course, not be fully efficient in sorting out the "right" customers and will not minimise costs; but they represent a compromise between costly universalism and discriminating selectivism.

While in the case of the universalism-selectivism dilemma a devotion to the Welfare State ideal demands partisanship for the more expensive method, it is probably just the other way round when the flat or proportional rate problematique comes up. This question is normally relevant when the welfare target is not the provision of some special services (like health, education) but the maintenance of income in general (sickness and unemployment benefit, old age pensions etc.).

Since the Welfare State ideology usually goes with a certain degree of egaliterianism and the wish to secure *basic* requirements for all individuals the cheaper method of flat rate benefits is – from this point of view – not only sufficient, it is also adequate. From a less egalitarian and more elitist point of view and/or when relative utilities are taken into account, income maintenance should bear some relation to customary living standards. This calls for earnings-related benefits[16]. Sometimes this principle is applied within certain limits as, for instance, with old age pensions and unemployment benefits. A compromise can be reached by a general, adequate flat-rate provision out of taxes and social security contributions coupled with insurance opportunities for additional (earnings-related) benefits based on individual insurance payments. This opens the way for economies without compromising the basic spirit of Welfare-Statism.

4. Concluding Remarks

Social policy (in the widest sense) has become an essential and irreplacable element in the political economy of all modern industrial states. But depending on political and moral views and the distribution of interests one finds restrictionist or expansionist views regarding the further development of social po-

---

[16] A good example of diverging views was the wide-spread discussion on family allowances that took place in England before their general introduction after World War II. The proposals stretched from children allowances for poorer families only, over flat rate payments, to a system (proposed by Harrod) of allowances rising with rising incomes in order to contribute to the higher educational costs of upper-class families.

licy. The latter attitude is characterised as a positive "Welfare State" attitude in this paper and the author has written it from such a viewpoint.

There are at present no signs that Welfare State activities have reached an absolute or relative maximum or that they have *by themselves* (apart from inefficient design) *net* harmful effects on economic efficiency or economic growth. More knowledge and analysis in this direction is certainly desirable in order to improve the efficiency of financing and providing welfare services. An "Economic Theory of the Welfare State" can be of great help in this respect and it can rely heavily on existing branches of economic and other theories such as the theories of public finance, public goods, public administration, organisation, as well as sociological and psychological theories of group action and structures of needs and satisfaction.

Not only are there continuing possibilities for further extensions of the Welfare State, there are also pressing needs. Poverty continues to exist, unemployment is once again rampant, quickening technological and structural change and environmental hazards create new victims, and there are, of course, innumerable tasks once one looks at the world at large.

At the same time we are experiencing at present a wave of conservatism in economic and political ideas which – by exaggerating the undeniable shortcomings and abuses of present-day welfare systems – turn against the Welfare State in principle or try to cut it back in favour of radical anti-inflationary targets and of military expansion. This policy is helped by the fact that, in our democracies lobbies and organised group interests have a stronger grip on parliaments and on mass media than in former times, while disprivileged groups happen to be badly and poorly organised. Thus, while social policy will no doubt continue for existential reasons of political stability, the wider idea of the Welfare State is in crisis. If it is to be saved it requires political will and political action. But this can be helped by hard scientific effort to learn from past mistakes and to develop efficient methods which are adapted to the needs and circumstances of our times.

Appendix

Table 1

*Per Capita Public Expenditures on Health and Education and Per Capita GNP
Ranking of 16 Industrial Countries, 1977*

	With Respect to per Capita		
	Public Health Expenditures	Public Education Expenditures	GNP
Sweden	1	1	2
Denmark	2	5	3
Germany	3	14	7
Netherland	4	4	9
Norway	5,5	3	5
Canada	5,5	2	6
France	7	11	10
Switzerland	8	8	1
Finland	9	9	14
Belgium	10	7	8
USA	12	6	4
Austria	12	13	13
Australia	12	10	11
Japan	14	12	12
UK	15	15	15
Italy	16	16	16

Source: SIVARD [1980], Table III.

Table 2

*Real Public Expenditures on Health and Education and Real GNP
in 15 Industrial Countries, 1970 and 1977*
(Million $ on the basis of 1976)

	Health and Education Expenditures		GNP	
	1970	1977	1970	1977
Australia	6 100	11 722[a]	80 026	99 021[a]
Austria	2 714	4 171	31 935	40 620[a]
Belgium	3 455	6 157	54 810	68 172
Canada	18 144	24 876[a]	142 967	191 197[a]
Denmark	3 315	3 983[b]	33 139	36 242[b]
Finland	2 226	3 421	22 641	27 514
Germany	17 516[c]	29 568[a]	362 968[c]	446 346[a]
Italy	7 747	10 641[a]	144 511	169 991[a]
Japan	17 261	30 485[b]	401 500	522 241[b]
Netherlands	5 779	8 238	72 598	91 742
Norway	1 574	2 434	22 218	32 062
Sweden	8 078	9 925[a]	65 145	73 975[a]
Switzerland	3 193[d]	4 508[a]	59 519[d]	58 424[a]
UK	17 972	27 951[a]	198 286	222 088[a]
USA	131 534	173 359	1 440 902	1 776 685

Source: US ARMS CONTROL AND DISARMAMENT AGENCY [1979].
[a] 1976   [b] 1975   [c] 1969   [d] 1971.

References

ABRAMOVITZ, M. [1981], "Welfare Quandaries and Productivity Concerns", *American Economic Review*, 71, 1–17.

BEVERIDGE, W.H. [1942], *Social Insurance and Allied Services*, Report by Sir William Beveridge to the Interdepartmental Committee on Social Insurance and Allied Services, London.

GLENNERSTER, H. [1975], *Social Service Budgets and Social Policy*, London.

LAMPERT, H. [1980], *Sozialpolitik*, Berlin – Heidelberg – New York.

LITTLE, I.M.D. [1950], *A Critique of Welfare Economics*, Oxford.

MÜLLER-ARMACK, A. [1946], *Wirtschaftslenkung und Marktwirtschaft*, Hamburg.

MYRDAL, G. [1960], *Beyond the Welfare State. Economic Planning in the Welfare States and its International Implications*, London.

SIMON, J.L. [1974], "Interpersonal Welfare Comparisons can be Made – and Used for Redistribution Decisions", *Kyklos*, 27, 63–98.

SIVARD, R.L. [1980], *World Military and Social Expenditures 1980*, Leesburg, Virginia.

SLEEMAN, J.F. [1973], *The Welfare State. Its Aims, Benefits and Costs*, London.

TITMUSS, R.M. [1968], *Commitment to Welfare*, London.

US ARMS CONTROL AND DISARMAMENT AGENCY [1979], *World Military Expenditures and Arms Transfers 1968–1977*, Washington.

WATRIN, C. [1979], "The Principles of the Social Market Economy: Its Origin and Early History", *Zeitschrift für die gesamte Staatswissenschaft*, 135, 405–425.

WIDMAIER, H.P. [1976], *Sozialpolitik im Wohlfahrtsstaat*, Reinbeck.

WILENSKY, H.L. [1975], *The Welfare State and Equality*, Berkeley, Cal.

[22]   254-70
             [1986]
KYKLOS, Vol. 39 – 1986 – Fasc. 3, 359–376

'Left' and 'Right' in 'Federal Europe'

Kurt W. Rothschild*

I. INTRODUCTION

The problem of the relations between politics and economics – so neglected in 'pure' economics or 'pure' politology – has attracted increasing attention in several quarters in the postwar period and particularly in the past two decades. The interconnections between economics and politics – running in both directions – are manifold and therefore the term 'Political Economy' today covers a wide variety of models and approaches ranging from classical and Marxist 'Political Economy' to system analysis and other modern methods[1]. In a narrower sense the term 'Political Economy' has recently been frequently used for three special segments of the wider field: (1) the so-called political business-cycle, i.e. the question of economic manipulation as a function of vote maximising and electioneering behaviour, (2) the question of the influence of economic factors on voting behaviour and the popularity of political parties, and (3) the question of how far changes in the political composition of the government, of parliament, and/or of social organisations have an influence on macro-economic outcomes[2]. Problem (1) has mainly attracted the attention of economists, while problems (2) and (3) have found a greater echo among political scientists and sociologists.

The present paper deals exclusively with problem (3). It is a modest empirical contribution to the debate which is motivated (or, is to be excused) by the following considerations. Firstly, the question as to

---

* Professor emeritus, Universität Linz.

1. See, for instance, the classification of different approaches to 'Political Economy' in FREY [1979].

2. 'Political Economy' in this more restricted meaning is, for instance, reflected in the title and contents of HIBBS and FASSBENDER's 'Contemporary Political Economy' [HIBBS and FASSBENDER 1981].

359

KURT W. ROTHSCHILD

whether important macro-economic processes and results differ significantly under different regimes is by no means answered unanimously in different studies. Thus further material can help to sharpen the picture. Secondly, new analyses become desirable, because we now have longer series for *both* the 'golden' years of the sixties *and* the more stagnant period since the mid-seventies, and a comparison of these two divergent 'states of the world' might be informative. Thirdly, there is no clear-cut methodology for the treatment of this problem so that it might be useful to experiment with a slightly different approach. And finally, for an economist the problem deserves increasing attention in a world which becomes more and more integrated. The question of whether and how much room exists for a national economic policy in a unified world economy becomes increasingly relevant. It has to be seen against the background of recent theories about small open economies on the one hand and rational expectation theories on the other, both of which point to the limitations if not impossibility of an effective national policy.

II. LINES OF RESEARCH

While it is fairly straightforward to ask the question whether the politics of the government in power (or some other sociopolitical configuration) has an influence on macro-economic outcomes, there is an almost unlimited number of ways in which one can try to tackle the problem. First of all there is the choice of the variables to be investigated. On the 'input' side we find – as already mentioned – party affiliation of the government (or of the prime minister in case of coalition governments), strongest party in parliament, trade union strength, or combinations of these factors. The variables on the 'output' side are chosen because they are considered as economically very relevant and/or because they are differently weighted in the programs of the parties. The most frequently used variables are GNP growth rates, inflation, unemployment, size of public sector, tax and transfer policy, and – occasionally – the balance of payments. In this paper I shall restrict myself to political composition of the government on the one hand and GNP growth, inflation, and unemployment on the other. This is typical for a great proportion of such studies.

LEFT AND RIGHT IN FEDERAL EUROPE

A very tricky problem is the question of linking 'inputs' and 'outputs'. Let us illustrate it with the relationship between government ('Left' or 'Right') and unemployment. The question is whether Left or Right makes a difference. This can be studied for a single country or for a group of countries. If a single country is taken this necessarily involves time series analysis. One tries to find out whether *periods* of Left governments show different results from periods of Right governments. Two problems arise. One is the very general one of our insufficient knowledge of lag structures. Different assumptions about the lags between government action and economic effects will lead to different results[3]. The second problem arises from the constant change in the national and international economic scene which affects the conditions under which the different governments have to achieve results. Even when one tries to make some allowance for these external factors, comparisons and interpretations remain precarious.

This last problem can be partly overcome by making a cross section analysis over several countries (which is more typical in this field). But here, again, one meets with difficulties. If one limits the study to one specific period of time (a certain year) the linkage of various national governments to national unemployment rates is – apart from the lag problem (this year's or last year's government?) – quite unequivocal. But one cannot be sure how far this special year gives typical results. Thus the more common precedure is to take averages over several years. And here we find two different approaches stemming from different hypotheses. One results from the simple averaging of the government-unemployment links of the several countries over several years. This excludes the danger of choosing an atypical year but reintroduces the problem that Left and Right did not always work under equal world conditions. Another method – such as, for instance, HIBBS' [1977] study which acted as a strong influence on later discussions – correlates the *average* unemployment rate over a longer period in each country with the *average* party composition over a longer period[4]. Here one tests not so much

---

3. For instance MADSEN in his study of Norway experiments with linking quarterly unemployment rates to government composition in various previous quarters (1 to 4). See MADSEN [1981] pp. 273/274.
4. In HIBBS [1977], for instance, average unemployment rates for 1960–1969 in twelve countries are related to the percentage of years in which socialist/labour parties were in the executive during the period 1945–1969. A negative correlation is obtained.

KURT W. ROTHSCHILD

what *direct* influence emanates from the government's political affiliation but rather whether the prolonged rule of a certain ideology creates a
'climate' which affects employment policy.

While cross-section studies can eliminate or reduce the problem of
time-dependent changes in external conditions they are affected – as
single country studies are not – by differences in historical and institutional factors. They point, therefore, in the direction of including non-
economic and country-specific influences and constraints[5]. This, however, complicates the picture and makes it more difficult to obtain
clear-cut results with regard to the political factor.

All these problems and intricacies, reinforced by the fact that different studies cover different countries and periods[6], contribute to a
wide variety of opinions as to the effect of 'Left' and 'Right' on
macroeconomic outcomes. While there is fairly good evidence and a
wide consensus that the size of the public sector and socially oriented
tax-transfer policies tend to be positively correlated with left-wing
government, the picture becomes blurred when it comes to growth,
inflation, and unemployment where external conditions are far more
influential than in the case of fiscal arrangements. Here we find a wide
spectrum of results and interpretations which reach from strongly
affirmative to largely negative answers regarding the role of government
composition for the variables just mentioned[7]. An intermediate position

5. A good example for an economic analysis which takes this problem seriously is
HULSMAN et al. [1983].

6. A good discussion of the influence of period choice and of most of the other
problems mentioned above is contained in SCHMIDT [1982], Section 3.3.

7. 'Political life, then, is far more than an occasional random shock to a self-con-
tained, isolated economic system; rather economic life vibrates with the rhythm of
politics' [TUFTE 1978, p. 137]; 'The results do not lend much credibility to a partisan
view of macroeconomic policy' [MADSEN 1981, p. 273]. Even where the same data are
used the interpretation may differ. Thus HIBBS' figures on average unemployment in
twelve countries and their relation to the average duration of socialist/labour executive participation result in a scatter diagram which permits HIBBS to point out a
negative relationship between unemployment and socialist/labour government.
MADSEN, by stressing that the United States and Canada belong to a 'different world'
because they do not have the close interaction between trade unions and left-wing
parties which is typical for Western European countries, looks at the same diagram but
leaves out the United States and Canada. As a consequence the relationship seen by
HIBBS has more or less vanished.

LEFT AND RIGHT IN FEDERAL EUROPE

is taken by some studies which make differential government results dependent on certain combinations of government composition and socio-political structure as for instance the existence of a united or divided opposition, the existence or absence of strong links between trade unions and political parties, etc.[8] It is this 'openness' of the question and the constant change in world economic conditions which make a constant return to these questions desirable.

III. THE METHOD

The usual method of the multi-country studies is to compare the achievements of the various single countries. If a relationship between achievement and political composition can be found, the effectiveness of political influence is taken for granted and vice versa. What is tested is whether different autonomous governments can and do follow special policies. In the present study a different 'basic philosophy' is adopted. When we look at the main economic indicators (growth, unemployment, inflation) in the developed Western European countries the first and strongest impression is that of a *parallel* movement. This is not particularly surprising. Both commodity and financial markets in Europe have become highly integrated, and world economic conditions are a very strong factor in shaping national fortunes. The room for manoeuvring in single countries has become rather narrow.

This situation suggests an experiment with an approach which differs from the usual method. We can look at Western Europe (Europe for short) as an integrated economic unit with a dynamic development, and can regard the individual countries as 'provinces' in this 'federal' Europe. Just as we can ask in a federal country with autonomous regions ('states', provinces, etc.) how far the different political compositions of the regions are reflected in regional developments, so we can approach the European scene from a similar angle. True, the position of national governments with their wider legal powers and their national currencies provides a far greater autonomy than any region in a federal country can hope for. But the fact remains that the general economic conditions are a

8. For a presentation of this view see, for instance, ESPING-ANDERSEN [1985], particularly pp. 494ff.

KURT W. ROTHSCHILD

very strong and common external force. This makes acceptable the picture of a common frame in which limited action might or might not be possible (which is to be tested).

We can now turn to a description of the adopted procedure. Our period of observation is 1960–1984 and the coverage is 'Federal Western Europe' consisting of twelve developed industrial countries (Austria, Belgium, Germany, Denmark, Finland, France, Great Britain, Italy, The Netherlands, Norway, Sweden, Switzerland). Growth, unemployment, and inflation rates for each country and for each of the 25 years are the basis for the calculations. (The detailed tables containing these data can be obtained from the author on request.) In each year Europe is split up into different regions according to political 'colour', and the question is asked whether systematic differences in performance and development can be observed.

The detailed procedure is as follows. The political factor ('input') in each country is represented by the party affiliation of the government. Four groups are distinguished (with symbols used in brackets): Left (L), Right (R), Left Coalition (C_L) and Right Coalition (C_R). Left governments consist of social democratic parties and parties to the left of social democracy, right governments come from liberal and conservative parties. Coalition governments are called left or right depending on the party affiliation of the prime minister[9]. The four groups also appear in combinations. C_L and C_R combine into C, i.e. coalition governments as opposed to 'pure' left and right governments. Alternatively we get a dichotomic classification into 'Left' and 'Right' in a wider sense (symbols: $\bar{L}$ and $\bar{R}$) by combining left and left coalition governments on the one hand ($\bar{L} = L + C_L$) and right and right coalition governments on the other ($\bar{R} = R + C_R$). This latter division will later be mainly used in order to avoid groupings which are too small.

For each year the countries are divided into these (two, three or four) groups (see Appendix) and for each group unweighted averages of the economic outcomes (growth rates, unemployment, inflation) are calculated from the respective country data. We thus obtain a time series of the

---

9. An exception was made in the case of Switzerland. Switzerland has a system of coalition government where government members (from different parties) take the prime minister's seat in turn. Considering the main lines of Swiss policy I have included Switzerland among the right coalitions throughout the whole period.

economic results for the combined left and right 'provinces' in Europe. This is the material we shall discuss in the following section. This section concludes with two additional remarks.

First, the lag problem ist just as tricky in this study as in all others. Some decision has to be made as to which government is held to be 'responsible' for the economic results of a given year (only annual data are used). Is it this year's or last year's government? In many cases this won't matter since – Italy excepted – governments tend to stay in power for a few years. But whenever changes occur, a decision has to be made. I have chosen the following simple rule. If a government of a given 'colour' was in power in the first quarter of a year, the country is allocated to this political group, the idea being that the main lines of development for this year would have been laid and could not be quickly changed by a new government[10]. If, on the other hand, there was a change of government within the first quarter, the government which ruled longest during that year determines the political allocation of the country.

Secondly, it will be seen that a specific characteristic of this method is that the *composition* of the groups which are compared (Left, Right) over the years is changing all the time both in numbers and countries. The advantage of this procedure is twofold. Firstly, by *always* comparing 'left' achievements and 'right' achievements (irrespective of country) in the *same* year we cut out the problem of different external conditions facing the governments, a problem which besets some of the previous studies where the experiences of left and right countries are compared at (partly) different periods (or in *one* possibly unrepresentative year). Secondly, the repeated changes in the composition of the groups reduce to some extent the danger of biased results stemming from (non-included) special institutional and social influences in individual countries. Because the countries shift between Left and Right the neglected factors are less troublesome than in studies where the individual countries are compared directly.

10. Practically in all cases where a government did only rule in the first quarter and was dislocated later, it had been in power for quite a while in the preceeding year(s) so that a lasting influence is probable.

KURT W. ROTHSCHILD

IV. THE RESULTS

In the following discussion the results of our calculations are shown in a condensed form (five-year averages and four-year moving averages). The data are given in two groupings: (a) a tripartite division into pure left, pure right and coalition governments (L, R, C), and (b) a bipartite division into 'Left' and 'Right' in the wider sense ($\overline{L}$, $\overline{R}$). In the interpretation of the results I shall restrict myself mainly to the second division since in the first case some groups are very small in some years so that the results could be too much influenced by a single country[11]. If nothing else is said, Left and Right (without quotation marks) will, therefore, always refer to the combined pure and coalition governments dominated by the Left or Right ($\overline{L}$, $\overline{R}$).

It does not take long to summarise the results, because the data present a fairly clear picture (see *Tables* and *Figures 1–3*). If we look at GNP growth rates *(Table 1, Figure 1)* we find a fairly clear-cut division into two periods: the 'golden' years from 1960 into the early seventies and the years after the 'Wende' (the turnabout) in world conditions and policy targets. In the first period right governments show on average higher growth rates than left governments. Closer inspection of annual and country data reveal, however, two things: (1) the averages hide considerable shifts in growth leadership from year to year; (2) the lead of the right 'provinces' partly reflects the 'economic miracles' in the war-devastated countries Austria, Germany and Italy who – during the sixties – belonged continuously to the right group. The picture changed quite clearly and unequivocally when the change in conditions, policy targets, and economic paradigms became effective. While growth rates declined everywhere, they remained at a higher level – year after year, without exception – in the leftist part of Europe from 1972 onward.

An analogous picture is obtained when we look at unemployment *(Table 2 and Figure 2)*. In the full employment period of the sixties the generally low unemployment rates are even lower in the right-wing countries than in the left-wing countries. The switch sets in in 1970. With

11. In one extreme case (left government in France in 1984) a group (L) consists of only one country. If we take the 'Left'-'Right' division ($\overline{L}$, $\overline{R}$) the number of countries per group never falls below three.

LEFT AND RIGHT IN FEDERAL EUROPE

Table 1

Annual growth rates of real GNP by political groupings
(five-year unweighted averages)

	L	C	R	L̄	R̄
1960–1964	5.1	5.6	5.6	5.2	5.6
1965–1969	3.3	4.8	4.8	4.0	4.7
1970–1974	3.9	4.3	3.9	4.3	4.0
1975–1979	3.1	1.9	1.9	3.1	1.0
1980–1984	1.5	1.6	1.2	1.9	1.1

Note: L = 'pure' left governments, R = 'pure' right governments, C = coalition governments, L̄ = left and left coalition governments (L + C$_L$), R̄ = right and right coalition
governments (R + C$_R$). See also text.

Figure 1

Growth rates of real GNP: four-year moving averages

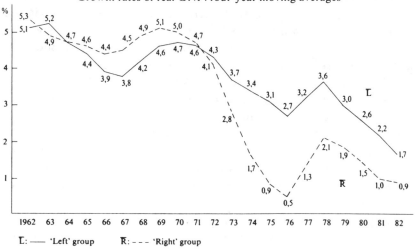

L: —— 'Left' group   R: - - - 'Right' group

the exception of 1973 the Left shows lower rates in all the years following
the switch. The picture becomes even more tilted towards the left
performance when we exclude Switzerland where special conditions
(financial centre, high and flexible quota of foreign labour) kept un-

367

KURT W. ROTHSCHILD

Table 2

Unemployment rates by political groupings
(five-year unweighted averages)

	L	C	R	L̄	R̄	R̄ excl. Switzerland
1960–1964	1.4	2.4	1.5	2.2	1.7	2.0
1965–1969	2.1	2.0	2.0	2.2	2.0	2.3
1970–1974	1.9	1.9	2.8	1.9	2.3	2.8
1975–1979	2.8	4.7	5.3	4.1	4.6	5.1
1980–1984	6.1	6.0	8.5	5.9	8.0	8.6

See Note in *Table 1*.

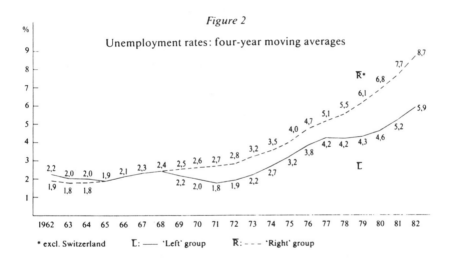

Figure 2

Unemployment rates: four-year moving averages

* excl. Switzerland   L̄: —— 'Left' group   R̄: - - - 'Right' group

employment at zero or near-zero rates most of the time. When this is done the left unemployment rate begins to fall below the right one as early as 1965 (with 1967 as an exception)[12].

12. Leaving out the coalition governments and comparing only the 'pure' left and right groups the switch to lower unemployment rates in the left domain occurred in the wake of the 1967/1968 recession. While unemployment rose between 1967 and 1968 from 2.2 to 3% on the Right, it fell from 2.5 to 2.3% on the Left.

LEFT AND RIGHT IN FEDERAL EUROPE

Table 3

Inflation rates (consumer prices) by political groupings
(five-year unweighted averages)

	L	C	R	L̄	R̄
1960–1964	3.4	3.5	3.2	3.7	3.2
1965–1969	4.4	3.6	3.9	4.7	3.7
1970–1974	7.7	7.2	8.6	7.4	8.3
1975–1979	9.2	7.1	10.9	8.6	9.5
1980–1984	8.8	7.5	9.3	8.6	8.3

See Note in *Table 1.*

Figure 3

Inflation rates (consumer prices): four-year moving averages

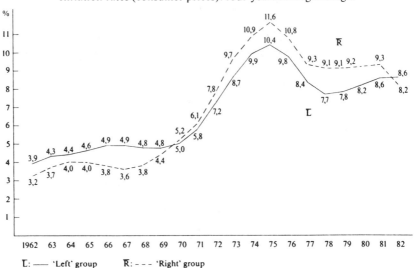

L: —— 'Left' group   R: - - - 'Right' group

Finally we come to inflation *(Table 3* and *Figure 3).* Here no clear picture is visible and least of all an 'expected' picture (with higher inflation rates in left quarters). With inflation rates rising everywhere right up to the mid-seventies, average levels move with varying speed on both sides so that 'leadership' changes frequently and irregularly. In the

KURT W. ROTHSCHILD

five quinquenniums the Left shows a higher average in three and the Right in two periods with levels lying fairly close together. When we look at annual data the Right has higher inflation rates in 15 years against the Left's 9 years (there is a 'draw' in 1972). Moreover, this pattern applies both to the early and the late period. During 1960–1972 the Right inflation rate is higher in 7 years (Left: 5), and during 1973–1984 in 8 years (Left: 4). It may, however, be significant that in all five-year periods except the first one (1960–1964) the group of coalition governments (C) has distinctly lower inflation rates than the 'pure' types of government of the Left *and* of the Right (L, R). This might be an indication that under coalition governments there is a better chance to achieve an income-policy-like compromise to slow down the wage-price spiral. There is also an indication of a stronger anti-inflationary trend in the right countries starting in 1980. Between 1980 and 1984 the inflation rate in the 'pure' right sphere declines steeply from 14.6 to 5.3% against a fall from 9.9 to 7.7% in the 'pure' left 'hemisphere'[13].

It was pointed out earlier that one of the weaknesses of empirical political-economic analyses of the kind we have before us lies in the neglect of additional factors which may affect the result. As I have mentioned, this weakness is somewhat reduced by the method I have adopted. Because of the continuous change in the composition of the analysed groups the institutional factors become to some extent 'randomized' and their influence should be less decisive. The following remarks are meant to support this 'hope'.

While the high integration of the world economy normally ensures that the main economic indicators in the various countries move *in the same direction*, historical and institutional factors can have a lasting influence on *the level* at which these movements take place. Some countries tend *generally* to higher growth, unemployment, inflation, etc., than other countries irrespective of actual political conditions. That this can be a strong factor is illustrated in *Table 4*. In this Table I present again quinquennial averages of GNP growth, unemployment and inflation

---

13. The decline in the (pure) right group is slightly dramatised because in 1980 the group included the high-inflation country Italy but not the low-inflation country Germany while in 1984 the position was the other way round. But even if we exclude Italy and Germany from the calculation we are still left with a decline in the inflation rate from 13 to 5.9%.

LEFT AND RIGHT IN FEDERAL EUROPE

Table 4

Growth, unemployment and inflation in countries with low values (L)
and high values (H) in 1960–1964
(five-year unweighted averages; six countries in each group)

	Real GNP growth rates, in %		Unemployment rates, in %		Inflation rates, in %	
	L	H	L	H	L	H
1960–1964	5.1	6.0	0.9	2.8	2.7	4.0
1965–1969	3.9	5.0	1.4	2.8	3.5	4.4
1970–1974	4.0	4.4	1.6	2.7	7.2	8.3
1975–1979	2.6	2.0	3.7	5.1	7.7	10.5
1980–1984	1.4	1.4	6.0	8.5	7.1	10.2

Note: For the countries in the L-group see Footnote 14. The remaining six countries are in the H-group.

rates, but using a different grouping of countries. In the three cases I compare two fixed groups of six countries each where the L-group consists of the six countries with the lowest values of the respective rates in the 1960–1964 period and the H-group of the six countries with higher values[14]. As can be seen the initial level continues to be (on average) a determining factor in the case of unemployment and inflation. While the movements of L- and H-countries run parallel, the former remain consistently on a lower level than the latter. In the case of growth no clear pattern emerges.

The question emerges whether such 'institutional' differences in levels might not lie behind the different developments which we have attributed to political factors. Could not the observed changes be the result of (systematic!) changes of L- and H-countries into certain poli-

14. In the case of growth rates the L-group consists of Austria, Belgium, Denmark, Great Britain, Norway, Sweden with rates ranging from 3.8 to 5.5% (5.6–7% in the H-group); for unemployment the L-list is Germany, Finland, France, Netherlands, Sweden, Switzerland with 0 to 1.4% (1.5–3.7% for H); and for inflation we have Austria, Belgium, Germany, France, Great Britain, Switzerland with 1.8 to 3.2% (3.3–4.9% for H).

KURT W. ROTHSCHILD

tical groupings? To shed some light on this question the following simple 'test' was made. For each country two separate (linear) trends were calculated both for growth and unemployment rates[15], one trend for the period 1960–1972 and one for 1973–1984 (to allow for the very different conditions in the two periods). Actual annual growth and unemployment rates in each country were then expressed as deviations (in percentage points) from trend. These deviations were then summed and averaged over the (annually changing) political groups. In this way the problem of different absolute and permanent ('institutional') levels is eliminated. If a political factor exists one would expect that *on the whole, but rather weakly*[16] there should be more years where the difference between the Left's and Right's trend deviations are positive for growth rates and negative for unemployment rates. This is indeed the case. For growth we find that the Left fares better (measured in deviations) in 16 years, the Right in 9 years. In the case of unemployment the Left scores better in 14 years, the Right in 7 years with four years of equal deviations.

V. CONCLUSIONS

Starting from the idea that in the highly integrated Western European economy the economic development in all countries must be fairly uniform we investigated whether deviations from the common path could be connected with the changing political composition of the European regions. The data suggest that while differences between Left and Right with regard to growth, unemployment and inflation were slight and irregular during the booming sixties, they became quite distinct with the turn in economic conditions and policies after 1970/ 1973. This is particularly true for unemployment where the change in policy emphasis between Left and Right has been greatest. Partly as a consequence of this and partly directly, a similar, though less pronounced division can be seen in the development of growth rates.

15. Inflation was left out because the political factor had not proved significant.
16. We can only expect a *weak* result for the following reason. If we have countries where the 'colour' of the government seldom or never changes then we get *necessarily* positive and negative deviations from (this country's) trend values. This problem applies to quite a number of countries (with Switzerland as the only country to stay *permanently* in the right camp).

LEFT AND RIGHT IN FEDERAL EUROPE

No clear division on political lines emerges in the inflation field. This looks surprising if one considers how important monetarist doctrines and anti-inflationary sentiments were for the spread of conservative politics after 1970. There may be two reasons why no obvious partisan split in inflationary developments can be detected (excepting perhaps the period 1980–1984). Firstly, inflation had become a sufficiently serious problem after 1970 to be attacked vigorously by all governments even if the fight against inflation did not obtain top priority. Secondly, in spite of flexible exchange rates and dirty floating, there exist – at least within Western Europe – sufficient economic interrelations and political inhibitions to currency manipulations to ensure a high degree of international price coordination. Comparatively, there is somewhat more room for national action with regard to employment and – to a minor extent – growth.

KURT W. ROTHSCHILD

APPENDIX

Political affiliation of government in 12 Western European countries, 1960–1984

	L	C$_L$	C$_R$	R
1960	N, S	DK	A, CH	B, D, F, GB, I, NL, SF
1961	N, S	DK	A, CH	B, D, F, GB, I, NL, SF
1962	N, S	DK	A, B, CH, I	D, F, GB, NL, SF
1963	N, S	DK	A, B, CH, I	D, F, GB, NL, SF
1964	N, S	DK	A, B, CH, I	D, F, GB, NL, SF
1965	DK, GB, N, S	–	A, B, CH, I	D, F, NL, SF
1966	DK, GB, S	–	A, CH, I, NL	B, D, F, N, SF
1967	DK, GB, S	SF	CH, D, I	A, B, F, N, NL
1968	GB, S	SF	CH, D, I	A, B, DK, F, N, NL
1969	GB, S	SF	B, CH, D	A, DK, F, I, N, NL
1970	GB, S	D, SF	B, CH, I	A, DK, F, N, NL
1971	A, N, S	D	B, CH, I, SF	DK, F, GB, NL
1972	A, DK, N, S, SF	D	B, CH	F, GB, I, NL
1973	A, DK, S	B, D, SF	CH	F, GB, I, N, NL
1974	A, GB, N, S	B, D, NL, SF	CH, I	DK, F
1975	A, GB, N, S	D, DK, NL, SF	CH, I	B, F
1976	A, GB, N, S	D, DK, NL	CH, SF	B, F, I
1977	A, GB, N	D, DK, NL	CH, SF	B, F, I, S
1978	A, DK, GB, N	D, SF	B, CH	F, I, NL, S
1979	A, N	D, DK, SF	B, CH	F, GB, I, NL, S
1980	A, DK, N	D, SF	B, CH	F, GB, I, NL, S
1981	A, DK, N	D, SF	B, CH, I	F, GB, NL, S
1982	A, DK, F	D, SF	CH, I, NL	B, GB, N, S
1983	A, F	SF	CH, I	B, D, DK, GB, N, NL, S
1984	F	A, I, SF	CH	B, D, DK, GB, N, NL, S

Notes:

(a) L, R are left and right governments respectively, C are coalition governments with either a left prime minister (C$_L$) or a right prime minister (C$_R$). In years of government change the government ruling in the first quarter was chosen. (For details see text.)

(b) Country abbreviations: A = Austria, B = Belgium, CH = Switzerland, D = Germany, DK = Denmark, F = France, GB = Great Britain, I = Italy, N = Norway, NL = The Netherlands, S = Sweden, SF = Finland.

Sources: P. FLORA and others: *State, Economy, and Society in Western Europe 1815–1975,* Vol. I, Frankfurt/London/Chicago 1983, ch. IV; and *Archiv der Gegenwart,* several volumes.

LEFT AND RIGHT IN FEDERAL EUROPE

REFERENCES

ESPING-ANDERSEN, G.: 'Der Einfluss politischer Macht auf die Entwicklung des Wohlfahrtsstaates im internationalen Vergleich', in NASCHOLD (1985), pp. 467–503.

FREY, B.S.: 'Ansätze zur Politischen Ökonomie', in POMMEREHNE and FREY (1979), pp. 1–34.

HIBBS, D.A. JR.: 'Political Parties and Macroeconomic Policy', *American Political Science Review*, Vol. 71 (1977), pp. 1467–1487.

HIBBS, D.A. JR. and FASSBENDER, H. (eds.): *Contemporary Political Economy*, Amsterdam: North-Holland, 1981.

HULSMAN, W.; SNYKER, W.B.C. and VAN WELZENIS, G.: 'Recent Economic Perform-ances and Policies of Smaller European Countries. An Assessment for Austria, Belgium, Denmark and Switzerland', *De Economist,* Vol. 131 (1983), pp. 609–633.

MADSEN, H.J.: 'Partisanship and Macroeconomic Outcomes: A Reconsideration', in HIBBS and FASSBENDER (1981), pp. 269–282.

NASCHOLD, F. (ed.): *Arbeit und Politik. Gesellschaftliche Regulierung der Arbeit und der sozialen Sicherung*, Frankfurt: Campus, 1985.

POMMEREHNE, W.W. and FREY, B.S. (eds.): *Ökonomische Theorie der Politik*, Berlin: Springer, 1979.

SCHMIDT, M.G.: *Wohlfahrtsstaatliche Politik unter bürgerlichen und sozialdemokra-tischen Regierungen. Ein internationaler Vergleich*, Frankfurt: Campus, 1982.

TUFTE, E.R.: *Political Control of the Economy*, Princeton: Princeton University Press, 1978.

[23]

KYKLOS, Vol. 42, 1989, Fasc. 2, 257–259

271-73
(1989)
P61 0242
D62 0244

The Economist as Preacher
A Note on YEW-KWANG NG's Article on Economic Efficiency versus Egalitarian Rights H23

KURT W. ROTHSCHILD

Economics is – hopefully – a positive science. It should help us to understand the complicated mechanisms and trends of the economic universe. But it is also a social science which touches deep and conflicting concerns of human beings. Thus it is only natural that the economic agenda comes into frequent contact with political and ethical propositions and that economists are drawn willy-nilly into normative remarks and considerations. Assuming that economists are 'normal' human beings this is probably unavoidable; it is also not particularly tragic (or harmful to the 'positivity' of economic theory) as long as one adheres as strictly as possible to MYRDAL's prescription that the chosen normative criteria ('values') should be explicitly stated so that their limited and relative validity is quite clear.

The trouble starts when economists display an implicit tendency to assume that they are in possession of a superior and over-riding normative standard, viz. 'economic efficiency'. Just as there is a tendency to extend the methodology of mainstream economic theory to the entire sphere of social science ('Beckerism'), so we can also detect as a further branch of 'economic imperialism' the tendency to ascribe particular weight to 'efficiency' when it comes to ethical considerations.

A good example for such a tendency can be found in and between the lines of the very thoughtful and stimulating paper by YEW-KWANG NG in a recent issue of this journal[1]. NG tries to persuade his readers that the allocational efficiency of the price system as defined by the economist (Pareto-optimality) should be accorded a far greater standing as a guiding principle in social decision-making than is the case at present where in many cases other forms of distribution (free public and merit goods, equal treatment, rationing, queueing, formal restrictions etc.) are deemed more appropriate. To some extent this may be due to the fact that people do not understand the nature and effects of the price system and insofar as this is the case NG is, of course, quite right to plead for a better education in economic principles. But what NG seems to neglect is that it is not just economic ignorance which prevents people from accepting his advice as to 'what should be' [p. 234], but that they may take a different view of some of the axioms on which economists rest their 'scientific' valuations[2].

---

1. NG, YEW-KWANG, 'Economic Efficiency versus Egalitarian Rights', Kyklos, Vol. 41 (1988), pp. 215–237.
2. 'The modern economy is too complicated for non-economists to understand. Just as we have to call in experts to deal with nuclear reactors, the society should consult economists even on apparently purely ethical questions of fairness, at least for those that are related to economic issues' [p. 234]. But the point is that physicists talk about reactors and not about 'fairness' or some abstract definition of global efficiency.

257

KURT W. ROTHSCHILD

The reasons why NG assumes that the 'economic principle of allocation and distribution' in the market and price system should be regarded as a normative rule rest essentially on three basic elements.

1. Firstly, 'economic efficiency' is firmly based on and defined in terms of individual welfarism. Social choice is to be based solely on individual preferences which can only be judged and expressed by the individuals themselves.
2. The preferences are well represented by the willingness to pay and this is generally recognised. 'At the economic end (i. e. outside politics etc.), most people accept the use of economic principles of resource allocation and distribution of private goods, including the use of the unweighted willingness (and ability) to pay as the measure of benefit' [p. 216]. Thus the price system is a good vehicle for welfarism.
3. Insofar as distributional outcomes of the market process are regarded as unsatisfactory, NG shows that under certain 'traditional' assumptions a Pareto-superior allocational position can always be reached by taxes and subsidies rather than by interfering in the market process itself.

This is the 'infrastructure' on which NG builds his powerful plea for accepting the economist's basic value of 'efficiency' as a pervasive normative imperative. If people do not always appreciate the qualities of the price mechanism as the ultimate rule it can – in NG's view – only be a consequence of either ignorance or 'procedural preference', i. e. a positive liking for some non-market forms of transaction (or disliking of market transactions).

Let us now look at the strength of these arguments by taking the various elements in turn. The choice of subjective welfarism as a standard has, of course, a long and useful tradition in economic theory as a framework and as an axiom for decision-making. But there is no reason to regard it as the only possible basis for social choice and ethical valuation. Quite apart from social interlinkages via external effects, prisoners' dilemma situations etc. which may necessitate collective action there is no reason why ethical considerations should not introduce general values, interpersonal comparisons etc. which go beyond individual welfarism. This is what actually happens and what lies at the basis of discussions and conflicts outside the economist's vocabulary. In fact, NG himself has great difficulties in sticking to this principle of subjective welfarism when he tries to explain why it is defensible to ban slavery or whipping even if an individual is willing to sell himself into servitude or agrees to be flagellated. Reluctant to recognise that society's ethical values forbid such actions as such he takes refuge to a roundabout reasoning by saying that 'while we allow most individuals freedom to choose and make mistakes, servitude for life is too big a mistake. On balance, it is in the interests of most individuals to disallow slavery altogether in case they make such a silly mistake at times of unclear mind' [p. 226]. This is obviously the thin end of a wedge which can undermine welfarism as the 'ultimate ethical principle' [p. 227]. Here strangely enough NG can suddenly speak of 'mistakes' in another person etc. How does *he* know it is a mistake? And if he wants to save individuals from 'mistaken' decisions in the case of slavery, why not in the case of drinking and smoking (through prohibition or taxes)? Where is individual welfarism absolute and where is social discussion permissible?

258

THE ECONOMIST AS PREACHER

As to the supposed general acceptance of welfarism and the price system by the public NG's whole paper is more or less proof for the fact that such a general acceptance does not exist. If it did he would not have to plead so urgently for its generalised utilisation. The fact, of course, is that people accept the price system in ordinary life partly because it is – in many cases – obviously the best and most convenient method, but partly just because it is the traditional way. In the latter case they are not necessarily *satisfied* with it (just as they are not satisfied with some bureaucratic methods which they nevertheless 'accept') and they express preferences for other methods of transaction (being scolded by economists for such 'irrational' preferences).

Insofar as dissatisfaction with the price system concerns distributional questions they could be – the third point above – repaired by subsequent taxation and subsidies. But as NG himself concedes these may not always be enforceable. And even where appropriate taxation is possible at present this may give less certainty for the future than the establishment of some definite principle like 'free higher education'.

NG is, of course, aware that people have various non-economic motivations. 'I perfectly agree that material gain is not everything, that fame, friendship, love, etc. are important' [p. 222]. But this only leads him to ask us 'that we should not ignore the value of these in our calculus of economic efficiency' [ibid.]. This comes very near to turning 'economic efficiency' into a loose tautology, since we can hardly measure the 'efficiency' of transactions so motivated. In any case, these motives may often lead to *deliberate* choices of non-price mechanisms which NG then acknowledges as 'permissible' procedural preferences though he tries to play down their importance when he warns us that 'the (procedural) preference may be due to tradition, dogmatism, or other sources of ignorance and/or irrationality' [p. 218]. But he fails to explain why an adherence to a tradition should be irrational while the insistence on the 'dogma' of 'economic efficiency' is rational.

In short, NG – like many other economists – takes the economists' ideas of welfarism and efficiency too much as the 'ultimate ethical principle' [p. 227]. While preferences of the individuals are given highest weight there is one preference which they are not permitted to have: a preference for non-market transactions. 'Inefficiency' becomes the ultimate sin. Of course, economists should instruct people about 'economic efficiency' in general and about its significance in particular situations: this is their duty as experts. But are they supposed to talk people out of other modes of decision and action?

KYKLOS, Vol. 44, Fasc. 2, 233-239

A Note on Insiders, Outsiders and the Two-Thirds-Society

Kurt W. Rothschild*

In the various attempts to explain wage rigidities and persistent unemployment within the framework of neoclassical theories a number of special theories have recently emerged in quick succession. Search theory was followed by implicit contracts which in turn were overshadowed by efficiency wage theories. The latest 'fashion' is an insider-outsider approach (for recent representative examples see LINDBECK and SNOWER [1988]; BLANCHFLOWER et al. [1990]; COE [1990]; NICKEL and WADHWANI [1990]). The main idea of this approach, which proves rich in modifications and applications, is that workers already employed in a firm ('insiders') have — either by themselves (because of their specific training) or through their union — the power to fix wages at a level above the equilibrium wage so that 'outsiders' who would be willing to work at lower wages remain unemployed. Insiders and/or unions are usually depicted as following purely egotistic aims neglecting the interests of the outsiders[1]. When this behaviour is characteristic for wide areas of the economy a tendency towards unemployment hysteresis arises leading to the emergence of a 'Two-Thirds-Society' where a minority of the population is permanently disadvantaged. Assuming that the insider-outsider picture is in fact a relevant representation of the *macroeconomic situation*[2], I want to show that such an insider (union) policy *can* be pareto-optimal seen from a working class (employed *plus* unemployed) point of view if we accept the economic neoclassical

*Emeritus Professor, University of Linz, Austria.

1. For instance: 'The basic assumption is that the outsiders are disenfranchised in the wage determination process and the insiders are mainly concerned with their own wages and job security' [COE 1990, p.164]; 'Consider a utilitarian monopoly union which cares only about insider members' [BLANCHFLOWER et.al. 1990, p.147].
2. The insider-outsider theory is, of course, fairly easily acceptable in its more restricted application to certain branches of industry. Indeed, many observations in the segmented labour market literature can be covered by this approach.

233

KURT W. ROTHSCHILD

axioms of income maximisation and individualistic preferences, but that it (and the resulting Two-Thirds-Society) would be a very questionable social arrangement.

I shall put my argument in the simplest possible terms. Frequently the insider-outsider story is presented as a dynamic process: As productivity rises (e.g. in a beginning boom) insiders manage to appropriate the productivity gains through higher wages even if unemployed persons are available, who would have been absorbed at the original level of real wages. I restrict myself to a static picture since it suffices to show the gist of my argument.

I accept, for the present discussion, the traditional neoclassical assumption of a one-to-one relationship between real wages and employment with a falling demand curve for labour following the course of marginal revenue productivity. The decline in marginal productivity can have different reasons: increasing difficulties in substituting labour when the capital stock is fixed, applications of additional labour to capital of older vintage, imperfect goods markets with falling prices when output rises, a non-homogenous labour force with each subsequently installed worker being slightly less efficient than the previous one. I shall take the latter case as the basis for my example (though other combinations could be used as well). That is, I assume a small open economy with one or several tradable goods whose prices are fixed on the world market where any surplus production (above domestic needs) can be disposed of. Average and marginal running costs (and average and marginal productivity) are constant for labour of a given quality. But labour is non-homogenous so that we obtain the 'normal' falling marginal productivity and labour demand curve DD' as depicted in *Figure 1* (where w represents the real wage and L stands for labour). Assuming that L^* is the given (and fixed) labour supply, full employment is obtained when the real wage is fixed at w^*, at which all workers are prepared to work.

If we now assume that at a certain moment only N people are employed, then these insiders (or their union) can enforce a wage w_n without having to fear that they will lose their job. But $(L^* - N)$ people will remain unemployed and this could be a permanent position. This is normally taken as a clear example that the union (or insiders) are concerned exclusively with their own welfare without taking any consideration for the outsiders. Now while this may very well be the case it can be shown that a wage above w^* may also be optimal for a union which cares for the entire labour force.

When deciding on the wage to be fixed the union (being constrained by the firm's labour demand curve) can either decide for w^* leading to full employment with the income of *all* workers equal to w^* or it can fix the wage at w_n with some workers obtaining a higher income (w_n) while the unemployed

INSIDERS, OUTSIDERS AND THE TWO-THIRDS-SOCIETY

workers have to depend on unemployment benefits. But these benefits will be to some extent a burden on the employed workers, since they will have to be covered by taxes. Let us assume that these taxes are levied entirely from the employed workers and cannot be shifted to other sectors[3]. This tax burden has to be taken into account in a fully informed union strategy. If we further stipulate that the unions *do* care for the unemployed then a sensible and rather ambitious

Figure 1

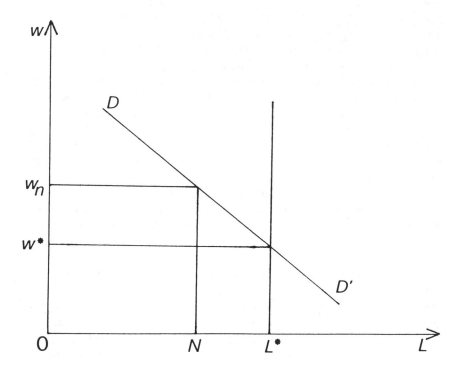

3.   This is, of course, the least advantageous situation for the unions and the workers. It was fully the case in the 19th century when the unemployed members were supported by the unions and it is still true to a considerable extent in today's tax and social insurance systems.

KURT W. ROTHSCHILD

target could be that the outsiders should financially not be worse off than they would have been if a full employment policy had been persued.

Collecting these assumptions we obtain the following picture. We start with a macroeconomic production function with nonhomogenous labour as the only non-fixed input

$$Y=aN-(b/2)N^2 \tag{1}$$

with Y for real output and N for employed workers. The marginal productivity and labour demand function is

$$w=a-bN \tag{2}$$

where w represents the real wage per worker. Assuming that L^* is the given fixed labour supply the union (seen as a wage fixer) has to set the wage at $w=a-bL*$ if it wants to secure full employment. Alternatively it can ask for a higher wage with the consequence that employment N will be less than L^* and that wage income has to be taxed to cover the costs of unemployment benefits. Writing u for the unemployment benefit per unemployed worker the total costs of unemployment for any given level of employment N is

$$u(L^*-N)$$

and the tax levied on each employed person is

$$u(L^*-N)/N \tag{3}$$

Thus if the wage is fixed above w^* the *net wage w'* which employees can take home is

$$w'=a-bN-u(L^*-N)/N$$

or

$$w'=1/N \ [N(a+u)-bN^2-uL^*] \tag{4}$$

236

INSIDERS, OUTSIDERS AND THE TWO-THIRDS-SOCIETY

If the union were not interested in the fate of the outsiders it would prefer low unemployment benefits to keep deductions from wages low. But since we assume that the union does care for the outsiders and wants to compensate them *fully* for not being able to work under full employment conditions, it 'votes' for unemployment benefits equal to the full employment wage. Thus we obtain

$$u=a-bL^* \tag{5}$$

Substituting (5) in (4) we get

$$w'=1/N\ [N(2a-bL^*)-bN^2-(a-bL^*)L^*] \tag{6}$$

An 'optimal' union policy would now be to maximise this 'constrained' net wage w' (constrained by the condition of 'full employment benefits'). Differentiating w' with regard to N we get

$$dw'/dN=1/N^2(-bN^2+aL^*-bL^{*2}) \tag{7}$$

and setting the numerator equal to zero we have

$$N^2=(a/b)L^*-L^{*2} \tag{8}$$

Equation (8) determines the optimal union-insider wage-employment strategy with benefits fixed at the full employment wage. It will lead to less than full employment whenever $L^* > a/(2b)$. Before discussing the result I want to illustrate it with a simple numerical example. We take a labour force of 280 persons ($L^*=280$) and 'technical' coefficients equal to $a=200$, $b=0.5$. *Table 1* shows the results one obtains in the full employment case and the 'optimal' strategy respectively. Formula (8) delivers an optimum solution with 183 employed and 97 unemployed persons. The corresponding wage is fixed at 108 compared with a full employment wage of 60. The unemployed still get the 60 as unemployment benefit, which involves a tax payment of approximately 32 for each employed person leaving them with a net income of 76,7 which is still well above the full employment wage[4].

---

4.   This is the 'optimum' result achievable under the assumption maintained throughout this paper that a single wage rate applies to all workers.

KURT W. ROTHSCHILD

If only income counts and if the unions feel themselves only responsible for the position of the working population (employed and unemployed) then the 'optimal' strategy is clearly pareto-superior to the full employment situation. The insiders are better off and the unemployed not worse off than under full employment. This 'miracle' is, of course, achieved because the shift to the 'optimal strategy' involves a considerable decline in profits[5]. But the usual insinuation that an insider policy *necessarily* implies the neglect of *workers'* interests is not substantiated if we remain within the limits of our assumptions. In fact, if the policy were changed just a little bit so that the unemployed get slightly more than 60, the unemployed themselves would have to be opposed to a return to full employment.

Table 1

	Full Employment	'Optimal Strategy'
Employment (N)	280	183
Unemployed	-	97
Real Output (Y)	36 400	28 228
Gross wage sum	16 800	19 856
Unemployment payments	-	5 820
Gross wage per employee (w)	60	108.5
Net wage per employee (w')	60	76.7
Unemployment benefit per unemployed	-	60
Profits	19 600	8 372

Where is the flaw in the above story? After all, even if we accept the idea that the union (or insiders) has (have) the power to set wages unilaterally and that it is politically feasible to raise unemployment benefits to a 'basic wage' (that is, what it amounts to!), it is difficult to imagine that a Two-Thirds-Society with 'optimal' unemployment would be applauded by the *total* working population. The reasons for this are not difficult to find. They lie in the differences between labour and goods markets: labour services are not just commodities, and wages are not just prices. By concentrating on wages, wage income, and individual preferences for income maximisation we have left out some very

5. This means that employers will normally strongly resist such a strategy. But in this paper we are only concerned with the question of union policy choice under the assumption that the union can enforce its wage demands (with employers determining the corresponding employment level).

INSIDERS, OUTSIDERS AND THE TWO-THIRDS-SOCIETY

decisive factors. Firstly, we live (or should we say: *still* live?) in a 'work society' where participation in *paid* work confers social status and social contacts. Secondly, preferences, too, have a social dimension. It is not only absolute income that counts, but also relative income. This is partly also a status question, but it follows additionally from 'demonstration' effects. An income of 60 gives more satisfaction if it enables me to share the consumption habits of my 'equals' than if some of them constantly 'demonstrate' a higher living standard.

When these factors are taken into account it can be seen that the insider-outsider question takes on a different perspective. Unemployment must be seen as a problem in itself and cannot just be regarded as an income problem. The Two-Thirds-Society is socially questionable quite apart from the poverty problem[6]. A union policy geared to the interests of all workers will have to take its aim at wages *and* employment as two separate though interdependent targets. This means that the fields of a simplified 'pure' marginal productivity theory have to be abandoned and note has to be taken of macroeconomic employment theory and policy options which will have to include considerations regarding effective demand, technology and education, institutional constraints etc. But that is another story.

REFERENCES

BLANCHFLOWER; D.G., OSWALD; A.J. and GARRETT, M.D.: 'Insider Power in Wage Determination', *Economica*, Vol. 57 (1990), pp. 143-70.
COE, D.T.: 'Insider-Outsider Influences on Industry Wages', *Empirical Economics*, Vol. 15 (1990), pp. 163-83.
LINDBECK, A. and SNOWER, D.J.: *The Insider-Outsider Theory of Employment and Unemployment*, Cambridge (Mass.) and London: MIT Press, 1988.
NICKEL, ST. and WADHWANI, S.: 'Insider Forces and Wage Determination', *Economic Journal*, Vol. 100 (1990), pp. 496-509.
ROLAND, G.: 'Gorbachev and the Common European Home: The Convergence Debate Revived?', *Kyklos*, Vol.43 (1990), pp. 385-409.

6.   While I do not want to stress the following point too much I would nevertheless venture to remark that what has been touched in this paper is not completely without relevance for (past) East-West differences. In the Soviet Union and other Eastern European countries full employment was given high priority without much consideration to its effects on individual wages. While I do not want to belittle the many other factors which had a dampening effect on productivity, this employment policy may have contributed to it. In the West, on the other hand, there was a greater stress on productivity which provided a basis for higher wages but was partly achieved by sifting out less productive workers and pushing them into long-term unemployment or into the circle of the 'working poor' thus threatening the advent of a Two-Thirds-Society. These strategic differences play some role in the present economic ajustment processes in the East (see, e.g,. ROLAND [1990])

Cambridge Journal of Economics 1993, 17, 259–266

(1993)

P 21
Germany

Like a *Lehrstück* by Brecht: notes on the German reunification drama

Kurt W. Rothschild*

Perestroika and its consequences took the world by surprise, experts and ordinary citizens alike. Overnight, a whole system was given notice and a transformation from dictatorship to democracy and from a Soviet-style ('planned') economy to a Western-style ('market') economy begun. While it was possible to put political reforms into place fairly quickly—at least formally—it was clear from the onset that economic transformation would require more time and encounter much greater difficulties. While switches from authoritarian to democratic regimes have been made before and do not require fundamental changes in material structures, the transformation of entire economic systems—and by this time badly functioning and deteriorating ones—presented a far more formidable task. It quickly became obvious that neither experience nor theory could provide secure guidance and that the transition would involve far more in the way of trial and error, dispute and compromise. Mistakes are unavoidable; but there may be more mistakes than necessary with dire economic and social consequences. The early history of the East German transformation process seems to fit this latter case.[1] This, I believe, will become clear from the following account.

Although it is common to refer to the transformation process and transformation problems of the Soviet bloc as a whole, it should not be forgotten that the circumstances of the various countries are rather different. The former Soviet Union and its territories are clearly a chapter in themselves. But the other countries also have specifities which must be kept in mind. This is particularly so in the case of East Germany, the only region which ceased to remain an independent country with an economic policy of its own.

Manuscript received 19 October 1992; final version received 23 March 1993.

*University of Linz. The literature on the economic unification of East and West Germany is substantial. The bibliography of this literature published by the library of the Institut für Weltwirtschaft in Kiel is itself a book-like product. Instead of an extensive reference list (which would still be selective) I want to mention as useful critical studies just the book by Gerlinde and Hans-Werner Sinn, *Kaltstart. Volkswirtschaftliche Aspekte deer deutschen Vereinigung* (Tübingen, J. C. B. Mohr, 1991, 2nd edn, 1992) and a series of books under the general title *Probleme der Einheit* (Marburg, Metropolis-Verlag, 1991, 1992). A much discussed early study in English is G. A. Akerlof, A. K. Rose, J. L. Yellen and H. Hessenius, 'East Germany in from the Cold: The Aftermath of Currency Union', *Brookings Papers for Economic Activity*, Nr. 1, 1991, pp. 1–105.

The empirical data used in the present paper are predominantly from various issues of *Wirtschaft und Statistik*, the monthly publication of the German Federal Office of Statistics (Statistisches Bundesamt), from Bulletins of the major economic research institutes, particularly the DIW (German Institute of Economic Research in Berlin), and from the OECD *Economic Survey of Germany 1991/92*.

[1] The official German terminology distinguishes between *alte und neue Bundesländer* (old and new federal provinces), the 'old provinces' referring to West Germany and the 'new provinces' to the former German Democratic Republic (GDR). For the sake of brevity I shall refer to West and East Germany.

0309–166X/93/030259 + 08 $08.00/0

260   K. W. Rothschild

It may be useful to point out the main differences between the East German situation and that of the other nations concerned. Let me begin with the favourable aspects. Together with Czechoslovakia and to a lesser extent Hungary and Poland, East Germany has the advantage of a notable industrial past and a skilled labour force. Despite the lag in the development and modernisation of its industrial base, it has the potential for a fairly quick take-off towards full participation in developed world markets. Added to this, of course, are the advantages of becoming part of a powerful country which is in a position to offer various forms of assistance and with markets unhampered by language and legal barriers. From this point of view the prospects for a quick East German upswing looked (and still look) much brighter than for all of the other transformation candidates.

But the very advantages of being adsorbed into the most powerful West European economy bring with them a number of special drawbacks. One of these, as we shall see, is due not so much to the absorption as such, as to its suddenness and comprehensiveness. The question whether a gradual transformation strategy would have been preferable to the 'big bang' strategy adopted is still an open one, but the fact remains that no other country has been exposed to such a big bang as East Germany. This necessarily created problems and, from the very beginning, closed off many avenues for learning and experimenting in the adjustment process. But even apart from the question of speed, the fact of being fitted fully and completely into the existing West German legal and economic structure rules out for East Germany certain strategies of linking change to existing institutions, behavioural traditions, experiences etc, which are open to the other transformation countries. Furthermore, the facts of a common language and organisational environment and other contacts with the West, previously counted as advantages, also increase the problem of discontent with the slowness of adjustment and can intensify unsettling demands and migration tendencies.

So much for the general background. We give next a short presentation of the main events and economic outcomes. As far as the basic political and economic conditions—the framework of the drama—are concerned, events followed each other with breathtaking rapidity. Though the story should start with Gorbachev's rise to power in 1985, we shall turn immediately to 1989 when the pace really started to quicken. In the Spring of that year the western frontier of Hungary became 'leaky', enabling East German 'tourists' to escape to the West, at first in small groups but then in quickly growing numbers, driven not only by a search for better conditions but also by the fear that such an opportunity would not last for long. At the same time, dissent and unrest spread within the country leading to the Autumn 'soft revolution' which culminated in big demonstrations, particularly in Leipzig. In November the frontier to West Germany was opened and a new GDR government signed an agreement of cooperation with West Germany, followed (in January 1990) by the readmission of private enterprise and joint ventures. A further important shift followed in March 1990. The nationalised enterprises were formally turned into joint-stock companies, private banking was permitted and the *Treuhandanstalt* (THA) established to look after the entire state property (land and industry) and prepare it for successful adaptation to a market environment (see Priewe, this issue).

March 1990 also saw the first free parliamentary elections in the GDR, which resulted in a clear victory for the conservative CDU (Christlich-Demokratische Union). The CDU had the closest links to the western German government from whose (promised) help a quick change-over to unity and a higher living standard was expected. Two months later a state treaty between the two German governments (West and East) was signed (to come into force on 1 July), combining the two countries in a single economic, currency and social union. Shortly before this union came into being—in June—the 'right to work' was removed from the constitution of the GDR, most price controls were abolished and, in a revision of the law concerning the THA, emphasis was laid on a speedy privatisation of state enterprises with reorganisation of promising enterprises as a subsidiary provisional measure. The closing-down of non-competitive enterprises provided a third choice.

Immediately after the establishment of the union of 1 July the unification of the currency on the basis of the western Mark (DM) came into force. The terms on which the East German Mark, which had stood at about 7 eastern Marks for 1 DM on the black market (partly because of speculative overvaluations of the DM), should be converted into DM was a difficult and hotly debated question. With free trade between the two regions, the exchange rate had to reflect purchasing power considerations, taking into account both the lower wages and the lower productivity in East German enterprises. As far as wages were concerned (lower in the East than in the West in the respective currencies) they should stay lower because of the lower labour productivity. On the other hand, if they were kept too low this might encourage the survival of outmoded enterprises with poor future prospects. Also, low wages might fuel further heavy migration to the West, though the same danger could be expected from high wages leading to unemployment. Finally, there were problems connected with savings, which should not be overly devalued, in order not to disappoint raised hopes, while at the same time the accumulated purchasing power should not be allowed to threaten a continuing policy of price stability and a strong DM.

In the end, the following compromise solution (with a not very happy central bank) was adopted. One possible currency *reform*, which would have frozen part of the eastern money stock for some time, to be released later in line with growing adjustment, was rejected—not least for political reasons (the hopes and expectations which had been raised in the unification campaign should not be disappointed right at the very start of the change). Instead, a differentiated system of exchange rates was established for the exchange of the eastern Mark into DM. A rate of 1:1 was granted for money holdings up to 2000 Marks for children under the age of 15, up to 4000 Marks for people between 15 and 59 years of age and up to 6000 Marks for older people. Money holdings (M3) beyond these amounts and financial obligations were exchangeable at the rate of 2:1. Finally a rate of 3:1 was applied to Mark holdings in other countries and to certain speculative hoards. As far as current money flows were concerned, a rate of 1:1 was applied to price and wage contracts and to old age pensions (calculated on the basis of eastern wages).

As compared with the black market exchange rate of about 7:1 before the conversion, this seemed an extremely favourable exchange arrangement and was criticised as a potential source of inflation. But the black market rate had not been based on purchasing power parities but rather on expectations about the availability of goods and on speculation about imminent currency reform. The price differences between East and West were difficult to judge in view of very different price and cost structures, but they did not correspond at all to the black market rate. Though the eastern Mark was certainly somewhat over-valued in the exchange process, the feared inflationary push in Germany as a whole did not take place (the consumer price index rose only by 2·8% in 1990).

Three months after the establishment of economic and currency union the complete unification of the two Germanies took place, on the basis of a unification treaty agreed upon in August 1990 and sanctioned by the occupation powers in both regions. Contrary to earlier plans to unify the two German countries in a (lengthy) process of finding a common basis for the new Germany, it was decided to adopt a 'crash' solution, with East Germany being absorbed into West Germany by taking over all its laws, regulations and

262   K. W. Rothschild

institutions lock, stock and barrel.[1] Thus, within the space of a single year, enormous political and economic changes had pushed the GDR from a state-dominated system into a highly developed and differentiated private market system.

Momentous as these shocks and changes were, their effects were even more dramatic. Between 1990 and 1991 the real gross domestic product (GDP) of East Germany declined by almost 30%.[2] In 1992 a slow upward movement set in, leading to a gain of about 8% over the previous year and it looks as though a similar figure may be attained in 1993. But there is still a considerable way to go to reach the 1989 East German level, let alone to catch up with the West German productivity and activity levels that politicians had promised would be attained within four years of unification.

Even more dramatic than the decline in GDP was the breakdown of the manufacturing sector. While building and services (particularly retail trade, restaurants, civil service, etc) were able to maintain and sometimes even expand their locally protected activities, the unprepared manufacturing sector was fully exposed to the sudden and unimpeded inflow of western goods and the loss of its traditional eastern markets. In the second half of 1990 manufacturing output fell to half the level of the first half, followed by a further decline in 1991 to about a third of the former level. Only by 1992 were there signs of a slow recovery. The value of exports declined by 59% between 1989 and 1991 and began to rise slowly in 1992, although now with rather better prospects once the world-wide slowdown of growth has been overcome.

These dramatic inroads into output, which surpassed anything that had been experienced in the great depression of the 1930s, was only partly mirrored in the unemployment situation. Employment shrank by 23% within a year of the reform; at the end of 1992 it was 40% below the end of 1991; and it will probably decline—because of further rationalisation and liquidation measures and public savings programmes—by a further 9% in 1993 (OECD estimate). Unemployment figures, however, rose far more slowly. Migration to the West, short-time working subsidies (occasionally with zero-hour working weeks), early pensioning off of dismissed workers, and a growing use of active labour market policies slowed down the rise of registered unemployment. Even so, the unemployment rate in East Germany, where people had been unfamiliar with this problem, rose from practically zero to more than 10% in 1991, 15% in 1992, and with a probable further rise to about 20% in 1993. 'Genuine' open and hidden unemployment (including discouraged female workers who lost their factory nurseries) has been estimated to have affected 40% of the former labour force.

In stark contrast to this picture of an economy in decline, the years since 1990 have seen an unbroken and even slightly rising level of final demand. This 'miracle' has been achieved by huge transfers from West Germany to the eastern *Länder*, which far surpassed the sums which had originally been thought necessary for a fast and successful unification process. Added together, western transfers (from federal and provincial governments, labour administration, unification fund etc) came to 170 bn DM for 1991 and approximately 218 bn DM for 1992. These figures correspond to 5·5 and 6·5% of Germany's GNP respectively, and should be compared with West Germany's share in the Marshall Plan, which amounted to approximately 2% of GNP. Of the 1992 contributions, about 55% were intended for consumption expenditure and consumption subsidies, 25% for

---

[1] A provisional exception was made with regard to abortion laws, where East Germany was permitted to retain her more liberal regulations.

[2] These figures rest on rough estimates of the Deutsches Institut für Wirtschaftsforschung (DIW) in Berlin. The Federal Statistical Office does not yet publish estimates of East German GDP.

investment and investment subsidies, and 20% for various other purposes. Of the transfers, 40% benefit private households directly, thereby financing about one third of East German private consumption. Hopes that such transfers would only be a short-term necessity have been abandoned. In March 1993—after considerable political controversy—a 'solidarity pact' was adopted, with plans for increases in taxation and cuts in government expenditure in order to finance additional transfers for many years. These sums will amount to billions of D Marks each year.

Thanks to these massive transfers, East Germany has been able to run a large import surplus and to absorb resources (private and public consumption and investment plus changes in stocks) far exceeding domestic production and income. The excess of absorption over GNP amounted to 40% in the second half of 1990 and rose to almost 90% in 1991 and 1992. Higher wages, pensions and transfer incomes based on this support enabled the maintenance of aggregate demand, a large part of which went into imports and into supporting the inflation of the (lower) East German price level (consumer prices rose by 14% in 1991 and by 11% in 1992).

It is this sharp contrast between a catastrophic decline in production and a fairly unchanged standard of demand and purchasing power which constitutes the outstanding difference between East Germany and all the other transformation countries. The lesson to be learnt is that one can afford the luxury of a 'big bang' strategy only if one has a rich uncle (whether it be America or Germany). But while East German transformation just about weathered the rough treatment it had to undergo, it could not be called a success. The high hopes that had been raised before unification by promises from the western government that nobody would be worse of after the unification, that taxes would not be raised, that East Germany would soon blossom and attain western standards in a few years, were badly disappointed. Unemployment and fear of unemployment on the one side, and unexpected burdens on the other, have created an atmosphere which contrasts sharply with the euphoric climate of 1990 and adds to the difficulties of finding a way out of the present impasse.

What are the reasons for the poor economic performance of East Germany since 1990? How far were they inevitable, how far 'home-grown'? It is obvious that changes of the magnitude of the transformation of the eastern European economies cannot be achieved without initial setbacks, even under favourable conditions. But conditions in East Germany were (and are) anything but favourable: inadequate infrastructure, partly obsolete capital stock, technological gaps, ecological neglect etc, all contribute to an intensification of adjustment difficulties and costs. But these factors alone cannot account for the dramatic setbacks since 1989 although, until recently, the German government tended to blame the past for all the shortcomings and disappointments since unification.[1] The severity and persistence of the set-back was greatly exacerbated by a number of miscalculations and omissions which were only slowly admitted and are still more slowly being corrected.

The most important negative shock occurred right at the beginning in July 1990, with the sudden and simultaneous opening of western trade and the switch to the DM. I have already mentioned that the currency measures were intended to achieve a variety of targets: to stop migration to the West, to integrate the eastern economy into the world economy under competitive conditions, to safeguard to some extent the immediate usability and purchasing power of eastern private savings, to maintain existing debt

---

[1] At the celebrations for the second anniversary of unification in October 1992, the German prime minister Kohl admitted (or had to admit) that policy mistakes had been made in the transformation process.

structures etc. It is obvious that no conceivable exchange arrangement—and quite a number were discussed—could have met all these targets at the same time. To achieve this it would have been necessary to adopt an intermediate regime of differentiated regulations. As it was, an exchange arrangement was adopted which could meet the expectations of the savers to some extent, but which involved an overvaluation of the eastern currency. This by itself had a severe dampening effect on the entire sector of internationally traded goods: exports were impeded, imports were encouraged.

But the overvaluation is not even half the story, particularly since—with a very different cost and price structure and lower wages—some of the eastern enterprises were in principle able to compete with western ones. But with the simultaneous complete freeing of western trade, price competitiveness counted for little in a world of imperfect competition and heterogeneous goods. Western products, with their different qualities and much more sophisticated marketing techniques (unheard of by eastern managers), rapidly mopped up eastern demand. The savings and the transfers going to the East stimulated the economies of West Germany and other western European countries. On the export side not only was the overvaluation a hindrance, but even more important was the loss of the dominant eastern European markets to whose needs the East German export industry had been adapted. With payments to East Germany to be made in hard DM-currency, the motivation to buy there was greatly reduced, with a consequent break-down of export sales, which could not easily be redirected to the West, for whose needs a different pattern of products and product qualities was required (see Heseler, this issue).

Though some people in West Germany regarded and still regard the big bang of 1990 as the ideal solution, many politicians and economists admit that a more gradual transition, on both the trade and the currency side, would have been preferable. But they maintain that the sudden, definite step was essential for political reasons, firstly in order to put a stop to mass migration from East to West Germany (where DMs could be earned) and secondly because of fears that the moment favourable to unification might slip away with changes in the Russian political landscape. It is doubtful how compelling these arguments are. Political unification was already seen as unavoidable internationally and could have proceeded with dual economic regimes. As far as migration is concerned, a serious and convincing programme with clearly defined steps to future full economic integration might have been possible and more productive than the euphoric march into immediate and complete unification.[1]

But be that as it may, if the quick change-over was a *political* necessity, particular attention should at least have been paid to the probable economic consequences and problems and a combination of measures to ease the situation provided. But though warnings regarding the possible dangers were raised here and there—ranging from the president of the Bundesbank to Oscar Lafontaine, a leading Social Democrat—these were drowned in the euphoric promises of the unification days. No proper strategy for meeting foreseeable difficulties was developed. Instead, all hope was pinned on the quick privatisation and modernisation of the East German economy and on the market forces which were supposed to lead in a relatively short time to full integration into the German and world economic network.

As already mentioned the reformed Treuhandanstalt (THA) was assigned the task of selling off the former state enterprises and, secondarily, of reorganising and restructuring firms that were felt to be viable but could not be sold immediately, and liquidating those

---

[1] Since instant unification could not remove the wide disparity between western and eastern wages and living standards an incentive for migration remained. Unemployment is of course an additional factor.

that were not. As the activities and performance of the THA are discussed at length elsewhere in this issue (see Priewe), I shall not go into detail here. Suffice it to say that the THA faced a strong buyer's market and that potential investors were anything but keen. After the more attractive enterprises had been sold the THA, under pressure to privatise, was driven into making worse and worse deals. Prices had to be lowered drastically and various concessions made. Even so, privatisation proceeded at a much slower pace than expected. By March 1992 the THA had privatised 42% of its 11,555 firms (including sales to municipalities) with another 6% returned to former owners; about 10% of the firms were liquidated, leaving more than 40% still to be privatised (including most of the 'difficult' cases).

The emphasis on privatisation led to neglect of the reorganisation and liquidation functions of the THA. Intent on early privatisation, the reorganisation of potentially viable firms (all firms had to prepare reorganisation plans) was seen only as a limited, short-term task. Limited credits were granted, enabling firms to maintain a nucleus of activities but no or few opportunities were created for the development of new products, for R&D and marketing activities (which are badly needed). This not only involved the loss of jobs and the migration of skilled personnel to the West but also reduced the chances for efficient privatisation. In time, some of these mistakes and shortcomings were recognised and gradual reforms were made in the THA, such as the acceptance and furtherance of management buy-outs, more liberal credits for future-oriented activities or participation in the establishment of 'employment companies' (temporary employment for communal needs outside ordinary market processes and for qualifying activities for dismissed workers). But the fact remains that the construction of and the reliance on the THA and its privatisation priority has contributed to the general difficulties mentioned above rather than alleviating them.

Basic difficulties and 'wrong turns' thus combined to throw the East German economy into deep recession. At present it looks as if the upturn may have begun, though—with world prospects not at their best—it looks more like a crawl than a march. It will clearly take some time before 1989 eastern levels are regained, let alone western levels. Whether they will ever be attained, or whether the ruined eastern landscape will remain a German *mezzogiorno*, is still an open question.

It is not possible to discuss here what alternative policies might have been adopted and what they could have achieved. But it is a fact that warnings were brushed aside and possible alternatives hardly discussed beforehand, only later being reluctantly taken up under the pressure of actual events. That politicians and interested lobbies should paint a rosy and oversimplified picture of the unification process may be understandable. Ignorance and political and economic sectoral advantages flowing from the expansionary possibilities stimulated such a policy. But that many, though not all, economists jumped on the band-wagon is hardly excusable. This is not the place to discuss the relative merits and shortcomings of mainstream, Keynesian, institutional and other types of economic theory. They probably all have something to say on different aspects of western-style capitalist market economies. But to use them, or rather one version of them, as the decisive guiding principle for the transformation problem was bound to create difficulties.

Though it was frequently stressed that we do not have a proper theory of the transformation of state-regulated eastern into market-style western economies, few hesitated to analyse the process from the perspective of neoclassic market theory, property rights analysis, and other building blocs of mainstream economics. These elements are, however, at best suited to the study of behavioural relations under an historically given

266   K. W. Rothschild

institutional framework and marginal adjustments to a slowly changing environment. Both these conditions are absent when a completely different system is imposed on an entire community overnight, destroying not only physical but also human capital in production and administration, and demanding deep inroads into behaviour and institutions going far beyond the elements of market processes and privatisation illusions contained in 'normal' economic theory. In fact, what is being experienced is a repetition of the mistakes which characterised the early discussions of economic policies for developing countries, when theoretical structures of the 'pure' economics of developed capitalist countries were applied with little discrimination to the very different problems of the less developed nations.[1] There can be little doubt that a 'political economy' paying more consideration to political, institutional, sociological and psychological factors, with their effects on timing, mobility, expectations etc, could have provided a better background for decision-making and might have mitigated the steep fall into depression and unemployment which will take a long time to repair. In the meantime, a 'lost generation' beats up foreigners and recalls visions of early Nazi days.

[1] Myrdal criticised this approach very aptly in his monumental study *Asian Drama* and what he said there can be applied *mutatis mutandis* to the case under discussion. 'Economic theorists', he wrote, 'more than other social scientists, have long been disposed to arrive at general propositions and then postulate them as valid for every time, place, and culture. There is a tendency in contemporary economic theory to follow this path to the extreme. For such confidence in the constructs of economic reasoning there is no empirical foundation. But even apart from this recent tendency, we have inherited from classical economics a treasury of theories that are regularly positioned with more general claims than they warrant ... As long as their use is restricted to our part of the world this pretense of generality may do little harm. But when theories and concepts designed to fit the special conditions of the Western world [in normal peace times, one should add, K.W.R.] ... are used in the study of underdeveloped countries in South Asia, where they do *not* fit, the consequences are serious' (Gunnar Myrdal 1968. *Asian Drama. An Inquiry into the Poverty of Nations*, Vol. I, pp. 16/17 New York, Pantheon).

[26]

2 89 - 99

1994

Austro-Keynesianism Reconsidered

Kurt W. Rothschild

Austria

E62
E66

E12

The 1978 Economic Survey of Austria by the OECD (Organization for Economic Cooperation and Development) opened with the following sentence: "The most remarkable feature of the Austrian economy of the last few years has been the simultaneous achievement of a progressive reduction of inflation and continued growth of employment" (5). It expressed the surprised recognition—soon to be shard all over the world--that little Austria, once an economic problem area par excellence, seemed to have charted a course which after 1970 ran counter to the unfavorable experiences in most of the other countries where economic growth had slowed and unemployment had returned as a pressing and growing problem. While after 1970-72 unemployment rose everywhere—and increased dramatically in the 1975 world-wide set-back—Austria was able to maintain a satisfactory growth record and to cut unemployment to the lowest postwar levels. Austria's unemployment rate, which in 1970 had stood (with 2.4 percent) above the average level of 2 percent in nine developed Western European countries (Austria, Belgium, Germany, Italy, Netherlands, Norway, Sweden, United Kingdom) fell to 1.9 percent.[1] Among Western European countries only Sweden, Norway and Switzerland had lower, but not declining unemployment in the 1970s. Moreover, this favorable employment record was achieved without serious inflationary consequences. Austria's inflation rate, which had stood at 4.4 percent in 1970 amounted to 6.4 percent in 1980 compared to 5.8 percent (1970) and 11.3 percent (1980) for the average of the aforementioned nine countries.

This success story of the 1970s and early 1980s which later (in 1979) was christened "Austro-Keynesianism was the result of a variety of factors. Like "Reaganomics," "Austro-Keynesianism" is not a clear-cut, theoretically-defined concept but rather an afterthought systematizing a pragmatic development and its results (with important differences *in content* between the two cases!). Here we have to restrict ourselves to a very brief sketch of the main aspects of Austro-Keynesianism, which will allow us afterwards to judge its significance from today's perspective.

A decisive reason for the divergent developments in the Austrian economy during the 1970s lies in the political sphere. Just at a time when the Western world (with few exceptions) turned conservative—both politically and economically—Austria stepped in the opposite direction. In the 1970 elections, the Socialist party overtook the conservative People's party, replacing the conservative government by a socialist-led coalition government. This government was replaced in 1971 by a purely socialist government after the Socialist party had won an absolute majority. This change of government had a decisive influence on the main directions of economic policy. While in most other countries, the rise in inflation rates and the "monetarist revolution" which preached the advantages and curative powers of "free markets" induced conservative governments to cut back public engagement and intervention for economic growth and full employment which had been typical in the preceding years, the Austrian government and not least its head, Bruno Kreisky, remained faithful to a full employment target, even increasing the emphasis in view of the economic disturbances of the mid-1970s.

While a determined political will to maintain production and employment was an important precondition for the course of events, it could not be decisive by itself. It had to be translated into an effective policy. This was achieved not so much by a clear-cut concept but rather by a more pragmatic policy-mix, though theoretical considerations as well as practical and historical experiences served as important guides. The main elements of this policy mix can be summarized as follows.

First, it was taken for granted that a certain steadiness of final demand is necessary if a cumulative deterioration in production and employment is to be avoided. Since the slow-down in the world economy threatened exports and with them the entire demand basis, public efforts were needed to prevent major set-backs from this side which at the time were considered a purely temporary disturbance in a fundamentally prosperous world development. Thus, a policy of "diving through" was adopted. Public demand was upheld and even increased in spite of falling revenues; budget deficits and a quickly-rising public debt were permitted to develop in the hope that they could easily be reversed in the coming return to world prosperity. In addition, special help was granted to industries and regions whose difficulties could develop into a threat for a wider circle of sectors and regions. These "demand-side" measures were supported by the extension of already existing "supply-side" measures such as special depreciation allowances, tax rebates, interest rate subsidies and the like to provide a prop for investment.

The challenge of growing inflation, which after the 1960s existed in Austria just as much as in other countries, was not met by a deflationary assault with its depressive affects on economic activity, but by a rather original combination of exchange rate and income policies. A "hard currency policy" was adopted that maintained a fixed exchange rate between the Austrian schilling (AS) and the German deutschmark (DM). This policy had two consequences. First, it removed all exchange rate risks vis-à-vis Germany, who is Austria's largest trading partner by far, both on the expert and on the import side. Second, it meant that the schilling—in line with the deutschmark—appreciated vis-à-vis the dollar and other currencies, mitigating world-wide inflationary tendencies. This proved particularly important in the wake of the two oil price shocks in 1973 and 1979.

But this hard currency policy (making Austrian commodities expensive for "weaker" currencies) could have been a threat to Austria's foreign transactions, stimulating imports and hampering exports. This threat was to a considerable extent met by a special Austrian institution, the so-called "Social Partnership," a rather informal body of cooperative contacts between the big and influential organizations of industry (employers' organization, Chamber of Trade), employees (trade unions, Chamber of Labor), and agriculture which had developed in the postwar years to come to terms with the tasks of reconstruction and normalization. Regular contacts in this framework permit a certain degree of steering market developments, and particularly wage-price processes, keeping them within certain bounds and preventing run-away developments. That such "corporatist" structures can be a help in stabilizing economies has been a wide-spread experience (with Germany, Switzerland, Sweden as typical examples in addition to Austria). This framework enabled Austria to maintain its international competitiveness in spit of the hard-currency policy. Wages and prices were on the whole sufficiently constrained by compromise and consensus to support the viability of the currency policy and its anti-inflationary effects.

We can now indicate in what respects the term "Austro-Keynesianism" is justified and what it signifies. A prominent Keynesian aspect was the obvious insistence on the role of effective demand and its stabilization (as far as possible) even at the cost of rising budget deficits and a certain degree of inflation. Another Keynesian or Post-Keynesian element was the attempt to contain inflation by some sort of income policy rather that through a policy of deflation and high interest rates. Finally, the stimulating effects of this declared public policy of maintaining high employment on business confidence and investment were also in the spirit of Keynesian ideas about the need to reduce uncertainty and risk.

The specific "Austro-"aspects in Austro-Keynesianism can also be summarized under three headings. First, the policy was not a dogmatic, one-sided Keynesian strategy with all the stress laid on demand maintenance and demand support. "Supply-side" measures, providing direct incentives to business and investment, were intensively used as an additional stimulus. Second, introduction of a hard-currency policy via the DM-connection was a very special approach to apply competitive pressure as a constraint on price. And finally, the historically-grown Social Partnership provided a framework that permitted a special type of income policy and market regulation.

This Austro-Keynesianism mixture that got going after 1970 and evolved during the following decade began to decline after 1980 and has practically disappeared as a special characteristic of Austria. The country has fallen into line with general Western European and world development. While between 1973 and 1979 the real GDP (gross domestic product) per capita had grown by three percent per annum in Austria against two percent in the European part of the OECD, growth rates fell and the difference shrank to two percent in Austria and 1.7 percent (OECD) between 1979 to 1989. Full employment ceased to exist. Though an expanding labor force led to further increases in employment, unemployment reached a level of 5.9 percent in 1992, still somewhat lower than the Western European average (7.9 percent) but far above previously accepted targets.

Several reasons contributed to the fading out of the Austro-Keynesian practice and pragmatism. A basic reason was that one of the main premises on which this practice had relied turned out to be false. The idea that a full employment policy connected with a rise in budget deficits and balance of payment problems (caused by a high import level) should be accepted was based on the expectation that the world-wide stagflation and recession would only be a temporary deviation from the growth path of the preceding years. This expectation was widely held at the time, not only in Austria. When it became clear (particularly in the 1981 recession) that a quick return to false, growth-high employment conditions in the international sphere was unlikely, the idea of "diving through" had to be discarded. A certain adaptation to the new situation was necessary.[2]

One obvious problem was that the sufferance of growing budget deficits had led to steep rise in the government debt. From a mere AS 47 billion (12.5 percent of GDP) in 1970 the debt had risen to AS 261 billion (26.2 percent of GDP) in 1980, with a strong rising tendency that ultimately stabilized a round 48 percent of GDP ten years later. While this is not an abnormal level as compared with other countries, the interest burden which it involves made it necessary to pay more attention to the size of deficits with consequent constraints on fiscal policy in general and on employment policy in particular.

These constraining budget effects were intensified by a change in the political background. After 1982 the Socialist party lost its absolute majority, and though still the strongest party in Parliament, it could only rule in coalition with one of the more conservative parties. This—together with the real difficulties and the international "climate"—led to a marked shift in policy targets. Reducing the budget deficit and containing government expenditure became top priorities pushing the employment target into the background. Keynesian skepticism with regard to automatic tendencies toward employment equilibrium was replaced by the more fashionable belief in the self-healing qualities of free, competitive market processes.

But even if these political changes had not taken place and the old priorities had remained unchanged, modifications in the policy would have been required. Originally designed (as far as we can speak of a "design") as a short-term strategy to avoid large-scale unemployment during a period of passing difficulties, it concentrated largely on demand maintenance wherever production and employment were threatened and on the extension of public and private services. But with the persistence of the external stagnation this policy of employment conservation threatened to become a hindrance to structural change which demanded a decline of some of the older industries and an accelerated creation and growth of new industries and products to fit into a changing world scene. While some change in this direction took place, its speed was rather moderate. A continued employment policy would have required a new Austro-Keynesian policy-mix with greater provision for long-term developments and structural change.[3]

A final factor contributing to the dissolution of Austro-Keynesianism is the general decline in opportunities for autonomous national economic policies in the wake of a growing international economic integration and the liberalization of capital movements. This factor, to which we shall return again later on, weighs particularly heavily in a small, open economy like Austria's where external transactions occupy a prominent place (exports including services: 41 percent of GDP; imports 40 percent).

When we come to an evaluation of the Austro-Keynesianism episode and try to derive some lessons from it, a separation between an Austrian and a more general perspective seems in place. As far as the Austrian perspective is concerned, we must distinguish between the situation as it presented itself in the 1970s and as it presents itself today. We must not forget that the premise on which the Austro-Keynesian strategy was built, namely, that the world-wide break in prosperity and growth would only be a short disturbance in a continuing trend, was a reasonable assumption at the time and was shared by many (though not all) economists and politicians all over the world.[4] Seen from this angle, the policy was certainly a success and was recognized as such by other countries and by international organizations. The "Austrian model" which managed to maintain full employment in the midst of a stagnating world with increasing unemployment and which could achieve this without paying the price of higher inflation was studied as an important experiment in several studies and conferences. The fact that this policy was accompanied by a quick expansion of the public debt and by structural inertia was not sufficiently noted to begin with; but it could also be regarded as a reasonable cost, considering the assumption that these drawbacks could easily be repaired in a coming period of regained world prosperity.

The picture changes when we look at the Austro-Keynesian story form a somewhat later perspective. In the later years of Austro-Keynesianism, say after 1980, reasonable doubts about the short-term nature of the stagnant international tendencies and about a return to the "golden era" conditions of the 1960s could no longer be suppressed. They should have led to a serious analysis and reconsideration of the established policy-mix and to attempts to modify it so as to meet the new situation and its longer-term aspects. This would not have required a renouncement of the full employment target as a top priority; but the policy-mix would have required adaptations and changes. Among the things to be done, it would have been advisable (and possible) to create a more flexible budget policy that would allow budget deficits and budget surpluses to be fitted better to the fluctuating economic situation (and so to achieve the desired demand effects at lower rates of debt accumulation); to supplement and modify the employment-oriented, supply-side supports (low interest rates, subsidies and the like) with structural considerations (including ecological needs); to "soften" the hard-currency policy to be able to meet structural balance of payments problems; and to help the Social Partnership to be better prepared for new problems in a changed environment.

The neglect of this need for reforms and (constant) adaptations led to a certain hardening of the earlier approaches, making the policy less effective in later years and creating the already mentioned problems of a quickly-expanding government debt and of structural disequilibrium which then—together with the shift in political weights from 1983 onwards—led to the end of a clearly distinguishable Austrian-type policy. As in other countries, reductions of deficits, containment of the government dept, price stability and international competitiveness became the leading targets, though employment has continued to play a somewhat more prominent role than in some other countries.

It must, however, be stressed that even an adapted and rejuvenated Austro-Keynesianism would have lost effectiveness in the 1980s in view of the loss of sovereignty in economic policy connected with the complete liberalization of capital movements, international integration, and particularly with Austria's membership in the European Economic Space and her intended membership in the European Community. Already today, but to a far greater extent in the future (in case the ECF achieves its aims of currency and political union) a small open economy will have very few opportunities to follow an economic policy of its own with a target-mix that differs from that of the Community as a whole. Fiscal, monetary, and trade policies, will be closely tied to the general trend of Community action. This does not mean that no national action at all can be taken and that small-country governments will be reduced to mere passive policy-takers; but the range of opportunities will be very modest indeed. Perhaps the people of Denmark will be glad one day that their negative vote to the extensive Maastricht plans secured for them a certain degree of monetary and policy flexibility which offers them a somewhat wider freedom of choice in their economic affairs.

A further valuative view from an Austrian standpoint can be taken when one looks back from 1993 asking whether the country *today* is better or worse of because of the special Austro-Keynesian walk taken in the 1970s and early 1980s. From an empirical point of view this is an idle question: we can never satisfactorily construct the alternative past, the answer to the question, what would have happened *if*. But one can speculate. And there the opinions differ.

Some people regard the past events as a failure because the fixation on the employment target had got the country into the habit of accepting budget deficits that lasted too long and that are responsible for the present interest burden, which—together with the structural distortions of the employment-oriented policies—is responsible for some of the present difficulties (including unemployment). This seems to me too one-sided a picture. While the heritage of a high debt and structural imbalance has to be admitted, it cannot be ascribed totally to the Austro-Keynesian elements in Austria's past. Increases in budget deficits and public debt have occurred in most countries as a consequence of cyclical and long-term disturbances though without turning them to employment-augmenting use. Moreover, with 48 percent of GDP, the present size of the Austrian government debt is neither alarming nor excessive when compared with that of other countries (for example, 39 percent on Germany, 28 percent in France, but 93 percent in Italy and 106 percent in Belgium). And as far as structural problems are concerned, most of them could not have been avoided because of the uncertainties in a rapidly changing world scene. Here, too, Austria's achievements and problems do not seem to differ markedly form the average of Western European countries.

On the other hand, the concern about employment in the Austro-Keynesian period has left a positive heritage that is still felt today. Though unemployment increased rapidly after the policy-change in the early 1980s—*relatively* quicker than the Western European average—the fact that the formation of a hard core of basic unemployment was avoided in the 1970s has left its mark on later developments. As mentioned before, Austria's present unemployment of roughly six percent lies still below a Western European average of about eight percent.

What general lessons can be learned from the Austro-Keynesian episode? In particular, how are these lessons of interest for other countries? One point must be stressed right away. Regardless whether one considers Austro-Keynesianism a success or a failure, it could not be an exact model to be followed (or avoided) by other states. Some of the prerequisites for the finally emerging policy-mix had been historically-grown institutions and attitudes that cannot be easily created or transferred to other countries.[5] Among these one has to mention particularly the existence of highly organized and centralized bodies representing the main socio-economic interest groups (employers, employees, industry, agriculture) and their regular contacts (extending to government participation) in the so-called "Social Partnership." Close and fairly smooth contacts between the Central Bank and the government also belong to this picture. This was a precondition for combining a hard-currency policy with a corresponding wage and price policy (an "income policy") which provided a certain balance between employment, price stability, and international competitiveness.

Though the particular institutional and traditional set-up just mentioned is a specific Austrian phenomenon, a general conclusion that may be derived from it and that is supported by studies covering several advanced industrial countries is that a certain amount of corporatism added to the forces of "free" markets can help to stabilize economic development, employment, and inflation.

But other lessons may also be derived from Austria's experience though they have all to be interpreted with care and are not independent of time, place, and current conditions. While the lack of clear-cut concepts in Austria's policy was certainly a drawback, the use of a pragmatic and non-dogmatic policy-mix had its advantages. By attacking several problems (inflation, unemployment, balance of payments) with a variety of weapons in varying proportions Austria reduced the danger of running into extreme errors and enhanced the possibility of correcting a wrong course. Of course, mixing wrong policies would not be helpful. But considering the uncertainties about future developments and about the exact affects of specific policy instruments an open-minded policy-mix seems to be a recommendable strategy.

Another lesson to be learned is the obvious fact that it is easier and less problematical to deviate for a short time from the general trend of the world economy than to achieve a long-term separation from the trend. Over short periods one can use rather heavy medicines to arrive at special results, even if they cannot be maintained for longer periods. In the longer run, the maintenance of a separate course becomes more difficult and requires modifications of the policy which in its first stages had to achieve a shift to a new basis. The neglect of this fact was certainly one of the main shortcomings of Austro-Keynesianism.

But perhaps the main secret behind the (comparative) success of Austro-Keynesianism that would have to be heeded by would-be successors was the strong political will to foster full employment supported by a broad social consensus. Making employment a high priority target did not just mean the enactment of certain employment-promoting measures but led to an infusion of employment considerations into a wide spectrum of policy actions. This added a distinct employment bias to economic policy as a whole. It is very likely that such a basic determination is at least as important as a sound theoretical and institutional foundation. In this connection it is worth quoting the noted British economist Austin Robinson who—when reviewing in 1945 Lord Beveridges' classical "Full Employment in a Free Society" which recommended a Keynesian policy for post-war Britain—made the following remark:

> They (i.e. the proposed instruments to fight unemployment) are not so very different from, nor so very much greater than those with which we failed to defeat unemployment in the thirties that we can feel absolutely confident of success. But what, *more than anything else*, was lacking was an overwhelming national determination to defeat unemployment. (Italics added. K.R.)

Replacing "1930s" by "1980s and 1990s" might explain part of today's problems.

Yet there is one important difference for Western European countries in general that has made it far more difficult to try to get off the band-wagon of general events. The increased integration of the European economies in the European Economic Space and the European Community with their "four economic freedoms" (mobility of goods, services, capital, labor) and their unification of many rules and targets makes life easier for transnational companies but sets severe limits on special national actions in economic targeting and economic policy. Such limits have already been clearly visible in Mitterand's efforts to follow a separate, employment-oriented French route, and they have contributed to the decline of the Swedish welfare state program. They are likely to grow with the intensification of the integration process.

It is obvious that such limits are particularly severe for small countries where above-average expansionary efforts can fritter away in the open space. An Austro-Keynesian policy in the old style may not be repeatable today. The tail cannot wag economically more potent states. There may still be some force in the "locomotive theory": by their own, though restricted attempts to set developments going, they might be able to have an effect on the integrated area as a whole. But in the end, if and when a European Union with a unified currency and policy evolves, the fate and the policy of the Union as a whole (and last but not least the world development) will alone be decisive—for better or worse.

NOTES

1. The unemployment percentages correspond to the ILO procedure relating unemployment to the *dependent* labor force (wage and salary earners plus unemployed). The OECD figures are lower because they calculate unemployment as a fraction of the *total* labor force (including self-employed persons).

2. "Austria has been fortunate to be able to operate a consensus-oriented policy, thus maintaining a better performance than other countries. However, not surprisingly, given the slow growth of activity in other countries, the difficulties in sustaining full employment and maintaining social consensus have increased" (OECD Economic Survey on Austria 1982, 49).

3. Some steps in this direction were taken in the 1980s through special incentives and credits for research and development and the establishment of future-oriented production.

4. Significantly, an international economic conference held in London in 1967 dealt with the question "Is the Business Cycle Obsolete?" Proceedings edited by Martin Bronfenbrenner (New York: John Wiley, 1969).

5. This is a consideration which applies to many types and aspects of economic policy. A neglect of this fact lies behind many shortcomings and failures of Western advice for the transformation processes of the Eastern European countries.

Bibliography of Kurt W. Rothschild's Writings in English

Articles included in this volume are marked thus: *

1942   'The degree of monopoly', *Economica*, n.s. **9**(33), February, 24–39.

1942   *'A note on advertising', *Economic journal*, **52**(206), April, 112–21.

1942   'Advertising in war-time', *Oxford University Institute of Statistics bulletin*, **4**(8), 6 June, 169–75.

1942–3   *'Monopsony, buying costs, and welfare expenditure', *Review of economic studies*, **10**(1), 62–7.

1943   'A further note on the degree of monopoly', *Economica*, n.s. **10**(37), February, 69–70.

1943   'Point rationing of foodstuffs' (with J. Goldmann), *Oxford University Institute of Statistics bulletin*, **5**(8), 5 June, 129–33.

1944   *'The small nation and world trade', *Economic journal*, **54**(214), April, 26–40.

1944   'Public expenditure in the national income: a note', *Economica*, n.s. **11**(41), May, 19–22.

1945   *'Rationing and the consumer', *Oxford economic papers*, **7**, March, 67–82.

1945   'Wages and risk-bearing', *Oxford University Institute of Statistics bulletin*, **7**(11–12), 1 September, 193–8; reprinted in Rothschild, *Employment, wages and income distribution*, 1993, 118–24.

1945–6   'Migration and the distributive trades' (with S. Gillespie), *Review of economic studies*, **13**(34), 81–3.

1946   *'Further comment' [on K.E. Boulding, 'In defense of monopoly'], *Quarterly journal of economics*, **60**(3), August, 615–18.

1946–7   *'The meaning of rationality: a note on Professor Lange's article', *Review of economic studies*, **14**(1), 50–52.

1947   *'Price theory and oligopoly', *Economic journal*, **57**(227), September, 299–320; reprinted in G.J. Stiglcr and K.E. Boulding (eds), *Readings in price theory*, London, Allen & Unwin, 1953, 440–64.

1947   *Austria's economic development between the two wars*, London, Muller.

1950   *The Austrian economy since 1945*, London, Royal Institute of International Affairs.

1954   *The theory of wages* (Oxford: Blackwell; reprinted New York, Kelley, 1967).

1954   *'The wastes of competition', in E.H. Chamberlin (ed.), *Monopoly and competition and their regulation* (London: Macmillan), 301–14.

1957   'Approaches to the theory of bargaining', in J.T. Dunlop (ed.), *The theory of wage determination* (London: Macmillan), 281–91; reprinted in Rothschild, *Employment, wages and income distribution*, 1993, 108–17.

1957   'A note on the rationality controversy', *Soviet studies*, **9**(1), July, 28–31.

1957   'Aggregative wage theory and money illusion', *Journal of political economy*, **65**(5), October, 442–5.

1958   'Actual and implied exchange rates', *Scottish journal of political economy*, **5**(3), October, 229–33.

1959   *'The limitations of economic growth models: critical remarks on some aspects of Mr. Kaldor's model', *Kyklos*, **12**(4), 567–88; reprinted in J.E. King (ed.), *Economic growth in practice and theory: a Kaldorian perspective* (Aldershot: Elgar), 159–78.

1960   'Size and viability: the lesson of Austria', in E.A.G. Robinson (ed.), *The economic consequences of the size of nations* (London: Macmillan), 168–81.

1961   'Some recent contributions to a macro-economic theory of income distribution', *Scottish journal of political economy*, **8**(4), October, 173–99; reprinted in Rothschild, *Employment, wages and income distribution*, 1993, 236–60.

1964   'The old and the new: some recent trends in the literature of German economics', *American economic review*, **54**, March, supplement, 2–33.

1964   *'Cobweb cycles and partially correct forecasting', *Journal of political economy*, **72**(3), June, 300–305.

1964   'A note on the long-term planning of new industrial developments', in *On political economy and econometrics: essays in honour of Oskar Lange* (Warsaw: Polish Scientific Publishers), 523–33.

1965   'Themes and variations – remarks on the Kaldorian distribution formula', *Kyklos*, **18**(4), 652–69; reprinted in Rothschild, *Employment, wages and income distribution*, 1993, 276–89.

1965   'Illusions about money illusion?', *Journal of political economy*, **73**(3), June, 298–9.

1967   'Chamberlin and German economics', in R.E. Kuenne (ed.), *Monopolistic competition theory: studies in impact* (New York: Wiley), 275–91.

1967   'Socialism, planning, economic growth: some untidy remarks on an untidy subject', in C.H. Feinstein (ed.), *Socialism, capitalism and economic growth: essays presented to Maurice Dobb* (Cambridge: Cambridge University Press), 162–75.

1969   'Austria and Switzerland', in M. Bronfenbrenner (ed.), *Is the business cycle obsolete?* (New York: Wiley), 225–46.

1971   *(ed.) *Power in economics* (Harmondsworth: Penguin).

1971   'Different approaches in distribution theory: a note on Mr. Ferguson's two-sector variant of Kaldor's distribution model', *Kyklos*, **24**(1), 10–29; reprinted in Rothschild, *Employment, wages and income distribution*, 1993, 261–75.

1971   'The Phillips curve and all that', *Scottish journal of political economy*, **18**(3), August, 245–80; reprinted in Rothschild, *Employment, wages and income distribution*, 1993, 125–61.

1971   *Development of income distribution by factor shares in Western Europe* (Paris: OECD).

1972 *'Stagflation and intensified inflation: a primitive hypothesis', *Economic journal*, **82**(328), December, 1383–7.

1973 *'Distributive aspects of the Austrian theory', in J.R. Hicks and W. Weber (eds), *Carl Menger and the Austrian school of economics* (Oxford: Clarendon Press), 207–25.

1973 'Military expenditure, exports and growth', *Kyklos*, **26**(4), 804–14.

1974 'Friedman, expectations and the Phillips trade-off: a reply', *Scottish journal of political economy*, **21**(3), November, 303–8.

1975 'Export structure, export flexibility and competitiveness', *Weltwirtschaftliches archiv*, **111**(2), 222–42.

1975 'Inequality: is income distribution an adequate measure?', in J. Lecaillon (ed.), *La répartition du revenu national* (Paris: Edition CUJAS), 182–97.

1976 *Social sciences policy in Norway* (Paris: OECD).

1978 'Kahn on Malinvaud', *Cambridge journal of economics*, **2**(4), December, 407–8.

1979 'Peace and security via interdependence and cooperation in Europe', *Österreichische zeitschrift für aussenpolitik*, **19**(1), 14–25.

1979 *Social sciences in policy-making* (a report by twelve experts) (Paris: OECD).

1980 'A note on female labour supply', *Kyklos*, **33**(2), 246–60.

1981 'Futurology and the economist', in N. Assorodobraj-Kula, C. Bobrowski, H. Hagemeyer, W. Kula and J. Los (eds), *Studies in economic theory and practice: essays in honour of Edward Lipinski* (Amsterdam: North-Holland), 63–70.

1981 *'Schumpeter and socialism', in H. Frisch (ed.), *Schumpeterian economics* (New York: Praeger), 113–25.

1982 *'A note on some economic and welfare aspects of working-time regulation', *Australian economic papers*, **21**(38), June, 214–18.

1982 *'Observations on the economics, politics and ethics of the welfare state', *Journal of institutional and theoretical economics*, **138**(3), September, 565–82.

1982 'Expenditure function and devaluation in a small open economy: a note on the Prachowny model', *Weltwirtschaftliches archiv*, **118**(3), September, 571–8.

1985 'Some notes on Weintraub's eclectic theory of income shares', *Journal of post Keynesian economics*, **7**(4), Summer, 575–93; reprinted in Rothschild, *Employment, wages and income distribution*, 1993, 290–305.

1985 'Exports, growth and catching-up: some remarks and crude calculations', *Weltwirtschaftliches archiv*, **121**(2), 304–14.

1986 *'"Left" and "right" in "federal Europe"', *Kyklos*, **39**(3), 359–76.

1986 'Economic theory: US-European linkages – a journal analysis', *Weltwirtschaftliches archiv*, **122**(3), 566–74.

1986 'Capitalists and entrepreneurs: prototypes and roles', in H.J. Wagener and J.W. Drucker (eds), *The economic law of motion of modern society: a Marx–Keynes–Schumpeter centennial* (Cambridge: Cambridge University Press), 186–96.

1986–7   'Is there a Weitzman miracle?', *Journal of post Keynesian economics*, **9**(2), Winter, 198–211; reprinted in Rothschild, *Employment, wages and income distribution*, 1993, 173–84.

1987   'The neglect of employment in the international economic order', *Annals of the American Academy of Political and Social Science*, **492**, July, 49–60; reprinted in Rothschild, *Employment, wages and income distribution*, 1993, 52–64.

1988   *'Micro-foundations, ad hocery, and Keynesian theory', *Atlantic economic journal*, **16**, June, 12–21.

1988   'Life in a complex system: remarks from a social science point of view', in K. Vak (ed.), *Complexities of the human environment* (Vienna).

1988   Discussion of A. Heertje, 'Schumpeter and technical change', in E. Hanusch (ed.), *Evolutionary economics: applications of Schumpeter's ideas* (Cambridge: Cambridge University Press), 90–94.

1989   *'Political economy or economics? Some terminological and normative considerations', *European journal of political economy*, **5**(1), August, 1–12.

1989   *'The economist as preacher: a note on Yew-Kwang Ng's article on economic efficiency versus egalitarian rights', *Kyklos*, **42**(2), 257–9.

1989   'Some reflections on the growth of a female labour supply and the tertiary sector', *International review of applied economics*, **3**(2), June, 232–42; reprinted in Rothschild, *Employment, wages and income distribution*, 1993, 65–74.

1989   Comment on A.L. Thimm, 'On co-determination in the German steel industry', in H.G. Nutzinger and J. Backaus (eds), *Codetermination* (Berlin: Springer-Verlag), 157–61.

1990   *'A note on some socioeconomic and normative aspects of risk', *Review of political economy*, **2**(3), November, 359–65.

1990   Comment on P. Kugler, U. Müller and G. Sheldon, 'Technical change and the demand for skills in West German manufacturing 1970–1984', in E. Matzner and M. Wagner (eds), *The employment impact of new technology* (Aldershot: Avebury), 99–102.

1991   *'Glimpses of a non-linear biography', *Banca Nazionale del Lavoro quarterly review*, **44**(176), March, 3–13.

1991   *'A note on insiders, outsiders and the two-thirds society', *Kyklos*, **44**(2), 233–9.

1991   'The Austro-Keynesian experiment: unemployment in Austria in the seventies', in C. de Neubourg (ed.), *The art of full employment* (Amsterdam: Elsevier), 353–66.

1992   'Kurt W. Rothschild (born 1914)', in P. Arestis and M. Sawyer (eds), *A biographical dictionary of dissenting economists* (Aldershot: Elgar), 472–7.

1992   'The end of history? Afterthoughts to an article by Rudolf Richter', *Kyklos*, **45**(4), 555–9.

1992   'Economics and the social problem', in U. Reifner and J. Ford (eds), *Banking for people* (Berlin: de Gruyter), 49–54.

1993 *Ethics and economic theory: ideas–models–dilemmas* (Aldershot: Elgar).

1993 *Employment, wages and income distribution: critical essays in economics* (London: Routledge).

1993 *'Like a *Lehrstück* by Brecht: notes on the German reunification drama', *Cambridge journal of economics*, **17**(3), September, 259–66.

1993 'New world economic order', *International review of applied economics*, **7**(3), September 243–52.

1993 *'Oligopoly: walking the Sylos-path', in S. Biasco, A. Roncaglia and M. Salvati (eds), *Markets and institutions in economic development* (London: Macmillan), 155–71.

1994 'Josef Steindl: 1912–1993', *Economic journal*, **104**(422), January, 131–7.

1994 *'Austro-Keynesianism reconsidered', *Contemporary Austrian studies*, **2**, 119–29.

1994 'Power (II)', in G.M. Hodgson, W.J. Samuels and M.R. Tool (eds), *The Elgar companion to institutional and evolutionary economics L–Z* (Aldershot: Elgar), 173–7.

1995 'In search of a European identity', *Kyklos*, **48**(2), 273–7.

Name index

Allen, R.G.D. 208
Andrews, P.W.S. xiv
Arrow, K.J. 182

Bain, J.S. 189
Baran, P.A. xi, 224
Bauer, O. 228
Becker, G.S. 179n
Berle, A. 96
Bertrand, J.L.F. 94, 188
Beveridge, W.H. 240n, 297
Bismarck, O. von. 239
Böhm-Bawerk, E. von 4, 28n, 159–74
Bombach, G. 136n
Boulding, K.E. xiii, 86–9, 139n, 157n
Brady, R.A. xi
Braithwaite, D.C.M. 55
Buchanan, J.M. 51n

Cairncross, A. 6
Cairnes, J.E. 78
Carey, H.C. 120
Chamberlin, E.H. x, xii, 7, 55, 65, 90,
    93n, 95, 112–13, 115, 175, 188
Clark, J.B. 160, 166, 175
Clark, J.M. 119
Clower, R.W. 31
Cournot, A.A. 94, 188, 189
Cowling, K. xiv

Devletoglou, E.A. 148
Dickinson, H.D. 113
Dixit, A. 189
Dobb, M.H. 125n, 139n
Domar, E.S. 143
Douglas, P.H. 175
Downs, A. 52
Duesenberry, J.S. 139n

Edgeworth, F.Y. 42, 91, 182, 208
Elster, J. 35n
Engels, F. 25n, 27, 224
Eucken, W. 22n

Fellner, W.J. 143, 157–9
Feyerabend, P. 13, 36
Frey, B. 43
Friedman, B. 182

Friedman, M. 22n

Galbraith, J.K. xi, 47
George, H. xi, 27
Grunberg, E. 146–7

Haberler, G. 4, 5
Hahn, F.H. 31, 33
Hall, R.L. 90n
Hamilton, W. 90n, 95n
Harrod, R.F. 87n, 100n, 126, 143
Harsanyi, J. xi
Hayek, F. von x, 4, 5, 113, 159, 164,
    168
Heilbroner, R. 44
Hermann, F.B.W. von 160
Hibbs, D.A. Jr. 256, 257n
Hicks, J.R. 23n, 31, 92n, 175, 208
Hicks, U.K. 37n, 59, 65n
Hilferding, R. 27, 228
Hirschman, A.O. 85, 142n
Hitch, C.J. 90n
Hobson, J.A. xi, 27, 109
Hutchinson, T.W. 44

Jevons, W.S. 158, 162, 166, 208

Kahn, R.F. 94n
Kaldor, N. xv, 126–45, 157, 210n
Kalecki, M. ix, x, xiii, xvii, 7, 47, 50,
    52, 88n, 234
Kautsky, K. 27
Keynes, J.M. ix, x, 6–7, 31–40, 47, 51n,
    52, 76, 127–8, 190, 224, 233,
    289–99
Knight, F.H. 8, 171n
Kreisky, B. 290

Lafontaine, O. 286
Lange, O. xi, 17–19, 52, 113, 234
Laski, K. 11
Lederer, E. 228
Lenin, V.I. 47, 109, 120, 224
Leontief, W.W. 169
Lerner, A.P. 11n, 113
Liepmann, H. 82–3
List, F. 120
Little, I.M.D. 242